The WASP Question

Andrew Fraser

The WASP Question:

An Essay on the Biocultural Evolution, Present Predicament, and Future Prospects of the Invisible Race

ARKTOS
MMXI

First edition published in 2011 by Arktos Media Ltd.

Copyright © 2011 by Arktos Media Ltd.

Printed in the United Kingdom

ISBN 978-1-907166-29-7

BIC classification: Social & political philosophy (HPS); Conservatism and right-of-centre democratic ideologies (JPFM); Nationalism (JPFN)

Editor: Kathleen R. Boehringer
Proofreader: Michael J. Brooks
Cover Design: Andreas Nilsson
Layout: Daniel Friberg

ARKTOS MEDIA LTD
www.arktos.com

Table of Contents

Introduction: The Anglo-Saxon as Pariah 7

I. Ethnogenesis: Toward a Biocultural History of English Constitutionalism

1. *Comitatus*: Kingship and Covenant in the Evolution of Anglo-Saxon Bioculture 27

2. *Republica Anglorum*: Religion and Rulership in Old England. 66

3. Metamorphosis: The Peculiar Character of the Early Modern Englishman 108

II. Pathogenesis: Anglo-Saxon Identity in the *Novus Ordo Seclorum*

4. *Homo Americanus*: A Post-Mortem on the First "White Man's Country" 167

5. Divine Economy: The Modern Business Corporation and the Lost Soul of WASP America . 228

6. Political Theology: How America's Civil Religion Fosters Anglo-Saxon Ethnomasochism. 270

III. Prognosis: The Return of the Repressed

7. Archeofuturism: Of Patriot Kings and Anglo-Saxon Tribalism in the Twenty-First Century . 329

8. Palingenesis: The Postmodern Rebirth of Anglo-Saxon Christendom 373

Subject Index 403

Name Index 415

Introduction:
The Anglo-Saxon as Pariah

This book seeks to explain why WASPs (a subtly, perhaps deservedly derogatory acronym coined sometime in the late Fifties to denote white Anglo-Saxon Protestants) rarely rise to the conscious, principled defence of their collective biocultural interests, even in the face of obvious aggression from their racial, ethnic, and religious rivals. One expects to find Anglophobia among other ethnic groups, most notably perhaps the Irish and Jews; such antagonism is the natural and ordinary consequence of inter-ethnic competition. WASPs, however, simply absorb such hostility; they, too, hold their ancestors responsible for uniquely monstrous crimes against humanity. Accordingly, self-loathing WASPs no longer look to an ethnoreligious community of memory as the indispensable source of collective meaning, value, and purpose.

Indeed, the few proudly Anglo-Saxon patriots scattered around the world are now political pariahs. By contrast, the thoroughly deracinated WASPs who eschew atavistic tribal loyalties are generally well-adjusted, other-directed characters eager to go with the flow. Few such "organization men" and even fewer "liberated" women possess the psychological independence necessary to flout convention and think for themselves, much less to express genuine solidarity with their co-ethnics, past and present. Denouncing and despising every explicit expression of in-group solidarity among their own kith and kin, WASPs have lost their collective soul. In an age of diversity, they are the invisible race. But their fate is not foreclosed; neither the gene pool nor the spirit of the Anglo-Saxon race is doomed to extinction. Over the next century, a saving remnant of Anglo-Saxon Protestant ethnopatriots, outcasts from a society in which the normal has become abnormal, will become a highly visible minority. Sooner or later, they will step out of the shadows to speak for a people reborn, an ethnonation like any other, requiring its own place in the sun.

Admittedly, such a prophecy is counter-intuitive. In present circumstances, any WASP who tries to revive older traditions of "British race
patriotism" immediately breaches the bounds of acceptable political discourse. Paradoxically, pariah status is now an essential precondition to
the rediscovery of collective identity among people of British ancestry.
Useful comparisons can be made between the newly emancipated Jewish
parvenu in Europe during the nineteenth century and the novel situation
facing WASPs who have become strangers in their own lands. Upwardly-
mobile Jews such as Karl Marx's father in Germany often foreswore open
solidarity with their own race and religion so as to gain admission to polite
society and the professions. Only a few isolated individuals insisted that
the emancipation of the Jews must amount to more "than an opportunity
to ape the gentiles;" they sought instead the "admission of Jews *as Jews* to
the ranks of humanity." In rejecting the "opportunity to play the *parvenu*,"
such men became "conscious pariahs." Today only a small minority of
WASPs dare to become conscious pariahs by refusing to renounce their
racial particularity. According to the Jewish scholar Hannah Arendt, this
is an intolerable state of affairs. In her view, it is a fundamental truth of
the human condition that an individual of any nation or race can enter the
"world history of humanity only by remaining and clinging stubbornly to
what he is." The systematic denial of that truth reveals the spiritual empti-
ness at the heart of modernity: The "normal," well-adjusted and utterly
deracinated liberal WASP passing in polite society as a cosmopolitan and
enlightened "citizen of the world" is actually "no less a monster than a
hermaphrodite."[1] The question arises: Why are so few WASPs willing to
cling any longer to who they are. The answer lies in the Anglo-American
tradition of constitutional patriotism, a civil religion that transformed
the abnormal renunciation of in-group solidarity among Anglo-Saxon
Protestants into the touchstone of political normality.

In her private and social life, Hannah Arendt clung stubbornly to
the particularistic bioculture and historic folkways of the Jewish people
even as she publicly prescribed a thoroughly secular and cosmopolitan
tradition of civic republicanism for her adopted country. She dismissed
as fanciful the notion that America is or ever was a Christian republic.
She claimed that the religious roots of the American republic are to be
found not in "the Christian faith in a revealed God" nor in "Hebrew
obedience to the Creator who was also the Legislator of the universe." If

---

1   Hannah Arendt, *Men in Dark Times* (New York: Harcourt Brace Jovanovich, 1968), 89; *id.*,
     The Jew as Pariah: Jewish Identity and Politics in the Modern Age (New York: Grove Press,
     1978), 67-68.

the founders "can be called religious at all," Arendt argued, it was only in "the original Roman sense" of the word "religion." According to Arendt, Roman religion had little to do with participation in the divine; it was more concerned with a pious respect for the halo of time shrouding the origins of the republic. One wonders, however, whether Arendt ever made the conscious calculation that the ethnic interests of her fellow Jews are best served by detaching the American republican tradition from the Anglo-Saxon blood and Christian faith of the nation's founding people.

Arendt, of course, is far from being the only political theorist to draw a bright line between the Christian faith and classical republicanism. JGA Pocock, a New Zealand-born WASP, is perhaps the most accomplished historian of the Atlantic republican tradition. He, too, distinguished between Christians who include the whole of humanity in their quest for eternal life and civic humanists. For the latter, the republic was universal only in that "it existed to realize for its citizens all the values which men were capable of realizing in this life;" it remained "particular in the sense that it is located in space and time." Both Arendt and Pocock presented the classical republic as a secular association of persons "formed with a view to some good purpose." Race and religion play little or no role in the work of either writer. Arendt concentrated on the abstract categories of work, labor, and action in her analysis of the constitution of the public and private realms in the Athenian *polis*.[2] In effect, she discovered the prototype of the "proposition nation" in the city states of pagan antiquity. In fact, she offered her modernist rendition of civic humanism as an antidote to the primeval urge to discover the divine in the blood and spirit of a particular people. She found a ready market for that prescription within the WASP intelligentsia. Certainly, both Arendt and Pocock exercised a profound influence on my own intellectual development.[3] Having fallen under the sway of their purely political civic humanism, I was ill-prepared to comprehend the scale of the immigration disaster unfolding before my eyes in Australia, Canada, and the United States.[4]

2   Hannah Arendt, *On Revolution* (Harmondsworth: Pelican, 1973), 198; and *The Human Condition* (Chicago: University of Chicago Press, 1958). JGA Pocock, *The Machiavellian Moment: Florentine Political Thought and the Atlantic Republican Tradition* (Princeton, NJ: Princeton University Press, 1975), 3; Aristotle, *The Politics* tr. TA Sinclair (Harmondsworth: Penguin, 1951), 54.

3   See, eg, Andrew Fraser *The Spirit of the Laws: Republicanism and the Unfinished Project of Modernity* (Toronto: University of Toronto Press, 1990); and, *Reinventing Aristocracy: The Constitutional Reformation of Corporate Governance* (Aldershot: Ashgate, 1998).

4   Cf. Peter Brimelow, *Alien Nation: Common Sense About America's Immigration Disaster* (New York: HarperPerennial, 1996).

Arendt sought to liberate political theory from the biological imperatives of natural necessity while providing a secular alternative to the alleged "wordlessness" of apolitical ethnoreligious communities grounded in Christian charity. Accordingly, she rejected the "German-inspired nationalism" that regarded "a nation to be an eternal organic body, the product of inevitable natural growth of inherent qualities," and explained "peoples, not in terms of political organizations, but in terms of biological superhuman personalities." Renouncing "all neo-romantic appeals to the *volk*," Arendt "maintained that one's ethnic, religious, or racial identity was irrelevant to one's identity as a *citizen*, and that it should never be made the basis of membership in a *political* community." Arendt was no less hostile to the theological image of the nation as "the incarnation of a divine absolute on earth," observing that "America was spared the cheapest and most dangerous disguise the absolute ever assumed in the political realm, the disguise of the nation." She recognized, of course, that the price *homo Americanus* paid for that release was severance from the blood and faith he shared with his kinfolk in the Old World.[5]

As a callow legal scholar steeped in both the chronic ethno-anaemia characteristic of the Canadian WASP and the civic culture of the American Republic south of the border, I, too, was proof against romantic appeals to the *Volk*. Indeed, in the earnestly bilingual and bicultural atmosphere of Canada in the late 1960s and early 1970s, I was simply bewildered by the ethnic grievance-mongering of newly empowered Québécois activists billing themselves as "the white niggers of America." It was perhaps natural to seek succor in Arendt's irenic vision of a political religion brought down to earth, one capable of creating public spaces in which the civic virtues of a self-selecting aristocracy would transmute the raw facts of social plurality into a common world transcending "the life-span of mortal men."[6]

My first encounter with Arendt's civic humanism came through two books, *The Human Condition* and *On Revolution*. I was only dimly aware of Arendt's Jewish identity; she barely mentions Jews or Judaism in either work. In retrospect, however, her political philosophy was inseparable from her identity as one of many German Jewish intellectuals transplanted to America as political refugees. It was easy for Arendt to conclude that a pariah people such as the Jews were safer in a pluralistic republic founded

---

5   Arendt, *Human Condition*, 52-53; *Jew as Pariah*, 156; Maurizio Passerin D'Entrèves, *The Political Philosophy of Hannah Arendt* (London: Routledge, 1994), 16; Arendt, *On Revolution*, 194-195.

6   Arendt, *Human Condition*, 55; Pierre Vallières, *White Niggers of America* (Toronto: McClelland and Stewart, 1971).

upon universal principles of constitutional law than in an organic nation grounded in the racial identity of a gentile majority.

To her credit, Arendt sought to hold Jews to the same standards she set for the American republic. She criticized Zionists repeatedly, both because they accepted the idea of "the Jew in general" as a biological creature and because they tied the goal of a Jewish homeland to an absolutist political theology of sovereignty. She insisted that "The real goal of the Jews in Palestine is the building up of a Jewish homeland. This goal must never be sacrificed to the pseudo-sovereignty of a Jewish state." Zionists, she believed, ought to recognize the rights of the Arabs already living in Palestine; turning the Palestinians into another pariah people in their own country could never be justified. Indeed, she held up America as a model for the sort of polity that should be created in Palestine.[7] It now seems clear that we were both doomed to disappointment; modern political and social life is utterly resistant to a revival of classical republicanism for reasons that are both biological and theological.

For those prepared to heed its lessons, the last fifty years have taught us a great deal about the intractable biocultural reality of racial differences and the consequent limits on pluralism in a modern republican polity. Certainly, the bloody and interminable conflict between Zionists and Palestinians suggests a certain naiveté in Arendt's view that "the very category 'Jew' is a human convention masquerading as a biological fact."[8] On the other hand, she had good reason to fear that the political theology of sovereignty would exacerbate racial, religious, and ethnic conflict in a self-proclaimed Jewish state ruling a multi-ethnic society. Meanwhile, experience in the "Anglo-Saxon countries" strongly suggests that European man alone bears the spirit of civic republicanism, a tradition still largely alien to other races and peoples.

The civil rights revolution combined with the reverse colonization of the West by the Third World has undermined the very possibility of a common world presumptively shared by the citizens of a republican polity. The corporate welfare state celebrates diversity, and thereby fosters, deepens, and strengthens the myriad biocultural divisions between men and women, homosexuals and heterosexuals, blacks and whites, Jews and Christians, Muslims and the entire Western world. It has become an axiom of postmodern politics that the perspective of any one group is

---

7   Arendt, *Human Condition*, 53; Hanna Fenichel Pitkin, *The Attack of the Blob: Hannah Arendt's Concept of the Social* (Chicago: University of Chicago Press, 1998), 76, 105; Arendt, *Jew as Pariah*, 192; See also, Hans Kohn, *American Nationalism: An Interpretative Essay* (New York: Collier, 1961).

8   Pitkin, *Attack of the Blob*, 72.

incommensurable with that of others. Representation of individuals must give way therefore to the representation of groups. The common good has been deconstructed as an illusion conjured up by powerful and privileged groups to protect their own particular interests.

Between-group competition is now an inescapable and ubiquitous feature of life for WASPs in a multiracial society. Unfortunately, even as racial and ethnoreligious tensions spill over into a low-intensity civil war, well-meaning but ineffectual WASPs remain resolutely blind to both the biological and the theological dimensions of their collective identity.

Nation of Nations

The major premise underlying this book was best articulated by Harold Cruse, easily the most incisive black nationalist thinker of the Sixties. Cruse recognized what most Americans of Anglo-Saxon ancestry are still loath to admit; namely that America is "a nation of nations," (an observation now equally applicable to Australia, Canada, New Zealand, and the United Kingdom.)[9] He identified Anglo-Saxons, Negroes, and Jews as the main players in the inter-ethnic struggles shaping the (re)distribution of prestige, power, and resources in American society and politics.

For my purposes, Cruse's most important insight is the following deceptively innocuous but explosively unorthodox proposition: American WASPs require and deserve explicit recognition as an ethnocultural group *comme les autres*—as an ethnonation *in* itself, if not yet *for* itself.[10] Unfortunately, as Cruse knew all too well, America is a nation that habitually lies to itself. Moreover, WASPs are the worst offenders. America is indeed a polyethnic nation of nations but Anglo-Saxon Protestants have—ever since the foundation of the Republic—refused to incorporate that patently obvious reality into their political, constitutional and theological discourse. The myth of the proposition nation has a long history.

In the well-ordered multinational America of Cruse's dreams, each of the major ethnic groups would "produce a native radical-intellectual trend,

---

9   Harold Cruse, *The Crisis of the Negro Intellectual: From Its Origins to the Present* (New York: William Morrow, 1967), 395.

10 *Cf.*, Karl Marx, *The Poverty of Philosophy* (New York: International Publishers, 1963), 173: "Economic conditions had first transformed the mass of the people of the country into workers. The combination of capital has created for this mass a common situation, common interests. This mass is thus already a class as against capital, but not yet for itself. In the struggle, of which we have noted only a few phases, this mass becomes united, and constitutes itself as a class for itself."

which trends should complement one another."[11] In effect, intellectuals provide each ethnonation republic with a corporate identity; every people acquires its own legal personality empowered to invoke as it is bound to respect three fundamental constitutional conventions of the multiracial republic: mutual recognition, consent, and continuity.[12] On Cruse's theory, it is the civic duty of every Anglo-Saxon, Negro, and Jewish intellectual to participate in the collective consciousness of his ethnonation. In practice, members of the Jewish intelligentsia alone volunteered—eagerly and often—to serve as the common (if rarely contrite) conscience of their proudly ethnocentric people. Highly educated Jews take their communal responsibilities seriously, ceaselessly working to promote a powerful spirit of in-group solidarity among their co-ethnics. As a consequence, the American Jewish community is not just a nation *in* itself; it is also an ethnic group famously ready, willing, and able to act *for* itself. In pursuit of their self-proclaimed mission to heal the world, Jewish activists moved quickly and decisively to forge an alliance with black Americans against an allegedly common foe, America's hegemonic WASP elites.[13]

The vast majority of American Negroes followed Jewish advice to forswear black nationalist strategies, as advocated, *inter alia*, by Booker T Washington, Marcus Garvey, and Harold Cruse. Such counsel may have been "good for the Jews" but Cruse was convinced that it poisoned the well-springs of political, cultural, and economic autonomy in black America. Negroes are now an ethnonation *for* itself only in the degraded sense that their leaders clamour incessantly to increase their entitlements under the federal Leviathan's racial spoils system. A race so (dare one say, slavishly) dependent upon governmental largesse hardly counts as a nation *in* itself.

Those enjoying the WASP lifestyle, on the other hand, represent a national group only *in* itself. Americans of British ancestry have never constituted an organic whole prepared to act *for* itself. Cruse predicted that the USA would pay a heavy price for the failure of WASP intellectuals (*and* their Negro counterparts) to recognize, promote, and defend their distinctive ethnonational identity. Cruse took it for granted that, in a multinational republic, every self-respecting, morally upright racial, religious,

---

11 *Ibid.*, 468.

12 James Tully, *Strange Multiplicity: Constitutionalism in an Age of Diversity* (Cambridge: Cambridge University Press, 1995).

13 Cheryl Lynn Greenberg, *Troubling the Waters: Black-Jewish Relations in the American Century* (Princeton, NJ: Princeton University Press, 2010).

and ethnic group will shoulder its collective responsibilities in the process of identity politics.

Jews were quick to grasp the proffered opportunity vigorously to defend their distinctive ethnocultural, economic, and political interests. Jewish leaders demanded and received public *recognition* of their right to a front row pew in the sacramental shrine of the Constitutional Republic. Accordingly, a triumvirate of Protestant, Catholic, and Jewish worthies now typically presides over the ceremonial expression of America's constitutional faith. And because corporate membership in the religion of the Republic carries certain privileges, it became axiomatic that Jews must *consent* to social and economic policy decisions affecting their group interests. Finally, Jewish intellectuals enlisted private, corporate, and governmental support to ensure their *continuity* as a self-governing ethnonation. Unfortunately, they have not always accorded reciprocal recognition to the biocultural interests and constitutional claims of other ethnic groups. On the other hand, neither Anglo-Protestant nor Catholic Americans have been particularly adept, much less highly principled players in the game of inter-ethnic competition.

In *The Slaughter of Cities* E Michael Jones describes the successful campaign by WASP and Jewish elites to cleanse American cities of Catholic ethnic enclaves.[14] Relocated to the suburbs, Polish, Irish, Italian and other Catholic ethnic identities were flattened into a homogeneous whiteness supposedly shared with Protestants and Jews. Like Cruse, Jones believes that America would be a better place today if Catholic ethnic intellectuals—not least of all those in the Church—had done their job, thereby enabling each of those distinctive ethnic groups to survive in and for itself. Instead, Catholic ethnics like WASPs and Negroes before them fell lock, stock, and barrel for utopian promises of health, wealth, and personal power marketed by the corporate welfare state as the American Dream. That Faustian bargain exacted a heavy price, spiritually if not materially, from America's constituent ethnonations.

This book is not, therefore, a narrowly ethnocentric piece of pro-WASP advocacy. On the contrary, it mounts an *attack* on my co-ethnics; namely the American WASPs who for over two centuries now have waged a reckless, revolutionary, and relentless cultural war on the ethnoreligious traditions which once inspired the Anglo-Saxon province of Christendom to greatness. American WASPs and their unruly ancestors have done much for which they ought to fear the wrath of God. Their salvation may depend

---

14 E Michael Jones, *The Slaughter of Cities: Urban Renewal as Ethnic Cleansing* (South Bend, IN: St Augustine's Press, 2003).

upon their willingness to renounce not just the statist idolatry rampant in the religion of the Republic but also the enchantments of Mammon for which they have sold their collective soul. It is well past time for WASPs to accept the responsibilities and burdens of ethnonationhood. In return, they will earn the right to bear, once again, the ethnonym of their illustrious Anglo-Saxon ancestors.

America's constitutional faith has been not good for the WASPs—or any other population group. In the medium- to long-term, even highly successful Jews will suffer if the WASP disease goes untreated. Anglo-Saxon Anglophobia is a spiritual disorder whose morally debilitating symptoms are highly contagious. Should WASPs fail to regenerate their historic ethnonation, such morbid ethnomasochism is sure to bring out the worst in other racial, religious, and ethnic groups.

Already America's rainbow republic exhibits dangerously high levels of Jewish hubris, Negro criminality, and Hispanic/Mexican aggression, as well as chronic moral decay within a rootless Catholic "faith community" desperately searching for its lowest common denominator in the mobile mass of the global multitude. The ethnopathology which laid *homo Americanus* low has spread to Anglo-Saxon Protestants outside the United States. Whether they realize it or not, the mental and physical well-being of WASPs in Australia, Canada, New Zealand, and even in England, is inextricably bound up with the fate of their co-ethnics in America.

Educated WASPs everywhere are remarkably resistant to suggestions that they, too, are an ethnic group. They prefer to imagine themselves as autonomous individuals. Sometimes—if the thorny issue of race comes up—they will, reluctantly, self-identify as "whites;" but mostly WASPs regard themselves as "plain vanilla" Americans, Australians, Canadians, and Britons. WASPs around the world disapprove of ethnonationalism—especially when it rears its ugly head among their own kith and kin. This book offers intellectual support to recovering WASPs in their inner spiritual struggle to overcome their ethnologically peculiar but politically correct and etymologically sound strain of homophobia.

Anglo-Saxon Anglophobia and the New Tribalism

WASPs are the canary in a multiracial mineshaft. Cracks and fissures snake around them as the transnational corporate welfare state digs ever-deeper into the precious stocks of social capital accumulated over centuries in the "Anglo-Saxon countries." Predictions of global anarchy are rife as nations break down into warring races and tribes. Ironically, bereft of a powerful sense of collective identity, WASPs face a future of individual isolation even as "the quest for the memory and spirit of the specific ethnic past has once again been renewed." It seems likely, according to Kotkin, that a new "tribalism…forged by globally dispersed ethnic groups" will shape the twenty-first century.[15] This book comes to a similar conclusion: Adapting themselves to the chaotic challenges of the twenty-first century, prudent WASPs will re-invent themselves as a global network of Anglo-Saxon tribes.

The only alternative to the self-conscious reconstruction of Anglo-Saxon ethnohistory, indeed of an Anglo-Saxon ethnotheology, is ever-deepening demoralization. The secular-minded WASP is now a tragi-comic figure, the object of both pity and contempt. Unless WASPs somehow recover the tribal spirit of early Anglo-Saxon Christians they will sink still further into ignominious impotence. A once-proud people will have been swept aside without a fight, just another sad story of defeat and dispossession ending not with a bang but with a whimper. But they may yet find their way back to an alternative future. During the first Dark Age, the Church served as the seedbed of the English nation; in our New Dark Age WASPs may discover that their salvation, on earth as in heaven, lies in a return to the Old Faith of medieval Christendom.

In Deuteronomy 26: 16-19, God recognized Old Covenant Israel as his "special possession." Biblical prophecies of a New Covenant creation were fulfilled in AD 70 when Christ came "on the clouds of heaven with great power and glory" (Matthew 24:30) to oversee the destruction of the Jerusalem Temple. The covenant world of the rebellious and stiff-necked Jews who had rejected Christ perished along with the physical structure of the Temple. A new heavens and a new earth appeared in which every nation (*ethnos*) was invited to enter into the Kingdom of God. The rulers of the pagan tribes of Anglo-Saxon England jumped at the chance. Alfred the Great and other Anglo-Saxon kings gladly recognized Jesus the Christ as their Lord. Their subjects soon conformed to the ways of the King of Kings.

By keeping his commandments, England became the Christian prototype of a holy nation; indeed the nascent English nation aspired to be a new Israel. In return, God raised England "high above all the nations which he has made," if only for a time. Contemporary WASPs must follow the example set by their remote ancestors in bringing "praise and fame" to God. By so doing, they can be reborn as "a people holy to the Lord."

15   Joel Kotkin, *Tribes: How Race, Religion and Identity Determine Success in the New Global Economy* (New York: Random House, 1992), 3.

Unfortunately, most WASPs today remain wedded to secular humanism, the civil religion which underpins the political economy of the modern state. So long as that bloodless faith survives, the lost souls of the invisible race fall under a collective life sentence of spiritual servitude.

WASPs are dead not just to their ancestral Christian faith but to the civic virtues essential to the constitutional health of the body politic. Forty years ago, Cruse charged that the then "dominant and representative" white ethnic group, "the Anglo-Saxons and their Protestant ethic" had abdicated "their creative and intellectual responsibilities to the internal American commonweal." Nothing since then has overcome the spiritual bankruptcy and ideological hubris, the "threadbare cultural heritage," associated with the steady hollowing out of Anglo-Saxon prestige, power, and influence.[16] The three-cornered ethnic competition between Negroes, Jews, and old-stock Anglo-Americans continues unabated, but with the addition of many new protected minorities an ever-expanding diversity industry now honeycombs the structures of state and corporate power.

In the business of inter-ethnic competition, there must be winners and losers. Cruse was not surprised when upwardly mobile Jews quickly stepped into the gaping intellectual vacuum left unattended by feckless WASPs; before long, he predicted, Jews would "dominate scholarship, history, social research, etc." WASP weakness was a critical factor in the vector of forces generated within the "fateful triangular tension" between Anglo-Saxons, Negroes, and Jews. Cruse was right to warn Anglo-Saxons that their "group must produce its representative radical-intellectual trend; or else social progress in America will be ethnically retarded, if not checkmated."[17] Well ahead of his time, he stressed that in at least one crucially important dimension the biocultural phenomenon of race is, indeed, a "social construct."

Race is a biological reality but not every racial difference represents the automatic, physical expression of particular gene pools. In fact, the social construction of race is always a work in progress, a job that can be done well or badly. A people can use its God-given genetic capital for good or for ill. WASP intellectuals deserve to be chastised severely; they refuse to pay attention to the peerless skill with which American Jews crafted a collective identity solidly anchored in the ancient moral imperatives of tribal loyalty. Well-schooled WASPs also turn a blind eye to shortfalls in the performance of non-European peoples. Conspicuous displays of altruism directed toward out-groups are valuable status markers for educated

---

16 Cruse, *Negro Intellectual*, 468.

17 *Ibid.*, 468, 483.

WASPs indifferent to the claims of in-group solidarity. The "selfish gene" has become incarnate in WASP intellectuals who routinely defect to the other side(s) in the game of identity politics.

Over the past century, the sheer ubiquity of such opportunistic behavior produced the terminal crisis of the Anglo-Saxon intellectual. Anglo-Saxon Protestants were on the ropes by the mid-Sixties. The collapse was not confined to the USA. Cruse probably never took much notice of Canada where Anglo-Saxons did manage, for a time, to create a native, conservative intellectual trend, under the aegis of the British monarchy. But, there too, Anglo-Saxonism had taken several body blows by 1965. That year marked the publication of George Grant's *Lament for a Nation*, a book mourning the defeat of an English-Canadian nationalist movement grounded in ancestral loyalty to British institutions rejected by the American Revolution. Around the same time, Britain's entry into the European Common Market broke the grip of "British race patriotism" on the politico-cultural imagination of opinion leaders in Australia and New Zealand, as well as on the English themselves.[18]

Anglo-Saxon Anglophobia is a mysterious affliction, becoming pandemic among WASPs in tandem with the rise of managerial multiculturalism. Official multiculturalism destroyed the common civic culture that WASPs absorb with their mother's milk. Apart from WASPs, it is now normal for virtually every significant social group to conceive its racial, religious, ethnic, gender, or lifestyle interests in accordance with the tribal logic of identity politics. WASPs stand outside the new tribalism. They cling instead to the scrupulously secular, color-blind, and gender-neutral norms of civic nationalism. WASPs don't "do" identity politics; their sense of belonging is based not on blood but on citizenship. Nor, needless to say, do they regard in-group solidarity as a sacred obligation. Unsurprisingly, therefore, in the second half of the twentieth century, Australia, Canada, New Zealand, the UK, and the USA ceased to be Anglo-Saxon countries, spiritually if not demographically.

In Search of an Anglo-Saxon *Volksgeist*

What is at work here is arguably a collective not an individual neurosis. In search of the deeply repressed *Volksgeist* of a disappearing people, we traverse the mundane domain of sociobiology—to establish that religion

---

18 See, George Grant, *Lament for a Nation: The Defeat of Canadian Nationalism* (Toronto: McClelland & Stewart, 1965); and, Stuart Ward, *Australia and the British Embrace: The Demise of the Imperial Ideal* (Melbourne: Melbourne University Press, 2001).

has secular utility—before ascending into the headier realm of Christian ethnotheology—to establish that a religion *of* secular utility is bad for the Anglo-Saxons.

Our story begins with the emergence of the English people as a socially cohesive ethnoreligious community; it also tells of their overseas expansion. The entire narrative recounts an ongoing historical process in which genes and culture co-evolve; throughout, the biocultural evolution of the Anglo-Saxon peoples, "at home" and in the diaspora, is evaluated in accordance with the orthodox Christian doctrine of nations. In other words, we look for the spirit animating the laws of God and man as it shines through or recedes from Anglo-Saxon biocultures widely separated in space and time.

The spirit of Anglo-Saxon Christendom manifested itself most publicly in laws and constitutions. This book rests upon a historiographical axiom laid down by Walter Ullman: "The history of jurisprudence is the history of civilization." Medieval Europe created a legal civilization, nowhere more obviously or successfully than in its Anglo-Saxon province. The English, like other Christian peoples, "were given their religion, their faith, their dogma in the shape of the law."[19] Accordingly, this book assumes that there is no better introduction to any period in Anglo-Saxon history and no more reliable mirror of their character than a study of the law enacted and practiced, first, in their island homeland and, now, throughout what remains of the civilization established by the British diaspora.

Another overarching theme revolves around the quest for the tragic flaw in the Anglo-Saxon character. How did a once-heroic people bring about their own downfall? Was the fatal flaw somehow encoded in their genes or their culture, or even both at once? My thesis is the social psychology of the Anglo-Saxons evolved in three stages, in a process of "punctuated equilibrium." The primitive, magicoreligious influences on the social character of the early Anglo-Saxon tribes were suppressed, first, by formal institutions (embryonic states and the Church) that fostered the dominant "tradition-directed" character type of medieval England; second, by the development of an "inner-directed" character adapted to the early modern bourgeois market economy; and, third, by the emergence of the "other-directed" character type among WASPs in the service of the modern corporate welfare state.

As we enter a period of deepening economic crisis, hitherto suppressed social and political tensions generated by the deliberate demographic transformation of the Anglo-Saxon countries seem certain to become more acute. Unmistakeable symptoms of acute racial polarization are already evident under the Obama administration in the USA. In this threatening atmosphere of political instability and economic insecurity, old-stock Americans, along with their co-ethnics in England, Canada, and Australasia, will be compelled, sooner or later, to join in the high-stakes game of identity politics. This book provides them with a game plan; it points, as well, to their greatest weakness—the disgraceful absence of the team spirit so central to the old-time religion of the fabled "island race."

Ten years ago, John Higham, a prominent WASP historian, observed that the full story of the "shattering defeat" of his own ethnic group in the mid-twentieth century "has never been told." Shortly afterwards, Eric Kaufmann set out single-handedly to fill that void with a masterful book on the rise and fall of Anglo-America. One reason for the previous absence of academic interest in the decline of American WASPs, Kaufmann remarked, is the unexamined presumption that it was "a demographic inevitability of only limited relevance to today's debates about whiteness and multiculturalism."[20] The conventional wisdom holds that WASPs were bound to be overthrown, sooner or later, by subaltern ethnic groups. In rejecting the dominant interpretation, Kaufmann took a giant step forward. This book builds upon his approach.

In several important ways, however, it represents a radical departure from Kaufmann's work. The most obvious difference between the two books is in their respective historical and geographic scope. Kaufmann confines his narrative and analysis to the rise and fall of *homo Americanus*. This book examines the ethnogenesis of the English nation; it also discusses the growth of the state and the companion system of political economy that powered English colonial expansion around the world.

Kaufmann and I agree that "the primary engine of dominant ethnic decline" is to be found in "cultural and ideological changes originating from *within* the Anglo-Protestant community."[21] But when Kaufmann celebrates the decline of the WASP, I decline to follow suit. Instead, this book laments the fall of Anglo-America (along with Anglo-Australia, Anglo-Canada, etc). Kaufmann sees in the "expressive individualism" of "the New York Intellectuals" positive signs that WASPs were reforming themselves over the course of the twentieth century. In my view, the rise of that cultural revolutionary movement signalled the onset phase of a malignant

---

20 Eric P Kaufmann, *The Rise and Fall of Anglo-America* (Cambridge, MA: Harvard University Press, 2004), 3.

21 *Ibid.*, 4.

ethnopathology decked out in the rituals and trappings of a false religion. On my analysis, the cosmopolitan creed embraced by Kaufmann is a clear and present danger to the inclusive fitness of WASPs everywhere, not least of all because it severs them from their ethnoreligious roots in the ancestral homeland of Anglo-Saxon Christianity.

My interpretation of world-wide WASP decline, therefore, reflects what might be termed an "insider's" perspective on Anglo-Saxon ethnohistory. Kaufmann, on the other hand, remains an "outsider" sympathetic to the demographic weight and biocultural interests of the Other, an interpretative stance explicitly linked to his ultra-cosmopolitan hybridity. He describes himself as "entirely secular and 'new' immigrant in origin: part postwar Jewish, part Chinese, part Hispanic." Born in Hong Kong, Kaufmann holds Canadian citizenship and apparently passes for a white, North American "Anglo." Wearing the latter hat, Kaufmann rejects the explicitly anti-WASP attitudes of the radical left; instead he upholds "the validity of both WASP and 'American' as important ethnic options," open in principle to anyone. Significantly, however, he denies Anglo-Saxon Christians an exclusive proprietary claim to the WASP brand.[22]

In advanced societies, Kaufmann believes, WASPs will become an upper-class status group in which whites and Asians (as well as mixed Eurasians) remain overrepresented. Ancestral ties to the British Isles will matter little: "In terms of authenticity, light skin and Anglo cultural characteristics might serve to dignify WASP ancestry—however partial and distant." In fact, he declares, "increasingly race and ethnicity is being superseded by transethnic cleavages based on status and ideology." He predicts "that racial boundaries, as with ethnic boundaries, will continue to weaken, thereby generating a symbolically fluid, highly privatized, post-ethnic social environment."[23]

Kaufmann's optimistic take on the future of managerial multiculturalism is a dangerous illusion. WASP identity is more than the leading lifestyle preference of the rich and famous; it is the biocultural expression of a deep-seated ethnopathology. We need to take sociobiology seriously. Contemporary WASP behavior is profoundly dysfunctional in circumstances of economic scarcity, social disorder, and political instability. If they are to survive and prosper, Anglo-Saxon ethnoreligious communities must refuse to reward individuals engaging in conspicuous public displays of out-group altruism. No longer can they afford to impose a high social price on the practice of ethnic nepotism within their own tribal

22 *Ibid.*, 283.
23 *Ibid.*, 309-311.

networks. Moral vanity of that sort is a sin; it is also a maladaptive mistake threatening the survival of an entire race.

Kaufmann believes that Anglo-Protestant *culture* can survive even if Anglo-Protestants cease to exist as a *people*. Of course, he is neither an Anglo-Saxon nor a Christian; nobody expects him to be moved either by the mystic moral magnetism of an ancestral faith or by the biological bonds of blood brotherhood to mourn the passing of a once-great people. It is quite another matter when prominent WASPs coolly contemplate the socially engineered extraction of the spiritual essence incarnate in the flesh and bone of their co-ethnics and its professionally managed transplantation into the dead heart of an ever-more alien nation. In such men, we see textbook examples of Anglo-Saxon Anglophobia. A case in point: a recent, best-selling book by the late Samuel P Huntington.[24]

Unlike Kaufmann who is, at most, an honorary "Anglo" by virtue of his Canadian childhood, Huntington was an *über*-WASP directly descended from early New England colonists. Despite his antecedents, Professor Huntington appeared unconcerned for the future of his people, expressing confidence that enlightened public policies can ensure the ideological hegemony of Anglo-Protestant culture in America even as those carrying the genes of the first English settlers shrink to an insignificant and voiceless minority. The thesis of this book is clear and unambiguous: In the absence of a really existing Anglo-Saxon Christian people, the civilizing influence of Anglo-Saxon Christian culture will be extinguished. Anglo-Saxon Christians are already an endangered species; their ethnoreligious community may simply wither away, leaving behind only a few scattered remnants of the faithful.

In its blindness, the rest of mankind will barely notice the cosmic tragedy implicit in the death and destruction of a unique bioculture born in the sacred light of faith, hope, and charity. In recalling the birth of Old England's *Volksgeist*, tracing its life cycle to its apparent end in modern America, and imagining its regeneration many decades hence, this book resurrects the long-since buried and forgotten corpus of orthodox Christian ethnotheology.

The *novus ordo seclorum* proclaimed at the creation of the American Republic was a major turning point in Anglo-American political and constitutional history; it also sealed the sorry fate of Anglo-Saxon Christendom. Until then, colonial Americans formed the vanguard of the Anglo-Saxon diaspora, thereby laying the biocultural foundation for

---

24 Samuel P Huntington, *Who Are We? The Challenges to America's National Identity* (New York: Simon & Schuster, 2004).

a trans-Atlantic ethnonation. My argument, following in the footsteps of George Grant and his Loyalist forefathers, is that by renouncing their ancestral allegiance to throne and altar, American revolutionaries committed something worse than a political or constitutional blunder. It was a mortal sin to deny and disown sacred bonds of faith, blood, and honour. (I do not mean to imply that King and Parliament were as pure as the driven snow. Readers will find ample evidence below to discourage any such inference.)

This book reminds contemporary WASPs that their advanced state of decay is visible proof that the wages of sin is death—a theological truth that applies to bodies politic no less than to bodies natural. But the death of the WASP is not the predestined end of this story. Like the risen Christ, the Anglo-Saxon people will be born anew as they shed the desiccated skin of the worn-out WASP. The final part of this book suggests that such a miracle may come to pass through the twenty-first century revival of Anglo-Saxon identity politics.

Writing in 1992 when the prospect of a "progressively more integrated worldwide economic system" seemed unstoppable, Joel Kotkin was convinced that "dispersed groups such as global tribes," along with "their worldwide business and cultural networks" were "particularly well adapted" for success. Today, as we ponder the impending collapse of our ever more unsustainably complex socio-economic systems, tribal networks offer an even more attractive bolt-hole. Tribes—the "organizational cockroach of human history"—have shown themselves to be highly adaptive collective survival mechanisms.[25] If only for such pragmatic reasons, WASPs might recall yet another age-old adage; charity begins at home. In the final analysis, however, home is where the heart is. Not so very long ago, the heart of the British diaspora remained "at home" in Old England. The natal narrative of that blessed realm can still provide much-needed inspiration to the postmodern rebirth of Anglo-Saxon tribalism.

---

25 Kotkin, *Tribes*, 3-4; see also, John Robb, *Tribes!* at: http://globalguerrillas.typepad.com/globalguerrillas/2009/03/manufacturing-fictive-kinship-.html. (March 6, 2009).

Part One

Ethnogenesis: Toward a Biocultural
History of English Constitutionalism

1.

Comitatus: Kingship and Covenant in the Evolution of Anglo-Saxon Bioculture

Introduction

Does the survival of an Anglo-Saxon culture presuppose the survival of an Anglo-Saxon people? Strangely enough, the answer provided by WASP managerial and professional elites is an emphatic "No!" One prominent exemplar of that paradoxical attitude is the late Samuel P Huntington.

As a Harvard professor, Huntington knew that Anglo-Protestant *culture* played a vital role in the development and survival of American national identity. But not even his distinguished pedigree as a descendant of Simon and Margaret Huntington who left England in 1633 to settle in America led him to accord Anglo-Saxons formal recognition as America's indispensable "founding race."[1] Instead, he flatly denied that people of British ancestry are the core ethnocultural foundation of the American nation. Rather, Huntington insisted that every American citizen is morally obliged to follow the example set by WASPs such as himself in transcending his merely contingent racial, religious, and ethnic identity. America's "greatest achievement," he declares, "is the extent to which it has eliminated the racial and ethnic components that historically were central to its identity," becoming instead "a multiethnic, multiracial society in which individuals are to be judged on their merits."[2]

---

1 Interview with Samuel P Huntington: http://www.booknotes.org/ Transcript/?ProgramID=1784.

2 Samuel P Huntington, *Who are We? The Challenges to America's National Identity* (New York: Simon & Schuster, 2004), xvii.

Faced with the rising tide of Third World immigration, Huntington urged all Americans, new and old, to "recommit themselves to the Anglo-Protestant culture, traditions, and values that for three and a half centuries have been embraced by Americans of all races." He declared that, so long as "that commitment is sustained, America will still be America long after the WASPish descendants of its founders have become a small and uninfluential minority."[3] Most likely that judgement is the fruit of Huntington's experience as a senior professor at Harvard University.

Founded in the seventeenth century, Harvard College was a resolutely Anglo-Saxon institution until well into the twentieth century. Its primary mission was to forge an overwhelmingly Anglo-Saxon ruling class.[4] That is no longer the case. In 2006, only forty-eight percent, or 3,197, of Harvard College students were "non-Hispanic whites."[5] Of that number, fully 2000—almost two-thirds of the total—were Jewish.[6] Clearly, descendants of the Anglo-Saxon Protestant founders of Harvard College have been reduced to an insignificant and uninfluential minority on that campus.

Do Harvard's admission policies deliberately and with malice aforethought set out to cleanse the college of old-stock American students? Practically speaking, the proof is in the pudding. The dominant ethnoculture at Harvard University is now more Jewish than "Anglo-Saxon Protestant." A troubling question arises for the future: should WASPs regard the Harvard experience (replicated at almost every Ivy League college in the United States) as a source of moral inspiration or, rather, as the grim harbinger of their impending defeat, decline and displacement around the world?

WASP elites react with calm indifference to the progressive exclusion of their co-ethnics from leading cultural, political, and economic institutions created by and for Anglo-Saxons. Such *sang-froid* is truly remarkable given the iron resolve of other peoples to defend their biocultural interests. Few Negro intellectuals, politicians or journalists, for example, believe that *négritude* would flourish if European, Arab, or Chinese settlers were free to remake sub-Saharan African societies in their own image. Nor do many Chinese want China to open its borders to non-Han peoples; with the example of the overseas Chinese in mind, they know only too well how alien tribal networks can seize control of the commanding heights of

---

3   Id.

4   Ronald Story, *The Forging of an Aristocracy: Harvard & the Boston Upper Class, 1800-1870* (Middletown, CN: Wesleyan University Press, 1980)

5   See: http://vpf-web.harvard.edu/budget/factbook/current_facts/2006OnlineFactBook.pdf;

6   See: http://www.hillel.org/HillelApps/JLOC/Campus.aspx?AgencyId=17431.

another nation's economy. Something rather special about Anglo-Saxon culture must account for the astonishing equanimity with which Anglo-Saxon elites greet the loss of their historic hegemony.

Neo-conservatives such as Huntington identify the primacy of the individual as the core concept in contemporary Anglo-American culture. They point to that fundamental idea—not ethnic solidarity—as the unifying element in the transnational, English-speaking, civil society sometimes called the Anglosphere. And individual identity, they insist, is rooted in culture not in genes. Like Huntington, they emphasize the ideological dimension of American national identity, pointedly preferring the term "Anglo-Protestant" to "Anglo-Saxon." On Huntington's reading, the core values of Anglo-Protestant culture emerged out of an historical accident; England became the happy beneficiary of a unique set of circumstances that established individual freedom as the foremost cultural and political value in that particular corner of the world. Freedom became a real possibility for "contact" peoples when the English exported the rule of law along with colonists bound to honor promises set down in contracts and covenants.

National identity, on this view, owes little or nothing to the genetic endowment of the American (or British or Australian or Canadian) people. Huntington remarks that the tradition of constitutional liberty that had its origins centuries ago in the insular history of the English nation "now belongs to Chang, Gonzales, and Singh, as well as to Smith and Jones." On this account, Anglo-Saxon Protestant culture boils down to the negative freedom of individuals to dissociate themselves from all collective identities, be they families, religions, racial or ethnic groups, political movements or corporations. The strong civil societies established throughout the Anglosphere owed their success to an individualistic culture whereas other societies denying individuals the freedom to shed their collective identities have remained "bogged down in ethnic, racial, or religious factionalism, nepotism, and economic systems such as the 'crony capitalism' so prevalent in East Asia and Latin America."[7]

In other words, Anglo-Saxon civil societies are successful because they are individualistic. One important by-product of that individualistic culture is the concomitant normative force of the anti-discrimination principle. It is *only* in such a society that anti-discrimination could become the *Grundnorm* of corporate culture and public law alike. The defining characteristic of WASPs is that they are much less ethnocentric than other

---

7   James C Bennett, *An Anglosphere Primer*:   http://www.pattern.com/bennettj-anglosphereprimer.html *passim.*

peoples; indeed for all practical purposes Anglo-Saxon Protestants appear to be all but completely bereft of in-group solidarity. They are therefore open to exploitation by free-riders from other, more ethnocentric, groups. It seems unlikely that nominally Americanized Changs, Singhs, and Gonzales are as committed in a practical sense to the anti-discrimination principle as Anglo-Saxon individualists. There is no shortage of evidence to suggest that the Changs, the Gonzales, and the Singhs (not to mention the Goldmans with their well-known animus toward WASPs) still practice forms of ethnic nepotism strictly forbidden to Anglo-Protestants.

In these circumstances, an interesting question arises: are contemporary WASPs entitled to recognition as an historic *people*? If not, why not? If so, do they, like other ethnonations, possess ancient constitutional rights requiring their collective consent to policies, programs, and prescriptions that affect the biocultural continuity of their racial, religious, and ethnic identity?[8] Are the few scattered voices calling upon their fellow WASPs to reverse the damage done to their biocultural interests simply "irrational" or unpardonably "racist"? How did WASPs lose the collective will to defend their biocultural interests? Do they lack a rational understanding of racial realities? Would a revival of Christian faith, hope, and charity help to cure the WASP disease; or did Christianity actually produce that ethnopathology? By examining the ethnogenesis of early medieval Anglo-Saxon tribes—the process that eventually created an English nation—we can begin to answer such questions.

We will now turn to the early history of that island race in the period running from the end of the Roman occupation of Britain in the early fifth century AD to the Norman Conquest and Papal Revolution of the eleventh century. Early Anglo-Saxon society was built upon the institutions of lordship and kinship as they developed among the Germanic tribes beyond the frontiers of the Roman empire. We will examine the role of law and the myth of sacral kingship among the Teutonic tribes which colonized Britain from the late fifth century onwards. A major watershed was reached when the Church Christianized those pagan kingdoms. The Church not the state became the nucleus around which the English nation first took shape. Anglo-Saxon England developed in embryo the distinctive constitutional forms transplanted around the world by the British diaspora; it was also the seedbed for a unique bioculture that found expression in widespread and enduring social practices such as oath-taking unknown to other cultures, notably the Chinese, then

---

8   *Cf.* James Tully, *Strange Multiplicity: Constitutionalism in an Age of Diversity* (Cambridge: Cambridge University Press, 1995).

or now. We consider how genes and culture interacted in the ethnogenesis of the Anglo-Saxon people. We conclude that the distinctive social character of the Anglo-Saxon race has an irreplaceable genetic basis that cannot be transmitted to persons from other gene pools simply through immersion in an Anglo-Protestant culture. In the next two chapters we examine the transformation of the Anglo-Saxon bioculture in the period from the Norman Conquest to the eve of the American Revolution.

The Germanic Origins of Anglo-Saxon Society

Under the Romans, Britain was a civilized and prosperous country boasting several large towns in which money, commerce and manufacturing as well as a complex class structure were well developed. In the towns and villages dotted throughout the countryside, large and luxurious villas had been established. Many "of the rich men, and very many of the villa owners, were British." During two centuries of intermittent warfare following the collapse of imperial authority, "the ordered world of Roman Britain was destroyed, or transformed."[9] In its place emerged not just a new and very different culture but a new people possessed of its own distinctive genotype. The Angles, the Saxons and the Jutes who overran the sophisticated Romano-British people were primitive, pre-literate, and pagan Germanic tribes. They lived as pastoral herdsmen before turning to settled agriculture. But they never lost their taste for making war. Tacitus advised that "You will find it harder to persuade a German to plough the land and to await its annual produce than to challenge a foe and earn the prize of wounds."[10]

Indeed, recent research on the Continental input into the English gene pool suggests that a relatively small number of Anglo-Saxon warriors enjoyed remarkable genetic success in Britain. Current estimates as to "the contribution of migrants to the English population range from less than 10,000 to as many as 200,000." The indigenous population numbered at least two million. Yet, despite their relatively small numbers, the Anglo-Saxons made a disproportionate contribution to the modern English gene pool. Noting that historical experiences of conquest and settlement are frequently associated with differential social status and reproductive isolation, scholars suggest that Anglo-Saxon overlords must have imposed

9   James Campbell, Eric John, Patrick Wormald, *The Anglo-Saxons* (Oxford: Phaidon, 1982), 9-11,20.
10 Cornelius Tacitus, *Tacitus on Britain and Germany*, trans with an introduction by H Mattingly (Middlesex: Penguin, 1948), 113.

an "apartheid-like social structure" upon native Britons. Elevated social and economic status enabled Anglo-Saxon invaders to enjoy "higher reproductive success" than the native population.[11] High social status and reproductive fitness alike were a function of an ethnoreligious solidarity demonstrably superior to that of the Britons.

It is possible to quantify, if only roughly, the social and economic advantage enjoyed by the dominant Anglo-Saxon minority over the majority population. In the seventh century, the laws of King Ine of Wessex set out the rates of *wergild* or "blood money" that could be claimed by the family of the victim of a killing as an alternative to a blood feud. The laws provided that the *wergild* payable for a Saxon was to be from two to five times more than that needed to compensate for the death of a "Welshman" (native Briton) of comparable status. When mating and intermarriage between the two groups occurred, higher-status Anglo-Saxon men were likely to attract more than their fair share of "poorer condition" native women. It would have been rare for low-status male indigenes to mate with, much less marry, Anglo-Saxon women and they were at a disadvantage in competing for their own women. The result was the replacement of indigenous Y-chromosones. A significant "degree of post-migration reproductive isolation" between ethnic groups was maintained from the middle of the fifth century until sometime around the ninth century.[12]

The laws of Alfred the Great dating from around 890 AD did not distinguish between Britons and Anglo-Saxons. By then, there was no need for such legal distinctions; in the fifteen or so generations since the mid-fifth century; formerly small bands of Anglo-Saxon invaders established their incontestable hegemony not just over the territory of England but also within the male-line ancestry of the emerging nation's gene pool. Native British men either were pushed physically outwards into the northern and western marches of the Anglo-Saxon kingdoms or remained as genetic fringe dwellers among a new island race. Like any other "race," the English had become "a large, partly-inbred extended family"[13] with its own increasingly distinctive traditions. After several centuries as a *Herrenvolk* in the British Isles, the Anglo-Saxons were distinguishable both genetically and culturally from the Germanic cousins they had left

---

11   Mark G Thomas, Michael PH Stumpf and Heinrich Härke, "Evidence for an apartheid-like social structure in early Anglo-Saxon England," *Proceedings of the Royal British Society* (doi: 10.1098/rspb.2006.3627.)

12   *Ibid., passim.*

13   Cf Steve Sailer, "It's All Relative: Putting Race in its Proper Perspective," http://www.vdare.com/sailer/presentation.htm.

behind on the Continent. Nevertheless, they remained a recognizably Germanic people.

There were, in fact, many Germanic peoples. Apart from Anglo-Saxons, there were Goths, Franks, Burgundians, as well as the Alamannic, Suevic and Vandal peoples, not to mention the Vikings of Scandinavia. Despite notable differences, these Germanic peoples had much in common. From Tacitus, generations of historians gathered the somewhat misleading impression that Anglo-Saxon democracy had its origins in the forests of Germany. On his account, tribal chiefs might discuss major issues in advance among themselves but the community as a whole maintained the power to decide. The sort of hearing accorded to a king or chief depended not on his authority but on whatever prestige attached to his "age, rank, military distinction or eloquence." According to Tacitus, the people would dissent loudly if a proposal displeased them but "if they approve, they clash their spears. No form of approval can carry more honour than praise expressed by arms."[14] Tacitus' image of tribal democracy among the Germans may have been exaggerated, but both German and Anglo-Saxon tribes clearly did possess powerful traditions of local self-government.

More recently, historians have debunked the nineteenth-century image of Anglo-Saxon England as a model of direct democracy in action. Few now doubt that "the effective government of the country remained in the hands of kings and princes supported by a powerful aristocracy." But the division of England into shires which were then subdivided into hundreds containing still smaller units known as tithings dated from the Anglo-Saxon period. Similarly, there was steady progress towards the emergence of a parish system in the Anglo-Saxon church.[15] Even so, the hundreds and parishes were so small and so numerous that their control could not have been monopolised by those of noble birth. Local government co-existed with government by kings and princes; it rested upon "a body of men small enough to have intimate knowledge of a small area and thus able both to attend to its affairs and to place ultimately upon the back of an individual his own share of the burdens and duties imposed by a king".[16]

An institutionalized predisposition towards both local autonomy and individual liberty is a deeply-rooted characteristic of Northern European peoples. Individualism is, of course, a feature of the Western

---

14 *Tacitus*, 109, 110.

15 HR Loyn, *The Governance of Anglo-Saxon England* (London: Edward Arnold, 1984), 58.

16 Peter Hunter Blair, *An Introduction to Anglo-Saxon England* (Cambridge: Cambridge University Press, 2003), 194-195.

world generally and can be traced back to the ancient Greek and Roman civilisations. All the markers of individualism are found uniquely within Western biocultures: namely, monogamy, nuclear families based upon consent and love with a consequent decline in the importance of extended kinship groups, representative government with individual rights against the state, moral universalism and a preference for reason and science over dogmatism and submission to in-group authority. But while the Christian West as a whole is markedly more individualistic than any non-Western civilisation, the people of north-western Europe, particularly the English, more often display such traits than other Europeans.[17]

This can be explained in terms of evolutionary psychology. Adapting to the harsh environment of the Ice Age, "the Nordic peoples evolved in small groups" and developed "a tendency towards social isolation". Natural selection favored inventive and resourceful people able to survive on their own or in small groups. Adaptations were "directed more at coping with the adverse physical environment than at competing with other groups". Under such circumstances, there emerged the paradoxical reality of an ethnocultural or racial group defined largely by the relative absence of an ethnocentric sensibility. In evolutionary terms, ethnocentrism is highly useful and adaptive in circumstances where survival depends upon the outcome of competition for resources between extended kinship networks and large, tightly-organised groups. While Northern European peoples remained hunter-gatherers in cold climates, they were unable to support large groups. Neither ethnocentrism nor extended kinship networks were of crucial significance in coping with harsh and unforgiving physical environments. Consequently, early Europeans were less likely than peoples in the Near East or in tropical lands to develop collectivist mechanisms for group competition. Instead, monogamy and bilateral kinship relationships in which both sexes made more or less equal contributions to the survival of small family units became the norm.[18]

Hunting as a mode of economic production required the male provisioning of females. This favors "pair bonding—the psychological basis of monogamy; in which there is cooperation between nurturing females and provisioning males".[19] The Germanic preference for monogamous families was noted by Tacitus. Almost uniquely among the barbarian peoples,

17   Kevin MacDonald, "What Makes Western Culture Unique?" in *Cultural Insurrections: Essays on Western Civilization, Jewish Influence, and Anti-Semitism* (Atlanta, GA: The Occidental Press, 2007), 271-299.

18   *Ibid.*, 287-292.

19   *Ibid.*, 289.

he remarked, they are "satisfied with one wife each." In Tacitus' view, no feature of Germanic morality deserved higher praise. [20] For good reason: monogamy was conducive to inclusive fitness. Successful hunting in northern areas required "considerable experience, quality education, and years of intensive practice". This led to a pattern of high investment parenting. Males could not easily provide for large families. Late marriages and low birth-rates were common, placing considerable pressure on females to ensure the survival and well-being of their children. Kevin MacDonald contends that this "simple household system is a fundamental feature of individualist culture." This culture favored the growth of liberty because each "family was able to pursue its interests freed from the obligations and constraints of extended kinship relationships and free of the suffocating collectivism of the social structures typical of the rest of the world."[21]

The existence of many small nuclear families among these Northern European hunter-gatherers encouraged the elaboration of various forms of non-kinship based reciprocity so that scarce resources such as meat were shared. This is not to suggest that extended families were unknown in Germanic biocultures. On the contrary, Roman observers noticed that, by comparison with the deracinated, culturally alienated individuals mixed together in the anomic urban environments of the Empire, the rural Germanic peoples were notable for their social cohesion and a high level of in-group solidarity. In the event of attack or famine, prehistoric Germans could not look to a bureaucratic empire for protection or assistance. The institution of the blood feud reflected the crucial importance of kinship networks. At the same time, the basic family unit typically consisted of husband and wife, together with minor sons and unmarried daughters and other legal dependents such as slaves or servants.[22] Moreover, solidarity among these small families was not based solely, or even mainly, upon extended kinship networks. On the contrary, non-kinship based forms of reciprocity were a vital source of collective security.

A unique feature of Germanic societies carried to Britain was the *Männerbund* or *comitatus*, "a band of young warriors led by a chief or king which was distinct from the other strata of society (i.e., the priests and the cultivators) and which exhibited in battle a remarkable recklessness

20 *Tacitus*, 115.

21 MacDonald, "Western Culture," 290.

22 Katherine Fischer Drew, *Law and Society in Early Medieval Europe: Studies in Early Medieval History* (London: Variorum Reprints, 1988), VIII 17.

and esprit de corps."[23] The vertical relationship between the chief and his picked band of followers was characterised as well by reciprocity. A chief whose courage in battle was surpassed by his followers would be disgraced, just as the followers were honor-bound to equal the courage of their chief. Lifelong infamy and shame would attach to any warrior who left the battle alive after his chief had been slain. The chiefs fought "for victory, the followers for their chief." That simultaneous verticality and reciprocity contributed to a high level of in-group solidarity. Leaders, no less than followers, had obligations. At the same time, the relationship between leaders and followers remained voluntary on both sides.[24]

The particular cohesiveness of the *comitatus* relationship became a substitute for or at least a complement to the solidarity experienced within the family. Marc Bloch remarked that in "tenth century Anglo-Saxon law, the lordless man is an outlaw unless his relatives are prepared to assume responsibility for him."[25] The oath of loyalty offered by warriors to their chieftain extended the bond of kinship beyond the limits of biological relatedness. Even the duty to avenge the death of a kinsman by "raising the feud" applied as well to relationships within the *comitatus*. "In fact", according to James C Russell, "the intensity of the *comitatus* bond seems to exceed even that of kinship."[26] Without such networks of voluntary relationships independent of and sometimes even in conflict with ties of blood, Northern Europe would not have developed successful civil societies.

Lordship and Kinship in Germanic Societies

Among the Germanic peoples of north-western Europe, the primary personal bonds of both lordship and kinship cemented the social structure and political order. The institution of hereditary kingship was as yet unknown. Instead, young warriors would attach themselves to temporary leaders for raiding parties. The order of companions or *comitatus* surrounding a chief had a rank ordering; according to Tacitus "there is intense rivalry among the companions for the first place by the chief, [and]

---

23 C Scott Littleton quoted in James C Russell, *The Germanization of Early Medieval Christianity: A Sociohistorical Approach to Religious Transformation* (New York: Oxford University Press, 1994), 117.

24 *Ibid.*, 119.

25 Marc Bloch, *Feudal Society: The Growth of Ties of Dependence* Vol I (London: Routledge & Kegan Paul, 1965), 224.

26 Russell, *Germanization*, 121.

among the chiefs for the most numerous and enthusiastic companions."[27] The more successful chiefs were able to establish themselves as "big men" able to organize longer-lived followings.[28]

But it was not possible to "maintain a large body of companions except by violence and war."[29] In practice, "the limit on the time span of big man leadership is set not by the leader's life so much as by his purse."[30] Loyalty was secured by dispensing gifts to the order of companions. Booty from raiding parties would provide one source of capital for that purpose. More ambitious conquests, particularly of settled agricultural territories would allow the leader to distribute those captured lands among his followers. But if the leader's largesse dried up, perhaps as the consequence of a protracted peace, young warriors might attach themselves instead to another chief in a different tribe where a war was afoot.[31]

Given the inherently transitory and unstable character of lordship in the Germanic tribes, the non-kinship based forms of reciprocity represented by the *Männerbund* were not capable alone of maintaining social order. For that reason, the kinship-based institution of the blood feud played a key role in Germanic societies. Indeed, the blood feud has been important to a wide range of primitive societies in which the state is either weak or non-existent. The blood feud "is the familial rather than the political means of maintaining order." In many parts of the world, family-based feud systems still provide a deeply-rooted bulwark against centralised political power and law-making authority.[32] The Northern European tendency towards social isolation imposed by an ecologically-adverse environment did not leave Germanic tribes totally bereft of collectivist mechanisms for group competition. Rather, those mechanisms were "relatively less elaborated, requiring a higher level of group conflict to trigger their expression."[33]

As Germanic tribes developed beyond the primitive hunting and gathering stage, new sources of conflict within and between groups became a fact of life. When the light of history first shone on them, kinship played an important role in Teutonic social organization. By then, of course, they had developed a more or less settled, if rudimentary, agrarian way of

---

27 *Tacitus*, 111-112.

28 Warren Winfred Lehman, "The First English Law" (1985) 6 *Journal of Legal History* 1 at 5.

29 *Tacitus*, 112.

30 Lehman, "First English Law," 6.

31 *Tacitus*, 112.

32 Lehman, "First English Law," 8.

33 MacDonald, "Western Culture," 287.

life. Their livestock and crops, together with their homes, were valuable forms of real and personal property, vulnerable to thievery from within and plunder from without the tribe. Cattle loomed very large in the lives of these rude folk. The loyalty of a warrior to his chief was secured by a gift of cattle known as a *feohgift* even if the gift exchange also involved armor or jewels.[34] Germanic society was a world of proud, self-possessed, violent—and armed—men. In the absence of a powerful public authority, a lordless or kinless man could be killed or robbed "with virtual impunity since no one was likely to take action on his account."[35]

In societies where the state is either weak or non-existent, the duty to avenge an injury suffered by an individual often falls on his kinfolk. Among the Germanic peoples, the blood feud functioned as a sort of proto-law in which disputes could be processed and resolved.[36] "The feud could also exist as a dispute system in its own right, independent of the law." Kin-based feuding was a more or less effective way of keeping the peace. Indeed, the law of the tribe as a whole might recognize the legitimacy of vengeance killings. Feud or the threat of it could also provide the force behind tribal law where it was the responsibility of the plaintiff and his kin to enforce judgements recognizing their right to compensation for the wrong committed by a defendant. The blood feud also provided an inducement for extended family networks to police themselves. Violent and unruly kinsmen could expose other members of the kin group to the threat of vengeance killings. People were encouraged "either to ensure themselves of their kin's support or to refrain from acting should their kin not approve of the course of action."[37]

Kin-based feuds impacted on the nature of the body politic. Because of its bilateral and ego-centered nature, the Teutonic kindred could never develop into a permanently compact group with a chief of its own. Any member of the tribe (ego) "could trace kinship through both male and female links and on both parents' sides." Since not everyone related to ego would be related to each other, the boundaries of the kindred fluctuated. A mother's brother and a father's brother would both be kin to ego but not to each other.[38] Despite the shifting character of the kindred, there can be no doubt that a "man who can at any moment surround himself with

---

34   Lehman, "First English Law," 5.

35   William Ian Miller, "Choosing the Avenger: Some Aspects of the Bloodfeud in Medieval Iceland and England" (1983) 1 *Law and History Review* 159 at 165.

36   Lehman, "First English Law," 8; Miller, "Choosing the Avenger," 160.

37   Miller, 161, 164-165.

38   *Ibid.*, 162.

a large group of persons all of whom are willing to make sacrifices for him, is in a very different position to one who has to depend on his own efforts and on those of his immediate family for protection against aggression." Small peasant proprietors within a cohesive kindred enjoyed social and political, not to mention economic advantages unavailable to isolated small landowners. Extended kinship networks served as insurance societies and stood guard over land belonging to members; if necessary, the kindred rallied around a kinsman threatened with a lawsuit. Wherever kindred maintained their solidarity it was more difficult "for a wealthy landowner, or even ecclesiastical foundations, to exploit the financial and social difficulties of a poor neighbour, by acquiring his lands or by extorting rights over him at a period of want."[39]

Changes in the balance of power between lords and kindred affected the evolution of political society among the Teutonic tribes. In particular, there were striking differences in the relative importance of lordship and kinship in Anglo-Saxon England as compared with southern Denmark and northern Germany from which the Angles, the Jutes and the Saxons originated. In Friesland and Schleswig-Holstein, throughout the Middle Ages there was a preponderance of free peasant proprietors with few great territorial lords endowed with seigneurial privileges. In England, by contrast, the prevalence of lordship was much more marked. The rigors of proto-feudalism in Anglo-Saxon times had been such that the modicum of independence enjoyed by free sokemen in northern and eastern England amounted to little more than the right to choose their own lord.

It may well be that the relative "absence of seigneurial rights among the nobility of Jutland, Schleswig, and Friesland" was "due to the strength of the kindreds; just as the growth of these rights in England" was caused by the absence there of cohesive kindreds. As a general rule, according to Phillpotts, "where cohesive kindreds persist into the later Middle Ages, there the peasant or townsman tends to be free." On the other hand, once the solidarity of the kindred disappears, the liberty of the individual suffers at the hands of lords asserting seigneurial rights over the peasantry.[40]

---

39 Bertha Surtees Phillpotts, *Kindred and Clan in the Middle Ages and After: A Study in the Sociology of the Teutonic Races* (New York: Octagon, 1974—orig. pub. 1913), 247-248.

40 *Ibid.*, 253-254.

Law in Early Anglo-Saxon England

The original home of the Germanic peoples from the Stone Age onwards appears to have been in southern Sweden, Denmark and northern Germany. It was there that "the solidarity of the kindred persisted longest." It was during the great migrations of the Teutonic tribes, the *Völkerwanderungszeit* (AD 375-568), that kindred cohesion began to break down. The kindred system of tribes whose migrations did not take them far from the old *Heimat*—the Frisians, for example—was not much impaired. Yet even those tribes who experienced years of wandering and of warfare on the Continent were better able to settle down and re-establish their extended kinship networks than those engaged in seaborne migrations to England and Iceland. Because it was very unlikely that a kindred group would build and man vessels for the purpose of transporting its own kinsmen exclusively, "any individuals wishing to join an expedition would rally to the first ship that was sailing and probably remain permanently associated with its crew in the new country."[41] Anglo-Saxons sailing in small groups across the Channel became separated from the extended families among which they were used to living. Kinship ties were weakened substantially.

Of course, kinship was not eliminated entirely, much less permanently, as a crucial factor in social organisation. Indeed, family was so central to Anglo-Saxon life "that the adoption of non-relatives was a common way of giving them a place in society." The blood feud remained a family affair but many individuals broke loose from ties of kin and pseudo-kin so that policing through feud and compensation were disrupted beyond repair.[42] The obligations associated with the feud had not changed but their burden had been "calculated for the backs of many individuals, not for one." When compensation to victims of wrongdoing was charged to a whole kindred, the price was comparatively cheap. By contrast, when *wergild* "was paid out of the cattle and household goods possessed by the individual slayer and his immediate family," it became a crushing imposition often leading to debt, serfdom, and poverty. A shift away from extended kinship networks increased the importance of lordship.

Expeditions setting out for England were led by kings who gathered around them an aristocracy of fighting men, or *comites* as Tacitus called them. The *comitatus* had always been a sort of surrogate family. In early Anglo-Saxon England, a lord assumed "the duty of providing for his

41 *Ibid.*, 262-263.
42 Lehman, "First English Law," 14-15.

followers what otherwise a young man's family would have been expected to do." Indeed, raising the feud actually worked to enhance the relative importance of lordship by imposing burdens too heavy to bear on small landowners. If a young man could not depend upon kinfolk for assistance in paying his *wergild*, or perhaps even his marriage portion, he was compelled to call upon his lord instead; in return, he was bound to accept specific obligations. Once the Teutonic *comites* reached a certain age, their aim was always to settle down on lands granted to them by the king. The ability of big men to exercise the seigneurial prerogatives of lordship over their neighbours depended very much on whether the countervailing power of kindred solidarity had remained intact. In England, the warrior nobility were much better placed than their Continental counterparts to establish themselves as territorial lords who "early gained rights over the neighbouring freemen in return for protection."[43]

The disruption of kinship ties associated with the sea-borne Anglo-Saxon invasion of England not only enhanced the role of lordship; it also helps to account for the early appearance of what might be described, somewhat misleadingly, as royal law codes. The weakening of kindred did not make the Anglo-Saxons any less disposed to seek revenge for killing or other injuries suffered by themselves or members of their immediate families. The only alternative to an endless cycle of tit-for-tat revenge attacks is a system of *wergild* compensation for wrongdoing. The more difficult it became for comparatively weak kindred to exact compensation from a wrongdoer's kinfolk, the greater the likelihood of increased random violence: "A man had neither the protection of kith nor kin to restrain him." In these circumstances, kings were well placed to enhance their authority by becoming actively involved in the settlement of feuds. Kings could provide go-betweens, who might be "either well-known, trustworthy men or specially designated officials" to induce a settlement supported by relatives from both sides of a dispute. In this way, early Anglo-Saxon laws appear, not as a radical substitute for feud, but as an integral part of the system, providing long lists of injuries for which compensation is prescribed.[44]

Anglo-Saxon law was not, however, a legislative codification of tribal custom. Nor, within the Anglo-Saxon tribes, did law have its source in a sovereign will. The "codes" proclaimed within several kingdoms were not positive enactments dictating the manner in which particular disputes should be resolved by judges acting in the name of the king. The

---

43   Phillpotts, *Kindred and Clan*, 253.

44   Lehman, "First English Law," 17.

fact that the laws were written did not signify the legislative primacy of the royal will. "Law was not law because the king announced it. Neither his words nor his intention were important to the law's force or meaning." The words of Alfred's code "did not limit the law but reminded the conscience." Something announced by the king would be right not because the king said so but because it accorded with the common conscience of the community.

Because there was never a legal priesthood in Anglo-Saxon England, both the king and the commoner were allowed "to search heart and head for law." Wisdom was an obvious prerequisite for such a task and kings were thought to be endowed with a more than ordinary wisdom.[45] Anglo-Saxon kings were credited with that special wisdom at least in part because their law codes were designed to foster that impression. In other words, the laws were intended not so much to provide a set of rules governing the effective resolution of disputes but to establish the ideological and symbolic hegemony of the kings who issued them.

The various codes are important vehicles "for the image which Germanic kings and their advisers, Roman or clerical, wished to project of themselves and their people: an image of king and people as heirs to the Roman emperors, as counterparts to the Children of Israel, or as bound together in respect for the traditions of the tribal past."[46] The Anglo-Saxon laws were part and parcel of the cult of kingship which helped to ease the transition from paganism to Christianity and which, in so doing, laid the foundations for English nationhood.

The Myth of Sacral Kingship

Before the great migrations, the Germanic peoples appear to have "had two sorts of kings, one essentially religious, the other military."[47] According to Tacitus, kings [*reges*] were chosen "for their noble birth, their leaders [*duces*] for their valour."[48] During the *Völkerwanderungszeit*, however, the two functions were merged in a magicoreligious cult centered on the worship of Woden and expressed in the regal role of the war-leader. Among the Anglo-Saxons, charismatic kingship was the political institution that

---

45   *Ibid.*, 12-13.

46   Patrick Wormald, *Legal Culture in the Early Medieval West: Law as Text, Image and Experience* (London: Hambledon, 1999), 38.

47   Patrick Geary, *Before France or Germany: The Creation of the Merovingian World* (New York: Oxford University Press, 1988), 55.

48   *Tacitus*, 106.

gave "cohesion to the realms established by the invading tribes." The often competing institutions of lordship and kinship were fused in the person of the king.

In one sense, kingship was the purest embodiment of the lordship principle; the relationship between a war-leader and his *comites* was rooted in non-kinship based reciprocal exchanges. But Anglo-Saxon kings were not mere mortals raised above ordinary folk by the simple accident of popular acclamation; they possessed a sacral quality by virtue of their royal blood. In every Anglo-Saxon kingdom, individual rulers were chosen from a particular lineage springing from earthly founders—the *stirps regia* or royal race—but almost always also claiming descent from a common divine ancestor, Woden, the god of kings and warriors. Indeed, the Anglo-Saxon word *cyning* for king originally meant "son of the *cyn* or family."[49] The cult of sacral kingship served as the foundation myth of Anglo-Saxon society.

In this context, the term "myth" is not used in a polemical or pejorative sense. Rather, a myth is an ideology or "political formula," a symbolic glue that maintains order and social cohesion. Political myths are always a mixture of truth and falsehood; they are not scientific theories but neither are they arbitrary. A successful political formula enables a nation, people or class to solve the real problems arising out of its own particular environment. Each successive regime in the history of the Anglo-Saxon people down to the present day has developed its own distinctive foundation myth.

Every society requires a political formula to justify the rule of whichever social class exercises effective control over its members. Ruling mythologies are always expressions of vital human interests, needs, desires, hopes, and fears. Whatever differences there may be between the political formulae employed in support of widely varying regimes, every foundation myth performs at least two functions: it must serve in some way the interests of the ruling class while arousing the most profound sentiments of the ruled classes.[50] The cult of sacral kingship in Anglo-Saxon society easily passed both tests.

As the intermediary between his people and the gods, the role of an Anglo-Saxon warrior-king combined religious and political functions in a seamless unity. Descended from a god, he was *heilerfüllt* (literally, "filled with the sacred") and so represented "the charismatic embodiment of the

---

49 William A Chaney, *The Cult of Kingship in Anglo-Saxon England: The Transition from Paganism to Christianity* (Berkeley: University of California Press, 1970), 14, 21, 7, 34.

50 James Burnham, *The Machiavellians: Defenders of Freedom* (London: Putnam, 1943), 72-74, 86-91.

'luck' of the folk." And it was in the realm of action that the king bound
the divine together with the fate of his tribe. The absence of a separate
caste of priests among the pagan Anglo-Saxons meant that it was the
king who sacrificed for victory and for good crops. Uniting priestly and
political functions, the king assumed the burden of ensuring a favorable
relationship with the divine. In effect, therefore, "the god is first of all the
god of the king...and only secondarily the god of the tribe whose 'luck'
is mediated by that of the ruler." As long as the king's luck or charismatic
power holds, the tribe is blessed by the deity; when he has lost his *heil* or
'luck' and is thus rendered powerless to secure divine favor, "his people
are justified, even obliged, to do the only thing possible, to replace him
with another who can make the office once more effective."[51]

The removal of a king reveals the reciprocal exchange at the root of the
relationship between an Anglo-Saxon lord and his followers. Reciprocity
found an especially ruthless expression in the practice of ritual king-slaying. Sacrifices offered to the deity by a king sometimes failed to deliver
temporal prosperity or victory to the tribe; a king who was seen to have
lost his 'luck' might be sacrificed himself. Faced with the threat of defeat
in battle, legendary Germanic kings were known to have offered themselves as a sacrifice in return for victory. The ritual sacrifice of kings was
a customary means of coping with tribal catastrophes "when the 'luck'
of the king and folk had deserted them; to restore the favor of Woden-
Othin the king, whose responsibility that favor was, was offered to him."
A traditional offering to appease the deity involved stabbing the king to
death and hanging him from the crown of a tree. Ritual king-slaying was
intended to restore the charismatic power of the royal lineage.[52]

That power, a *mana* from on high, permeated the entire Woden-
sprung clan from which kings were elected. Kingship was hereditary only
in the sense that any member of the royal race could be lifted out of the
rank of ordinary folk by virtue of his divine ancestry. The fact that any
member of the royal lineage was eligible to succeed to the throne sparked
recurrent fratricidal wars and struggles throughout Anglo-Saxon history.
By the same token, however, no individual prince of the blood royal possessed a right to the kingship independent of the popular will. Tribal election of a sacral ruler did not, however, represent a primitive prototype of
democracy in action. Rather, the tribe was asserting "the right to assure
itself the possession of the *mana*-filled, god-sprung king, selected from
the royal race for his obvious 'luck.'" The choice of potential kings was

---

51 Chaney, *Cult of Kingship*, 12.

52 *Ibid.*, 113-115.

"limited to the god-sprung family to which the 'luck'-giving *mana* was apparently confined."[53]

The fusion of religious and political authority embodied in Anglo-Saxon kings facilitated the conversion of their peoples to Christianity. This was true, most obviously, because the kings played a direct role in the coming of Christianity. Without royal support, conversion did not and could not occur. Nowhere in England did the common folk of a tribe convert before the conversion of their monarch. Some aspects of Christian theology were congenial to both the Anglo-Saxon kings and their peoples. The concept of God as a heavenly monarch dispensing rewards to his band of followers echoed the pagan theme of the god-sprung king. Portraying Christ as the Son of God also made it easy for Anglo-Saxon to understand his authority in terms analogous to Anglo-Saxon kingship. [54] Even the crucifixion of Christ could be assimilated to the pagan legends of ritual king-slaying, "portraying a young hero who ascends the tree of the cross to enter into combat with death and, while succumbing, prevails in the end."[55]

The ancient Anglo-Saxon tradition of the sacrificial king was maintained by newly Christian rulers acting to purify the folk. The pagan priest-king was expected to overcome any imbalance of nature and restore the 'luck' of his people. So too the Christian king had to mediate and, if necessary, suffer himself for the sins of his people.[56] The *mana*-filled royal dynasty was the purest manifestation of the Anglo-Saxon *Volksgeist* before and after the transition from paganism to Christianity.

The ethnogenesis of the English people was very largely a religious phenomenon, proceeding in tandem with the success of Christian missionaries working to convert pagan kings—who brought their people with them into the fold of the Church. Certainly, not even the strongest pagan kingdoms were able to establish secure or permanent hegemony over their rivals. Some of the smaller kingdoms in the east of England, it is true, did manage to achieve a measure of political power over other Anglo-Saxon tribes, probably because they were the spearhead of a colonizing movement. That superiority was not long lasting, however, since "turbulence among the settled groups and rivalries between them were much more characteristic of the early centuries rather than awareness of common purpose." Subordinating the native Britons became a joint enterprise of

53 *Ibid.*, 20, 16-17.

54 *Ibid.*, 167, 46, 19,

55 Russell, *Germanization*, 170.

56 Chaney, *Cult of Kingship*, 71.

sorts, providing an important counterbalance to the deep local hatreds among the Anglo-Saxon tribes.[57] But a shared interest in consolidating the colonial supremacy of the Teutonic tribes over the indigenous independent British peoples was not enough to create a united Anglo-Saxon kingdom. As the pagan Anglo-Saxon tribes squabbled within and among themselves, the bride of Christ became the womb within which the embryonic English nation began to quicken.

It was in the late sixth-century that the pope in Rome was inspired to send his emissary, Augustine, on a mission to convert the Angles. Among the Germanic tribes that had invaded Britain, the Angles may have been the most numerous and powerful. For whatever reason, it was their name that the founder of Anglo-Saxon Christianity fastened upon the nation that had already attained an ideal existence in his own imagination. Almost alone among the leading figures on the Continent during the sixth century, "Gregory the Great invariably described the pagans to whom he dispatched his mission as 'Angles'" destined to become "angels." As a consequence, "those distinguished by Germanic speech and heathen convictions from Britain's indigenous inhabitants became children of the mother church of the 'English' founded by Gregory's disciples at Canterbury."[58]

A Church for the *Angelcynn*

That powerful vision of a single Christian church for a single "*gens Anglorum*" was soon transformed into reality. By 679 the *Angelcynn*, or people of the English race, had their own archbishop in Canterbury. Not long afterwards, in about 730, the Venerable Bede wrote his *Ecclesiastical History of the English People*. Bede was well aware that a medley of Germanic tribes had entered Britain where they established a number of separate, competing kingdoms. His work demonstrates, however, that barely one hundred years after the conversion of the Angles, Saxons and Jutes to Christianity, those still-warring tribes had been fused into a single nation, the *gens Anglorum*, within a single church, if not yet ruled by a single king.

Within their own sphere of authority, Archbishops of Canterbury strove to achieve a political cohesion beyond the grasp of every earthly king in England. It was therefore in the interest of the archepiscopal see of Canterbury to promote the emergence of a political overlord whose

---

57   Loyn, *Governance*, 8-9.

58   Wormald, *Legal Culture*, 374.

authority could underwrite its own ecclesiastical hegemony. Carrying a vision of a common ethnocultural identity across tribal boundaries, the Church fostered a sense of spiritual unity among all Anglo-Saxons. It was the Church that first exposed the Anglo-Saxons "to a view of themselves as a single people before God—a people who, though they lived in 'Britannia' or 'Saxonia' and though they called themselves Saxons as well as Angles, were known in Heaven as the '*gens Anglorum*.'" It seems clear that Anglo-Saxon kings from Bede's time onwards inherited a sense of Englishness "which drew its strength from spiritual ideals rather than political realities."[59] In other words, the communal identity of the English people was grounded in a spiritual unity fostered by the Christian Church.

It would be a grave error to suppose, however, that the transition from paganism to Christianity represented a sharp break with Germanic traditions of religiosity. On the contrary, to make headway in Britain, missionaries readily accommodated Christian theology to pagan tribal traditions. The Christian Church had emerged in the urbanized environment of the Mediterranean *oikumene* of the late Roman Empire. Greco-Roman cities of that era were characterized by high levels of social disorganization, ethnic heterogeneity, and the widespread destabilization of family life. The result was an inescapable sense of anomie. Under these circumstances, the ethos of "brotherly love" among Christians attracted many culturally and spiritually alienated individuals ready to reject a world steeped in sin in the hope of heavenly salvation.

By contrast, Teutonic tribesmen settled in Britain led a rural existence notable for high levels of in-group solidarity. The other-worldly preoccupation with sin, salvation and religious humility that appealed to the lonely, fearful and isolated individuals of the urban Empire appeared merely plebeian and dishonourable to a nobility of warriors.[60] Germanic warriors were not alienated from their fellow tribesmen. Nor did they fear death and the other irrationalities of human existence. They did not turn to their religion to find a haven in a heartless world. On the contrary, they asked little more from religion than prayers for victory and good crops, protection against black magic and a swift and easy death carrying them directly into the Valhalla of tribal heroes.

To a very significant extent, the effort to convert Anglo-Saxon pagans would never have succeeded had Christian missionaries not recognized

59   Patrick Wormald, "Bede, the *Bretwaldas* and the Origins of the *Gens Anglorum*" in Patrick Wormald *et al* ed *Ideal and Reality in Frankish and Anglo-Saxon Society* (Oxford: Basil Blackwell, 1983), 126-129.

60   Russell, *Germanization*, 81-103.

the need to accommodate "the religiopolitical and magicoreligious orientation of Germanic religiosity." The Germans were Christianized but
only because Christianity was Germanized. "When the church encountered pagan elements that it could not suppress, it tended to give them
a Christian dimension, thereby assimilating them. One obvious example
is found in the ethics of heroism surrounding Christian knighthood that
found militant expression in the crusading movement of the High Middle
Ages.[61]

The policy of accommodation was adopted from the beginning of the
missionary efforts among the Anglo-Saxons. After "giving careful thought
to the affairs of the English," Gregory directed Augustine to ensure
"that the temples of the idols among the people should on no account
be destroyed." While the idols themselves could be smashed, "the temples themselves are to be aspersed with holy water, altars set up in them
and relics deposited there." Pagan sacrifices were forbidden but only if
the people were permitted to make similar offerings to God instead of to
idols. The result "was the emergence of a worldly, heroic, magicoreligious,
folk-centered Christianity."[62] As a consequence, the Anglo-Saxon cult of
kingship survived almost unchanged in the transition from paganism to
Christianity.

The Anglo-Saxon legal world was not divided into secular and religious compartments; "the purpose of the first written laws of the English"
was "to integrate the new religion into the already existing social structure." The relation of Christian kings to the Christian Church continued
the relation of the pagan king to the pagan religion. Like the sacrificial
priest-king of the ancient Germanic tribes, the Christian tribal king possessed a sacred character. "The elevation into sainthood of kings whose
'luck' was strong was a natural product of Germanic religious thought,
and the possession of the relics of these sacred rulers was an object of
rivalry." God and the king were fused together in a unitary world-view
reflected in Alfred the Great's biblically suspect claim that Christ had
"ordered that everyone should love his lord [hlaford] as He Himself did." [63]

The treatment of fidelity to one's lord as a religious duty had a profound impact on the institutional development of the medieval Church in
England. The warrior nobility, generally, and not just the king had a stake
in the sacral character of lordship, viewing "ecclesiastical offices, churches
and monastic foundations from a pre-Christian Germanic perspective, as

61   Ibid., 162, 168.

62   Ibid., 185, 189.

63   Chaney, Cult of Kingship, 185, 195.

sources of sacral charism and legitimation." Such considerations fuelled two important religiopolitical developments in the Middle Ages: the "proprietary" church system, or *Eigenkirchensystem*, and the proprietary monastic system, the *Eigenklostersystem*. That is to say, livings in churches and monasteries were in the personal gift of the landed nobility. Nobles were concerned less with inculcating orthodox doctrines among their people than with an ortho*praxy* tied to adherence to a set of cultic and ritual observances highlighting the *mana*-filled nature of lordship.[64]

An ironic contrast can be drawn between the early Church's need to accommodate itself to the magicoreligious character of Germanic folk-religion to win converts, and the renunciation by modern Anglicanism of its roots in the Anglo-Saxon *Volksgeist* in favor of a universalistic, secular humanist emphasis on the social gospel. Nothing could be more remote from the pacifist preoccupations of contemporary mainstream Christianity than the fascination that the blood-soaked war stories of the Old Testament held for early Anglo-Saxon Christians. From Bede to Alfred the Great literate Anglo-Saxons viewed their own history through the prism provided by the history of ancient Israel in the Old Testament. Reflecting on the long struggle of the Israelites to maintain their settlements in the Promised Land, Bede sought to identify the precise conditions under which his own people could maintain and extend the conquest of their own Land of Milk and Honey in the face of considerable opposition from its indigenous inhabitants.[65]

Bede and Alfred both understood the Anglo-Saxons as another chosen people. By contrast, the native Britons had proved themselves unworthy of the blessings of the Roman and Christian civilisations that had been bestowed upon them. The unbridled wickedness of the Britons caused God to abandon them and hand victory to the Germanic invaders. The *gens Anglorum*, like the Israelites before them, understood themselves as a covenant community. English nationhood was a gift of God; to secure the blessings of that gift the conquering people must remain obedient to God's laws. It was the Anglo-Saxon kings who bore primary responsibility in

---

64 Russell, *Germanization*, 154-155. Vestiges of the proprietary church system persisted into modern times in English law in the fossilized form of the advowson. In the eighteenth century, Blackstone placed the private right of presentation to a church or benefice on the same mundane level as other incorporeal hereditaments such as rents and annuities. But, by then, the ministers and bishops of the Church of England "had lost that faintly magical aura which could lurk behind even the least impressive medieval clerk."William Blackstone, *Commentaries on the Law of England* Vol II, (Chicago: University of Chicago Press, 1979), 20-24. See also, Keith Thomas, *Religion and the Decline of Magic* (Harmondsworth: Penguin, 1973), 188.

65 Judith McClure, "Bede's Old Testament Kings" in Wormald, *Ideal and Reality*, 76, 82.

remodelling the *Angelcynn* in the image of Israel.[66] Looking to the example of powerful kings such as Saul, David and Solomon who extended
their territories and brought alien peoples under their control, Bede and
Alfred understood that the spiritual destiny and political fate of their
people depended on the influence, ability and military strength of kings.
The biblical history of Israel demonstrated that only kings could "serve
as effective warleaders in maintaining and extending the position of their
own people against the encroachments of surrounding tribes with their
own hostile and aggressive kings."[67]

Undoubtedly, the English king most conscious of the divinely-ordained
responsibilities of rulership was Alfred the Great (849-899 AD). But he
acknowledged explicitly that a king cannot "get full play for his natural
gifts, nor conduct and administer government, unless he has fit tools,
and the raw material to work upon." Without "a well-peopled land" comprised of virtuous, diligent and intelligent "men of prayer, men of war, and
men of work," a king "cannot perform any of the tasks entrusted to him."
Accordingly, he portrayed the recurrent Viking invasions that plagued the
early years of his reign as "a scourge sent by God to recall his wayward people." Alfred believed that it was "necessary to rededicate himself and his
people to God." Unsurprisingly, it was Alfred, the most imaginative and
intellectual of West Saxon kings, who inspired the translation of Bede's
Ecclesiastical History of the English People into the vernacular. Alfred was
also the first ruler in England to style himself king of the Anglo-Saxons.[68]
Although Alfred never managed to unite the whole of England under his
reign, he took the decisive steps that led to the emergence before 1066 of
the prototype European nation-state in that country.[69]

The Origins of English Nationhood

It was once a staple of orthodox legal history that English exceptionalism
had its roots in the twelfth century emergence of the common law. It is
now beyond question that people all over "what is now England considered themselves English long before many of their neighbours considered

66   Wormald, *Legal Culture*, 376-377.

67   McClure, "Old Testament Kings," 87.

68   Richard Abels, *Alfred the Great: War, Kingship and Culture in Anglo-Saxon England*
(London: Longman, 1998), 8, 19, 259, 320-321.

69   Adrian Hastings, *The Construction of Nationhood: Ethnicity, Religion and Nationalism*
(Cambridge: Cambridge University Press, 1997), 39.

themselves French."[70] It is more accurate to locate "the decisive period of divergence" not in the twelfth century but in the tenth.[71] The basis for English unity was based, in part, on Alfred's success in repelling the Danish invasion which had destroyed other Anglo-Saxon kingdoms. But a deeper unity was revealed in the way in which Alfred brought the laws of several other kings together in his famous code, thereby revealing the existence of single political as well as ethnoreligious community.

It should be remembered that Anglo-Saxon law codes "rarely behaved and were seldom treated like the program for the day-to-day conduct of society and the remedy of its mundane disorders" provided by modern legislation. This is not to say that Anglo-Saxon kings were not deeply involved in dealing with the disputes and disorders of their people. Rather, the law codes themselves served a broadly political and ideological, not a narrowly jurisprudential, function; they underwrote and reinforced the cult of sacral kingship. Alfred's *domboc*, for example, was prefaced by selected extracts from the Mosaic Law—occupying over a fifth of the code as a whole—to demonstrate that Anglo-Saxon laws "belonged from the outset to the history of divine legislation for humanity." Alfred's subjects were called upon to fulfil their destiny as a new Chosen People. As an intellectual, Alfred conceived his code as one more contribution to the vernacular literature designed to have a symbolic "impact on the collective consciousness by juxtaposing familiar customs, judgements and decrees with perceptibly similar laws of God." [72]

The code was never intended to determine the manner in which judges were to resolve practical legal disputes. Anglo-Saxon law retained much of its oral character in practice; judgements were rendered through a communal and participatory process. There were no professional judges, professional lawyers or a professional legal literature. The conduct of Anglo-Saxon lawsuits remained an amateur affair: "the degree to which kings were able to dictate to their subjects did not by any means always depend on the use of written instructions." [73]

Of necessity, royal authority was devolved to local institutions but following the effective unification of the kingdom under Alfred and his successors, "the law of English kings intruded into their subject's lives to an extent that had no Anglo-Saxon precedent." Nor did the increasingly

---

70 Wormald, "Bede," 104.

71 Wormald, *Legal Culture*, 354.

72 Patrick Wormald, *The Making of English Law: King Alfred to the Twelfth Century* (Oxford: Blackwell, 1999), 417-429.

73 Wormald, *Legal Culture*, 304-306.

aggressive character of English royal law have any European parallel in the tenth century. By then, "English law was moving to the position where, metaphorically, if not literally, the king's writ would run throughout the realm."[74] Between the seventh and the tenth centuries, the inability of the traditional kin-based blood feud to maintain order in Anglo-Saxon England provided kings with the opportunity to expand their authority. "English kings no longer merely wrote themselves into the discords of society. They, in effect, re-orchestrated the whole symphony of feud in a royal key."

Early Anglo-Saxon law had been based on the demand for vengeance. Wrongdoing was conceived more in the manner of a tort demanding compensation than a crime calling for punishment. But even in the seventh century, the dependence of weakened kindred groups upon the regal role in maintaining order led to a situation where compensation entailed not just the purchase of security or life from an injured party but also a cut to the king whose peace had been breached. By the tenth century compensation was overwhelmingly owed not to the kindred of the victim but to God, Church, and the king or the community at large. At the same time, *wergild* had become payable for offences which did not directly or immediately threaten the king. For that reason, the kin-based terms that described the ancient Germanic way of life do not apply in late Anglo-Saxon society.[75]

A centralized *government* had become a defining feature of English nationhood even if the emergence of a centralized *state* in the full-blooded, modern sense of that term still stood a long way into the future. Contrary to popular belief, the Norman Conquest did not wipe out the national identity of the English people. In retrospect, it is remarkable "how rapidly the conquered digested the conquerors."[76] That process of reverse assimilation was assisted by the fact that Normandy itself had been conquered by sea-borne Teutonic invaders and, as a consequence, kindred groups had been weakened there just as they had been in England.[77] Anglo-Saxon men may have been disinherited by their Norman overlords but "their daughters married Normans and taught their children the meaning of Englishness."

Just as importantly, Norman rule was exercised both centrally and at the local level through institutions established by the Anglo-Saxon kings.

74   Wormald, *Making*, 478, 475, 483.

75   Wormald, *Legal Culture*, 61, 341-342.

76   Hastings, *Construction*, 43.

77   Phillpotts, *Kindred and Clan*, 263-264.

"The post-conquest regime was not run by equivalents of Cromwell's Major-Generals, but by the machinery, and at lower levels presumably the personnel, of the vanquished." There was no fundamental breach in the continuity of English history after the Conquest. "If the levers of power were in good enough order to work for William I and Henry I, the likelihood is that they worked quite smoothly for Cnut, Edward the Confessor and Harold II."[78] Before and after the Conquest, the strongest bond in English society was that between lord and man. The existence in Anglo-Saxon England of local communities dominated by landlords bound closely to the king provided a fertile seedbed in which the formal trappings and institutional regularity of Norman feudalism were to flourish.[79]

The Conquest set in motion a paradoxical dialectic: the Anglo-Saxon nobility was pushed aside by the rigid feudal order imposed by Norman barons, thereby setting the stage for the persistent oscillation between baronial power and royal authority that ultimately produced Magna Carta, the hallmark of English constitutional liberty. William created a systematic feudal hierarchy by granting vast demesnes to a handful of great magnates. In theory at least, all land was thereafter held of the king and tenure was conditional upon the performance of military services. The king's vassals were required to provide a set number of knights to follow the feudal host; they met their obligations through a process of subinfeudation. Fiefdoms were granted to men who swore fealty to the king's man as their own lord in a descending chain of personal dependence and loyalty. In the result, the Norman warrior nobility was set over a decapitated Anglo-Saxon society.

The king could and did discipline his vassals by disseising them for some failure, real or imagined, to perform their feudal obligations. Because the king's tenant could not invoke a superior jurisdiction, the king's disseisins were often avowedly no more than an arbitrary expression of the royal will. And this was but one of the perceived injustices that sparked the baronial revolt of the early thirteenth century. The victory of the barons over King John was enshrined in the great constitutional milestone known as Magna Carta. Magna Carta marked a crucial turning point in "the political development of England as a mature nation-state." In the somewhat romanticised language of Bishop Stubbs, it was "the first great public act of the nation, after it had realised its own identity." That view has been debunked by those who emphasize the role of the baronial

78 Wormald, Making, 19.

79 HR Loyn, Anglo-Saxon England and the Norman Conquest, Second Edition (London: Longman,1991), 309-310.

revolt in the genesis of the Great Charter. But the real significance of the document lies in the symbolism attached to repeated royal promises to respect the rights of the non-baronial "free man" together with the ritually acknowledged subordination of the monarchy to the nation and its fundamental laws.[80] Accordingly, the Great Charter declared "that the king should disseise only by judgement;" in doing so, it sought to make him treat his own men as his law already made them treat theirs. [81] For us, the significance of Magna Carta has less to do with its meaning in 1215 than with its subsequent career "as object of the kingdom's fundamental loyalty." It became the first formal and fully national manifestation of the tradition of constitutional patriotism that is characteristic of the Anglo-Saxon people wherever in the world they settled in large numbers.

Constitutional Forms and Ethnoreligious Loyalties

Of course, Anglo-Saxon constitutionalism has undergone many profound transformations in the eight centuries since the adoption of Magna Carta. Over most of that period, however, Magna Carta stood at the heart of a folk-centered civil religion. Even the haughtiest feudal barons knew that social cohesion among Englishmen of all the estates of the realm was essential when faced with competition from other ethnonations. Not always able to express the idea in words, they sensed—or felt—that English nationhood was a matter of common blood nourished by a common faith; that is to say, membership in the English nation was defined by shared descent from ancestors who had been washed in the blood of the Lamb. English noblemen shared with the common folk "an intuitive conviction" of their nation's tribal origins and distinctive ethnoreligious character. There was no talk in those days of inter-faith dialogues in ecumenical Judeo-Christian civilization. Everyone knew that English Christians and Jews belonged to nations bound to live separately and apart. Accordingly, Magna Carta explicitly named the Jews as the source of much predatory economic behavior. It imposed upon the king the obligation to defend English families from Jews resorting to unfair economic practices. Protection for the wives and children of Englishmen borrowing from Jewish moneylenders was given a prominent place in the Charter.[82]

---

80 Hastings, *Construction*, 50.

81 Loyn, *Norman Conquest*, 25.

82 Walker Connor, *Ethnonationalism: The Quest for Understanding* (Princeton, NJ: Princeton University Press, 1994), 202. Magna Carta provides in s 10 that "If anyone who has borrowed from the Jews any amount, great or small, dies before the debt is repaid, it

Strangely enough, the enthusiasm for constitutional patriotism displayed by contemporary WASP politicians, managers, and intellectuals is exceeded only by their conspicuous lack of interest in the specifically English character of the liberties enshrined in Magna Carta. According to the scrupulously deracinated philosophy of contemporary civic patriotism, it is not "common roots but law" which holds a society together. One prominent Canadian politician-intellectual insists that merely "by subscribing to a set of democratic procedures and values, individuals can reconcile their right to shape their own lives with their need to belong to a community."[83] Clearly, both the times and the character of Anglo-Saxon ruling classes have changed.

For thirteenth-century Englishmen, "common roots" were central to a shared national identity. Nor was there much doubt that the English king normally accepted "royal responsibility for the well-being of his subjects." Reciprocal hostility between Christians and Jews was built into the cohesive and highly exclusionary societies of medieval Europe; indeed, it provides many dramatic examples of the ethnocultural solidarity binding rulers to their subjects in that era. Like the king of France and the pope in Rome, English kings were compelled eventually to place definite limits on Jewish exploitation of their Christian subjects. Jews were clearly perceived not just as alien and rootless strangers but as highly competitive economic rivals, a "market-dominant minority" in modern parlance, with interests set in opposition to those of the indigenous folk.[84] Their notorious involvement in the practice of usury was greatly resented by many Englishmen as was their stubborn adherence to their own faith. But the Jews also made themselves very useful to European Christian societies. Because Judaism encouraged lending at interest to gentiles—a practice forbidden to Christians by the Church—Jews filled an economic niche important to both the English king and his noble vassals. Employed by the

---

shall not carry interest so long as the heir is underage, of whomsoever he holds...; s 11 provides "And if a man dies owing a debt to the Jews, his wife may have her dower and pay nothing of that debt; and if he leaves children under age, their needs shall be met in a manner in keeping with the holding of the deceased, and the debt shall be paid out of the residue, saving the service due to the lords..." James C Holt, ed *Magna Carta and the Idea of Liberty* (New York: John Wiley, 1972), 175-176.

83 Michael Ignatieff, *Blood and Belonging: Journeys into the New Nationalism* (New York: Farrar, Strauss and Giroux, 1993), 7.

84 For a discussion of "market-dominant minorities" in the modern context see, Amy Chua, *World on Fire: How Exporting Free-Market Democracy Breeds Ethnic Hatred & Global Instability* (London: William Heinemann, 2003). On the hostility towards the market-dominant Jewish minority in medieval Europe, see Kevin MacDonald, *Separation and its Discontents: Toward an Evolutionary Theory of Anti-Semitism* (Westport, CN: Praeger, 1998), 118-119.

feudal hierarchy as tax farmers and bankers, Jews incurred the resentment of the lower orders who produced the economic surplus upon which their betters battened. Christian kings soon found themselves torn between their "private," or feudal, interests and the "public," or regal, responsibilities owed to their fellow Englishmen. The case of Edward I (1272-1307) illustrates this tension.

Edward I was a pious man who took his role as a Christian king seriously. But he also benefited greatly from Jewish tax farming and banking. He faced resistance when the Church petitioned the King to protect his people from Jewish economic aggression. At first, Edward sought to resolve the problem by calling for the mass conversion of Jews to Christianity. That campaign failed miserably. Finally, in 1290, having received guarantees that lost tax revenue would be made good by the lords and the Church, Edward ordered Jews to leave England. Historians acknowledge that the refusal of Jews to assimilate was a major "factor in Edward's final decision to expel them from England."[85] The pressure on Jews to assimilate can be taken as a sign that the ethnocultural identity of the English people was not based exclusively on blood ties. Jews could become Christians by swearing an oath backed by the supernatural sanctions administered by the Church. Non-kinship-based forms of reciprocity solemnized by oaths played a larger role in the constitution of English identity than was the case elsewhere in medieval Europe.

In effect, the propensity to take and respects oaths was in the blood of every honest Englishman, as was the heroic and chivalrous spirit of the Christian faith. Certainly, Jews, then as now, readily grasped the subconscious linkage between consanguinity and the ethnoreligious identity of the English nation. No doubt, it was an "intuitive conviction" of the unique descent shared by members of the Jewish ethnonation, the sense that all Jews belong to a kindred group of their own, that accounts for their refusal to accept adoption into the extended family of the medieval English nation.

In modern times, Sigmund Freud's highly developed interest in the unconscious mind gave him special insight into the nonrational, emotional roots of his own Jewish identity. He acknowledged, however, "that the emotional wellsprings of national identity defied articulation." Beneath all public professions of religious belief and conscious expressions of national pride, Jewish identity was the product of "many obscure and emotional forces, *which were the more powerful the less they could*

---

85 Robin R Mundill, *England's Jewish Solution: Experiment and Expulsion, 1262-1290* (Cambridge: Cambridge University Press, 1998), 276.

be expressed in words, as well as by a clear consciousness of inner identity, a deep realization of sharing the same psychic structure." Freud was convinced that "blood binds more firmly than business."[86] Similarly, most Jews in the time of Edward I understood that the formal act of swearing an oath would make them Englishmen and Christians in name only. In a very real sense, oath-taking was an English thing; members of many other ethnonations simply did and do not understand its primordial significance.

The ritual practice of oath-taking still provides revealing glimpses into enduring aspects of Anglo-Saxon identity. Indeed that is why the now commonplace spectacle of Third World immigrants reciting oaths of allegiance at naturalization ceremonies is calculated to warm the hearts of WASPs committed heart and soul to the constitutionalist creed of civic nationalism. Oath-taking was one of the earliest defining characteristics of the Anglo-Saxon people. In other societies, even highly developed tradition-directed civilizations such as ancient China, oath-taking never played an important role in social or legal ordering. The presence or absence of oath-taking in a society is associated with important differences in national character.

The Bioculture of Oath-taking

Civilizations differ greatly not just in their social structures but also in their belief systems and cognitive processes. "Human cognition is not everywhere the same." Different systems of thought and perception have evolved in East Asia and Europe, for example, because the different environmental conditions and "historicities"[87] experienced by the populations favored the emergence of divergent forms of economic and social organization. Over millennia, Chinese and Anglo-Saxon societies trod evolutionary paths that rarely crossed. The result was the emergence of two distinctive approaches to the world so unlike each other that they have evolved into "self-reinforcing, homeostatic cognitive systems."[88] The oath

---

86 Connor, *Ethnonationalism*, 198-203.

87 George C Williams, *Natural Selection: Domains, Levels and Challenges* (New York: Oxford University Press, 1992), 6. Williams contends that "biologists interested mainly in unique evolutionary histories" are bound to treat organisms as a sort of historical "document." "The doctrine of historicity holds that the properties of the organic world, from the total biota to minute parts of animals and plants, are the results of unique historical contingencies, some of which are documented in features of the organisms themselves."

88 Richard E Nisbett, *The Geography of Thought: How Asians and Westerners Think Differently…and Why* (New York: Free Press, 2003), xvii, xx, 38.

in Anglo-Saxon society is a revealing outcropping of one such unique homeostatic system. Like the dog that didn't bark in the Sherlock Holmes story, the absence of oath-taking in the ritual life of ancient China tells us something we need to know.

Oaths of homage and fealty were an essential feature of both lordship and kingship in Germanic societies. The oath commending a man to his lord had always been central to the *comitatus*. The social bonds of loyalty and reciprocity established through oaths served to create a surrogate for kindred relations. Persons without kinsmen or lords to vouch for their good character were a threat to social order. For that reason, rootless traders roaming throughout the countryside were allowed to buy and sell only in the presence of trustworthy witnesses.[89] The prominence of oath-taking in Anglo-Saxon culture developed as a response to the disrupted dialectic of trust and mistrust that is a feature of societies based on kinship. In primitive societies an impersonal, neutral relationship with strangers is inconceivable; in inter-personal relations, there is either complete trust or complete mistrust. "Every family relationship defines a certain group of rights and duties, while the lack of a family relationship…defines enmity."[90] The weakened condition of kindred following the Anglo-Saxon invasion of England gave relatively greater weight to the roles played by lordship and kingship in fostering in-group solidarity than had been the case in the old Teutonic *Heimat*.

Like any other Anglo-Saxon lord, Alfred the Great "demanded hold-oaths from his commended men, including his advisors and agents."[91] The divine sanction behind the oath of allegiance reinforced the sacral character of Anglo-Saxon kingship. Indeed, once the Anglo-Saxon kings cast themselves as the earthly counterpart of Christ, their subjects were bound even more firmly to submission. "The sacred character of the Christian ruler, unlike that of the pagan sacrificial king, makes him, in theory, inviolable." But the sacral quality of the Christian rulers was balanced by the duties that they owed to their subjects. They were admonished "to obey their bishops heartily with great humility, because to these are given the keys to heaven, and they have the power of binding and loosing."[92] Kings, too, were bound by the solemn oath they made on ascending the throne.

---

89   RI Page, *Life in Anglo-Saxon England* (London: BT Batsford, 1970), 19.

90   Harold J Berman, *Law and Revolution: The Formation of the Western Legal Tradition* (Cambridge, MA: Harvard University Press, 1983), 57.

91   Richard P Abels, *Lordship and Military Obligation in Anglo-Saxon England*, (Berkeley, CA: University of California Press, 1988), 83.

92   Chaney, *Cult of Kingship*, 252, 255.

In their coronation oaths, Anglo-Saxon kings made a "tripartite promise to protect the Church, to punish malefactors and to do justice to all Christian people."[93]

Oaths played a critical role in resolving almost every sort of dispute in Anglo-Saxon society. "Sworn on holy relics, they drew upon a force more powerful than any wielded by an earthly king, the shared Christian belief that divine retribution would visit oathbreakers." Lacking a monopoly on coercive power, kings no less than their subjects had need of supernatural sanctions to secure promises. Certainly, the Church played a role of the utmost importance in counting the value of the oaths tendered by and on behalf of litigants.[94] "Oaths were administered by priests in churches, at altars, on relics, and through appeals to divine sanction against falsehood." False swearing put at risk not just the property and legal standing but the very soul of oath breakers.[95] Alongside ordeals, oaths were a principal mode of settling legal disputes. The determination of a "defendant's guilt or innocence did not depend upon an investigation into the facts of the case, as it would in a modern court of law, but upon his willingness to swear before God that he was innocent of the charge and his ability to produce the required number of oath-helpers to attest to his good faith." The oaths sworn by all of the parties and compurgators (oath-helpers) "had to be repeated flawlessly, 'without slip or trip,' if they were to succeed." This was no easy matter since they "were cast in poetic form, with abundant use of alliteration." Ordeals by fire, water or battle were mandatory for those "who had no kin to swear for them (or who for some other reason failed to produce the necessary oath helpers), and those of ill-repute whose oaths were wholly unreliable, as well as for certain designated crimes."[96]

Trial by ordeal appears utterly irrational to anyone accustomed to the modern Anglo-Saxon legal system. But it may well have served to compel confessions by criminals unnerved by the religious trappings and supernatural sanctions surrounding the occasion. At bottom, the ordeals reflected a core cultural presupposition; namely, that truth can and should be reached through a dramatic process of conflict and confrontation. It may also be the case that the "irrational" elements in the Anglo-Saxon process of compurgation have been exaggerated. "Oaths mattered, but so, to a much greater extent than hitherto appreciated, did what modern

93 Loyn, *Governance*, 85.

94 Loyn, *Norman Conquest*, 269.

95 Abels, *Alfred the Great*, 268.

96 Berman, *Law and Revolution*, 58, 65; Abels, *Alfred the Great*, 277.

justice would consider evidence, and such evidence was preferably in writing."[97]

The Anglo-Saxon *Weltanschauung* changed significantly after conversion to Christianity, but certain features of that world-view remained constant. Firstly, whether Anglo-Saxons believed that the truth was immanent in the nature of things and could be discovered through magical means or whether they accepted a transcendent notion of truth discoverable through the unaided use of human reason, Anglo-Saxon law always took for granted the central importance of truth itself. This is not a view shared by all cultures and peoples. The cosmology underlying Anglo-Saxon legal traditions is radically different from the world-view that emerged out of ancient Chinese civilization. Indeed, the Chinese have tended to react to the very idea of law with the greatest suspicion. Fearing that the mere act of promulgating a code of law breeds an attitude of disrespect for authority, ancient Chinese scholars recommended that rulers rely instead upon custom and administrative oversight to erect a "barrier of righteousness" against wrongdoing. They would have found the elaborate scale of blood-payments in the Anglo-Saxon laws foolish in the extreme. In their settled view, as soon as a formal legal code sets out prescribed punishments, a "litigious spirit awakes, invoking the letter of the law, and trusting that evil actions will not fall under its provisions."[98]

Litigiousness of any kind was frowned upon. "To take advantage of one's position, to invoke one's rights, was looked on askance, as it always has been in China." One was expected instead to cultivate a ritual moderation, giving "way on certain points and so accumulating an invisible fund of merit whereby one can later obtain advantages in other directions." Crimes and disputes were viewed "as ominous disturbances in man's connections with Nature" rather than breaches of a purely human code. When such ruptures occurred, responsibility was fixed not in terms of "who has done something" but of "what has happened." For the ancient Chinese, responding to crimes and wrongdoing through dramatized ritual ordeals of fire, water or battle would only make matters worse. The greatest priority was not to discover the true culprit behind the crime but to restore the harmony of things.[99]

For the same reason, the Chinese never relied on oaths to maintain order. Lordship and kingship in China did not rest upon reciprocal

---

97 Wormald, *Legal Culture*, 309.

98 Joseph Needham and Colin Ronan, *The Shorter Science and Civilization in China*, Vol I (Cambridge: Cambridge University Press, 1970), 276-280.

99 *Ibid.*, 282-284.

bonds of duty, loyalty and service as they did in Anglo-Saxon England. Government existed to control not to serve the people. Control was to be achieved through the inculcation of ethical standards not by either the promulgation of formal rules or oath-taking. The good man would maintain his honesty and dignity without the need for formal public promises.[100] To ask the good man to swear on oath to avoid wrongdoing was tantamount to recognising his freedom to engage in such conduct should he choose to do so. Individual freedom to break loose from the ties of kindred and community may have been a fact of life in Anglo-Saxon England. It was and is not so in China. This observation is confirmed by the fact that, when oaths do appear in China, they are associated with groups on the margins of China's clan-based society. Oaths have most often been a way of binding people from different clans with different surnames together into "secret societies" such as the Heaven and Earth Society or the Triads.

Elaborate ritual oaths involving the smearing of blood around the mouth created a surrogate community of memory and imagined blood. But precisely because such secret societies disrupted the enforced harmony of established social structures, they were driven to the margins. As an organization formed across clan lines, the Heaven and Earth Society was "not only viewed with antagonism by the clans, it was also suppressed by the authority of the state, which itself had a family-like structure." It was taken for granted that by "not placing their hopes and ambitions within their own clan," the members of secret societies "aroused antagonism between the rich and the powerful on one hand, and the poor and weak on the other." Not surprisingly, the concept of an artificial clan based on oaths came to play "an important role in folk legends about bandit heroes."[101]

By contrast, the oath in Anglo-Saxon society was an implicit affirmation of individual *agency*. That awareness of agency was closely associated with a strong sense of individual identity. Both have been reflected in the Anglo-Saxon fascination with dramatic battles between heroic protagonists not just as they were played out in the courts of the shires and the hundreds but on the theatrical stage as well. The Chinese have been much more preoccupied with the need for *harmony*. "Every Chinese was first and foremost a member of the collective, or rather of several collectives— the clan, the village, and especially the family." Individual Chinese were

---

100 Helen Silving, "The Oath: I" (1959) 68 *Yale Law Journal* 1329 at 1380-1381.

101 Sun Jiang, "Imagined Blood: The Creation of a Community of Memory Through Sworn Brotherhood" (2004-5) 37(2-3) *Chinese Sociology and Anthropology* 9 at 11-12.

not free agents maintaining a unique individual identity across social settings; they were interdependent beings defined by their relationships within a complex and harmonious social network. "Within the social group, any form of confrontation, such as debate, was discouraged."[102]

Conclusion

It is easy to document the existence of such radical differences between Chinese and Anglo-Saxon world-views. It is also possible to explain those cultural differences by reference to history and geography. As we have seen, the European environment favored the emergence of societies based on non-kinship based forms of reciprocity, a tendency reinforced by the circumstances of the sea-borne Anglo-Saxon invasion of England. Their favored occupations of hunting, herding, fishing and trade required relatively little cooperation with large numbers of other people. In China, where the landscape "consisted largely of relatively fertile plains, low mountains, and navigable rivers, both the growth of a populous agricultural society and its centralized control were relatively easy." The development of large-scale irrigation systems gave further impetus to both population growth and authoritarian government.

Civic patriotism never played a significant role in Chinese political or intellectual history. The question arises: Can large numbers of Chinese be assimilated into the civic cultures of Anglo-Saxon countries? It is hard to conceive a Chinese culture in the absence of the Chinese people. Why then is it easy to imagine an Anglo-Saxon culture continuing to thrive without Anglo-Saxons? The answer, in part, is that a belief in the ability of the unique individual to transcend the constraints inherent in any given society and adapt himself to the circumstances of a new society is an essentially Anglo-Saxon or, at most, a European conceit. By nature, Anglo-Saxons are much more resistant than Chinese to the notion that we are the products of a bioculture shaped not just by our environment but by our genes as well. WASPs seem congenitally reluctant to accept that who and what we are today and who or what we can become tomorrow depends not just on individual agency but on intractable biological relationships to distant ancestors.

It is more than likely that the ritual significance of oath-taking in England has an evolutionary basis. In particular, one might expect that men who remained faithful to their oaths and became known as

102 Nisbett, *Geography of Thought*, 4-6.

trustworthy individuals consequently enjoyed greater commercial and reproductive success than known perjurers and outlaws. Over generations, that pattern will produce a population characterised by high levels of trust and trustworthiness. Significantly, a stronger disposition to trust strangers is associated with enhanced levels of a hormone known as oxytocin in the body and the brain. Giving experimental subjects a sniff of oxytocin specifically affects their "willingness to accept social risks arising through interpersonal interactions." Oxytocin is also the key mediator in promoting maternal behaviors and is sometimes termed the "hormone of love," a tag that must be qualified. Far from being an indiscriminate "cuddle chemical," oxytocin has been shown to create "intergroup bias" by motivating "in-group favoritism and, to a lesser extent, out-group derogation." It seems then that trusting behavior has a biological basis and this suggests, in turn, that "the degree of trust could be ratcheted up or down in the course of human evolution by genetic changes that either increased individuals' natural production of the hormone or enhanced the brain's response to it."[103]

If that is true, then it may be that the oath-taking rituals of Anglo-Saxon society co-evolved with increased sensitivity to oxytocin among Anglo-Saxons. Other biochemical mediators and additional psychological and behavioral adaptations are in all probability in play as well. In China, by contrast, the intensely clan-based nature of society did not favor the evolution of trust towards strangers to the same degree; the result may have been a comparatively decreased sensitivity to oxytocin.

At this stage those hypotheses remain untested. But encouraging mass immigration from the low-trust societies of the Third World is probably not the most prudent or efficient way to test the alternative hypothesis that there is no biological basis for trusting behavior. It may be wise not to rely too heavily upon the good faith of the countless Chinese, Africans and other Third World immigrants who daily swear allegiance to Anglo-Saxon civic cultures that are permanently at odds with their own traditions and folkways. It seems likely that, the more genetically distant immigrants are from the host population, the less capable they will be *over the long term* of building or even sustaining the economic and social conditions characteristic of Anglo-Saxon societies.

WASPs are trusting souls. For that very reason, they can be exploited easily by those who promise one thing and do another. Such free riders

103 Nicholas Wade, *Before the Dawn: Recovering the Lost History of Our Ancestors* (New York: Penguin, 2006), 163; Carsten KW De Dreu, *et al* "Oxytocin Promotes Human Ethnocentrism" 10 January 2011, Proceedings of the National Academy of Sciences: www.pnas.org/cgi/doi/10.1073/pnas.1015316108.

"seize the benefits of social living without contributing to the costs."[104] Mass Third World immigration imposes enormous risks upon Anglo-Saxon societies grounded in unique patterns of trusting behavior that evolved in isolation over many centuries. If newcomers do not accept the burdens entailed by the civic culture of the host society—most notably the need to forswear one's pre-existing racial, ethnic and religious allegiances—they are bound to reduce the benefits of good citizenship for the host Anglo-Saxon nation. If infidelity to an oath of allegiance not only goes unpunished but is actually rewarded by the ethnic spoils system built into a multiracial polity, it will hasten not just the already projected disappearance of the Anglo-Saxon people but the final dissolution of Anglo-Saxon culture. Barring a revival of the ancient Anglo-Saxon folk-religion that bleak outcome may be inevitable.

Centuries of revolution have displaced the cult of sacral kingship from the hearts of the *Angelcynn*. WASP elites no longer even pretend to be *heilerfüllt*. Instead this self-serving, militantly secular, managerial-professional class preaches a hollow and legalistic constitutional patriotism, demanding that the Anglo-Saxon countries sacrifice themselves on the altar of universal human rights and free trade. Anglo-Saxons have cast off the spiritual moorings that once bound them to their ancestors and their descendants. Neither the state nor the Anglican Church represents any longer the political and spiritual unity of the *Angelcynn*. Civic nationalism now serves as the official ideology of the corporate welfare state while contemporary Anglicanism is steeped in a pious secular humanism. Both ostentatiously welcome as members all people, regardless of race, color, creed, gender, language or ethnicity. Having been stripped of his own church and state, the contemporary WASP is sorely in need of a sacrificial king prepared to die, if necessary, to defend the ethnic interests and ancestral homelands of his people. Without the miraculous appearance of leaders ready, willing and able to revive their old-time folk-centered religion, WASPs will suffer the consequences of prolonged spiritual, geopolitical and demographic decline. Their distinctively constitutional brand of patriotism, once a selective advantage, has become a tragic flaw in the Anglo-Saxon character.

We will now turn to the period between the Norman Conquest and the Puritan Revolution of the seventeenth century. The story begins 1066 AD. The Anglo-Saxon ethnonation created by Alfred the Great fell under the sway of William the Bastard, the upstart Duke of Normandy sponsored by the Pope in Rome. By the end of the period, we will see that the English

---

104 *Id.*

people had developed into a nation-state—the first such state in the history of the world. By the mid-point in that socio-political evolutionary process, the rise of secular humanism exposes the fault line dividing the embryonic civic culture of the *republica Anglorum* from the centralized *Kirchenstaat* created by the Papal Revolution of the eleventh century.

That rift signalled unparalleled changes to come in the social character of the English people. The very fact of Norman England already entailed significant changes in the bioculture of Old England. In the most general sense, the magicoreligious character of the ethnoreligious practices of the Anglo-Saxon people were substantially reworked so as to conform to the tradition-directed norms of late medieval Latin Christendom. But both the old and the new regime located the source of spiritual and temporal authority in its origins. Six centuries after the Papal Revolution, the inner-directed character of Protestant individualism shifted national attention away from the backward-looking veneration of tradition for its own sake towards a future of perpetual innovation. The *republica Anglorum* of Old England passed into history once and for all, along with the medieval Christian commonwealth of which it was a constituent part.

2.

Republica Anglorum: Religion and Rulership in Old England

Introduction

The Germanic warriors who invaded Britain following the departure of the Romans were intensely ethnocentric. They emerged out of a pre-historic world in which inter-tribal conflict provided each group with essential reassurance of its own indivisible identity. Warfare also grounded the socially embodied certainty that one's tribe alone lived in conformity with the real law. Every primitive people tell themselves that "ours is the only proper way to exist and we are the only ones worthy of being called human."

As an expression of the sacred bond between the tribe and its gods, that outlook was religious in the original and purest sense of the term. Bound together in the impenetrable mystery surrounding the origins of the natural and the supernatural world, the dead, the unborn and the living shared membership in a trans-generational community of blood, language and memory. The WASP attachment to secular humanism is the end product of the "progressive" movement over the past millennium away from the religious roots of ethnocultural identity. As citizens, workers, and consumers, we inhabit a self-contained temporal realm within which spirituality is sublimated into the commodified society of the spectacle. Otherwise, we are safely sequestered from the Old Faith of early medieval Christendom.[1] Indeed, anyone claiming to catch glimpses of the divine in the *Volksgeist* of Old England will be treated as an outcast bewitched by the original sin of "racism."

---

1   Marcel Gauchet, *The Disenchantment of the World: A Political History of Religion* tr Oscar Burge (Princeton, NJ: Princeton University Press, 1997), 42; Guy Debord, *Society of the Spectacle* (Detroit: Black & Red, 1970).

As the folk religion of their forefathers lost its hold upon the English imagination, the primordial ethnocentrism latent within every Anglo-Saxon country found a surrogate faith in loyalty to secular states. Once WASPs were "freed" from the old-time religion, Anglo-Saxon ethnic solidarity disappeared down the memory hole. Contrary to the conventional wisdom espoused by neo-pagan white nationalists, the conversion of the Anglo-Saxons from paganism to a Germanized Christianity did not weaken their ethnocultural identity; nor did it dissolve their warlike spirit. It was not the Christian faith shining through the heroic deeds of Alfred the Great but its subsequent theological perversion into the social gospel of the corporate welfare state that drained the divine from the world of the WASP.

For centuries after St Augustine's mission to the Angles, Anglo-Saxon Christianity nurtured an ethnoreligious community that incorporated several independent kingdoms. Thus, Anglo-Saxon England was an autonomous province of Christendom long before a unitary secular state came into being. Every Anglo-Saxon king carried his splendour into the life of the Church; as *fidei defensor*, he was a priest, as much as a monarch. By the same token, the king was bound to walk by the orthodox light of the Church. The Norman Conquest marked the end of an era, however. Slowly but surely, the magicoreligious, highly ethnocentric, Anglo-Saxon myth of sacral kingship lost its force. In the High Middle Ages the spiritual and temporal powers carved out separate and distinct and autonomous spheres of jurisdiction. Just as the sacred was severed from the secular realm, so too religion itself became a matter of reason not magic. Reflecting the prestige of scholastic rationalism, Catholic Christianity in England became more universalistic and less Germanic in its outlook. Meanwhile, the stage was set for the emergence of a tradition of perpetual and purposeful innovation sponsored by a modernizing monarchy hedging its ideological bets by paying lip service to the populist myth of the ancient British constitution.

In short, the narrative which follows tracks the political, constitutional, and religious history of England from the Papal Revolution of the eleventh century to the Puritan Revolution of the mid-seventeenth century. The main theme is conventionally described as the "secularisation" or "disenchantment" of the modern world. Of course, that begs the question of what it means to live in an "enchanted" world. We preface our narrative, therefore, with a discussion of the primeval religion practiced by primitive peoples such as the pagan Anglo-Saxons. It may surprise many readers to learn that one of the main actors in the "secularization" story was the medieval papacy.

The history of England after Pope Alexander II sponsored the Norman Conquest can be contrasted with the first millennium in the history of Christendom, the Age of Incarnation. In those days, Christians were entranced by the poetic vision of God become incarnate in a man sacrificed for the sins of his people. The thousand years since the Papal Revolution is best understood as the Age of Disincarnation, a period during which the earth became progressively more detached from God, whose heaven was projected somewhere beyond space and time.[2] The very model of a spiritual revolution from the top down, the Papal Revolution laid the groundwork for the secular revolution from the bottom up launched six centuries later by the Puritan saints of Protestant England. Over that period the social character of Englishmen was twice radically transformed. In the time of Alfred the Great, religion and magic were intertwined in the social practices of everyday life. The Papal Revolution set into motion changes that replaced magical incantations with legal traditions (common law, canon law, Roman law), all sanctified by a rationalist theology premised on the doctrine of the two swords, spiritual and temporal. But then the novel autonomy of the secular realm endowed human reason with a life of its own. Eventually, both *raison d'état* and the private actions of a multitude of inner-directed English Protestants fueled the permanently revolutionary forces which destroyed the tradition-directed world of the High Middle Ages.

Primeval Religion

The primeval religion of Anglo-Saxon paganism was premised on the inviolable permanence of the order to which men owe their existence. Whatever the differences between them, all primitive societies appear to share an "underlying belief...that we owe everything we have, our way of living, our rules, our customs, and what we know, to beings of a different nature—to Ancestors, Heroes or Gods." Primitive peoples believe that because "everything governing our 'works and days' was *handed down to us*" by the invisible divine beings immanent in the visible world of nature, we are bound to "follow, imitate, and repeat what they have taught us."[3] Among pagan

---

2   Fr Andrew Phillips, *Orthodox Christianity and the English Tradition* (Norfolk: English Orthodox Trust, 1995).

3   *Ibid.*, 23-24.

Anglo-Saxons, primordial religious belief revolved around the cult of sacral kingship. The ritual expression of that foundation myth generated a distinctive "social character" shared by members of every Anglo-Saxon tribe. In any society, the dominant "mode of conformity" ensures that its members *want* to act in the way that they would *have* to act to ensure the survival of the group.[4] Pagan Anglo-Saxons readily submitted to dominant characters in their tribes who were perceived to be emissaries of the magicoreligious forces lurking everywhere in the visible and invisible world.

The entire framework encompassing the practices of such a primitive society has its "origin in a founding past that ritual both revitalizes as an inexhaustible source and reaffirms in its sacred otherness." The fundamental imperative of its religion, then, is to safeguard what exists through conformity to an ancestral law. The mythical past is "accepted in its entirety and completely removed from man's grasp." It is only through the ritual recurrence of the sacred moment of origins that the drastic distance that separates primitive societies from their beginnings can be overcome. But the origin remains forever shrouded in mystery.

Primeval religion inculcated a profoundly anti-historical frame of mind. Religious hegemony was articulated around the absolute predominance of a founding past that predated the personal preferences of any living soul; it was also premised on the incapacity of humans to transform the organization of their world. Religion, therefore, was an indispensable ingredient in the foundation and maintenance of stable group identities. For that very reason, the primacy of the past was never traced to a "unique global event attributable to the sovereign will" of a creator God. The primordial function of religion was to maintain "a well-defined type of society based on the priority of collective organization over the will of the individuals it brings together." To conceive a transcendent deity separated from the human and natural world he had himself created would open up the possibility that men "here-below" were in some sense responsible for ordering their own existence.[5]

Even in the face of such vitally important changes as the Neolithic revolution, primeval religion insisted on the absolute dependence of the present on the mythical past. Everywhere, the momentous human achievement of agriculture was treated "as a gift from the gods, introduced in ancient times by a hero whose example was thereafter dutifully followed."[6]

---

4   Cf. David Riesman, et al *The Lonely Crowd: A Study of the Changing American Character* abridged edition (New Haven, CN: Yale University Press, 1961), 5-6.

5   Gauchet, 24-25, 30, 27.

6   *Ibid.*, 24.

From the perspective of Christianity and atheism alike, primeval religion dispossessed men of their innate capacity to do both good and evil. The foundation of their way of life was considered to be wholly other.

Paganism was diametrically opposed to the monotheistic conception of a God existing somewhere beyond space and time, a first mover responsible for the creation of the world. The primitive deities worshipped by Anglo-Saxons were feeble by comparison, having no capacity to control the destiny of their world. And this is the fundamental paradox in the history of religion: the weaker the gods, the more dependent humans are on the occult forces and invisible powers that lurk everywhere in the visible world. Conversely, "the greater the gods and the more extensive their power," the more opportunity humans have to develop ways of thinking that "aim to understand the world with an eye to its global control (from either the human subject's or the divine subject's viewpoint.)"[7] Nor does that power belong exclusively to the philosophical abstraction of mankind at large. Western law presumes that even the solitary individual possesses the power to act of his own free will; it follows that he must accept responsibility for the natural and ordinary consequences of his actions.

By contrast, primeval religion submerged the subjective consciousness of the individual in a group-mind knowing no clear boundary between the visible and invisible worlds. This was as true of archaic Greece as it was of early Anglo-Saxon England. When Homer wants to explain the source of an individual's strength or weakness, "he has no course but to say that the responsibility lies with a god." Homer never recognizes "genuine human decisions; even where a hero is shown pondering two alternatives the intervention of the gods plays a key role." Aristotle's "first mover" is as far removed from Homer's ken as the modern concept of the "mind" as the seat of the human capacity for self-control or self-direction. Homeric man "is unaware of the fact that he may think or act spontaneously, of his own volition and spirit." The spirit of primeval religion is utterly counter-subjective. Whatever "strikes" a man, "whatever 'thought' comes to him, is given from without, and if no visible external stimulus has affected him, he thinks that a god has stood by his side and given him counsel, either for his benefit or for his destruction." Unburdened by scruples or doubts, Homeric man does not "feel the weight of personal responsibility for right or wrong."[8] Similarly, the concept of *mens rea*, or the guilty mind, played no part in the Anglo-Saxon blood feud. The law of vengeance could be

---

7   Ibid., 31.

8   Bruno Snell, *The Discovery of the Mind: The Greek Origins of European Thought* (Oxford: Basil Blackwell, 1953), 1-23.

satisfied if compensation for the injury to the victim and his kindred was forthcoming; punishing the actual perpetrator of wrongdoing was never the point.

But the breakdown of kindred bonds in the wake of the sea-borne Anglo-Saxon migration to England pushed both kings and peoples along the path towards autonomous individuality. The rituals of oath-taking highlighted the importance of personal obligations and loyalties between lords and their followers. As the myth of sacral kingship came to outweigh the kindred as the constitutive principle of social order, the egalitarian structure of primeval religion was upset.

Strictly speaking, primeval religion exists prior to the emergence of social hierarchies organized around the exercise of power. There is no place for the political in a world founded by beings other than ourselves whose inviolable legacy we must preserve through the ritual repetition of their sacred teachings. "No one among the living could justifiably claim a privileged connection with the invisible foundation as it did not need anyone to gain universal acceptance." The revolutionary emergence of political power or the embryonic state embodied the divine within society in the form of representatives, administrators and interpreters of the law.[9]

Christian Kingship in Old England

Primitive religion separates men from their origins "in order to forestall the sudden appearance of a division between them." But such divisions become inescapable with the emergence of political power; henceforth, the "dominant ones are on the side of the gods while the dominated are not." The sacral king of the Anglo-Saxons was completely different from his fellow beings insofar as he "participated directly in the invisible sacred center fuelling collective existence." But the very fact that the coercive power of the gods is brought directly "into the midst of human affairs gives rise to a critically important corollary, namely, that the same gods are brought back within reach and, in practice, become socially questionable." Political domination introduces a dynamic of change. When a ruler *imposes* an order, even in the name of its inviolable legitimacy, he inevitably *changes* it, however quietly or surreptitiously. The order of things is no longer simply received, it is *willed*.[10] The structural imperative of change

---

9   Gauchet, 14.

10   *Ibid.*, 35-36.

gathered further momentum when the Anglo-Saxon kings sponsored the conversion of their pagan peoples to Christianity.

In the long run, Christianity shaped and was shaped by the social character of the Anglo-Saxons. The conversion experience had as much to do with Germanizing Christianity as with incorporating the Germans into Christendom. Significantly, conversion occurred only with and through the cooperation of Anglo-Saxon kings who continued to trace their ancestry back to the pagan gods. Rulers found as much support for the cult of sacral kingship in the wrathful image of the Old Testament God and the bloody history of ancient Israel as in the New Testament gospel of peace. If the ruler was the embodiment of the divine, then his power could only be enhanced through identification with an omnipotent God who existed beyond this world yet was somehow responsible for its creation. The comparison is compelling: On the one hand, "The old deities remained within the world without being able to act on it as a totality, whatever mysterious ability they had to influence the changing cycle of life and events."[11] On the other, the God of Israel created the totality of things from which he nevertheless remained absent, thereby leaving an autonomous space in which rulers could impose an order of their own making.

Anglo-Saxon kings were not slow to generate political capital from biblical stories of the trials and tribulations suffered by the Israelites after they triumphantly entered the Promised Land and became a kingdom. In their own promised land, the Anglo-Saxon tribes were ready to believe that they too were a chosen people whose initial victory over the native Britons was a sign that they were bound by covenant to an all-powerful God. Later, as catastrophes began to rain down on them, they could not help but wonder what they, like the Israelites before them, had done to invoke God's fearsome punishment. Not surprisingly, the most successful Anglo-Saxon kings turned their minds to the ways in which they might redeem themselves and their people in the eyes of God.

Even after their conversion to Christianity, Anglo-Saxon kings, no less than their people, remained rooted in a magicoreligious way of life. Their authority was charismatic in character. Max Weber used the term "charisma" to denote "a certain quality of an individual personality by virtue of which he is set apart from ordinary men and treated as endowed with supernatural, superhuman, or at least specifically exceptional powers and qualities." The charismatic leader is an exemplary figure whose magical powers are regarded as of divine origin. Having witnessed a miraculous sign or proof of the leader's charismatic mission, his followers are driven

---

11 *Ibid.*, 52.

by enthusiasm, despair or hope to recognize his authority. But charismatic authority is doomed to instability. Should proof of his charismatic qualification fail him for long, the leader may be deserted and rejected by followers.[12] Like the sacrificial kings of the Anglo-Saxons, the leader may even be killed and hung in a sacred tree to propitiate the gods.

The charismatic authority of Anglo-Saxon kings stood outside the mundane routines of everyday life. It must be distinguished from both the traditional and the rational-legal forms of authority characteristic of the late medieval and early modern eras respectively. Even Alfred the Great established only embryonic forms of bureaucratic and legal ordering. In his day, there could be no legal wisdom oriented towards judicial precedents. Like Alfred, every Anglo-Saxon king was a sort of prophet driven to manifest his *heil* by preaching, demanding or creating *new* obligations, imposed by his own will. Recognition of that charismatic authority was a duty but it always remained open to challenge by other members of the royal lineage claiming a charismatic sanction of their own. Such a contest could be resolved only by magical means or by an actual physical battle between the leaders.[13] Only when charismatic authority became routinized was the magicoreligious-directed character of the English ruling class finally replaced by a new way of life.

The routinization of charismatic authority in England was the product of a series of massive upheavals, beginning with the Norman Conquest. New forms of rationalized and traditionalized authority, oriented to the routine control of everyday behavior, made their appearance. As a consequence, the social character of the dominant classes in England was transformed. A new mode of conformity made its appearance: the tradition-directed character.[14] At the deepest level, the transformation in the social character of the ruling classes in England marked a new chapter in the history of religion in general and of Christianity in particular.

The transition from a magicoreligious-directed social character to a tradition-directed mode of conformity was not peculiar to England or even Europe. Ancient China underwent a similar transformation. But there was a radical difference between the cosmic harmony valorized by Confucian, Taoist and Buddhist traditions after the Chinese broke with their primordial religions and the formal logic of Christianity in England following the Norman Conquest. While Chinese religious traditions

12　Max Weber, *The Theory of Social and Economic Organization* edited by Talcott Parsons (New York: Free Press, 1964), 358-363.

13　*Ibid.*, 361.

14　Cf., Riesman, *Lonely Crowd*, 9-13.

aimed to unite body and spirit in a unity of opposites, a remodelled Roman Catholicism radically separated the spiritual realm from the world of nature.

In an effort to bridge the gulf between the sacred and the secular, Europeans, and Anglo-Saxons in particular, invoked the grandeur of human reason. The theological emphasis on the God-given faculty of reason unleashed human powers of innovation and control; and these eventually waged war not just on Christianity but also on the very idea of tradition itself. The institutional foundation for the tradition-directed character of medieval and early modern Englishmen—with its in-built psychological tensions and contradictions—was laid by the Papal Revolution of the eleventh century.

The Papal Revolution

When William the Conqueror captured the throne of England in 1066 he assumed the ancient Germanic mantle of sacral kingship worn by his Anglo-Saxon predecessors. Like Frankish emperors and kings on the Continent, William styled himself the "deputy of Christ." The pope, by contrast, was merely the "deputy of St Peter." As Bishop of Rome, the pope did enjoy primacy among the other bishops of the church. But that formal precedence did not alter the reality of imperial, royal and local lay leader-ship over the church throughout Europe. Pope Alexander II acknowledged the weakness of papal authority in the commission he granted William to reform the English church "by freeing it from local and feudal pres-sures and centralizing ecclesiastical authority in the hands of the king." Therefore, William was not engaged in an unlawful usurpation when he asserted the royal right to determine whether or not a pope should be acknowledged by the church in Normandy and England in his famous decree of 1067. Accordingly, ecclesiastical law was to be made by church synods convened by William while ecclesiastical penalties imposed on his barons and officials were subject to a royal veto power.[15]

In 1075, however, Pope Gregory VII launched a frontal assault on the cult of sacral kingship by declaring "the political and legal supremacy of the papacy over the entire church and the independence of the clergy from secular control." Defending the freedom of the church from control by lay lords and kings, the pope insisted not only that he must control

---

15 Harold J Berman, *Law and Revolution: The Formation of the Western Legal Tradition* (Cambridge, MA: Harvard University Press, 1983), 92, 255.

the appointment of bishops but that they "were to be subordinate to him and not to secular authority." Indeed, Gregory went on to assert "the ultimate supremacy of the pope in secular matters, including the authority to depose emperors and kings."[16]

The revolutionary movement begun by Gregory the Great did not realize all of its ambitions, least of all in England, but it did transform utterly the political, socio-economic, cultural and intellectual life of Western Europe from the late eleventh to the early thirteenth century. Beginning with the *Dictatus Papae* of 1075, the papal monarchy produced rapid changes that were sometimes cataclysmic and always shocking in a prolonged struggle between the Church and the emerging states of Western Europe.

The struggle between church and state in England ended in a compromise between the old and the new. For a considerable time, the old legal and political order grounded in the myth of sacral kingship resisted the revolutionary claims of papal authority. William the Conqueror and his two successors resolutely rejected papal claims to supremacy over the church in their dominions. But during the anarchy that characterized the reign of Stephen (1135-1154) the papal party made substantial gains in power and prestige. In a bitter struggle between Henry II (1154-1189) and the Archbishop of Canterbury, Thomas Becket, the freedom of the English church received reluctant royal recognition. In frustration and anger, Henry uttered his infamous words, "Will no one rid me of this pestilential priest?" leading four of his men to murder Becket. Henry's subjects were so shocked by this act that he was forced to submit to a papal legate and renounce the forms of royal supremacy over the church deemed most "offensive" to the papacy.[17]

In England and on the continent, the conflict between church and state produced an institutional separation of spiritual from secular authority. Nevertheless, both jurisdictions continued to overlap in important ways. Even more significantly, those who wielded spiritual and secular authority ceased to be reared within the mold of a magicoreligious-directed character type. New forms of legal-rational authority called forth a different sort of tradition-directed character among kings, nobles and prelates alike. In effect, the once-charismatic nature of both spiritual and secular authority was routinized. Each asserted its authority through a distinctive legal system: the canon law within the church and the common law in royal courts.

16 *Ibid.*, 87.
17 *Ibid.*, 255-269

A distinctive Western legal tradition grew out of that juxtaposition of several competing legal systems—canon law, royal law, feudal law, urban law, mercantile law—each giving expression to the distinctive logic and experience of its own more or less autonomous realm. The papal push to protect and preserve the freedom of the church from secular control had the paradoxical effect of freeing kings to expand their own powers and prerogatives. Moreover, the divine mandate to exploit to the full our earthly abode was carried out not just by feudal lords, their vassals and the lowly peasantry but by the Church, its monastic orders and the universities, not to mention the emerging towns and corporate boroughs with their rich merchants and artisan guilds.

Centralization of the papal monarchy paradoxically unleashed the dynamic potential inherent in medieval Christian civilization. That result was by no means a foregone conclusion. Certainly no spiritual power center comparable to the papacy appeared elsewhere. The Church grandly declared that "a universal God demands universal domination."[18] But only the conjunction of at least three factors made it possible for the messianic imperialism of the papal monarchy to establish itself in Western Europe. First was the absence of effective competition in the race to establish universal hegemony. The collapse of the Carolingian empire created a power vacuum in the heart of Europe. This circumstance allowed the Church to invent the prototype modern Western state while pressing its claim to universal domination. The Church became an independent, hierarchical public authority asserting the sovereign capacity to create new laws, enforceable through its own bureaucracy and judiciary.[19]

But the rise of the *Kirchenstaat*, or church-state, represented far more than an exercise in power politics; it also entailed a radical transformation in the relationship between God and man. More than just a state-building project; the justification of centralized spiritual authority required the reform of theological discourse in both form and substance. The need to satisfy that ideological imperative was the second critical factor. In fact, the papacy produced not just a strikingly original political formula but also a theology designed to hollow out the Anglo-Saxon Christian cult of sacral kingship.

Medieval scholasticism launched a frontal assault on the syncretic message that the early missionaries carried to Anglo-Saxon England. The newly-converted Anglo-Saxons had fused Christianity with their primordial belief in the ultimate unity of the visible and the invisible world. The

---

18   Gauchet, *Disenchantment*, 116.

19   Berman, *Law*, 106-119.

Old English cult of sacral kingship symbolized the close involvement of God in the world of his chosen people. By contrast, the Catholic theology that justified papal supremacy deliberately distanced God from his creation by endowing the church with a monopoly over the power to mediate between the beyond and here-below.

Finally, the gulf between the ideal and the reality of papal monarchy could only be bridged by a Christian people capable of constructing the intellectual, institutional and physical edifice of ecclesiastical power, a people ready, willing and able both to meet the challenges and to seize the opportunities presented by the de-spiritualization of nature implicit in the new-modelled Christian theology. In a very important sense, the Papal Revolution could not be confined to the spiritual realm. The radical separation of God from the world necessarily transformed the relationship of Christians with nature. Believers acquired a new freedom to act here-below. By channelling the relationship with the other world through the institutional structures of the church, the Papal revolution fostered a pervasive disposition among the laity to redirect energy back toward the appropriation of this world.[20]

The centerpiece of the papacy's revolutionary theology was its highly rationalized reworking of the orthodox doctrine of the incarnation. Medieval Christianity, like Judaism, Islam and Eastern Christianity, conceived God as the Creator of the universe. All of these traditions had gone beyond the primordial religious belief in the magical interpenetration of the visible world with the mysterious deities and occult forces influencing it. When they posited the radical separation of God from man, they nonetheless acknowledged a concomitant interconnection; all monotheistic religions conceive God as a judge governing his creation through divine law.[21] But in Judaism, Islam and Eastern Christianity, the emphasis on an omnipotent creator leads man either to seek a mystical escape from this world or to accept total submission to the revealed word of God. Those two solutions to the problem of man's relationship to God were rejected by the incarnational theology of the scholastic philosophers.[22]

---

20 Gauchet, *Disenchantment*, 72, 83.

21 Berman, *Law*, 178-179.

22 Gauchet, *Disenchantment*, 76.

Between Heaven and Earth

Roman Catholic theology made the seemingly contradictory claim that God is both transcendent and immanent. Inevitably, reconciliation of two self-substantiating orders of reality—the spiritual and the temporal—became a never-ending task. The emphasis on the incarnation as the central reality of the universe unleashed the dynamic interplay between these contradictions. When God became incarnate in the human form of his only begotten Son, "he emerged as wholly other, so different and remote that without the assistance of revelation he would have remained unknown to humans." At the same time, when the Word became flesh the terrestrial sphere acquired an autonomous dignity; the mystical union of human and divine in the figure of the Saviour created "an inexhaustible sustaining mystery" at the heart of Western Christianity. Two consequences followed: rejection of the world was now held to be unworthy of Christ's humanity. On the other hand, it was not possible simply to obey divine decrees because the vast abyss that separates us from God makes it difficult "to interpret his will and be assured of his truth."[23] An essential indeterminacy was inescapable; only through the God-man Jesus Christ can we gain an inkling "of the limitless nature of what lies beyond creation" but "what we receive is God's thought put in human language and we know that this thought surpasses human language."[24]

The papal monarchy strove to paper over this central indeterminacy by presenting the church itself as the essential intermediary between heaven and earth. In the sacrament of the eucharist the substance of the bread and wine is miraculously transformed into the "true" body and blood of the crucified Christ at the moment it is consecrated. Still, the fact is that the intersection of the human and the divine occurred in a historical space once occupied by the Son of Man that now stands out of reach in the swirling mists of time. The mystical re-enactment of Christ's arrival in the eucharist "is equally a commemoration of an absence, a ritualistic repetition of an unrepeatable event." Scholastic theology emerged in response to an institutional need for a body of men qualified to interpret God's otherwise unfathomable messages. Its task was "to demonstrate by reason alone what had been discovered by faith through divine revelation."[25] Theological reason effectively deprived established political authority of

---

23　*Ibid.*, 77.

24　*Ibid.*, 81-2.

25　Berman, *Law*, 175.

its religious function and character, reserving the spiritual realm as the exclusive province of the church.

Whatever temporal functions the church undertook, however, it was bound to remain, first and foremost, a spiritual community. For that very reason the papacy could never achieve supremacy in secular matters. Indeed, to the extent that the *Kirchenstaat* served as a model for the modern state, it remained a contradiction in terms. The *raison d'être* of the modern state derives, after all, from its divine-ordained mandate to exercise dominion over the secular realm. Equally, however, the specialized ecclesiastical hierarchy that enabled the papacy to assert itself independently of temporal powers also freed the secular sphere from a restrictive preoccupation with the supernatural. A huge gap opened up between the invisible realm of the divine and the mundane but now self-sufficient terrestrial sphere. While the church retained exclusive responsibility for souls, temporal bodies politic rushed into the gap, asserting to claim independence and power over the management of worldly affairs.

Primordial religion had integrated people into the cosmos. There was no fixed and impermeable boundary between the spiritual and the temporal. But once the scholastic interpretation of the incarnation reconceived divine otherness, a paradox revealed itself. Christ oriented his followers to the other world in a quest for eternal salvation. At the same time, the reality of his sacrifice highlighted the impossibility of fleeing this world. Christ's crucifixion in atonement for the sins of mankind demonstrated that men could seek salvation not by turning away from this world but by embracing its intrinsic autonomy and integrity. Men could store up a treasury of merit in this life by performing good works but they were also required to accept full responsibility for their sins within the ecclesiastical Body of Christ. The management of sin through the priestly offices of confession, absolution, and the granting of indulgences inserted the spiritual power deep into the conscience of every Christian.

The doctrine of purgatory provides a striking manifestation of the way in which spiritual authority was routinized in the mundane form of legal rationality. The concept of purgatory presupposes not just that life in this world has a purpose but that man is responsible for the realization of that purpose. In accounting for the conduct of one's life in purgatory, individual sins are weighed and penalties allocated according to an elaborate system of rules and standards. Sin was no longer understood as "a condition of alienation, a diminution of a person's being; it now came to be understood in legal terms as specific wrongful acts or desires or thoughts for which various penalties must be paid in temporal suffering."[26]

By contrast, in treating sin as a separation or alienation from God or one's neighbours, early Anglo-Saxon Christianity personified it as a manifestation "of the struggle between God and the devil for the soul of every man." In that context, baptism was of far greater importance than the eucharist. Baptism was the "great Christian mystery in which man, once and for all, dies to himself, renounces the devil, and is reborn as a citizen of the heavenly kingdom." Today, this is still true of Orthodox Christianity. For both Anglo-Saxon and Eastern Christianity, the focus was on the transcendence of God the Father, the Creator. Because Christ showed mankind the way to ascend to the infinite, the crucifixion had no significance apart from the resurrection. In the orthodox faith of the early Anglo-Saxon church, Christ was "seen primarily as the conqueror of death." But the emphasis on the crucifixion in the medieval doctrine of atonement cast Christ instead as "the conqueror of sin." While the early church fixed its gaze upwards to a communion of saints in heaven, the Papal Revolution took charge of a community of sinners on earth.[27]

In essence, scholastic rationalism reflected a bedrock "belief in incarnation of divine mysteries in human concepts and theories."[28] Law was no less important than theology in rationalizing the institutional structure of the papal monarchy. Theology taught "that the rational order of the universe requires that sins always be punished." A new legal science emerged to explain how divine justice could be manifested by asserting ecclesiastical jurisdiction over the earthly community of sinners. It is, of course, true that, almost from the beginning, the creators of Latin Christianity conceived the relations between God and man as legal relations, placed "in the framework of rights and duties and moulded into a Roman jurisprudential scheme."[29] The church always had ecclesiastical *laws* and a legal *order* but there had never been a "*system* of ecclesiastical *law*." It was only as a consequence of the Papal revolution that the system of canon law emerged as an "independent, integrated, developing body of ecclesiastical legal principles and procedures, clearly differentiated from liturgy and theology."[30]

---

26 *Ibid.*, 171.

27 *Ibid.*, 174-178.

28 *Ibid.*,178.

29 Walter Ullman, *Medieval Political Thought* (Harmondsworth: Penguin, 1975), 21.

30 Berman, *Law*, 202.

A theology transforming the incarnation into a philosophical abstraction provided the essential platform for "the rationalization and systemization of law and legality in the West."[31] Eastern Christianity did not follow this path. It is not true, therefore, that the systematic application of legal-rational authority to both the spiritual and the temporal realms was driven by the "logic" of Christianity. Not all Christians believe that the ultimate mysteries of their faith can be resolved through logic. It seems more likely that the legal-rationalistic theology of the incarnation was a cultural variant that the peoples of Western Europe were predisposed to receive. In the south of France and in Italy remnants of the Roman legal tradition survived the collapse of the Empire, thus providing a stable foundation upon which claims of papal supremacy could be erected. At the other end of Europe, among the Anglo-Saxons, a relatively centralized and powerful kingship had developed a tradition of folk-law readily adaptable to the new-found autonomy of the secular realm.

Anglo-Saxon kingship and law emerged from a Germanic society in which the blood ties of kinship had been weakened relative to the voluntary bonds that tied lords to their followers. The ties of dependence, loyalty and obligation between free men were based on freely given oaths supported by supernatural sanctions. However primitive and clumsy by the standards of a developed legal system, reliance on compurgators and trial by ordeal incorporated the assumption that legal procedures could and should punish those guilty of an offence against God or man. Once the church took charge of the community of sinners, the secular power was placed under pressure to recognize the responsibility of individuals for their crimes. From then on, criminals would be subject personally to punishment; no longer would kindred or lords be expected to compensate victims of wrongdoing. A major step away from the magicoreligious-directed character of Anglo-Saxon society had been taken.

The Distinctive Social Character of Western Christendom

Nowhere more effectively than in England did the religious revolution of the High Middle Ages foster an evolved social psychology of individual autonomy. By the thirteenth century, the English were already set apart from the rest of Christendom by their pronounced predisposition towards liberty, independence and individualism. Indeed, "within the recorded

---

31 *Ibid.*, 178.

period covered by our documents," Alan Macfarlane writes, "it is not possible to find a time when the Englishman did not stand alone."[32] The English spirit of individualism stands in even more striking contrast with ancient Chinese culture. In China, the long interaction between cultural and genetic evolution favored collective harmony over individual agency. The people of ancient China, too, possessed a tradition-directed character but that tradition promoted stability and harmony rather than innovation and individual autonomy.

The absolute separation of the spiritual from the temporal realm posited by the rationalist theology of late medieval Roman Catholicism was utterly alien to the Chinese. To conceive God as a personal, wrathful, yet merciful being seemed contradictory to them. If God has corporeal substance, he must have been created by some higher power; but if he was an incorporeal being, how could he abandon himself to passions such as wrath? "A being of perfect virtue does not lose his temper." God revealed his unseemly, egoistical nature to the Chinese by decreeing that only those who believe in the Lord Jesus can be saved. No such petty human whim bears comparison to the divine order of Heaven. Even the idea of God as a supreme lawgiver issuing the Ten Commandments seemed little more than vulgar and superstitious trick designed to upset and delude the world. Even more scandalous and absurd was the notion of a vulnerable God who died nailed to a wooden "construction in the shape of the number ten." If Jesus really was a man among men he could not have been the Master of Heaven. If he was the Master of Heaven it made no sense for him to have descended into one particular kingdom at one particular time leaving all the other kingdoms—past, present and future—to their misfortune.[33]

Like the other great world religions, Confucianism breaks with the primordial religious outlook in which the visible and the invisible are united. That rupture occurs whenever people begin to think about the totality of things. Like Jews, Christians and Muslims, Confucians recognized the division of the universe between presence and absence. They, too, were compelled to go behind the multiplicity of sensory perceptions in order to return to the underlying One, the fundamental ordering principle of the universe as a whole. Unlike Jews, Muslims and Christians, however, the Chinese never identified the One in terms of transcendent

32   Alan Macfarlane, *The Origins of English Individualism: The Family, Property and Social Transition* (Oxford: Basil Blackwell, 1978), 165-188.

33   Jacques Gernet, *China and the Christian Impact: A Conflict of Cultures* trans Janet Lloyd (Cambridge: Cambridge University Press, 1985), 222-225.

subjectivism or separated otherness. They chose another path; by locating their organizing principle in the midst of things, they established an underlying identity between body and spirit. Instead of a creator God, the universe is governed by an impersonal immanence uniting apparent opposites.[34]

The Western belief in "a personal and transcendent God of pure spirit…sets up an opposition between the earth below, where man plays out his eternal destiny, and a Beyond, which is totally incommensurate with it." The Chinese thesis, on the other hand, has been "that there is no meaning outside the world and that body and spirit cannot be separated." For the Chinese, the concept of Heaven merged the secular and the religious. Through its association with Earth, "Heaven produces all creatures and ensures their development." That cosmology has produced a culture and a people profoundly resistant to Western Christianity and its legal-rational model of both spiritual and temporal authority.[35]

The essential premise of Roman Catholicism—the radical separation of body and spirit—is deeply embedded in Western folkways, appearing in the most unlikely places. For example, twentieth-first century social scientists are not noted for their strong Christian convictions, but they cling to the belief that culture—the superorganic realm of spirit—and the materialist realm of Darwinist biology are unrelated to each other. The Chinese denial of such a binary opposition between mind and body probably renders them more open to the suggestion that biology and culture are much more intimately related than progressive WASPs prefer to believe. It seems likely that the profound religious differences between China and the West have been both cause and consequence in the long evolution of significant biocultural differences between the two civilizations.

A powerful sense of individual agency has been deeply-ingrained in Western cultures since at least the classical era in Greece. Manifested not just in the drama and philosophy of ancient Athens, it also found primitive expression in Anglo-Saxon folk-law. Nowadays the importance of agency is reflected, *inter alia*, in tacit assumptions about the nature of communication incorporated into modern Western child-rearing practices. "Westerners teach their children to communicate their ideas clearly and to adopt a 'transmitter' orientation." That is to say, speakers are expected to communicate in context-free terms readily understandable by their listeners. The contrast with Chinese practice is instructive. Chinese children

34 Gauchet, *Disenchantment*, 48, 217 n 37.

35 Gernet, *China*, 193-198.

are taught a "receiver" orientation in which it is up to the hearer to understand what is being said, perhaps by relying upon contextual clues rather
than the content of the speech itself.[36] Even more significantly, it appears
that the Western "transmitter" and the Chinese "receiver" orientations
are not just "cultural constructs." The differences appear to be hard-wired
into new-born infants. In one study, Chinese babies reacted placidly when
placed face down in a cot or when a cloth was placed over their noses,
forcing them to breathe through their mouths. Western babies, on the
other hand, were much more likely to cry or otherwise fight the manoeu-
vre.[37] If such studies provide a reliable indicator, the spirit of agency is
incarnate in the European gene pool.

Sharp differences between Europeans and Chinese emerged from a
process of natural selection in which the cultural adaptations of the two
widely separated populations co-evolved with their respective genotypes
over many generations. Both ethical individualism and collective harmony are products of a complex interaction between cultural and genetic
evolution taking place in very different environments.[38] The transmitter
response built into European culture and the very different Chinese pre-
dispositions towards the receiver mode express their respective genotypes.
While Europeans are primed genetically to respond to cues triggering
independent or individualistic responses, the Chinese are innately more
sensitive to interdependence cues.[39] Genetic evolution created a social
psychology that favored complex but very different cultural adaptations
such as the ideal of agency in Europe and the ideal of harmony in China.

The emphasis on harmony precluded the institutional separation of
the spiritual and the temporal realms in China; it also generated a normative order hostile to formal law. In 535 BC, a Chinese sage warned that
"when the people know that there are laws regulating punishments, they
have no respectful fear of authority. A litigious spirit awakes, invoking the
letter of the law, and trusting that evil actions will not fall under its provisions." In such circumstances, many scholars warned, government would
become impossible not because irresponsible individuals freely chose to
commit crimes and foster disputes but because tearing down the barrier
of righteousness in favor of a formal legal code would itself amount to a

36   Richard E Nisbett, *The Geography of Thought: How Asians and Westerners Think
     Differently…and Why* (New York: Free Press, 2003), 60.

37   Vincent Sarich & Frank Miele, *Race: The Reality of Human Differences* (Boulder, CO:
     Westview Press, 2004), 204-205.

38   Peter J Richerson & Robert Boyd, *Not by Genes Alone: How Culture Transformed Human
     Evolution* (Chicago: University of Chicago Press, 2006), especially 191-236.

39   Nisbett, *Geography*, 68.

disturbance in the Order of Nature.[40] No such inhibition prevented the growth of secular legal systems in the West, least of all in England.

The Political Theology of Medieval Monarchy

In England, the Papal Revolution produced a curious paradox. Scholastic theology dethroned the myth of sacral kingship; at the same time, it sanctified powerful and centralized secular monarchies. Nevertheless royal power was but one manifestation of the spirit of agency that drove the development of the English constitution in the medieval and early modern periods.

In effect, the Roman Catholic God left the tribes, nations, peoples, and tongues of medieval Christendom to fend for themselves. As a consequence, kings were compelled to identify themselves with the collective bodies subject to their power. Conversely, the legitimate organization of each self-sufficient terrestrial community required the active cooperation of its members. "Once the split between this world and the beyond has caused political authority to take responsibility for representing and organizing collective being, then individuals will soon exercise sovereignty, whatever royal trappings of authority remain."[41] The co-evolution of genes and culture from the eleventh to the thirteenth centuries favored the individualization of souls in the realm of faith; it also helped to generate the energy powering the practical individualism at work everywhere in the secular domain. The radical separation of the spiritual from the temporal sphere had the effect of reducing nature to mere matter, wholly adaptable to human needs and open to unlimited exploitation. Simultaneously, "the feudal reformulation of the hierarchical principle" entailed the complementary individualization of the "political" bonds of dependence, loyalty and obligation.

Even at the bottom of the feudal hierarchy labor was individualized in the domestic smallholdings of the peasantry. Although serfs were completely subjugated, they enjoyed an important measure of social autonomy in the ability to organize their labor. The "miniscule autonomization of the production unit" helped to generate a doubling of productivity between the ninth and the thirteenth centuries. Autonomous individualism enjoyed an even more striking selective advantage in the new urban

---

40   J Needham and C Ronan, *The Shorter Science and Civilization in China* Vol I (Cambridge: Cambridge University Press, 1970), 276-306.

41   Gauchet, *Disenchantment*, 58-9.

centers. The "remarkable compromise between the individual and the collective" characteristic of European feudalism created a new system of production and ownership, along with novel institutional forms such as guilds.[42]

The English common law tradition was another fruitful compromise; in this case, serving both private litigants and the public authority of the English crown. Unlike the codified system of Roman law that was revived on the continent, the common law was a body of judge-made case law. While Roman law was issued from the top-down by the will of a prince, the development of the common law was driven from the bottom up by litigants who made use of procedural writs to bring their private disputes into the royal courts. Both royal power and the property rights of free persons were enhanced by the growth of the common law. But the common law tradition also required an accommodation between the spiritual and temporal powers.

As we have seen, the revolutionary movement to endow the Church with sole jurisdiction over spiritual matters stripped Germanic priest-kings of their charismatic aura. In interpreting the Word-made-flesh, secular rulers were forbidden to trespass on the exclusive role assigned to the priesthood under the system of canon law. The struggle waged by the papacy to secure the freedom of the church in England began soon after the Norman Conquest and came to a head during the reign of Henry II. In this confrontation with the papacy, the institution of kingship was profoundly changed. It became axiomatic that a Christian monarch could not be both priest and king. After Christ, no king "could claim to occupy the pivotal point where the Natural and the Supernatural had come together in one body."[43] Kings were compelled to cede jurisdiction over the management of souls to the Church. By the same token, however, they were empowered to claim a "temporal" supremacy over the bodies of their subjects.

Anglo-Saxon kings had been "living embodiments of the sacred foundation and the divine law." Now, as a consequence of the Papal Revolution, the sacrality of secular authority no longer originated "in a personification of the invisible source of every rule and every life." But the Church had no wish to deny outright that temporal power had its own independent foundation in the law of God. After all, when the Church consecrated the coronation of a king, it ratified a divine decree governing an order of terrestrial sacrality outside its jurisdiction and "to which it had to piously

---

42   Ibid., 95, 88, 156.
43   Ibid., 139.

submit." Just as the Church asserted its originality as an instrument of salvation, "the political power was no less justified in claiming a sacrality, *sui generis*, directly dependent on God alone and free of any obligation to the spiritual power." [44] Kings were provided with both a strong incentive and the opportunity to gain both power and money by making royal justice supreme in temporal affairs.[45]

By asserting their divinely ordained independence from the Church, English kings took a fateful step toward the eventual disenchantment of political authority. The political disincarnation of the Holy Spirit also affected the character of the English people. No longer was royalty sacred in the primordial "ethnographic" sense. The pagan myth of sacral kingship made the divine present in human form. It had also underpinned the radical ethnocentricity of tribal identity: Anglo-Saxons had been placed securely at the center of the world by the magicoreligious, *heilerfüllt* character of their kings. No doubt the capacity of sacral kingship to reinforce English ethnic identity had already been weakened by the hegemony of the French-speaking nobility after the Norman Conquest. Indeed, even before William the Conqueror donned England's royal mantle, the charismatic aura surrounding sacral kingship must have been dimmed somewhat by the reign of Danish kings. But when the king no longer claimed to embody the divine presence in his person an altogether novel concept of kingship came into being.

Under the new theological dispensation, royal authority was a function of the king's temporal body politic; no longer was his natural body the medium through which an emanation of sacred *Heil* descended directly from the gods. A decisive step in that direction was taken by Henry II when he carved out a role as mediator "in a register removed from the spiritual power's control, the register of justice."[46] Through the medium of the common law, English kings gradually became the legal representative of the nation; as such, they were expected to employ their coercive power in the interests of the political community as a whole. By comparison with the primordial religion that gave birth to the myth of sacral kingship, the spiritual dimension of the common law was thin indeed.

44 *Ibid.*, 139-142, 89.

45 Berman, *Law*, 404-409.

46 Gauchet, *Disenchantment*, 142

Double Majesty in English Feudalism

The invention of the modern state was the necessary corollary of the Gregorian concept of the Church. The ascendancy of a territorial concept of kingship followed naturally from the institutional separation of a single, universal, spiritual association from a multiplicity of particularistic secular polities. Wherever royal power claimed jurisdiction over a defined territory, it sought increased authority over other secular polities—tribal, local, feudal, and urban.[47] But the king of England was not the sovereign locus of public authority. In a feudal society characterized by the "parcellization of sovereignty," the king could not exercise his authority directly over the population as a whole. The royal will had to be transmitted through the innumerable layers built into a complex hierarchy of feudal dependencies.[48]

Before and after the Norman Conquest, the political landscape in England was marked by divisions between local units and feudal units. The basic local unit was the village; groups of villages were known as hundreds. Shires or counties and the towns were the largest local units. The basic unit of production in medieval England was the manor in which free peasants and unfree villeins worked the land held by a feudal lord who presided over the manorial court. Many of the hundred courts had been taken over by feudal lords after the Conquest and became, in effect, manorial courts. Lords of the manor were themselves vassals holding their lands as tenants with an obligation to render military services to a higher lord. Vassals were subject to the jurisdiction of the seigneurial court over which their lord presided. The higher lords in turn were tenants of the chief lord—the king—who leased all the lands of England to his vassals in return for their military services. The feudal system of military tenures was introduced into England by William the Conqueror who distributed some 5,000 fiefs to occupy and hold down the country. It was not long, however, before the greatest of the feudal barons were in a position to challenge royal authority.

Once the Norman host ceased to be an occupying army and was more or less assimilated into the English nation, the "inherent ambiguity and oscillation at the vertex" of every feudal regime began to re-assert itself. At most, the monarch "was a feudal suzerain of his vassals, to whom he was bound by reciprocal ties of fealty, not a supreme sovereign set above his subjects." Royal authority "was necessarily different not in kind, but only

47   Berman, *Law*, 140.

48   Perry Anderson, *Passages from Antiquity to Feudalism* (London: NLB,1974), 150.

in degree, from the subordinate levels of lordship beneath it." Kings were endowed with a distinctive divinely-ordained role as the representative of the collective body of the political community as a whole. So long as they retained the support of the Church, English kings enjoyed an important edge in the "constant struggle to establish a 'public' authority outside the compact web of private jurisdictions." But that proto-public authority could expand in one direction only. No twelfth century king possessed the financial or even the imaginative resources necessary to carve out an "executive" role by constructing a permanent administrative apparatus to enforce the law. Similarly, kings were in no position to assert a "legislative" power to create new laws in a tradition-directed society marked by the fragmentation of sovereignty. Instead, Henry II chose to expand royal authority over the exercise of justice. This was a natural move in the royal struggle for supremacy over the feudal barons. "Justice was the *central* modality of political power" in medieval England.[49] Accordingly, the new forms of royal justice first sought to control the doings of lords in their own seigneurial courts.

But the fragmented organization and stubbornly local outlook of the feudal barons was resistant to that centralizing impulse. The expansion of royal power cut across the grain of deeply entrenched traditions. For centuries, legitimate authority in England had been based on the institution of the *comitatus*. The relationship of personal allegiance between the Germanic chieftain and his companions remained the template that shaped the aristocratic and military outlook of the medieval nobility. This was not an explicit, self-conscious political theory. Rather there was a tacit assumption that the foundation of authority and political legitimacy rested on the principle of "double majesty," meaning that "both the predominant elements of the social order, the king and his leading men, were thought to possess an independently grounded title to authority." Neither king nor nobility owed its standing to the other. Kings denied that their selection by the great men of the realm meant that kingship itself derived from such selection. Similarly, even if a given title or estate might have its source in a royal gift or grant, the order of nobility was not seen as the creature of royal authority. Indeed, aristocratic warriors who thought of their lands as rewards for services insisted that they ought to be exempt from taxation. The allegiance of the nobility to the king was personal not public; they believed, therefore, that the king ought to live from the revenue of his own

---

49 *Ibid.*, 151-153.

lands, just as they did.[50] The king, of course, could not view the alienation of royal lands in that manner: to do so would impoverish the monarchy and lead to its collapse.

Royal authority did have a significant advantage, however, so long as the greater nobility conceded that "the routine of government was the king's affair." Over time, the cumulative weight and strength of administrative routine created a situation in which baronial interests could only be effectively defended when barons became involved in the routine conduct of governmental business. But no stable rules governed such involvement. The king could summon anyone or no one for that purpose and when "a baron gave his assent, he did it as himself; he represented no one but himself." The feudal polity lacked integration and self-consciousness. Lacking an understanding of rationalized government, even the greatest of the king's subjects were bereft of civic consciousness or a genuinely public point of view. In their resistance to royal initiatives, the nobility "largely failed to act in conjunction." Whenever they "did unite temporarily in their disaffection, they could outmatch the king's military strength, but they were not often able to present a common front."[51]

Nevertheless, the procedural ideal of double majesty remained rooted in traditional usage. One thirteenth century writer acknowledged that "none may presume to debate the act of a king nor dispute his deed" but added immediately that the earls and barons "are called *comites* from *comitiva*, companionship" precisely because the king's companions "are bound to bridle him" when he acts rashly. Acts done by the king's authority must be "properly determined by the counsel of his magnates...after due deliberation and discussion thereon." The notion that the king should act "with and through the counsel and consent of the barons" was not so much a legal requirement as "a working arrangement which had its roots deep in the past."[52] The notion of double majesty was the nucleus around which the myth of the ancient constitution began to crystallize. The cult of St Edward the Confessor provided a bridge between the Anglo-Saxon myth of sacral kingship and the early modern cult of the ancient constitution. William I was the first of many early Norman monarchs to confirm the laws of his sainted Saxon predecessor.[53]

50 Donald W Hanson, *From Kingdom to Commonwealth: The Development of Civic Consciousness in English Political Thought* (Cambridge, MA: Harvard University Press, 1970), 41, 42, 44, 52-53.

51 *Ibid.*, 22, 52.

52 *Ibid*, 124-125, 128.

53 Janelle Greenberg, *The Radical Face of the Ancient Constitution: St Edward's "Laws" in Early Modern Political Thought* (Cambridge: Cambridge University Press, 2001), 36, 38.

The cult of St Edward, the penultimate Anglo-Saxon king (1042-1066) not only endowed the monarchy "with an essential measure of stability," lending legitimacy to efforts to construct a more centralized government; it also set standards of conduct against which kings could be measured. Barons who believed "that the right to judge royal actions rested in them and not the king alone" repeatedly invoked the cult to reinforce the tradition of double majesty. King John's barons based "their resistance on the coronation charters of Henry I, King Stephen, and Henry II, all of which carried royal promises to abide by St Edward's laws as amended by the Conqueror." Indeed, the reforms enshrined in Magna Carta were justified by King John's failure to abide by the good old laws of the Confessor.

By the early fourteenth century, an oath recognizing the practice of double majesty had been incorporated into coronation ceremonies. Kings were required to swear to uphold St Edward's law and to govern in accordance with the laws and customs that the community of the realm "shall choose."[54] No doubt the "community of the realm" was a convenient euphemism that referred to the baronial class and excluded the vast majority of ordinary folk. But, the crucial significance of the oath lay in its characterization of the political order "as the conjunction of two native and independent sources of legitimacy and, therefore, of...political initiative."[55]

This proto-constitutional framework of dual authority continued for centuries as the setting of both conflict and cooperation between kings and magnates. But an inherent ambiguity always surrounded the identity of those who were to be included as of right within the political "community of the realm." Thus, when the pressing financial and military needs of a rapidly developing political system created sufficient pressure on the king, he issued writs summoning "not only the great magnates but also knights representing the shires and burgesses representing the towns" to give counsel and consent to royal initiatives. Magnates were summoned individually but the knights and burgesses came as representatives of their constituencies. The representative character of the lesser men helped to make this parliament an important platform for the resolution of struggles between the king and his great men. This is not to say that parliament became the center of government in the middle ages. On the contrary, the heart of the king's government remained his council; parliament did not come into its own until the seventeenth century. But when the king and the nobility found themselves at loggerheads, both could attempt to

---

54 *Ibid.,* 39, 49-50.

55 Hanson, *Kingdom,* 43.

enlist the support of the commons thereby transforming the style and the techniques of opposition to royal authority.[56]

The political ideas and practices associated with double majesty served to limit not just the power of the king but that of the great magnates as well. During the fifteenth century, when effective central government nearly broke down, feudal barons could and did depose kings. They rushed into the resulting "vacuum to consolidate and expand their control of local affairs and contended among themselves to rule directly through the king's council." Even then, when "the medieval monarchy was most debased the magnates clung to the idea of its independent authority." And, because the political behavior of the barons was primarily oriented to local activity and interests, able kings were essential to deal with problems afflicting the kingdom as a whole. The royal lawmaking that dealt with such issues should not, however, be equated with modern legislative sovereignty. Medieval lawmaking "resembled the efforts of a carpenter to shore up a sagging beam more than the general plans of an architect." Even at its strongest, baronial ascendancy required royal authority. But by the same token, kings could "neither make laws nor impose subsidies on their subjects, without the consent of the Three Estates of the Realm."[57]

In the middle of the fifteenth century, the idea of double majesty was described by Fortescue as a *dominium politicum and regale*.[58] But this regal and political dominion had no room for a sovereign. Instead there was "a notion of kingship balanced by a complex institution which was assumed to have a representative relationship with the people, or with some of them, at any rate." In Fortescue's work the identity of the non-regal partner remains shifting and ambiguous, "described variously as the people, the three estates, parliament, and the chief men of the realm."[59] But the tradition of double majesty could never be set in stone. By the late fifteenth century, the weakness of the commons and endemic disunity among the great magnates combined with the growing wealth of the kingdom as a whole to present the new Tudor dynasty with an opportunity to establish kingship on a new footing. Before long, Henry VIII's imperial conception of kingship all but eclipsed the idea of double majesty.[60]

---

56 *Ibid.*, 154-5, 167.

57 *Ibid.*, 181-186, 210, 223.

58 Sir John Fortescue, *De Laudibus Legum Anglie* edited and translated by SB Chrimes (Cambridge: Cambridge University Press, 1942).

59 Hanson, *Kingdom*, 187, 224.

60 Walter Ullman, "This Realm of England is an Empire" in Walter Ullman, *Jurisprudence in the Middle Ages* (London: Variorum Reprints, 1980).

The theoretical question of *sovereignty* never came up, however, simply "because prince and people were at one on the major political questions until near the end of Elizabeth's reign." By the time the Tudor revolution had run its course, the idea of double majesty had been transformed: the medieval polarity between prince and people was replaced with a new emphasis on the inseparable duality of prince and law.[61] Despite its novelty, the royal supremacy asserted by the Tudor monarchs continued to draw upon the long-established medieval tradition that regarded the spiritual and temporal realms as radically separate.

The Tudor Revolution

It is one of the great ironies of Roman Catholic theology that its "sanctification of secular efficacy" provided doctrinal justification for the nationalization of the church in England. That movement began in earnest with the 1553 *Act in Restraint of Appeals* which eliminated papal jurisdiction in England not just in matters of faith and morals touching upon secular concerns such as marriage, legitimacy and the oaths involved in contractual exchanges, but also in equitable matters that alleged defects of justice in the king's courts. The Tudor Reformation rested upon the theologically-inspired obligation placed upon kings "to accept full responsibility for the whole of the collective life" of their kingdoms. In wresting control of the church away from Rome, English monarchs set out to establish "a connection between the parts of the social whole, from the top to the bottom." [62] The 1534 *Act of Supremacy* establishing Henry VIII as the supreme head of the Church in England was the logical corollary of that project.

But the regal assumption of papal prerogatives did not entail the rejection of the traditional distinction between the spiritual and the temporal realm. Instead lawyers such as Christopher St Germain employed the established canons of legal-rational authority to redraw the boundaries between spiritual and secular jurisdictions. Traditional legal materials were rewoven "into a novel fabric in which the dominant thread is royal supremacy." Although St Germain was prepared to concede, at least in theory, the existence of a spiritual realm beyond the authority of the King-in-Parliament, in practice, he deprived spiritual jurisdiction of any

---

61 Hanson, *Kingdom*, 232, 252.

62 Gauchet, *Disenchantment*, 78, 143.

purchase on the material matters and temporal interests at play in the terrestrial sphere.[63]

Henry VIII's quest for a terrestrial plenitude licensed by Catholic theology encouraged him to reconstruct the English Crown as an empire rivalling and imitating the Church. Royal usurpation of papal jurisdiction systematized the long struggle by the English Crown to establish a sacrality for itself equal to that embodied in the papal monarchy. In the end, a state religion in the form of a cult of the Nation raised terrestrial government to the level of a heavenly being by investing it with legal perpetuity. While flesh and blood kings are born and die, the Crown and the kingdom will last forever as mystical entities with celestial status. By installing Henry VIII as Supreme Head of the Church of England, parliament created a new category of sacred being, at once a collective apparition to which every Englishmen belonged and an immanent deity crushing anyone resisting its demand for devotion.[64]

The Tradition-Directed Character of the Ecclesiastical Polity

By the end of the sixteenth century, the theoretical justification underpinning the union of the church and the commonwealth of England had been spelled out in Richard Hooker's massive work, *Of the Laws of Ecclesiastical Polity*. Hooker pressed the theological separation of the spiritual from the temporal realm to its limits; in his view, God's gracious gift of salvation "remains absolutely invisible and transcendent." Therefore, the outward actions of men in this world have nothing to do with salvation and everlasting life remain "internal affairs of the heart and conscience which are known only to God." Those who are saved in Christ owe their redemption to "the secret inward influence of his grace;" it is through the outward profession of faith, not through its action, that the visible Church is constituted. According to Hooker, God does not expect the Church "to dive into men's consciences" because "their fraud and deceit (against God)" cannot "hurt any man but themselves." On the other hand, the Church does require men to submit their right to private judgement to lawful regulation. If individuals were free to act in accordance with their consciences,

63 Hanson, *Kingdom*, 263; Christopher St Germain, *Dialogue Between a Doctor of Divinity and a Student in the Laws of England* edited by William Muchall, (Cincinnati, OH: R Clarke, 1874), esp. 45, 309-346.

64 Gauchet, *Disenchantment*, 89-90.

society would collapse into total disorder. For that reason, "the Church and the commonwealth are…one society, which society being termed a commonwealth as it liveth under whatsoever form of secular law and regiment, a church as it hath the spiritual law of Christ."[65] For all practical purposes, the Church belongs entirely to this world. Even in matters of Christian religion, the Church is subordinate to the prince.

In Tudor England, "the categories of Church and commonwealth are completely interchangeable." Every member of the Church of England was also a member of the commonwealth.[66] According to Hooker, the self-contained integrity of the ecclesiastical polity was the product of "ancient ordnances, rites, and long approved customes, of our venerable predecessors." Clearly, from this perspective, papal supremacy within the Church of England had been a wrongful usurpation of the king's traditional prerogatives. No doubt the break with Rome was a product in part of an already well-established English national identity but the Reformation had the effect of intensifying that indigenous "self-consciousness, of driving Englishmen, when necessary, to manufacture the foundations of social life out of their own traditions."[67] Religious reformers "probed historical records for proof that the English church represented the one, true religion that papists had long ago corrupted." Determined to demonstrate that every area of the life of their common life was grounded in its own sovereign past, secular scholars turned to Saxon studies to confirm that the ancient constitution of the English nation was both Saxon and Protestant. By looking to their "glorious Germanic past," Englishmen could find the origins of England's "most precious institutions, secular as well as religious." Tudor antiquaries "paid special homage to St Edward's laws, and for the first time we see the body of Saxon laws taking precedence over the cult of his kingship." Once the "cult of the Confessor had been joined by the cult of the Confessor's laws" in the early sixteenth century, the basic building blocks of the myth of the ancient constitution had been set in place.[68]

Hooker devoted his life to defending the allegedly ancient constitution of the ecclesiastical polity against challenges arising from both papists and Puritans. Faced with the twin threats of Catholic reaction and Puritan radicalism, Hooker appealed to the authority of tradition. The presumed

65 David Little, *Religion, Order and Law: A Study in Pre-revolutionary England* (Oxford: Basil Blackwell, 1970), 151-153.

66 *Ibid.*, 155-156, 150, 153.

67 *Ibid.*, 133, 135.

68 Greenberg, *Radical Face*, 78-86.

antiquity of the old order signified its legitimacy and acceptability: "The love of things ancient doth argue stayedness, but levity and want of experience maketh apt unto innovations."[69] Hooker believed that what English tradition taught for Church polity would harmonize "readily with the needs of secular politics." It was an article of faith for him that every law at one time or another serves to institute "the conjunction of power ecclesiastical and civil." He failed to recognize that the state religion he preached, far from marking a return to the Anglo-Saxon myth of sacral kingship, represented a radical innovation in the political history of religion.

Infused with divine grace, Anglo-Saxon priest-kings incarnated the sacred in their persons. But the majesty of kingship in the Anglican ecclesiastical polity derived as much from the body politic of the kingdom as from the body natural of the king. Hooker declared "that the true source of power in the community is neither king nor parliament but the whole body politic."[70] Because England, like every other independent society, enjoyed full dominion over itself, it was free "to determine the kind of polity it will live by." Hooker was no democrat, however. Community consent could not be divined simply by listening to the loud voices of the living; the accumulated weight of the judgements made by past generations must be added to the balance. For him, law arises out of "the custom and continual practice of many ages or years" and is therefore the deed of the whole body politic. And, because kingship is based upon past common consent, it is identical with the rule of law. The law is a product of the realm and the realm is a product of the law. In this way, that rational, pre-established and natural order of law conformed to the ancient constitution.[71]

The charismatic, radically unstable, authority of pagan Anglo-Saxon kings could not be contained with the framework of a settled constitutional order. Their subjects were under the sway of invisible deities lurking everywhere in an enchanted world of magic and myth. Kings who lost their personal charisma forfeited any claim to the loyalty of their subjects. Under such circumstances, kingdoms were fragile arrangements built on shaky foundations. By splitting the spiritual from the temporal domain, the Papal revolution helped to institutionalize the distinction between kings and their kingdoms. When the Anglican Church declared its independence from Rome, the legal-rational authority of the state became supreme in all matters, secular and ecclesiastical.

---

69 Little, *Religion*, 158.

70 Hanson, *Kingdom*, 273.

71 Little, *Religion*, 163-5.

Identified fully with the law of reason, Hooker's ecclesiastical polity pushed purely spiritual issues out of sight into the private realm of conscience. For Anglo-Saxons moved by the myth of sacral kingship, reason had been all but irrelevant and powerless to control their common life; the principle of collective order was unknowable, emanating from beings forever beyond their ken but whose influence was palpably omnipresent. In the sixteenth century Englishmen were freed from subjection to unseen forces operating through and around them. They quickly learned, however, that henceforth they owed everything to the terrestrial transcendence of a royal authority. Royal authority was disconnected from the supernatural but it now aspired, in principle, if not yet in practice, to omnicompetence in worldly affairs.

It seems that Hooker was saying, "God is in his heaven and all will be right with the world as long as the traditional order of Church and commonwealth remains undisturbed." But, even as he wrote, Hooker knew that such complacency was unwarranted. As a consequence of the major changes set in motion by the Tudor revolution, fundamental challenges to the newly established order were already brewing. The reign of Henry VII did much to tame the great magnates and refine the legal and administrative methods of centralized government. Henry VIII made good use of those techniques to displace papal authority and confiscate the wealth of the Catholic Church. But, through the dissolution of the monasteries and the sale of their land, the king vastly increased the property of the gentry class now represented in the House of Commons. Over the course of the sixteenth century, the political influence of the landed gentry increased relative to that of the nobility and clergy with the result that a new constitutional balance was struck between the king, lords, and the commons.

Under the new regime, the traditional notion of double majesty was recast by Hooker and others into the language of law thereby exposing the tension at the heart of the myth of the ancient constitution. Hooker's version of double majesty asserted that regal authority derives from the law but also that the law locates supreme jurisdiction in the king. Double majesty had been "a loose working notion about the appropriate terms of political cooperation" between the king and his companions; it hardened into an insoluble legal dispute. Under the Tudors, the king's duty to insure that justice was done was elaborated and refined into a set of principles and practices that amounted to "a surrogate for the idea of sovereignty."[72] When the Stuarts employed the royal prerogative in the sweeping exercise of that equitable jurisdiction, it came into conflict with the property rights

---

72 Hanson, *Kingdom*, 280, 253.

of the landed gentry. The result was legal deadlock. Both sides appealed to tradition in defence of their position; both sides also encouraged a spirit of innovation that resulted in the collapse of the traditional order.

Fracturing the Tradition of Innovation

During the Middle Ages when opportunities to engage in trade and commerce were limited, English society was comprised of autonomous, more or less self-sufficient households, landed estates, shires, boroughs, guilds, and parishes, each of which served, in effect, as a little school of self-government. As a commercial civil society began to take off on a self-sustaining course of development during the sixteenth century, households and localities became steadily less self-sufficient while the expanding powers of the state undermined their capacity for self-government. Demand for agricultural products was increased by the growth of towns and cities, especially London. The woollen industry, building construction, coal mining and improvements in transportation provided even more economic opportunities. An expanding overseas market developed for grains, dairy products and wool.[73] Faced with a complex and unprecedented array of problems thrown up by the rising wealth and prosperity of an emergent market economy, government was compelled to respond. Its response prompted an equal and opposite reaction. On the one hand, a new breed of *statesmen* emerged as counsellors to the king; together they sought to cope with a thoroughly novel situation by remodelling the traditional materials available to them. On the other, the modernized mobilization of royal authority was resisted by common lawyers who invoked supposedly ancient principles of constitutional liberty to defend the property interests of an emergent landed gentry and its mercantile allies.

Almost from the moment of James I's accession to the throne of England, the latent conflict between princely prerogatives and the common law of the land came to the surface. Waged in the language of law, the clash was a symptom of a schizophrenic split within English society that set "traditionalist modernizers" in bitter opposition to "modernizing traditionalists." Both royalists and common lawyers were, by definition, traditionalists. James I himself appealed to long standing traditions of biblical authority and Christian theology in support of the divine right of kings; he also readily acknowledged that he was bound to rule in

---

73   Reinhard Bendix, *Kings or People: Power and the Mandate to Rule* (Berkeley, CA: University of California Press, 278-279.

accordance with the fundamental laws of the realm. But he was also committed to transforming the royal prerogative into an effective instrument of both executive and legislative power. On the other side, the parliamentary opposition routinely invoked the hoary traditions of the common law to defend the property interests that were fuelling the anarchic disorder of an early-modern market economy. For decades no clear line of division separated the two camps. Instead there was "a common denominator of constitutional and political thought from which each side drew and advanced its own views."[74] Over time, the friction generated by that entrenched ideological stalemate robbed the ethnoreligious mythology of the ancient British constitution of its power to sustain political unity. Thereafter, sovereign authority was justified not by its origins but by its results. By setting out to modernize the theory of royal power, the Stuart kings and their advisers challenged the ideological hegemony of the common law. In doing so, they de-stabilized the traditional constitutional order.

The most famous ideological strategy adopted by the Stuarts drew upon the language of theology to assert the divine right of kings to rule as God's lieutenants on earth. James I claimed that the "state of monarchy is the supremest thing upon earth". Even by God himself, he declared, kings "are called gods" because "they exercise a manner or resemblance of divine power upon earth." Like God, kings "make and unmake their subjects: they have power of raising and casting down; of life, and of death, judges over all their subjects, and in all causes, and yet accountable to none but God only."[75] Closely related to divine right theory was the patriarchal view of the king as *parens patriae*. Fathers and kings alike exercised a natural authority ordained by God. The most sophisticated versions of patriarchal theory did more than draw an analogy between patriarchal and regal authority: they portrayed monarchy as an outgrowth of the patriarchal authority ordained by God. Both patriarchal theory and the divine right of kings maintained "that God created an ordered universe in which all things had their pre-determined place in a complex hierarchy." But precisely because both ideological moves presupposed "the immutably hierarchical nature of the political world,"[76] they could not provide a

74 Margaret Atwood Judson, *The Crisis of the Constitution: An Essay in Constitutional and Political Thought in England, 1603-1645* (New York: Octagon, 1971), 13-14.

75 James I, "Speech to Parliament" 21 March 1610 in JP Kenyon, ed *The Stuart Constitution: Documents and Commentary* (Cambridge: Cambridge University Press, 1966), 12-14.

76 Glenn Burgess, *The Politics of the Ancient Constitution: An Introduction to English Political Thought, 1603-1642* (London: Macmillan, 1992), 133-134.

political formula appropriate to the needs of royal absolutism in a rapidly developing commercial society.

Both divine right and patriarchal theories endowed the ancient constitution with a *genetic* legitimacy. The one explained the subject's duty to obey his king by reference to the divine origins of governance; the other in terms of its inter-generational continuity. That traditionalist orientation toward the genesis of political obligation implies a rejection of historical change as a source of normative standards. The most far-sighted royalists understood that simplistic traditionalist theories of patriarchy and divine right kingship were obsolete. For that reason, royal ambitions did not rely solely, or even mainly, upon the backward-looking authority of origins. On the contrary, James I drew heavily upon the work of "progressive" statesmen-legislators such as Francis Bacon who produced a prototype of the modernist jurisprudence of control. Under their supervision, the English state began to invoke novel, *telic*—i.e., results-oriented—norms of constitutional legitimacy.

Bacon was a key figure in the history of the modern idea of change precisely because his work embodies the contradictory character of the Anglo-Saxon tradition of innovation. He entered royal service to promote his "central ambition: to reform the apparatus of governance so as to create what he believed were the conditions for an imperial monarchy."[77] He insisted that he was "launching a totally new enterprise" but "he builds meaning powerfully from traditional contexts." Drawing "on authority and examples from history," his writing features "arresting and often imaginatively interpreted" quotations from ancient poets, philosophers, historians or jurists.[78] In the jurisprudential realm, Bacon's program deliberately aimed to hollow out the myth of the ancient constitution. He attacked the confusion and uncertainty, the excessive litigation and the tangled procedures of the common law. Nor did he " hesitate to draw on the principles of Roman law where he found them useful."[79]

Roman public law declared that *quod principi placuit legis habet vigorem* (ie whatsoever has pleased the prince has the force of law). Bacon believed that law reform required "the further consolidation of royal power in the state: did the king rule, or did the judges?" He recommended that the king appoint committees of legal experts to sift through the law

77   Julian Martin, *Francis Bacon, the State, and the Reform of Natural Philosophy* (New York: Cambridge University Press, 1992), 4.

78   Charles Whitney, *Francis Bacon and Modernity*, (New Haven, CN: Yale University Press, 1986), 10-13, 57.

79   Perez Zagorin, *Francis Bacon*, (Princeton, NJ: Princeton University Press, 1998), 189.

reports and statute books with a view to collecting, collating and arranging the distilled and rational essence of the law into a digest which would then receive the royal imprimatur. What Bacon hoped to create out of this process "was a code, and he was perfectly explicit that it would be modelled on the law code of the Romans."[80] This reformed law would owe more to the enlightened will of the statesman-legislator than to common law judges whose independence was to be substantially curtailed. In Bacon's view, law was to become an integral part of a new science firmly rooted in the philosophy of progress.

Bacon defended the royal prerogative in the most aggressive terms as the necessary precondition for the transformation of England into a mighty empire. A reformed legal order would endow kings with the power "to sowe greatness to their posteritie and succession."[81] To the extent that royalists embraced Bacon's philosophy of law, they were riding the wave of the future. Unfortunately for them that wave broke over the rocky resistance thrown up by those determined to defend the jurisprudence of liberty enshrined in the myth of the ancient constitution.

Sir Edward Coke was a persistent thorn in the side of both Bacon and James I. He identified "the fundamental law of England" with the common law, which was "the law that had been applied by the courts of King's Bench, Common Pleas, and Exchequer since their establishment in the twelfth and thirteenth centuries."[82] Steeped in the history and traditions of the common law, Coke was a formidable antagonist. Better than any other person alive, he could cite—and, when necessary, fabricate—innumerable strong legal precedents in support of the subject's property and rights. Coke was determined "to limit and whittle down the personal jurisdiction of the king, the jurisdiction of chancery and of the ecclesiastical courts, to the point where such jurisdictions would be definitely dependent on the all-controlling determination of the common law courts."[83]

Faced with such intransigence, Bacon resolved to help the king write the absolute prerogative into law. Bacon's rationalism was manifested in his belief that careful study of both nature and the law would reveal their inner workings. Moreover, the systematic organization of our knowledge of law and the natural world was the means to dominion. Both Bacon and James I were convinced that the law could be understood through

---

80   Martin, *Bacon and Reform*, 126-128.

81   *Ibid.*, 134.

82   Harold J Berman, "The Origins of Historical Jurisprudence: Coke, Selden, Hale," (1994) 103 *Yale Law Journal* 1651, at 1681.

83   Judson, *Crisis*, 118-119.

the natural reason possessed in greater or lesser measure by every human being.

Coke did not deny that the common law was based upon reason; he did, however, reject the king's claim that in matters of law "he and others had reason as well as the Judges." His Majesty was not learned in the laws of England "and causes which concern the life, or inheritance, or goods, or fortunes of his subjects, are not to be decided by natural reason but by the artificial reason and judgement of law, which law is an act which requires long study and experience, before that a man can attain to the cognisance of it."[84] Even if all the natural reason dispersed into the several heads of the most brilliant lawyers of the present day were united into one, it would not be possible to replicate the artificial reason of the common law. Only through "many successions of ages" was "it fined and refined by an infinite number of grave and learned men" into "the perfection of reason."[85] The mass of formal precedents embodying the *letter* of the law might appear tangled, confused and contradictory to the layman; nevertheless, learned members of bench and bar could be relied upon to resolve the particular matters coming before them in a manner consistent with the *spirit* of the law.

Bacon, by contrast, was confident that natural reason could be deployed to purge the common law of its confusion and contradictions, distilling its essence into a set of consistent *regulae juris*. Bacon dismissed Cokean claims that the professional socialization of common lawyers was, in effect, a spiritual experience binding the living, the dead and the unborn together in a trans-generational community of memory.

In Coke's estimation, successful lawyers were bound to preserve a corporate fidelity to the permanent ideals of that community even as they accommodated the law to ceaseless change in the circumstances of everyday life. Indeed, for him, the history and traditions of English law were an integral part of the nation's secularised civil religion. There can be little doubt that the seven years that Richard Hooker spent as chaplain to the Inns of Court had significant influence on Coke's thought. He was frequently among Hooker's congregation at the Temple church. For both men, no doubt, history "was not a science but a faith." In opposition

---

84   Sir Edward Coke, "Prohibitions del Roy" 1607, in Kenyon, *Stuart Constitution*, 180-181.

85   Sir Edward Coke, quoted in JW Tubbs, "Custom, Time and Reason: Early Seventeenth-Century Conceptions of the Common Law," (1998) 19 *History of Political Thought* 363 at 388-389.

to Bacon's "emphasis on innovation and modernity, the myth of 'old England'—the older the better—became a dominant ideological force."[86]

By contrast, Bacon was a materialist who denied "the existence of a spiritual realm separate from the universe of matter." On that view, the traditions of the legal profession were mere social conventions rather than ideals rooted in the nature of things. The underlying premise of Bacon's "thought is that matter or body is all that exists in nature." It follows that the spirit of the laws must also be understood as a form of matter, a thin and invisible physical reality "whose action upon other bodies is explainable by physical causes."[87] Bacon wanted to understand how spirits, like any visible phenomenon worked. In law, as in natural philosophy, "knowledge becomes power in the service of appetite." No longer expressing the inner nature or social character of a particular people, law was destined to become a tool in the hands of "a vast bureaucracy designed to promote economic activity."[88]

Ironically, Bacon's materialism is best understood as a secularized version of a soteriological-eschatological, other-worldly, future-oriented Christian metaphysics. Just as Christians looked forward to the salvation and the final triumph of the kingdom of God, Bacon "saw in the historical-temporal process itself a potentiality for growth, renewal and the expansion of knowledge that fortified his belief in the future kingdom of man."[89] Bacon's philosophy of time and change announced a doctrine of progress premised on the conquest of nature, including, inevitably, human nature as well. It is probably no accident that the Stuart regime plunged into its final crisis when it heedlessly pushed Bacon's future-oriented materialism to the point where its egalitarian and universalist premises were revealed.

Public Prerogatives versus Private Property

It may seem odd to identify royal absolutism with the egalitarianism that became the hallmark of legal modernism. But the despotic pretensions of the Stuart monarchy were tied to a theory of sovereignty according to which all subjects were equal in the allegiance they owed to the king. So long as feudalism persisted, there was no clear distinction between private and public law, between ownership and *dominium*. The bonds

---

86 Berman, "Historical Jurisprudence," 1687; Little, *Religion*, 147-149.

87 Zagorin, *Francis Bacon*, 113-114.

88 Richard M Weaver, *Ideas Have Consequences* (Chicago: University of Chicago Press, 1984), 38.

89 Zagorin, *Francis Bacon*, 204.

between lord and vassal were based upon personal relations of dependence, subordination and tenure. The king's authority over his subjects was mediated through several complicated and interlocking layers of subinfeudation. Outside Parliament, the authority of the English king to levy taxes depended on the existence of these highly particularized feudal ties and obligations. For example, the Crown did possess powers to require the provision of ships or contributions to maintain them. But such powers were limited and local in character, originally resting "on the service which coastal towns like the Cinque Ports had been obliged by tenure to provide."

By the sixteenth century, such parochial limitations constrained the development of a modernizing state; the Crown began to assert a broader prerogative power to requisition, "treating the merchant shipping of the country as an adjunct to the royal fleet." No concerted opposition to this policy arose so long as it applied only to coastal towns and districts. In the famous *Ship Money case*, the Crown, in effect, asserted that all of its subjects, those who lived in inland counties as well as those on the coast, were equally subject to the prerogative power to requisition either ships or money to help build ships for the use of the royal navy. Clearly, the inhabitants of inland counties had no tenurial obligation to provide ship money. But it was not at all clear why maritime districts alone should bear the fiscal burdens associated with the naval defence of the realm. Accordingly, obligations specifically based upon tenure fell into desuetude and the Crown rested its prerogative power on the broader ground of allegiance.[90] In doing so, the Crown asserted an impersonal, public authority that placed it in a direct relationship with its subjects, each one of which owed a duty of allegiance to the Crown in return for its protection.

The modernizing logic of such a revitalized royal prerogative, operating outside the framework of parliamentary consent to taxation, posed a clear and present danger to the spirit of the ancient constitution. The expansion of a regal power modelled on the Roman *imperium* necessarily implied that all private individuals were equally subject to kings acting in the name of the collective welfare. Additionally, the incipient egalitarianism inherent in the doctrine of allegiance eventually undermined "private" property rights. John Hampden and other opponents of the ship money levy were right to insist that property is an essential bulwark of liberty against the threat of tyranny. Once public law is based on the maxim *salus populi suprema lex*, property rights lose their absolute character. No longer possessed of a genetic legitimacy grounded in immemorial

---

90   DL Keir, "The Case of Ship-Money," (1936) 52 *Law Quarterly Review* 546.

custom, all manner of proprietary interests become contingent upon their contribution to the collective welfare.

Leading a revolution from above, the most ambitious royalists hoped that the universalistic principles of Roman public law would help them to usher in an empire of reason liberated from the fetters of tradition and the mindless veneration of the past. Their philosophy of progress left a permanent mark on the constitutional culture; legal rationalism, philosophical materialism and universalistic egalitarianism were set in permanent opposition to the spirit of liberty rooted in the particular history and distinctive character of the English people.

The age-old spirit of English liberty was sanctified by the myth of the ancient constitution. Equality, even equality before the law, was always subordinate to the liberty that had its material foundation in the common law institution of property. Before it came under sustained challenge from the royal prerogative, the common law had established the foundation for a mixed and balanced polity. That mixed constitution presupposed the existence of a stable and ordered hierarchy of households, localities and corporate bodies politic, whose autonomy, jointly and severally, depended upon the secure possession of landed and personal property. Coke recognized that the letter of the common law alone could never defeat the gathering force of a modernized prerogative power. But, by maintaining that the common law had its origins in an ancient British constitution, Coke was able to resolve even the most mundane disputes between property and the prerogative in a manner consistent with the spirit of liberty. But, in so doing, Coke, too, helped to unleash dynamic forces in an emergent market society that would produce a fatal rupture between the spirit of innovation and the prescriptive force of tradition.

In *Darcy v Allein*, the court was asked to uphold a royal patent that granted Darcy the sole right to make playing cards within the realm for a period of twenty-one years. The court held instead that the patent was an unlawful monopoly. Coke's report of that decision declared that Magna Carta guaranteed that the defendant Allein could not be deprived of his "freedom or liberty" to produce playing cards except "by the lawful judgement of his peers." In fact, of course, the "liberties" protected by Magna Carta, at the behest of powerful feudal barons, were more in the nature of "immunities and franchises," precisely the vested right that the plaintiff in *Darcy* sought to protect against unlawful usurpation. But Coke was ready to invent precedents, if need be, to safeguard the spirit of individual liberty in his own day.[91]

He was no less willing to defy centuries of established precedents if they constrained the liberty of individuals to enter a lawful trade. In both the *Tailors of Ipswich case* and *Dr Bonham's case*, Coke undercut the traditional authority of guilds (tailors in the one case, physicians in the other) to discipline individuals who failed to comply with the prescribed formalities that governed their respective trades. Such guilds derived their powers from royal charters. Whatever justification these two guilds might once have had as guarantors of quality and high standards in a closed community, Coke concluded that in an emergent market economy they were acting as combinations in restraint of trade. Here, too, upholding the prerogative power posed a threat to individual liberty.[92]

Conclusion

But not even Coke could hold his finger in the dike forever. Because, he, too, was committed to the tradition of double majesty, he recognized the king's absolute prerogative to make war and conduct international relations.[93] It was precisely that prerogative that the king's justices invoked in deciding the *Ship Money Case*, thus demonstrating that the common law alone could not defend the goods and liberties of the subject against a determined royal assault. To maintain, as Coke did, that the king was bound to seek parliamentary approval to meddle in matters of *meum et tuum* turned out to be a futile exercise because judges very early "learned how to use the doctrines of reason of state and national emergency in domestic affairs." The result "was to deprive men of their property without the consent of parliament."[94] Rhetorical appeals to the ancient constitution were not enough to cause most of His Majesty's judges to renounce their sworn allegiance to the Crown. As it happened, even Coke's formal acknowledgement of royal prerogative was not enough to prevent his dismissal from the bench in 1616. Common law judges, he was reminded, served at the king's pleasure.

---

91 Samuel E Thorne, "Sir Edward Coke, 1552-1952," in Samuel E Thorne, *Essays in English Legal History* (London: Hambledon Press, 1985), 225-233.

92 *Ibid.*; see also, Harold J Cook, "Against Common Right and Reason: The College of Physicians Versus Dr Thomas Bonham," (1985) 29 *American Journal of Legal History* 301.

93 Judson, *Crisis*, 26.

94 Hanson, *Kingdom*, 307.

It was left to Parliament to defend the ancient liberties of the free-born Englishman against the absolutist pretensions of the Crown. In the end, royal tyranny was defeated but in taking up the cudgels in defence of the ancient constitution, parliamentary forces paved the way for "a very English absolutism," the unchallenged sovereignty of Parliament itself.[95] The *republica Anglorum* underwritten by the myth of the ancient constitution collapsed as a consequence of civil war and revolutionary upheaval.

After decades of instability, a reformed regime much more consistent with Bacon's preference for a modernist jurisprudence of control began to take shape. Parliamentary sovereignty became the foundation myth of that new regime. Significantly, the destruction of the Stuart monarchy did not come at the hands of traditionalist defenders of the ancient constitution. Rather the deadlock between royalist modernizing traditionalists and the common law traditionalist modernizers exhausted both sides and allowed a third force to tip the balance, plunging the nation into revolution and civil war. It was the Puritan refusal to recognize the established Church of England as the synergistic unity of society, politics and religion that finally sealed the fate of the *ancien régime* in England.

Puritans rejected the past-oriented, this-worldly, folk religion of their Germanic ancestors and embraced instead a future-oriented, salvation history of sin and redemption in which the "Godly" were radically estranged from conventional society. Separating themselves from their "lukewarm" neighbours, Puritans withdrew into select, independent and voluntary communities composed solely of equals. Their virtuous communities of the elect existed in a state of grace that knew no national boundaries.

The Puritan revolt against royal absolutism was not a movement to defend the ancient constitution. On the contrary, the Puritans radicalized a revolution begun by Bacon and his absolutist patrons. In their view, the royalists were both too materialistic and not sufficiently universalistic and egalitarian. Along with the modernist canon of Baconian rationalism, royalist pretensions toward absolutism, and a runaway market economy, the Puritan Revolution helped to transform the character of the English people. Once the dust settled after decades of civil war and revolution in England, the tradition-directed character-type became an anachronistic anomaly among ambitious members of the political nation. The world was truly turned upside down as the traditional vices became modern virtues.

---

95 Michael Mendle, "Parliamentary Sovereignty: A Very English Absolutism," in Nicholas Phillipson & Quentin Skinner, *Political Discourse in Early Modern Britain* (Cambridge: Cambridge University Press, 1993), 97.

3.

Metamorphosis: The Peculiar Character of the Early Modern Englishman

Introduction

Republica Anglorum: the phrase conjures up the civic spirit of classical antiquity transposed into an English Renaissance landscape. Even though Sir Thomas Smith's well-known book on sixteenth century England was written in English, its Latin title accorded with established usage.[1] In framing his account of England's uniquely successful polity, Smith drew upon an Aristotelian tradition of political philosophy rooted in the ancient republics. Despite its explicitly classical antecedents, however, Smith's headline reference to the *republica Anglorum* is seriously misleading, especially for modern readers. That is partly our own fault; nowadays, the term "republic" is typically defined as a state in which sovereignty resides in the people rather than in a monarch. Political philosophers in classical antiquity learned to distinguish between "democracies," in which the people ruled themselves, and "republics," the latter involving some form of mixed and balanced government combining monarchical and aristocratic elements with popular participation in government. A more substantive source of confusion arises out of Smith's own translation of the word *republica* into English not as "republic" but, rather, as "commonwealth." Concealed in that apparently innocuous choice of words was an implicit departure from the classical republican tradition, a break that became a yawning gulf a century later in the Puritan Commonwealth imposed upon England by the Lord Protector, Oliver Cromwell, and his army.

---

1   Sir Thomas Smith, *De Republica Anglorum: A Discourse of the Commonwealth of England*, edited by L Alston (Cambridge: Cambridge University Press, 1906).

Smith defined a commonwealth as "a society or common doing of a multitude of free men collected together and united by common accord and covenauntes among themselves, for the conservation of themselves as well in peace as in war." Like Aristotle, Smith believed that the polity had its germ in private households which then gathered together into villages before becoming developed bodies politic. Once isolated households acquire a common civic identity, private concern for private property can be transformed into a public concern. In Smith's view, the commonwealth existed mainly to secure the common *wealth*: "it is profitable to everie common wealth…to be kept in her most perfect estate." Indeed, it "is not so farre out of the way" to equate justice with "the profite of the ruling and most strong part…of the Citie or common wealth." [2] In England, there can be little doubt that the commonwealth "assumed the disguise of an organization of property holders who, instead of claiming access to the public realm because of their wealth, demanded protection from it for the accumulation of more wealth." At the same time, however, the political imagination of some Englishmen had been captured by the recently redis-covered classical republican tradition of political thought. In that tradi-tion, men rose into the public realm for much less mundane motives. No wonder, since the classical *polis* "was permeated by a fiercely agonal spirit, where everybody had constantly to distinguish himself from all others, to show through unique words and achievements that he was the best of all (*aien aristeuein*)."[3] While few of those on either side of the long running conflict between king and parliament were moved to rise above concern for their property, it is likely that the ancient constitution of the *republica Anglorum* was rejuvenated by an infusion of civic humanism stirring on the continent.

Indeed, in June 1642, only two months before the outbreak of the civil war, two of Charles I's advisers persuaded him to issue a document drawing on the language of classical republicanism to portray the English polity as a mixed and balanced government vested in three estates, the king, the lords and the commons. *His Majesty's Answer to the Nineteen Propositions of Both Houses of Parliament* has been described as a drastic departure from the divine right theory of kingship that "was both consti-tutionally incorrect and a disastrous tactical error in royalist polemic."[4]

---

2   *Ibid.*, 20.

3   Hannah Arendt, *The Human Condition* (Chicago: University of Chicago Press, 1958), 68, 41.

4   JGA Pocock, *The Machiavellian Moment: Florentine Political Thought and the Atlantic Republican Tradition* (Princeton, NJ: Princeton University Press, 1975), 361.

Leaving aside the question of how this document may have contributed to the downfall of the monarchy, historians generally agree that its classical republican vision of a mixed and balanced constitution was not an accurate depiction of either the Tudor or the Stuart regime or even their medieval predecessors. As we have seen, Donald Hanson contends that the noble order of medieval England was too fragmented and too preoccupied with purely local and familial pursuits and loyalties; barons were far too interested in the possession of land and the cultivation of their military prowess to develop a civic consciousness. Only the king focused his "political attention and sustained activity at the level of the central governmental institutions of the society."[5]

Civic consciousness, on this view, was the product of the long, grinding crisis of the constitution in the early seventeenth century when parliamentarians and common lawyers were compelled to enter the public realm to defend their liberty and property against the threat of royal absolutism. In somewhat oversimplified terms, "Englishmen, denied civic consciousness by the prevalence of 'double majesty,' were pitchforked into it by the trauma of 'double majesty's' collapse."[6] It might be more accurate to suggest that the Puritan Revolution of the seventeenth century foreclosed the possibility that Smith's Anglican commonwealth would be remodelled in line with the classical republican model presented by King Charles I and his advisers.

Even in the sixteenth century, prominent humanists such as Thomas More and Thomas Smith reflected a growing civic awareness; both men served as counselor to his prince. The civic humanist figure of the counselor appeared in growing numbers in the guise of "the country gentleman, representing a shire or borough to counsel his prince in parliament, under a writ which enjoins him to treat of all matters affecting the realm and to serve as the representative of the whole body politic."[7] The appearance of such role models was an important step towards the constitution of the *res publica* in England; these men appeared in public where their words and deeds could be seen and heard by everybody who mattered and where they received the widest possible publicity. But the revival of the civic traditions of classical antiquity required something more as well.

---

5   Donald V Hanson, *From Kingdom to Commonwealth: The Development of Civic Consciousness in English Political Thought* (Cambridge, MA: Harvard University Press, 1970), 5, 17.

6   Pocock, *Machiavellian Moment*, 338.

7   *Ibid*, 340.

It presupposed the existence of boundaries between the private and the public realm.

The ancient republics created a common world belonging to all members of the political nation that is clearly distinguishable from their privately owned place in it. Arendt argues that "the existence of a public realm and the world's subsequent transformation into a community of things which gathers men together and relates them to each other depends entirely on permanence." The public realm of the *res publica* "must transcend the life-span of mortal men."[8] By contrast, the sixteenth century humanists who "discoursed of the common weal" formulated their advice to the prince only for the sake of the living. Many dedicated themselves to understanding the economic forces at work in their society; indeed, they promoted "ideologies of dynamism" likely to undermine the seemingly static and medieval ideals "maintaining the realm as a hierarchy of degree."[9]

Tradition-directed characters such as Richard Hooker resisted the tendency to subordinate the ecclesiastical polity of the *republica Anglorum* to activities formerly banished to the private realm of the household. But his opponents in the Puritan movement pushed for the revolutionary transformation of the old order. Hooker's vision of the commonwealth retained elements of a Christian cosmology that provided the main traditionalist alternative to the renaissance of classical republicanism. The *Puritan* commonwealth turned the tradition-directed world of the *republica Anglorum* upside down. Even after the restoration of the monarch in 1660, the public realm was occupied by private interests which were "essentially much less permanent and much more vulnerable to the mortality of their owners than the common world" of Hooker's ecclesiastical polity.[10] Steeped in autochthonous ecclesiastical traditions, the *Anglican* commonwealth grew out of the past and was intended to last for future generations.[11] Its revolutionary overthrow created the conditions in which a radically new social character took hold, particularly among a merchant class influenced by Puritanism.

By the late eighteenth century, the widespread diffusion of the Puritan, "inner-directed" character type facilitated the progressive *embourgeoisement* of English elites. The Puritans were the vanguard of a bourgeois

---

8   Arendt, *Human Condition*, 52, 55, 68.

9   Pocock, *Machiavellian Moment*, 339.

10   Arendt, *Human Condition*, 68.

11   Richard Hooker, *Of the Laws of Ecclesiastical Polity* edited by Arthur Stephen McGrade (Cambridge: Cambridge University Press, 1989); Arendt, *Human Condition*, 68.

revolution that transformed the nature of both the English people and the regime governing them. The change from tradition-direction to inner-direction was the greatest social and characterological shift in the history of the Anglo-Saxon peoples. Its impact was far greater than the biocultural innovations associated with the routinization of charismatic authority. Neither in the early Anglo-Saxon era when magical forces and mysterious deities reigned over the visible world nor in the tradition-directed societies of medieval Christendom had there been any need to develop a pronounced individuality of character; behavior was governed by "prescriptions...objectified in ritual and etiquette." The inner-directed character was a necessary adaptation to the rise of modernity with its increased personal mobility, accelerating technological shifts and, above all, endless expansion, both geographically and in the production of goods and people. Such a society presented individuals with many novel situations that required individual initiatives which could not be encompassed in advance by traditional codes of behavior.[12]

Under the new bourgeois regime, the common *wealth* steadily undermined the durability of the common world. This outcome could not be reversed, even by the accumulation of "wealth...to a point where no individual life-span can use it up, so that the family rather than the individual becomes its owner." By its very nature, "wealth remains something to be used and consumed no matter how many individual life-spans it may sustain." Puritans famously displayed an in-built resistance to temptation, resolutely refusing to consume the very considerable wealth generated by their religious devotion to a calling. Early in life their elders had implanted an "inner" source of direction oriented "toward generalized but nonetheless inescapably destined goals," thereby giving birth to the spirit of capitalism. In Puritan hands, "wealth became capital whose chief function was to generate more capital." Driven by the spirit of accumulation, private property came close to acquiring "the permanence inherent in the commonly shared world." However, this permanence was of a different nature; it was the permanence of a process of perpetual change rather than the permanence of a stable structure. The entry of the inner-directed bourgeois individual into the public realm became a means to an end—the accumulation of capital—rather than an end in itself as it had been for the citizens of the ancient republics. The bourgeois commonwealth never became "common in the sense we speak of a common world; it remained, or rather was intended to remain, strictly private. Only the government

---

12 David Riesman, *The Lonely Crowd: A Study of the Changing American Character* (New Haven, CN: Yale University Press, 1961), 14-15.

appointed to shield the private owners from each other in the competitive struggle for more wealth, was common." In the new-modelled *republica Anglorum*, the only thing people had in common was their private interests.[13]

The Puritan Revolution not only foreclosed the possibility that the Anglican commonwealth might develop into a classically republican, mixed and balanced polity, it also suppressed the folk memory of the cosmology that had been the spiritual seed-bed for the fusion of the civic and early Christian cultures of classical antiquity. Only when we understand the kinship between Anglo-Saxon paganism, the myths and deities of classical Rome and Greece, and the Germanization of medieval Christianity can we begin to grasp the radical nature of the rupture with European traditions that was engineered by the Puritan "revolution of the saints."

The distinctive social structure of medieval Christendom displayed remarkable continuity with the ethnoreligions practiced by many, widely separated pagan peoples of the ancient world. Christianity formally proscribed the old religions but it did not uproot the social ideals embodied in the pagan gods. Even after the Papal Revolution, tradition-directed English Christians preserved the trinitarian cosmology that their Anglo-Saxon ancestors shared with the Celts, the Scandinavians and the Romans.

The Puritan spirit of capitalism not only turned that ancient worldview on its head; it also launched Anglo-Saxons into a *novus ordo seclorum* that brought religion down to earth in an economy enchanted by the cornucopian myths of modernist Mammonism. Nowadays, we are all too familiar with that mythology: we now owe everything to the inscrutable operation of an impersonal world-system that is no less absolute than the invisible gods governing pagan peoples. Before we can hope to escape our self-imposed domination, we must understand how the Puritan Revolution flattened the foundational myths of the trifunctional social order characteristic of all Indo-European societies.

The Trifunctional Social Order

We know that there were people living in the British Isles 26,000 years ago. We also know that their descendants were forced south by the onset of the Ice Age 8,000 years later. When the glaciers retreated, people returned to what are now the British Isles. But they were forced to retreat once again

---

13   Arendt, *Human Condition*, 68-69; Riesman, *Lonely Crowd*, 15.

when the ice returned sometime around 9000 BC.[14] Seeking refuge in the south of France, Italy and elsewhere in southern Europe, the northern peoples encountered each other. It is clear that the mingling of those populations with others already settled in the south of Europe accounts for the high level of genetic similarity among Europeans, making them the most homogeneous of the major continental races. It also appears that many English, Irish, Welsh and Scots are descended from maternal lineage groups whose generations-long migration moved along the north coast of the Mediterranean, through the Straits of Gibraltar and up the Atlantic coast before reaching Britain and Ireland. Other lineages arrived via eastern and the central Europe. Either way, the shared ancestral experience of displacement and migration left a lasting legacy of ethnic kinship clearly reflected in the distinctive tripartite cosmology of many widely dispersed Indo-European peoples.

One manifestation of a shared Indo-European cosmology is the remarkable congruence between the gods of ancient Rome and Scandinavia that also extends to the Vedic religions of India 3,000 years ago. In each case, gods were divided into three ranks, each playing its own distinctive role in the cosmos. In the first rank were the gods representing the sovereign function of maintaining unity and harmony. In the Vedic religion Mitra was closest to man in this world while Varuna represented the immense ensemble of the other world. Contract, a form facilitating treaties and alliances between men, was the mode of action associated with Mitra. Varuna was conceived as a grand sorcerer whose magic created form itself and seized the guilty through an irresistible power. In Rome, making due allowance for the more utilitarian and patriotic character of its culture, it appears that the Mitrian role was played by Dius Fidius, the luminous god of fidelity, of loyalty and of oaths, while the Varunian function was performed by Jupiter. The analogy to the Indian gods of the first rank was even more striking in Scandinavia where Odin and Týr shared the sovereign function.[15]

The second type of god commonly found in Indo-European mythology was associated with war. In Scandinavia, a portion of the warrior role was annexed by Odin but Thor remained the Thunder God, the god of violence, a function performed by Indra in Vedic religions and Mars in Rome. Gods of the third rank performed the functions that provided the foundation for the two other roles. In this grouping were found the

---

14   Sykes, *Blood*, 14-17, 137-138.

15   Georges Dumézil, *Mythes et Dieux des Indo-Européens*, edited by Hervé Coutau-Bégarie (Paris: Flammarion, 1992), 155-165.

gods of fecundity and abundance, associated, *inter alia*, with Freyr in Scandinavia and Quirinus in Rome. If the third function was the most humble, it was the essential precondition permitting the superior gods to perform the functions of sovereignty and war. How could sorcerers and warriors live if not supported by farmers and pastoralists?[16] The trifunctional character of the pantheon presupposed the interdependence and unity of the three ranks of gods and goddesses. The boundaries separating the three functions were not set in concrete precisely because interaction and interpenetration of the three divine archetypes was essential to produce a harmonious equilibrium.

The inescapable need to achieve a stable balance between the three functions formed the central theme in the legends surrounding the origins of Rome. Only when the distinctive attributes and virtues of the three constituent tribes combined could the foundations of Rome be securely laid. Romulus—*rex* and *augur*—and his companions are the repositories of sovereignty and the auspices; they are also the protégés of Jupiter. Indeed, Romulus is favored by the two premier gods of the triad because he is also the son of Mars. As such, he can make good use of his Etruscan allies who are specialists in the military arts. His enemies, the Sabines, are averse to war but, because they are well-endowed with women and rich in herds, they are able to avoid it. In this legend, Quirinus is treated as a Sabine god because that tribe is seen as bearers of the third function.[17]

The tripartite structure of Indo-European ethnoreligions embodied a social ideal that was translated at one time or another, with greater or lesser fidelity, into the organization of social life. It is true that the ancient Greeks departed significantly from a trifunctional cosmology; that might reflect the influence of earlier civilizations in the Aegean and eastern Mediterranean but is more likely a product of their uniquely critical, innovative and creative character. Even so, the three classes in Plato's ideal *Republic*—the philosophers who governed, the warriors who defended the state and the third estate which created wealth—bear a powerful resemblance to the Indo-European ideal. Other more conservative peoples, most notably Germans and Scandinavians, also translated the social ideal embedded in their religions into the structure of everyday life.[18]

One might be tempted to dismiss the interplay between the tripartite theology and social structures of the Indo-European peoples on the ground that the functions of sovereignty, of war-making and of material

---

16 *Ibid*, 137, 176-177, 192.

17 *Ibid*, 141.

18 *Ibid*, 55, 92.

provision must, of necessity, be performed in every society. But the striking fact is that non-Indo-European peoples have *not* made those functions the explicit foundation either of their cosmology or of their social organization. The only exceptions have been the product of contact with an Indo-European people that can be precisely dated and located. It is in vain that one looks for an independent replica of Indo-European tripartition among the Finnish, the Siberians, or biblical Hebrews. Instead, one finds undifferentiated nomad societies where every man is both fighter and pastoralist. In ancient China or early Mesopotamia there were also theocratic regimes where a king-priest or emperor was supported by a mass of subjects hierarchically organized along a gradual continuum that was homogeneous only in its servitude and humility. In other societies, the sorcerer was merely one speciality among a great many others. None of them reproduced, in theory or in practice, the distinctive Indo-European hierarchical structure of three functional classes of both gods and men: those who ordered the visible and invisible worlds, those who fought, and those who worked.[19]

With the conversion of the Anglo-Saxons to Christianity, the divine triad of the pagans was driven underground. But the pre-historic ideal of a trifunctional social structure retained its imaginative power to shape the organizational life of Old England. Alfred the Great invoked the trifunctional theme in the translation of Boethius' *On the Consolation of Philosophy* of which he claimed to be the author. At the time the translation was being prepared, God was subjecting Alfred's kingdom to cruel tribulations. Faced with mortal danger from foreign invasion, the translators chose to add a brief commentary in the margins of Boethius' text. Just as a man, they wrote, cannot practice a craft without materials and the tools of his trade, the king cannot govern without "a well-populated land; he must have men of prayer, men of war, men of labor." Those "three pillars of the community" are the ruler's tools; as for materials, he must have enough land to provide an adequate supply of arms, food and clothing. Otherwise, the king "cannot keep these tools, and without these tools he cannot do any of the things he is responsible for doing."[20]

Even before the Roman conquest, the triadic schema of social organization was "probably familiar to the people of the British Isles."[21] The structure was never rigid or inflexible, however. Alfred's conception may

---

19 *Ibid*, 86, 93.

20 Georges Duby, *The Three Orders: Feudal Society Imagined* (Chicago: University of Chicago Press, 1980) 100.

21 *Ibid*, 102.

reflect a necessary accommodation of the older Germanic ideal to the transformation of the sacred after the Anglo-Saxon conversion. The pagan priest-king of the Teutonic tribes represented both aspects of the premier function, magic and sovereignty; he might also represent a mélange of elements drawn from all three functions, particularly the second since he was invariably drawn from the warrior class.[22] In Alfred's schema, however, the king is presented as above and apart from the trifunctional structure sustaining the throne just as three legs support a stool. The three pillars were not self-sufficient in Alfred's model; besides the tools and the materials necessary to practice the craft of rulership, the king required "one more thing, wisdom. Because, of course, matter must be dominated by spirit." The three values embodied in the system "were combined, owing to deeply rooted mental habits, in the person of the sovereign, wherein they reached their culmination."[23]

Such triadic complexes had "deep roots in traditional Celtic political imaginings." They continued to have an influence in England throughout the medieval era and beyond. Well after Alfred's death, in times "when people sensed that evil and disorder were on the rise in Anglo-Saxon and Frankish kingdoms alike…anxious intellectuals were working desperately to locate the sources of the troubles so that they could quell the disturbance and restore peace." The church played an important role in reminding men "that society consisted of three categories that cooperated and exchanged services among themselves." Translated into Latin, the three functions were identified in terms identical to those employed by Alfred: those who prayed, *oratores*, those who fought, *bellatores*, and those who worked, *laboratores*. At the same time, the hierarchical character of the trifunctional postulate was clearly recognized. "While each of the functions was indispensable to the other two, this did not mean they were all equally noble." It also meant that the nobility itself was bifurcated: just as a warrior ought not to engage in manual labor, "a consecrator of the host ought not to fight." As nobles who shared the blood of kings, both *oratores* and *bellatores* had the duty to protect and the right to exploit the ignoble *laboratores*. But however impure the laborer might be, one thing "was certain: this world could dispense with neither armed men nor toiling men." It was no less certain that the three orders of men inhabited a common world ordained by God.[24]

---

22 Dumézil, *Mythes*, 113.

23 Duby, *Three Orders*, 100, 276.

24 *Ibid*, 108, 102-103, 117, 165-166.

The Common World of the *Republica Anglorum*

The Papal Revolution did not go unchallenged within medieval Christendom, even in the West. There were those who maintained that the clergy should be placed under the tutelage of a community of friars. Monastic orders which inhabited a kingdom not of this world reflected a triadic vision quite different from the Indo-European norm which united those who prayed, those who fought, and those who worked in a common world. During the eleventh century, monks vigorously defended their own triune hierarchy of merit based upon sexuality. Accordingly, they "distinguished among three degrees of sexual purity: that of virgins [ie those closest to God], that of the continent, and that of the married couple." Sexually impure married couples engaged in the worldly business of production and reproduction occupied the lowest rank on that scale. By conspicuously devaluing the temporal order, the three orders of merit inscribed within the monastic ideal contradicted the functional logic of the Papal Revolution. The papal monarchy had clearly recognized the autonomy and integrity of the temporal world, both by setting out to restore episcopal authority over the monastic orders, of bishops over abbots, and by asserting the freedom of the church in spiritual affairs. Reformist bishops in northern France and England decried the excesses of a monastic movement that denied the very possibility of a common world in the here and now. Like those who preached equality, "those proud, mad people who dared to claim that they were free of sin and fancied themselves escaping the human condition" were going too far, too fast and would inevitably generate disorder. Bishops, no less than abbots, wanted "to clear the way for the ultimate transformation" in the world to come but "they wanted to do it in a different way." They were convinced that mankind ought "to arrange itself in proper order, to form up in ranks, so as to be able to pass through the gates of the true life without panic, without a scuffle."[25]

Ecclesiastical efforts to preserve the proper order of medieval Christendom contributed to the resurrection of the trifunctional social order within the newly independent terrestrial realm, both as an ideal and as a *social reality*. The pagan trinity remained embedded within a Christian cosmology but it lost much of its spiritual depth once it was brought down to earth. Much, but not all: the relationship between those who pray, those who fight, and those who work was clearly ordained by God. The civic spirit of those defending the *republica Anglorum* endowed

---

25 *Ibid*, 81-82, 145.

the secular realm with a sacred aura of its own. Historians often overlook the contribution to the English republican tradition made by those whose function was to fight. No doubt it was true that the medieval English nobility thought of themselves as warriors bound to protect and preserve their local propertied interests, leaving to the king the responsibility to safeguard the interest of the realm as a whole. The nobility was not, however, altogether bereft of a civic consciousness. In fact, the tripartition of the secular realm in medieval English society should be seen as an inchoate expression of civic humanism. "This was a consequence of its terrestrial, incarnate aspect." The trifunctional ideal joined those who prayed, those who fought and those who worked in a common world here below; in doing so, it rejected monastic "illusions of otherworldliness, of flight into the timeless beyond."[26]

The role of medieval knights, therefore, was to defend the common world of the *res publica*. In the service of the king, the duty of the nobility was to restrain the appetites of the powerful and to protect the poor. No doubt the purpose of the ideal was to justify the seigneurial mode of production which, after all, was the material foundation on which the kingdom rested. The point of social trifunctionality was to establish a civil code, to show that the distribution of services and privileges was equitable. But the proto-republican character of chivalric codes must not be exaggerated. The civic consciousness of the warrior is not that of a citizen, nor does the priest or the laborer think of himself in such terms. The world they inhabit in common is hierarchical and functionally differentiated but it most definitely belongs to the secular city of man just as priests and monks occupy the spiritual realm. "For the earth is here the be-all and the end-all, and responsibility for ensuring stability rests entirely with the *princeps*." Christian knighthood and its needs were clearly coupled with royal prerogatives in the idea of double majesty. But the significance of double majesty must be located within the "whole ungainly edifice" of the trifunctional social ideal "with its two wings, corporeal and spiritual," an ideological system intended "to prove that knighthood is entitled to be 'served' by the other two categories, the people and the clergy."[27]

In the course of the Tudor revolution during the early sixteenth century, the ability of the great feudal barons to raise their own private armies independently of the Crown was sharply curtailed. As a consequence, double majesty—of king and nobility—was subsumed into the complex interplay between the prince and the law. That transformation

---

26 *Ibid*, 165.

27 *Ibid*, 275-276, 305.

was incorporated into the revised version of Richard Hooker's Trinitarian theology. In that Anglican schema, "politic *Society*" was divided into two distinct corporations: the first was "the *Church* of *Christ*" housing "those who pray"; the other was "the *Commonwealth*" exercising the functions of sovereignty.[28] "Those who fight" were now identified wholly with the regal functions of governance. Hooker revealed the harmonious interdependence of the traditional triadic ideal not just in the organization of society as a whole but also within the internal structures of both Church and Commonwealth. He attributed the strength of the body politic to its fabrication as "a threefold cable, consisting of the king as a supreme head over all, of peers and nobles under him, and of the people under them." The "second wreath of that cable" consisted "as well of lords spiritual as temporal: nobility and prelacy being by this means twined together." Hooker warned that, if Puritans succeeded in their campaign to tear the lords spiritual away from the lords temporal, both would be weakened which must "impair greatly the good of all."[29]

Both Church and Commonwealth necessarily rested on and included the people as the indispensable third element which supported the entire edifice. All "those who labor" were simultaneously members of the Church of England and of the Commonwealth, creating "a figure *triangular*" in which "the base does differ from the sides thereof" but in which every line is "both a base and also a side" depending on the perspective from which it is viewed.[30] Hooker was no egalitarian however. His conception of the tripartite order reflected a traditional vision as fundamental to the sensibilities of the ancient Romans and Greeks as it was to the Teutonic tribesman who had invaded England in the fifth century. Like the ancients, he believed that men are by nature part "animal" but they also have a "divine" quality that distinguishes them from other creatures and which must govern their baser instincts. His "triangular" figure replicated the hierarchical equilibrium between three functions that regulate the order of the cosmos. Plato had identified three elements in the human soul and body which play a role analogous to the three classes described in the *Republic*. The first divine function is incarnated in the head which becomes the "acropolis of consciousness and spirituality." It is superior to the other two parts. The second element, located in the heart, relates to action and military valour. It serves as an ally of the head in the struggle to

---

28   Hooker, *Laws*, 130.

29   David Little, *Religion, Order, and Law: A Study in Pre-Revolutionary England* (Oxford: Basil Blackwell, 1970), 157.

30   Hooker, *Laws*, 130.

maintain control over the third "animal" function located in the stomach, the seat of appetites and desires.[31] Hooker shared that determination to ensure that those who toiled were governed by those who embodied the highest virtues of wisdom and courage.

He recognized that men "seek a triple perfection, first, a sensual, consisting in those things that very life requireth either as necessary supplements, or as beauties and ornaments thereof." Those who devote the whole of their lives to satisfying such needs "have no God but only their belly." There were also those whose aim is to cultivate "the law of moral and civil perfection" in this life. But that worthy endeavor cannot satisfy our "spiritual and divine" needs for "those things whereunto we tend by supernatural means here, but cannot here attain unto them." Hooker was in no doubt that, while riches may "be a thing which every man wisheth, yet no man of judgement can esteem it better to be rich, than wise, virtuous and religious."[32] In the Christian cosmology that Hooker opposed to materialism, "the superior could not be explained by the inferior, morality by heredity, politics by interests, or love by sexuality."[33] Hooker was certain that his Puritan adversaries represented a mortal danger to the traditional order. He was fortunate not to have had to witness the triumph of the Puritan Commonwealth which turned the trifunctional social ideal on its head. The Puritan Revolution set into motion a process leading to the unshakeable supremacy of the belly over both the heart and the head.

The World Turned Upside Down

The inversion of the trifunctional social order did not occur overnight. Indeed, it was the work of centuries to extinguish the last residues of the trinitarian ideal embedded in the social organization of Anglo-Saxon Christendom. War, for example, was still the occupation of the nobility and the gentry until the last quarter of the nineteenth century. "By tradition, by training, and by temperament, the aristocracy was the warrior class." Not only did the landed classes grow up riding horses, hunting foxes, and firing shot-guns, they "knew how to lead, how to command, and how to look after the men in their charge." The patrician attributes of courage and chivalry, gallantry and loyalty, along with a thirst for honor and glory were second nature to officers recruited from the aristocracy

---

31 Dominique Venner, *Histoire et Tradition des Européens: 30,000 Ans d'Identité* (Paris: Éditions du Rocher, 2004), 18.

32 Hooker, *Laws*, 103.

33 Venner, *Histoire*, 48.

and the gentry. But there was no room for heroic cavalry charges amidst the barbed wire and poison gas, the machine guns and massed artillery deployed on the Western Front during the First World War. Learning that lesson came at a high price. Patricians who were either professional soldiers or among the first to volunteer suffered losses that "were, proportionately, far greater than any other social group."[34]

A half century earlier, during the War for Southern Independence, another entire class of predominantly Anglo-Saxon gentlemen-planters had marched into the maw of the Yankee war machine. In their heroic defence of the Lost Cause of the Confederacy, the Cavaliers of the Old South recalled the highest ideals of European chivalry. Indeed, even before the war, pro-slavery writers such as George Fitzhugh were struggling to articulate a vision of Southern plantation society that would unite those who worked with those who prayed and those who fought in an organic community superior to the soulless materialism of Northern capitalism. By immolating traditionalist ideals in a storm of fire and steel, the Yankee descendants of the Puritan Roundheads made their own revolutionary contribution to the transformation of the Anglo-Saxon character.[35] Patrician elites remained in place somewhat longer in England, as compared with the United States where, as a consequence of the Civil War, the absolute hegemony of the levelling, acquisitive and utilitarian society pioneered by the Puritan Revolution was firmly entrenched. But the Puritan spirit did not triumph overnight; nor was it an immaculate conception that sprang forth fully-formed from the mind of John Calvin in sixteenth century Geneva. The doctrinal seeds of Anglo-Saxon Puritanism had been sown long before in the theological faculties of medieval universities.

The Papal Revolution posited the church as the essential mediator between the spiritual and temporal realms. God was the other separated from our world "whose very being was revealed to us in the person of his son, and whose enigmatic withdrawal we would never stop questioning, from the moment of his annunciation." The church claimed to embody the meaning of the God-man's intervention into history "by locating it in the living present while maintaining its presence throughout the ages." But, in its never-ending effort to define the theological ground for its own existence, the church inevitably paved the way for a completely personal quest for, and reception of, divine wisdom. In effect, the church "could

---

34 David Cannadine, *The Decline and Fall of the British Aristocracy* (New Haven, CN: Yale University Press, 1990), 73-74, 264-265, 274, 276, 83.

35 Eugene D Genovese, *The World the Slaveholders Made: Two Essays in Interpretation* (New York: Pantheon, 1969); William R Taylor, *Cavalier and Yankee: The Old South and American National Character* (New York: Harper Torchbooks, 1969).

only maintain its position by creating conditions for surpassing it, in the form of faith developing independently of it. When that happened, personal mediation turned against institutional mediation." A challenge to the church's mediating legitimacy could be made at any time in the name of divine truth's transcendence and the very interpretative problem that justified the ecclesiastical hierarchy. In other words, the Protestant Reformation was the inevitable second stage of the secular revolution launched by the medieval papacy.[36]

In its Puritan guise, that revolutionary movement overthrew not just the canonical order of the Roman Catholic Church but also the ecclesiastical polity of the *republica Anglorum*. Indeed, Puritan preachers attacked the "dregs of popery" still to be found in the established Church of England: ceremonies, ritual ornaments and priestly gowns; all were condemned as symbols of institutional corruption. In the exercise of its monopoly over spiritual mediation, the papacy had been all too willing to accommodate itself to the sinful ways of a fallen world. Anglican clerics who wore "the Queen's livery" were open to the same charge. One Puritan condemned the surplice as "the defiled robe of the Anti-Christ" because it confused "weak consciences" and discouraged a final break with "idolatry." Such men demanded a new ecclesiastical order in conformity with the law of God. For them, the inner mediation of the Word's incarnation not only sufficed but was absolutely essential if God's will was to be done. Not only did Puritan ministers refuse to reverence the Anglican episcopacy, they refused to read the prayers appointed by the hierarchy. They would not be bound "to any set form of prayers invented by man," preferring instead to pour "forth hearty supplication to the Lord...as the spirit moved them."[37] No traditional society could contain or satisfy their unbridled enthusiasm for the Word of God.

English Puritans held to Calvin's teaching that Christ, as the "living Word of God," was the incarnate command of God and the "Head" of the true social structure. Only through the redemptive power of Christ could all things be brought into their proper order. Social confusion or disorder have their source in the heart (or will) of man. Harmony between the will of God and the will of man can be achieved only by those who voluntarily respond from the heart to God's command, as Christ Himself had done. Within the Church, therefore, the only tolerable authority is the voluntary, conscience-driven obedience to the Word of God. The Law of God,

---

36 Marcel Gauchet, *The Disenchantment of the World: A Political History of Religion*, trans Oscar Burge (Princeton, NJ: Princeton University Press, 1997), 82-83.

37 Walzer, *Revolution*, 118-121.

as propounded by Puritan dissenters, demanded a *new* obedience and a *new* order.[38] Their Reformed vision of biblical law literally flattened the trinitarian social structure of medieval Christendom. The Puritan elect drew no moral distinction between those who prayed, those who fought and those who worked.

In the traditional hierarchy, humble men earning their daily bread by the sweat of their brow were destined to serve the higher orders distinguished by their inborn wisdom and exemplary courage. But, in the new order established by the saints, labor acquired a radically different significance. Puritan theology was built upon the premise that "the rational order of the universe is the work of God and the plan requires that the individual should labor for God's glory."[39] Individuals were expected to "conduct themselves as energizing centers of ethical action."[40] In the Puritan pattern of order, free conscience was the engine driving God's plan towards fulfilment. Every individual was expected to pursue his own freely-chosen "calling." Working together in a fellowship realized through the fruitful division of labor, every member of the church would contribute in his own fashion to the coming of the Kingdom. Idleness and poverty were evidence of the fallen nature of corrupt men. Even the monastic celebration of voluntary poverty attracted disapproval from the Puritan divines who roundly condemned, as well, the undisciplined and dissolute lives of both the idle rich and the undeserving poor. In their view, man was created by God "for voluntary labor that is offered in a spirit of uncompelled devotion to the service of God and the community."[41]

The Revolutionary Conscience

Puritans were scandalized by the Church of England's "carelessness in the use of the means of grace, the words and Sacraments." For traditional Anglicans, such as Hooker, sacraments were the means by which Christ's saving grace could be extended, in a partial and inchoate way, to every professed Christian. In other words, questions of salvation and everlasting life were looked upon as "internal affairs of the heart and conscience… known only to God."[42] Puritans were convinced that such clerical indul-

---

38 Little, *Religion*, 48-49, 88-89.

39 RH Tawney, *Religion and the Rise of Capitalism* (New York: Mentor, 1947), 199.

40 Gertrude Huehns quoted in Walzer, *Revolution*, 218.

41 Little, *Religion*, 58.

42 *Ibid.*, 151, 154.

gence could only encourage men to believe that grace was being offered promiscuously to everyone, whether or not he belonged to the church and no matter how he might live. In their view, the law of God required the church to *institutionalize* an independent sphere of behavior, thereby establishing the standard by which traditional patterns of family, economic and social life "must be tested anew." The whole of life was to be "subordinated to the overriding claims of the coming order." Obedience to God's command amounts to the fulfilment of his social-structural design for the harmonious arrangement of all things. In Calvin's doctrine of predestination, even those who voluntarily devote and submit themselves to the new order owe their decision to "the freedom of the sovereign will of God over the creation of order." It is the "free grace" of God that accounts for the fact that "some men truly obey and some do not."[43]

The Puritan quest for God commenced in the inner depths of an individual's conscience, not in the outer world of nature. The community of the elect with their God was realized as they became conscious of God working through them. "That is, their action originated from the faith caused by God's grace, and this faith in turn justified itself by the quality of that action." The Puritan saint "could not hope to atone for hours of weakness or of thoughtlessness by increased good will at other times" as could the Catholic or even the Anglican. Catholics had long been accustomed to the very human "cycle of sin, repentance, atonement, release, followed by renewed sin." Puritans scorned the idea that single good works were enough to secure one's place among the elect; their God demanded nothing less than "a life of good works combined into a unified system."[44]

Laborare est orare: to work is to pray. That was the Puritan way to salvation. Work was essential to the health of the soul and the ethical duty to labor in his calling continued "long after it has ceased to be a material necessity."[45] What was required was an ascetic discipline as rigorous as that imposed upon any monastic order—with one crucial difference. The more strongly asceticism gripped the monk, the further away from everyday life he was driven "because the holiest task was definitely to surpass all worldly morality." Puritans, too, were required to live a holy life; but their "passionately spiritual natures which had formerly supplied the highest type of monk were now forced to pursue their ascetic ideals within

43 *Ibid.*, 127, 49.

44 Max Weber, *The Protestant Ethic and the Spirit of Capitalism* (New York: Charles Scribner's Sons, 1958), 113, 117.

45 Tawney, *Religion and Rise*, 200-201.

mundane occupations."[46] Only through systematic labor could ordinary men transform themselves into saints. "Work was a test for which men must volunteer." When those sunk in idleness and poverty shirked their duty, it "was evidence that they had not been called." The need to prove one's faith in worldly activity "substituted for the spiritual aristocracy of monks outside of and above the world the spiritual aristocracy of the pre-destined saints of God within the world."[47]

Puritans established a close connection between the new moral order ordained by the church and economic modes of expression. Each member of the Church had a specific secular vocation and it was through "the integration and harmony of all the differentiated functions" performed by the elect that the common good was served. Calvin himself regularly employed economic language and imagery to describe the life of the saint, affirming that "The life of the godly is justly compared to trading." A man's God-given talents are a sort of "merchandise" to be employed for gain in a calling. In discharging the office assigned him, each man will be "engaged in trading" with others in a process of barter and exchange. Prosperity was the likely consequence of unrelenting labor and, as such, a sign of God's blessing.[48]

It was an article of faith for Puritans that God had subjected both religious life and material life to the same order. It followed that "those who are obedient members of the Church are the *true citizens* of the new order." A man's usefulness would "be judged, finally, on the basis of his obedience to the Church." If Anglicans readily accepted the subordination of the church to the state, Puritans were no less insistent in their conviction that "the state must become fashioned according to the Body of Christ until ultimately (or eschatologically) it ceases to be needed as a constraining agent." The elect were determined to construct a radically new model of harmonious social integration based upon the free exercise of individual conscience. In pursuing that ambition, Puritanism became the first modern revolutionary movement that strove to bring about the withering away of the state.[49] As a revolutionary ideology, Puritanism set out to strip away the aura of sanctity surrounding the established political traditions and religious practices of the *republica Anglorum*.

The internal order of the church, in particular, was to emerge from heartfelt human participation and response to "an open and clear

---

46　Weber, *Protestant Ethic*, 121.

47　Walzer, *Revolution*, 218; Weber, *Protestant Ethic*, 121.

48　Little, *Religion*, 127, 59,119-121, 64.

49　*Ibid*, 97, 99, 104.

profession of the trewthe." Everything turned on the voluntary decision of the Christian about the order of God. "The Word of God is a radical equalizer: it places all on the same footing before God." In the new community, the traditional social distinctions of the old order counted for nothing. Election by God was the basis of membership. A preaching ministry replaced the episcopal hierarchy, but the authority of the minister was inseparable from the electing consent of his congregation.[50] And it was precisely this egalitarian principle—that congregations could elect or choose in matters of church government—that provoked misgivings among Anglican figures such as Hooker. It "may justly be feared," he wrote, "whether our English Nobility…would contentedly suffer themselves to be always at the call, and to stand to the sentence of a number of mean persons assisted with the presence of their poor teacher" from whom, in the absence of any ecclesiastical hierarchy, "no appeal may be made to anyone of higher power."[51]

Puritans extended the principle of voluntary consent from the realm of church governance into the domestic sphere of the family. Indeed, they portrayed the family not as a natural association but as a "little church" and a "little commonwealth" in which fathers governed as magistrates whose authority was to be tested by the Word of God. Inherited paternal authority was "nothing but a succession of consents." Carrying the consensual principle to its logical conclusion, women were recognized as potential saints. "Souls have no sexes," according to one writer. "In the better part they are both men." Consequently, a marriage between two saints would be a "spiritual union" rather than "the prescribed satisfaction of an irrational heat" deplored by Milton. Prospective partners were entitled to appraise one another's potential godliness and marriage required the voluntary agreement of both parties. This convention subtly undermined the authority of parents. An agreement to marry was a secular, contractual bond that "tended to move the two individuals most involved outside the range of extended familial connection." Not only did the emphasis on voluntary consent sharply reduce kinship obligations, it also contradicted the traditional idea that marriage, celebrated as a sacrament, was an indissoluble bond. Divorce was accepted as a legitimate response to marital breakdown, at least in cases of adultery and desertion if not necessarily of incompatibility.[52]

---

50   Ibid, 113, 92.

51   Hooker, Laws, 37-38.

52   Walzer, Revolution, 183-187, 194-195.

It would be a grave error, however, to confuse the Puritan tolerance of divorce with a narcissistic quest for personal fulfilment. Puritans were certainly consistent in the application of their view that society should be based on contractual relations "entered into voluntarily by formally free men, whose calling was sufficiently certain and whose activity was sufficiently sustained for them to make long-term promises and agreements."[53] Similarly, there can be no doubt that Puritan religiosity was a matter of personal feeling, powerfully reinforcing an already strong sense of individualism among the English. But the desperate hope of salvation and nagging fear of damnation generated an omnipresent atmosphere of emotional tension in which the individual is "trying to create God *in himself* and in the world."[54] Every Christian had to wear spiritual armor to ward off "armies" of devils, lusts and temptations. Just as young people were encouraged to seek out godly partners, well-meaning preachers advised servants to shun profane and wicked masters. An individual saint could never relax his guard in the face of the many adversaries besetting him, "as infidels, idolators, heretics, worldlings, all sorts of persecutors, yea, and false brethren." For the Puritan, faith and God were both internalized; he heard the voice of God through his conscience. Among the elect, that inner voice never left them in peace for "the world's peace is the keenest war against God."[55]

The lesson was clear. *Orare est bellare*: to pray is to fight. The Puritan clergy in England was an independent and cohesive social force profoundly alienated from the "corruptions" of their native land. Puritan radicals refused "to submit religion to either civil law or national allegiance." In the sixteenth century, many had become exiles, "men who had abandoned 'father and fatherland' to enlist in Christ's army." This was an army capable of making war ruthlessly; "it had nothing but contempt for the world within which it moved." The Lord was a man of war in Puritan cosmology and that "warlike God made warlike men." One Puritan preacher proclaimed that God loves soldiers above all creatures and "above all actions he honors warlike and martial design." No longer was war to be the specialized function of a noble caste. "Whoever is a professed Christian… is a professed soldier; or if no soldier, no Christian." Saints were to be soldiers but, in fact, "All degrees of men are warriors, some fighting for the enlargement of religion and some against it." That this military rhetoric

---

53   *Ibid*, 213.

54   Zevedei Barbu, *Problems of Historical Psychology*, (London: Routledge & Kegan Paul, 1960), 185, 207.

55   Walzer, *Revolution*, 195, 279-280.

was no mere metaphor became plain when Cromwell's New Model Army pioneered the use of the modern citizen army in warfare.[56]

To work was to pray; to pray was to fight: the traditionalist trifunctional social ideal was swept aside by the ideological force and military might of the Puritan Revolution. *Oratore, bellatore,* and *laboratore* were fused in the single, inner-directed character of the Puritan saint. Not only did the saints provoke a political revolution which toppled the established order of the *republica Anglorum,* they esteemed and cultivated a particular type of character embodying the utilitarian moral attitude typical of early modern English society.[57] In the figure of the saint one can recognize "the first outlines of what was going to be the English national character."[58] While English Puritanism was not solely responsible for the decline of the older, tradition-directed English character; it was a crucial "agent of modernization."[59] Indeed, Puritanism did not endure as a central creative force in England after the restoration of the monarchy in 1660; but, in the preceding period of crisis and upheaval, it successfully subverted the foundations of the traditional way of life.

Once the ideological passions driving the Puritans into revolution and Civil War had subsided, interest in arcane theological disputes waned among propertied Englishmen. But the saints' moral discipline continued to exert a powerful influence on English culture. Methodical endeavor and tight self-control became central tenets of the expansionist gospel of wealth preached at every level of eighteenth century English society. Both "at home" and in the American colonies, the Puritan character was a highly successful cultural variant with two distinguishing features: the ability to defer gratification and to rationalize behavior. Able to displace their emotions, brushing aside the carnal satisfactions, pleasure, elation or prestige that could be had through money, seeking instead "the inner experiences derived from effort, thrift, diligence and frugality," Puritans visibly compounded the rewards of their industry.

Puritanism also encouraged the social conditioning of individuals toward regular patterns of behavior. Individual members of Puritan congregations made an unusual effort to establish their own inner discipline, to see clear goals in their lives and to engage in sustained effort to achieve them. The evident utility of the Puritan cultural variant encouraged many ambitious persons to adopt successful saints as role models.

---

56 *Ibid,* 96, 130, 278-279.

57 Tawney, *Religion and Rise,* 188, 202.

58 Barbu, *Problems,* 186.

59 Walzer, *Revolution,* 300.

The ubiquitous "Books of Improvement" that instructed individuals how to perceive and react to most life situations in the service of practical rational goals also promoted the cultural transmission of Puritan character traits in a more didactic fashion.[60] Those who devoted themselves, heart and soul, to a calling were rewarded with better than average reproductive and material success; natural selection, therefore, appears to have played a significant role in diffusing that inner-directed character type more widely in the English population.[61]

Puritans and their less pious epigones tapped into seemingly inexhaustible stores of psychic and physical energy to produce material abundance beyond ancient dreams of avarice. Worldly success came, however, at a high spiritual price. In fact, the hidden costs are only now due for payment—not coincidentally, at the moment when our civilization is running short of cheap energy. Unfortunately, in order to settle that account, we cannot draw on the spiritual capital bequeathed by English Puritanism and their Anglican co-religionists; it was squandered by their WASP descendants. The saintly secularism of the Puritan has degenerated into the nonchalant nihilism of the postmodernist.

The Secular Commonwealth

As his countrymen reeled from the impact of revolution and civil war, the English philosopher, Thomas Hobbes, ushered them into the antechamber of modern materialism. Hobbes' political theory posits a state of nature in which every man is pitted against every other man in a perpetual state of war. In the absence of a sovereign authority, isolated individuals are driven by the sole imperative of self-preservation. While deploring the ideological excesses of Puritan preachers, Hobbes recognized in their potentially anarchic, inner-directed character type the *Grundnorm* upon which a realistic political theory must be premised. His bleak picture of human nature reveals the extent to which the Puritan personality had become the template for the transformation of the English national character.

Exploiting the failure of the Puritan Revolution, Hobbes encouraged his fellow Englishmen to imagine an all-but-complete exit from

60   Barbu, *Problems*, 188-201.

61   Peter J Richerson and Robert Boyd, *Not By Genes Alone: How Culture Transformed Human Evolution* (Chicago: University of Chicago Press, 2006), 58-98; Gregory Clark, *A Farewell to Alms: A Brief Economic History of the World* (Princeton, NJ: Princeton University Press, 2007).

Christianity. They had been set on that path long before, of course, by the late medieval celebration of the autonomy and integrity of the terrestrial sphere. The English Puritans affirmed even more emphatically the compatibility of their sacred values and the worldly concerns of the body politic; their bloody failure gave Hobbes the opportunity to herald the final triumph of secular humanism. Puritan Englishmen believed that they served the greater glory of God through voluntary, conscience-driven labor in a worldly calling. Hobbes went one giant step further, observing that even sinners can claim to be moved by the inner voice of God. Hobbes' radical naturalism asserted that there is no fundamental conflict between the conscience of the saint and the instincts of the sinner. Inevitably, the secret, inner dialogue between conscience and desire leads to "considerable confusion between the voice of God and that of man." Hobbes was convinced that what "the individual believes to be the will of God is often his own will in disguise."[62] If so, he reasoned, any commonwealth erected in place of the collapsed *republica Anglorum* must have a wholly secular character.

Hobbes was in no doubt that clerical agitation had plunged England into civil war. He even pondered whether it might not have "been much better that these seditious ministers, which were perhaps not one thousand, had been all killed before they had preached?" That would have been "a great massacre, but the killing of 100,000 [in the civil wars was] a greater one."[63] The Reformation had spawned a multitude of bickering sects, "ranging from Presbyterian sobriety to millenarian ecstasy" all of which had been "nurtured on…doctrines of private judgement, private conscience, and the priesthood of all believers. All England seemed ablaze with inner lights." In their unending strife and fanaticism the sects plunged Anglican Christianity into a state of anarchy that soon precipitated the collapse of the whole society into a state of nature. Hobbes roundly condemned the claim made by Christians of all stripes to have privileged access to the voice of God. Their vainglorious efforts to proclaim as truth what could be nothing more than "private knowledge of good and evil" could not "be granted without the ruin of all government."[64]

Hobbes sought to reconstitute the *res publica* as a sort of theological King Canute, commanding Christians to roll back the tide of interpretative freedom unleashed by scholastic theology. Seeking the lowest common

62 Barbu, *Problems*, 206-207, 209.

63 Walzer, *Revolution*, 114.

64 Sheldon S Wolin, *Politics and Vision: Continuity and Innovation in Western Political Thought* (Boston: Little, Brown, 1960), 258.

denominator of Christianity, Hobbes maintained that "belief in Jesus as the Christ is sufficient for salvation."[65] He portrayed Christianity as a system of prophecy. Speaking through the prophets, God had pronounced certain words which, "together with other happenings to which they refer, constitute a series of divine acts in past time." Christians believe that God performed those acts, and in his promise of a resurrection, because they believe the words which the prophets have relayed to them.

Protestantism, for Hobbes, was a religion of the word, of *logos*. Because *logos* is a system of communications through time, salvation and even eternity must be grounded in the temporal realm. It followed that the church cannot exist on an autonomous spiritual plane communicating between time here below and an eternal now beyond time and space.[66] Until "the coming again of our blessed Saviour," we are bound to rely solely on our senses, experience and natural reason to establish "Justice, Peace, and true Religion."[67]

The worship of God, therefore, ought to be conducted in public in accordance with a uniform rule prescribed by the secular authority of the Commonwealth. Political order, no less than religion, depended upon "a sensitive system of communications dependent upon a system of verbal signs, actions and gestures bearing generally accepted meaning." Common meanings in the language of both politics and religion depended "on a ruling power capable of enforcing them." For that reason, "the Right of Judging what Doctrines are fit for Peace and to be taught the Subjects, is in all Common-wealths inseparably annexed...to the Sovereign Power Civill." Because the Sovereign is the Supreme Pastor of the Commonwealth, "it is by his authority that all other Pastors are made, and have power to teach, and perform all other Pastorall offices."[68]

Hobbes was a philosophical materialist but that, in itself, did not suffice to place him outside the mainstream of Protestant thinking. He simply pressed to their logical conclusions long-established Catholic doctrines that recognized the autonomy of the terrestrial sphere. "In a universe consisting of matter and motion 'spirit' may be the name of an extremely subtle corporeal substance, or a metaphor helping to express the state of a man's thoughts or feelings" but "there can be no justification for using

---

65   Paul A Rahe, *Republics Ancient and Modern: Classical Republicanism and the American Revolution* (Chapel Hill: University of North Carolina Press, 1992), 385.

66   JGA Pocock, *Politics, Language and Time: Essays on Political Thought and History* (Chicago: University of Chicago Press, 1989), 178-179.

67   Thomas Hobbes, *Leviathan*, edited by CB Macpherson (Harmondsworth: Penguin, 1968), 409.

68   *Ibid*, 405, 567, 569; Wolin, *Politics*, 259.

it…to describe any medium of communication between God and man." Protestants had long portrayed the pope as the Antichrist because he claimed to represent the presence of God, acting from the beyond, in the here and now. Any spiritually-based challenge to secular authority could be attacked, in principle, as the work of the Antichrist. One after another Romish priests, Anglican bishops and Scottish presbyters were arraigned on such charges. In the Puritan claim to "a spiritual authority, election, or illumination, not accessible to other men," Hobbes saw another "threat to the secular community in its spiritual role that was basically of the same order."[69]

In effect, Hobbes "employed the arguments of radical Protestantism to demonstrate the impossibility of any earthly agency's exercising an authority peculiarly derived from Christ between his ascension and his return, or one immediately derived from God between the Mosaic theocracy that had ended with the election of Saul and the theocracy that would be exercised by Christ following his return and the resurrection of the dead."[70] The papacy, along with Protestant presbyters and bishops, was guilty of spiritual usurpation in claiming an authority derived directly from God on the basis of divine law or grace without the intervention of the civil sovereign. Spiritual jurisdiction was condemned by Hobbes as a fallacy resting on the confusion of time and the timeless. Even the Puritan saints supposed "that because a kingdom was promised for the future they could exercise in the present an authority that could only exist when the kingdom was restored." Like the pope, the saints set themselves up as the "lieutenants within time" of a kingdom existing outside time. Hobbes mocked those who set up that sort of "*Ghostly Authority*" against the civil sovereign, scornfully dismissing their position as little more than a childish belief "that there walketh (as some think invisibly) another Kingdome, as it were a Kingdom of Fayries, in the dark."[71]

Hobbes' acerbic attack on the autonomy of the spiritual sphere was but one prong of a comprehensive assault on classical political traditions, both ancient and medieval. In England, from the Anglo-Saxon era to the high middle ages, those who prayed and those who fought had been treated as the highest representatives of their people. After all, only the superior wisdom and courage of the higher social orders justified their right to rule over the subordinate classes condemned to a life of toil. Plato's *Republic* adopted a tripartite functional order to structure the life of society around

---

69 Pocock, *Machiavellian Moment*, 396.

70 *Ibid*, 397.

71 Hobbes, *Leviathan*, 370.

an ideal pattern of individual and collective existence.[72] Indo-European peoples, generally, believed that the triadic social ideal was inscribed in the very nature of things, a belief reflected in the strikingly similar functional ordering of the pagan pantheon almost everywhere in Europe. Hobbes issued a radical challenge to that cosmology by positing an original state of nature from which both gods and kings were banished. If civilized men were deprived of the protection of an established sovereign authority, Hobbes was sure that no gods of their own imagining could restore a stable civil society. In the disenchanted state of nature, every individual would stand or fall on his own. Priests and philosophers had propagated the illusion that the cream would always rise to the top of a natural social order. Hobbes was determined to demolish that complacent conviction.

The Political Theology of Possessive Individualism

Hobbes' vision of the state of nature was not about the "natural" condition of "primitive" man in pre-historic times prior to the rise of civilization. Rather, Hobbes wanted to discuss "the hypothetical condition in which men as they now are, with natures formed by living in civilized society, would necessarily find themselves if there were no common power to overawe them all." He sketches a picture of a society bereft of industry, agriculture, navigation, arts, architecture, or letters in which the life of man would be "solitary, poore, nasty, brutish, and short." Without a common power to hold them in check, Hobbes had no doubt that civilized men would soon find themselves at war with each other. Men in the state of nature would "desire not merely to live but to live well or commodiously." Left to fend for themselves, every individual would be forced into a violent competition "to make themselves Masters of other mens persons, wives, children, and cattell."[73] At the same time, they would be forced to defend themselves against similar aggression from others while holding themselves ready to avenge any real or imagined insult to their honour or self-esteem. In Hobbes' thought experiment, civilized men thrown into a state of nature were expected to behave in accordance with the norms of the possessive individualism fostered by an emergent bourgeois society.

---

72 Dumézil, *Mythes*, 92-93.

73 CB Macpherson, *The Political Theory of Possessive Individualism: Hobbes to Locke* (Oxford: Oxford University Press, 1962), 18-19, 24; Hobbes, *Leviathan*, 185-186.

Given the rough equality in the faculties of mind and body of men, Hobbes was sure that, in the absence of the civil sovereign, the classical tripartite hierarchy of social orders could never re-emerge spontaneously. Every individual would be driven by imperious appetites and blind passions to seek power over all other men without distinction. Of course, one man might be stronger while another is quicker of mind but, all things considered, the differences are not so great that any one person could claim a benefit without being open to challenge from others. In the state of nature, even "the weakest has strength enough to kill the strongest, either by secret machination, or by confederacy with others." When all men, however courageous they might be, "live without other security, than what their own strength, and their own invention shall furnish them," those who fight could never constitute themselves as a privileged caste set apart and above ordinary mortals. Internal quarrels would quickly tear asunder even the most fearsome gang; if not, temporary success would attract the attention of other marauding bands. Ordinary men would be even less likely to submit to cognitive elites of wise men. Hobbes ridiculed the Aristotelian belief that the possession of wisdom made some men by nature fit to command others. In the state of nature, "all men are equall" and "there are very few so foolish, that had not rather governe themselves, than be governed by others." Even when men are, in fact, unequal in intellect, those "that think themselves equall, will not enter into conditions of Peace, but upon Equall termes." No end to lawless chaos would be possible until even the best and the brightest finally conceded that "it is not Wisdom, but Authority that makes a Law."[74]

For Hobbes, the humble hordes of those who worked would play the decisive role in escaping from the state of nature. By itself, the fear of death would not incline men to seek peace. Even without a common power to over-awe them, civilized men would retain the self-discipline and goal-oriented behavior that is rewarded with success in a possessive market society. They would still be moved by the "Desire of such things as are necessary to commodious living; and a Hope by their Industry to attain them." Only by erecting a common power could such men provide for their mutual security. Only by covenanting together "to conferre all their power and strength upon one Man, or upon one Assembly of men," a conflicting multitude of wills can be transformed into one will, thereby ensuring "that by their owne industrie, and by the fruites of the Earth,

---

74 Hobbes, *Leviathan*, 183, 211; Thomas Hobbes, *A Dialogue Between a Philosopher and a Student of the Common Law* edited by Joseph Cropsey (Chicago: University of Chicago Press, 1971), 53-54.

they may nourish themselves and live contentedly."[75] But individuals would be disposed to enter into a covenant relationship only if it created a Commonwealth that protects industry and secures to each individual the fruits of his labor. In thus identifying labor and industry as the *raison d'être* of the common-wealth, Hobbes revealed that the Puritan work ethic had taken on a life of its own, stripped of its Christian trappings. In Hobbes' common-wealth, the classical tripartite social order disappears; the higher orders which once represented wisdom and courage are transformed into the merely ideological superstructure of an administrative machine. This move is prefigured in the novel character of the covenant by which men first agree to create civil society.

On one level, Hobbes' account of the creation of Leviathan seems to reflect the central role played by covenant in the foundation of the *comitatus* in Anglo-Saxon England. In that era, the covenant between a lord and his companions had assumed greater importance than kindred relationships in the maintenance of social order. But the Hobbesian covenant differs in several important respects from its Anglo-Saxon precursor. First of all, the party structure of Hobbes' covenant is horizontal rather than vertical. In other words, the several parties seeking security for their lives and possessions covenant, not directly with the sovereign, but with each other. One man, M, surrenders his absolute right of self-rule to X, the civil sovereign, only on condition that Y promises to do the same. "The covenant achieves the condition of peace aimed at because it divests Y of the power to inflict harm on M without reprisal by X, the civil sovereign." The authority of X to rule over us derives from our voluntary agreement with each other to surrender our natural right to a third party, X. Strictly speaking, the sovereign, X, is a third party beneficiary rather than a party to the covenant itself. X acquires "the right to take any action, not contrary to the covenant, which may operate on any and all parties to the covenant." The sovereign's "right to rule does not lie in any power, capacity, or virtue which he possesses in his natural aspect."[76] He merely occupies an office created by the covenant, a sort of hired hand taken on so individuals do not have to engage in personal combat to defend their lives and property. Taxes become "the Wages, due to them that hold the publique Sword, to defend private men in the exercise of severall Trades, and Callings."[77]

---

75   Hobbes, *Leviathan*, 188, 227.

76   Frank M Coleman, *Hobbes and America: Exploring the Constitutional Foundations* (Toronto: University of Toronto Press, 1977), 78-79.

77   Rahe, *Republics*, 393.

For Hobbes, the authority of the civil sovereign is neither traditional nor charismatic. Men recognized that authority purely and simply as a matter of enlightened self-interest. Individuals remain bound to perform their obligations under the covenant only "(1) to the extent that other parties to the covenant do, (2) to the extent that the sovereign is able to provide the subject with safety in performance." If those conditions are not satisfied individuals may choose to prefer their private interests in life and property over the claims of public order. A soldier conscripted into the sovereign's army "who throws down his arms and flies from the field of battle may perform an act of cowardice but not of injustice." A volunteer, on the other hand, would be bound to fight as long as his unit "keeps the field, and giveth him means of subsistence." But should his commander be defeated, it becomes a matter of *sauve qui peut* so that any soldier "may seek his Protection wheresoever he has most hope to have it," without any fear of dishonor.[78] The contrast with the heroic spirit of the Anglo-Saxon *comitatus* is stark and unmistakeable. Tacitus reports that just as "it is a disgrace for a chief to be surpassed in valour by his companions," the companions were expected to match "the valour of their chief." Certainly, there could be no question of "leaving a battle alive after your chief has fallen, *that* would mean lifelong infamy and shame."[79] For the Germanic warrior, dying well was more important than living dishonorably.

Chivalrous ideals of self-sacrifice have little place in a Hobbesian common-wealth; possessive individuals are disposed to civil obedience mainly through their "Desire of Ease, and sensuall Delight."[80] Unfortunately, by enshrining the supreme value of self-interest in place of classical traditions of nobility and civic virtue, Hobbes also devalued the idea of community. In a "society of egoists," the only way to legitimize authority was for each subject "to accept the commands of the sovereign 'as if' they were his own." Conversely, the sovereign would promote the advantage of his subjects only because he had an interest in ensuring that they remained fat and happy. Conflict between public and private ends was eliminated in a society of egoists by "the creation of a public, institutionalized ego." The result was power without community. Not only did the Hobbesian covenant drain the sovereign of his *heilerfüllt* charisma, it also detached the common-wealth from its ethnocultural roots. Hobbes rejected utterly the classical view of man as a political animal by nature. He portrayed

---

78 Coleman, *Hobbes*, 80; Hobbes, *Leviathan*, 270, 272.

79 Tacitus, *Tacitus on Britain and Germany* trans by H Mattingly (West Drayton: Penguin, 1948), 112.

80 Hobbes, *Leviathan*, 161.

society as "the product of an explicit agreement between individuals whose commonalty resided solely in each having made the same choice." The common-wealth remains external to individuals whose diffuse fear of each other is replaced by a determinate fear of the sovereign. The abstract principle of sovereignty becomes the "soul" of a commonwealth otherwise bereft of common identity or corporate unity.[81]

Fears of Corruption

Amidst the horrors of civil war and revolution, Hobbes' dystopian vision was at least plausible. Certainly, from a postmodernist perspective, the nihilism of his deracinated commonwealth appears remarkably prescient. Nevertheless, when peace returned and the monarchy was restored in England, there was a sharp traditionalist reaction against Hobbes' political theory. But, in the long run, traditionalists could not turn the clock back. In fact, many of Hobbes' contemporary critics, men who could not stomach his conclusions, actually shared his view of society as a market, along with his analysis of human nature.

By the late eighteenth century, there could be little doubt that both England and the new American republic were the world's premier bourgeois market societies. As exemplified by the autobiography of Benjamin Franklin, possessive individualism became the highest expression of the Anglo-Saxon character.[82] The individualist world-view of the forward-looking propertied Englishman or American clearly owed more to the Puritans and Thomas Hobbes than to the trifunctional social order of their remote Anglo-Saxon ancestors. Even before the English civil war, it had been obvious that the tradition-directed character of the English people was changing; afterwards, the question was how to interpret the transformation: Did the emergence of *homo oeconomicus* betoken the material efficacy of a new morality or a spiritual descent into the corruption afflicting even the greatest republics in times past?

Following the Restoration, propertied Englishmen rejected every sort of experimental and arbitrary government. Only a return to the rule of law, they believed, "could guarantee to the property-owner the enjoyment of his historic rights." Few were willing to accept the Hobbesian claim that law was nothing more than the command of a self-perpetuating sovereign

---

81 Wolin, *Politics*, 272-279.

82 Benjamin Franklin, *The Autobiography of Benjamin Franklin* (New York: Washington Square Press, 1955).

will. After the Glorious Revolution of 1688 which replaced James II with William and Mary, the political class told itself that the governing authority in England's parliamentary monarchy was subject to a fundamental law. At the same time, Hobbes' staunchest critics could hardly deny that Parliament was supreme and that there was no *legal* limit to its legislative capacity. "Parliament knew quite well that it could enact and make into law whatever it chose; but its laws might, nevertheless, be wrong."[83] The landed classes needed "a sovereign state to sanction the right of possession;" they also needed to maintain control over membership in that sovereign body, lest it pose a threat to their property.[84] Eighteenth century English society, as a consequence, took on the character of "*an open aristocracy based on property and patronage.*"[85]

As Hobbes predicted, the desire for "commodious living" became the animating principle of eighteenth century England. Rights and liberties were almost always conceived in terms which implied individual proprietorship. The legitimacy of law and government rested on confidence that every man would be left to the absolute and safe possession of the fruits of his labors. At all levels of society, the "acquisition of wealth was the route to social acceptance and political power." Anglican clergymen were apt to dismiss Hobbes' work as "a farrago of Christian atheism,"[86] but those who prayed were no less in thrall to property than the bourgeois classes directly engaged in labor and industry. The Church of England routinely subordinated the spiritual purposes of religion to the propertied mentality of the time. There was little difference between clergy and laymen in the way they treated their material resources. Indeed, the church became notoriously vulnerable "to strictly commercial exploitation by clergy and laymen alike." Especially scandalous were the blatantly commercial dealings in the right of presentation to clerical livings.[87]

Those who fought were also tarnished as the organization of the militia was shaped by the scramble to accumulate property. Before 1750, propertied families had been responsible for contributing men and material to the militia in proportion to their wealth. Afterwards, service in the militia "was determined by a ballot of all able-bodied males between the

---

83   JW Gough, *Fundamental Law in English Constitutional History* (Oxford: Clarendon Press, 1961), 140-141.

84   Macpherson, *Possessive Individualism*, 94-95.

85   Harold Perkin, *The Origins of Modern English Society, 1780-1880* (London: Routledge & Kegan Paul, 1969), 17.

86   Rahe, *Republics*, 384.

87   Paul Langford, *Public Life and the Propertied Englishman, 1689-1798* (Oxford: Clarendon Press, 1994), 2, 9, 15, 18.

ages of 18 and 50, regardless of social standing." But anyone "who chose not to serve was permitted to hire a substitute by private negotiation or to buy exemption for £10." At the same time, officers' commissions were obtained by purchase, with senior ranks available only at a higher price. Such measures certainly gave landowners a commanding position in the ship of state. But making "mere cash" a qualification for military leadership might do more to attract men of fortune rather than gentility, another worrying symptom of the corruption so characteristic of the eighteenth century English polity.[88]

It would be a great mistake, however, to believe that the dramatic commercial and colonial expansion of England, especially from the early eighteenth century onward, made the country any less warlike. In the seventeenth and eighteenth centuries, "the intimate interdependence of war and trade" achieved an almost law-like status; "throughout the period trade leads naturally to war and war fosters trade." The object of England and its European rivals "was now to increase its trade, not by waiting upon the wants of mankind, but by a wholly different method, namely, by getting exclusive possession of some rich tract in the New World."[89] Colonial expansion not only generated vast wealth for supporters of the commercially-minded Whig oligarchy presiding over the era, it also opened up new fields of endeavor for the restless ambitions that drove inner-directed Britons across the sea in search of new lands to settle.

Not everyone, however, welcomed the economic and social changes associated with war, commerce and the exploitation of the New World. Indeed, a bitterly persistent political struggle in the early eighteenth century set the parliamentary faction known as the Country party in opposition to Court Whigs who supported the first minister, Robert Walpole. The most effective intellectual firepower behind the Country opposition to Walpole's Robinocracy was provided by Henry St John, Viscount Bolingbroke. All of Bolingbroke's political and historical writings were organized around a persistent theme. He warned his readers that the fierce, indomitable spirit of liberty animating the British constitution from ancient times now seemed on the verge of succumbing to the insidious corruption and ubiquitous influence of a novel form of government. Bolingbroke worried that his contemporaries had been blinded by complacency. It was easy to believe that the "spirit of liberty transmitted down from our Saxon ancestors" had defeated, once and for all, the tyrannical

---

88   *Ibid*, 266-267, 302-303.

89   Sir John Robert Seeley, *The Expansion of England: Two Courses of Lectures* (New York: Cosimo Classics, 2005), 109-111.

pretensions of the Stuarts in the Glorious Revolution of 1688. In fact, however, the linkage between war and trade had endowed the English government with new forms of public finance that posed an even greater danger to British liberties than the prerogative power in the hands of an absolute monarch.

Bolingbroke drew attention to the new constitutional order implicit in the creation of the Bank of England in 1694, the concomitant rise in the national debt, and the great moneyed corporations such as the East India Company and the South Sea Company. Together, these developments amounted to a "financial revolution" that provided those acting in the name of the Crown with the means effectively to subvert the "independency of Parliament." Because "the power of money, as the world is now constituted, is real power, and that all power, without this, is imaginary," Bolingbroke charged, the threat of corruption was becoming "more dangerous than prerogative ever was" under the Stuarts. Under the Whig ascendancy of the early eighteenth century, "the prince who gets prerogative alone, gets a phantom; but...he who gets money, even without prerogative, gets something real." The new system of managing the public revenues had armed the King's ministers with "all that is necessary to employ the expedient of corruption with success."[90]

Court versus Country

As portrayed by Bolingbroke, the Country opposition to Walpole was a party that abhorred the division of the nation into parties. Formed "on principles of common interest", the Country party was not based on the particular prejudices or interests "of any set of men whatsoever." Bolingbroke claimed that a "party, thus constituted, is improperly called party. It is the nation, speaking and acting in the discourse and conduct of particular men."[91] Its victory would mean the end of parties.

This non-partisan ideal reflected the logic of royal government as long as the king remained the actual head of the government with the unchallenged right to choose and dismiss his ministers. Under such circumstances, opposition to the king's ministers could easily be taken for opposition to the king himself. As a consequence, any "formed opposition" to the government of the day was of doubtful legitimacy. But Bolingbroke

90 Viscount Bolingbroke, "A Dissertation upon Parties" in David Armitage, ed *Bolingbroke: Political Writings* (Cambridge: Cambridge University Press, 1997), 82, 186, 183, 3.

91 *Ibid*, 37.

and his friends denied that they were setting themselves against the king. In their view, Sir Robert Walpole, the chief minister, had effectively usurped the legitimate influence of the Crown and concentrated power in the executive.[92] It was this embryonic prime ministerial regime, not the king in whose name it acted that was the object of Bolingbroke's ire.

From the outset of the Whig ascendancy, Bolingbroke charged, Walpole's Court party "had given their whole attention…to the project of enriching themselves, and impoverishing the rest of the nation." By corrupt means they sought to establish "their dominion under the government and with the favor of a [royal] family, who were foreigners, and therefore might believe, that they were established on the throne by the good will and the strength of their party alone."[93] The King had ceased to be the true proprietor of the royal authority delegated to Walpole.

For Bolingbroke, the very fact that Walpole appeared to be exercising the powers of a prime minister was conclusive evidence that the essential balance of the constitution had been upset. Far from being the servant of the Crown, Walpole "seemed to be the essential energy of the government, engrossing all functions and holding the Crown captive." At this time, the office of prime minister was associated with absolute monarchies where the prince invested one man "with the sole management and direction of all his affairs." Bolingbroke struck a popular chord then when he concluded that Walpole had "all the essential power of a monarch, without the pomp and the name." Such a ministerial tyranny had to be resisted in all its forms and guises if the free constitution of Britain was to be preserved intact.[94]

In Parliament and through the press, the Country opposition pressed its case against Walpole. Certain issues rapidly assumed prominence in oppositional rhetoric. Widespread fears that a standing army was an open invitation to despotism led Country politicians to demand its replacement with a militia under the leadership of independent country gentlemen. Repeated efforts were made, as well, to eject placemen—persons who held office under the Crown—from Parliament and to prevent the ministry from rewarding its supporters with pensions and patronage. After the passage of the *Septennial Act* in 1716, the call for more frequent parliamentary elections became another staple item of opposition discourse. All of these issues figured prominently in the essays written by Bolingbroke for *The Craftsman* and later published as *A Dissertation upon Parties*.

---

92   Archibald Foord, *His Majesty's Opposition* (Oxford: Clarendon Press, 1964), 147

93   *Ibid*, 148, 206.

94   See, Kramnick, *Bolingbroke*, 114.

In mounting his attack on the Whig regime, Bolingbroke drew a clear distinction between the government and the constitution. The "constitution is the rule by which our princes ought to govern at all times; government is that by which they actually do govern at any particular time." By "constitution" he meant "that assemblage of laws, institutions and customs, derived from certain fixed principles of reason, directed to certain fixed objects of public good, that compose the general system, according to which the community hath agreed to be governed." A good government would operate in "strict conformity to the principles and objects of the constitution." Bad governments were administered on other principles. It followed that those "friends of the government" who made "it a capital point of their wicked policy to keep up a standing army" were actually the "real enemies of the constitution."[95] Because "Parliaments are the true guardians of liberty", Bolingbroke saw placemen, pensions and the infrequency of parliamentary elections as the most serious threat to the survival of the constitution.[96]

But the money power was also undermining the government of the household among the landed classes. Within families, the manic pursuit of paper values drove a wedge between the generations; the living readily sacrificed the interests of the dead and the unborn to their own present desires. The stability of the hereditary landed estate was at stake in a system tending to devalue real estate in favor of mobile property. The heady growth of funds invested in stocks, bonds, and public debt encouraged the gentry to mortgage their landed properties in search of ready cash. Even in peacetime the ordinary expenses of government, too, were "defrayed in great measure, by anticipation and mortgage." Bolingbroke wondered what would "happen when we have mortgaged and funded all we have to mortgage and to fund?" Would the process continue until "we have mortgaged all the product of our land, and even our land itself," thereby undermining the material foundations of civic virtue?[97]

It was widely recognized that the gap between business classes and landed families was being narrowed by the mutability of landed property. Paper wealth "was portrayed as an illegitimate, counterfeit pretender to the title and authority properly enjoyed only by land." For Bolingbroke, landed men were the "true owners of our political vessel" and moneyed men were "no more than passengers in it." Because commercial property was inherently movable, its holders were regarded as inherently

---

95 Bolingbroke, *Dissertation*, 88-89, 92.

96 *Ibid*, 93.

97 Bolingbroke, *Dissertation*, 181.

undependable. Those who held land had a unique and irreplaceable stake in their country but the owners of mere riches could "pick up their property on their backs and leave the country in the twinkling of an eye."[98]

But, for Bolingbroke, the crisis of the constitution produced much more than a structural shift in the balance between different forms of property; it meant as well the slow death of the hitherto indomitable spirit of English liberty. He was convinced that self-imposed and self-inflicted forms of tyranny and oppression would cause the spirit of liberty to vanish from the hearts and minds of the English people. Britons would become the prisoners of their own vicious desires and the victims of their own petty ambitions.

The great gobbets of wealth flowing into the coffers of the state with the assistance of the stockjobbers allowed government to base itself on parties of professional politicians rather than on independent landed gentlemen. When Bolingbroke called for the restoration of the original principles of the ancient constitution, he was calling upon the landed proprietors to cease regarding themselves as agrarian capitalists and to return to their civic responsibilities as landed gentlemen responsible for the conduct of public affairs. Such a conception of the ancient constitution made sense only to those who still thought of landed property as the material foundation of the civic virtues rather than a private economic asset to be developed in an efficient and productive manner.

But, for landowners preoccupied with the productive use of their private property, it made good sense to leave the conduct of public affairs very largely to their representatives in parliament while minding their own private business. For such people, parliament was the supreme lawmaking authority in "the broad-based propertied society which it served." In their complacent view, parliamentary power "was deployed in response to the demands of interests, groups and communities, not so much imposing a sovereign will as providing a legal service." In delivering that service, parliament took care to protect powerful groups and respect the interests of propertied people.[99] Bolingbroke would not be surprised to learn that the political class in England eventually established itself as a reasonable facsimile of Hobbes' self-perpetuating sovereign—a secular process that reached its apogee in our own time.

---

98 Langford, *Public Life*, 40-41, 58-60.

99 Langford, *Public Life*, 139-140.

An Ethnohistory of British Liberty

Bolingbroke witnessed the frenetic onset of a biocultural metamorphosis that transformed the character of the English people. He did not fully grasp the irresistible logic of capitalist modernization or the political imperatives of state-building at work in the corruption of the Commons. Nevertheless he recognized that oppositional forces urgently required a myth of common origins or descent precisely because English society under the leadership of presumptively enlightened statesmen-legislators was embracing what we know as the "creative destruction" characteristic of modern capitalism.[100]

One of the paradoxes of modern "society is its appetite for expansion coupled with a deep nostalgia for the past." Deprived of a secure anchorage in religion and a traditional way of life, many took to the idea of posterity to ensure that "deeds live on and memories are kept alive." But that aspiration only makes sense "within a chain of like deeds and memories, which stretches back into the mists of obscure generations of ancestors and forward into the equally unknowable generations of descendants."[101] Bolingbroke adopted the form of "exemplary history" in addressing himself to the English political nation.[102] In doing so, he presented his readers with an ethnohistory relating the dramatic story of the recurrent conflicts between the English nation and its rulers.

Only those who possess a sense of "anamnestic solidarity" with their ancestors, only those who feel duty-bound to honour their memory, are likely to be at all concerned with the good opinion of posterity.[103] Exemplary history is based upon the premise that there is an essential thread of continuity binding the present to both the past and the future. As an historian and a political thinker, Bolingbroke recognized that the political community includes not just the living but also those of our blood who have passed away and those as yet unborn. Lacking a concept of ethnic genetic interests, Bolingbroke portrayed the bond between the successive generations of the English people in spiritual terms. For him, the spirit of liberty enshrined in the ancient British constitution defined the essence of English nationhood. Bolingbroke was convinced that if that

---

100 Joseph A Schumpeter, *Capitalism, Socialism and Democracy* (New York: Harper & Row, 1942).

101 Anthony D Smith, *The Ethnic Origins of Nations* (Oxford: Blackwell, 1988), 174, 176.

102 GH Nadel, quoted in Editor's Introduction to Bolingbroke, *Historical Writings*, xvi.

103 Christian Lenhardt, "Anamnestic Solidarity: The Proletariat and its Manes," *Telos* 25 (Fall 1975), 133-154.

patriotic spirit waned, if the ethnoreligious kinship between the archaic Anglo-Saxon nation and eighteenth century Englishmen and, through them, to posterity was lost to consciousness, then the constitution would be destroyed. Each generation would suit itself, heedless of and indifferent to the interests of either the dead or the unborn. He reminded his readers that it had been the distinctive spirit and enthusiastic patriotism of the Roman people, transmitted from generation to generation, that had enabled their empire to endure as long as it did. Yet when "this spirit decayed, when this enthusiasm cooled, the constitution could not help, nay, worked against itself."[104]

In contending that the history of the English nation displayed an essential continuity, Bolingbroke did not deny that the past had been blighted by long periods of tyranny and oppression. The Norman Conquest, for example, had broken the Saxon constitution and invaded the liberties of the people. Under the regime of the conqueror, "the government was entirely monarchical and aristocratical, without any exercise of democratical power." The spirit and the letter of the ancient constitution were violated and suppressed; nevertheless, "the law of liberty retained its primeval power." Although "the branches were lopped and the tree lost its beauty for a time, yet the root remained untouched, was set in good soil, and had taken strong hold in it: so that care and culture and time were indeed required, and our ancestors were forced to water it, if I may use such an expression, with their blood; but with their care, and culture, and time, and blood, it shot up again with greater strength than ever, that we might sit quiet and happy under it."[105]

Bolingbroke urged his readers to listen to the voice of their ancestors, taking care to preserve the precious gift of liberty that been bequeathed to them in trust for their own descendants. In so many other countries the "sacred fires" of liberty had been extinguished; "here they have been religiously kept alive." Now that the danger from the prerogative power had been eliminated, the British constitution "cannot be destroyed, unless the peers and the commons, that is, the whole body of the people unite to destroy it, which is a degree of madness, and such a monstrous iniquity, as nothing but confirmed and universal corruption can produce." Should the British people passively permit the decay of the constitution they would "incur greater blame, and deserve by consequence less pity, than any enslaved and oppressed people ever did." They would have failed in their duty to past and future generations of Britons. "The virtue of our

104 Bolingbroke, *Dissertation*, 131.
105 *Ibid*, 154.

ancestors, to whom all these advantages are owing, would aggravate the guilt and the infamy of their degenerate posterity."[106]

Like other ethnohistories, Bolingbroke's historical writings became "both a moral teacher and a temporal and terrestrial drama of salvation." What counted, for Bolingbroke and his audience, was "never a disinterested inquiry into the past 'as it really was,' but a yearning desire to re-enter into a living past." He sought to make the past respond to the needs of the living by recreating the peculiar atmosphere and distinctive setting associated with the English people and no other. The object was to teach the English people who they were by defining the nation in the course of its dramatic development and by directing the nation towards a visionary goal. Anthony Smith has suggested that every ethnohistory "must supply a history and metaphysic of the community, locating it in time and space among the other communities on the earth." In his *Dissertation upon Parties* and other works, Bolingbroke does just that. He also generates the sort of "ethic and blueprint for the future" found in the ethnohistories of other nations.[107]

By calling for the restoration of the ancient constitution, Bolingbroke enabled his audience to identify with an idealized past and at the same time helped it "to transcend a disfigured and unworthy present." The romance, mystery and drama of the ancient constitution are to be found not just in its origins and evolution through time but in its decline and rebirth. The ancient constitution is either "betrayed" from within the nation or "subjugated" from without.[108] Either way, the natural remedy requires a return to the original principles upon which the nation was founded. The questions then arise: What were the original principles of the ancient constitution and how could they be restored?

One can be sympathetic to Bolingbroke's attack on the Whig regime while wondering whether he fully understood the relationship between the problems facing his nation and the ethnoreligious origins of the English people. Such sympathy deviates radically from the dominant historiographical approaches to Bolingbroke's political thought. Because WASP academics remain wilfully blind to the decay and corruption of our own thoroughly deracinated, transnational managerial regime; they are ill-equipped to appreciate Bolingbroke's struggle to defend the ancient constitution against what appears to be the sheer unstoppable power of modernity. According to the conventional academic wisdom, the forms of

106 *Ibid*, 112-113, 186, 112.

107 Smith, *Ethnic Origins*, 179, 180, 182.

108 *Ibid*, 182-183, 191.

behavior which Bolingbroke denounced as corrupt were simply harbingers of a new morality. In his resistance to modernity, Bolingbroke, himself, is portrayed either as a hidebound reactionary or a cynical opportunist.

Virtue Transformed

Most professional historians today dismiss Bolingbroke's fear that "universal corruption" was sapping the foundations of English liberty as overblown, foolishly alarmist rhetoric. Shelley Burtt, for example, is prepared to acknowledge only "that the emergence of a new system of public credit was a significant political and economic innovation." Bolingbroke's "story...in which a resentful gentry corrupts itself to maintain social equality with a collection of financial parvenus" does not ring true to her. It may have made "for good reading in the coffeehouses," but it "does not provide convincing evidence that the rise in the stock market was responsible for the decline in public virtue."[109] She finds Bolingbroke's call to return to the original principles of the ancient constitution even less compelling.

Bolingbroke worried that the new system of public finance would corrode the political community of memory, language and blood; he took it for granted that the ethnocultural solidarity of nation and state is a positive good. Burtt, on the other hand, ignores the context of the financial revolution; namely, the emergent system of political economy even then spreading its tentacles around the globe. Certainly, she shows little concern over the long-term impact of the new world order on the relationship between the Anglo-Saxon peoples and their rulers. Like many academic historians, Shelley Burtt is an enthusiastic xenophile; for her, the practice of interracial adoption is a modern expression of "civic virtue."[110] Having thus rejected racial homogeneity as an essential element of family life, she is unlikely to mourn the erosion of the core ethnocultural identity of erstwhile Anglo-Saxon nations. Those unwilling to dissolve the racial identity of their families and nations have good reason to reject Burtt's reading of Bolingbroke; we can still find in his work important clues as to the causes of our present discontents.

The financial revolution marked a fateful shift in the constitution of the English nation. It facilitated the quickening of an embryonic political

---

109 Shelley Burtt, *Virtue Transformed: Political Argument in England, 1688-1740* (Cambridge: Cambridge University Press, 1992), 102.

110 Shelley Burtt "Is Inclusion a Civic Virtue: Adoption, Disability and the Liberal State" paper delivered at Florida State University Conference on Virtue and Social Diversity, March 3-4, 2007. http://www.fsu.edu/~philo/Burtt%20abstract.pdf

and economic system in which permanent revolution became a way of life. Land, trade and credit became interdependent when "money and war...speeded up the operations of society." The result was that evaluations of the public good constantly had to be translated "into actions of investment and speculation." Political behavior then came to be "based upon opinion concerning a future rather than a memory of the past."[111] Rational political behavior in the new world order had little to do with maintaining a sense of solidarity with ancestors or winning the approval of posterity. In Bolingbroke's time, progressive Englishmen came to define the political nation as a collection of lives in being exclusively preoccupied with their own material interests in the here and now. Past and future generations were left to look out for themselves.

In every Anglo-Saxon country, this chronic constitutional amnesia became more debilitating with every passing generation. Burtt misses the vital ethnohistorical dimension of Bolingbroke's thought when she complains that he "reduces the notion of political liberty to the maintenance of formal constitutional structures: an independent parliament and a balanced constitution." She cannot understand why Bolingbroke condemns any deviation from this ideal, even when "the actual political experience of English citizens" prepared them to accept such innovations.[112] For Bolingbroke, it was a matter of patriotism; it was about the love of fathers. To give those of us in the present a political licence to violate the trust of our predecessors and to ignore the interests of our descendants is to corrupt the spirit of the ancient constitution.

We can easily recognize Bolingbroke as a practitioner of ethnohistory. But, for him, it was no easy matter to understand either the ethnogenesis of the English nation or the nature of ethnocultural identity in general. To achieve such an understanding, one would have had to break free from the constraints that biblical literalism imposed upon Christian ethnotheology in seventeenth and eighteenth century England. Drawing on the Book of Genesis, sacred history "associated the peopling of the world with the Japhetan descendants of Noah." Biblical "accounts provided a recognized point of departure not only for the study of ethnicity but also for the construction of national identities."[113] In that context, the common genesis of all members of the human race was a fundamental article of faith, as was a chronology that fitted the development of all peoples, nations, and tongues within a space of around six thousand years. Bolingbroke

---

111 Pocock, *Machiavellian Moment*, 440.

112 Burtt, 60, 86.

113 Kidd, *British Identities*, 120.

was one of the first English historians to express deep scepticism about the capacity of Old Testament genealogies to provide a universal narrative of the peopling of the world.[114] But he was in no position to provide an alternative account.

Bolingbroke's brand of exemplary history was not concerned overmuch to establish what really happened. He knew, however, that unless historical writing had "a certain degree of probability and authenticity... the examples we find in it would not carry a force sufficient to make an impression on our minds," much less to illustrate and "strengthen the precepts of philosophy and the rules of good policy."[115] Nor did Bolingbroke see stark differences between the various peoples who played a role in the development of the English nation. In his view, the Celts, Danes, Normans and Saxons all "came out of the same northern hive." For that reason, Bolingbroke saw no obvious distinction between "ethnic patriotism" and "constitutional patriotism." The differences between the "two German nations founded, at no great distance in time, in Britain and in Gaul" had mainly to do with institutions. In Gaul, the German commoners settled there "were little better than slaves" while in Britain "another constitution was formed, and another spirit prevailed."[116] Believing that British identity was grounded in an institutional spirit of liberty, Bolingbroke's intuitive kinship lay with the great republics of classical antiquity.

It is commonly said that Bolingbroke used "language that we now identify as within the tradition of classical republicanism or civic humanism to persuade contemporaries that the policies and practices of Walpole's ministry were both corrupt and corrupting."[117] Faced with such a threat to the civic virtues of the British people, Bolingbroke called upon all "friends of the constitution" to contribute all they could "to prevent the ill effects of that new influence and power which have gained strength in every reign since the Revolution."[118] The rhetorical force of the paired opposition of "virtue" and "corruption" accounts for the public impact of Bolingbroke's language. The particular meaning he attached to those terms reflected the influence of earlier classical republican writers such as James Harrington; it also bespeaks the cumulative authority of older civic humanists in a tradition that stretched from Aristotle and Polybius to early modern figures

114 Lord Bolingbroke, *Historical Writings*, edited by Isaac Kramnick (Chicago: University of Chicago Press, 1972), 35-48.

115 *Ibid*, 58.

116 Bolingbroke, *Dissertation*, 152-153.

117 Burtt, *Virtue*, 88.

118 Bolingbroke, *Dissertation*, 184.

such as Machiavelli. This civic republican language was premised on a conception of the polity as "both an institutional and a moral structure." Each class of citizens in a mixed and balanced polity that united the one, the few and the many had its own particular virtues in the common activity of decision-making. Each citizen was bound to pursue his own particular goods but citizenship could persist only if he remained concerned for and aware "of the common universal good." Because the survival of the republic rested upon the freely willed actions of its citizens, corruption "was an ever-present possibility."[119]

The fate of every republic, then, depended on the maintenance of the laws regulating the activities of its citizens as well as "on the continuance of the external circumstances which made those laws possible." This meant that there were countless variables at play "and the name of the force directing the variations of particulars was Fortune." The inescapable confrontation between "virtue" and "fortune" or "corruption" was the decisive factor in the life of every republic. Every republic was forced to confront "its own temporal finitude" as it sought "to remain morally and politically stable in a stream of irrational events conceived as essentially destructive of all systems of secular stability."

By the eighteenth century, the "role of fortune was increasingly assumed by the concepts of 'credit' and 'commerce.'" In these circumstances, fortune was no longer thought of as just a random, irrational, and deforming set of external circumstances. Rather, corruption became a historically specific and dynamic system with the capacity to sustain a novel way of life with a normative force of its own.[120]

The Political Economy of Corruption

In such unprecedented circumstances, Bolingbroke could not sustain the ideological hegemony of a single, all-embracing paradigm of civic humanism. The meaning of "virtue" and "corruption" became radically unstable as the imperatives of the new political economy came to make themselves felt in the course of everyday life. In the realm of statecraft, the practice of corruption was first seen as a matter of making a virtue out of necessity. Given the new system of political economy, the constitution could no longer be conceived as a *natural* balance between the various estates of the realm. Instead, it came to be understood as a *functional* balance justified

---

119 Pocock, *Machiavellian Moment*, 73, 74, 76.

120 *Ibid*, viii, 405.

by its capacity to realize social purposes. National power and prosperity was now seen to depend upon the consolidation of executive influence in government. No one believed that support for the policy objectives essential to the national welfare would emerge spontaneously from the disinterested benevolence of the Commons. Instead, it was necessary for the executive to enlist selfish passions and private interests in the service of policy. Indeed, in recognition of the compelling need to concentrate the effective political will of the sovereign, Hume declared all that influence going under "the invidious appellations of *corruption* and *dependence*" to be an essential part of the weight maintaining the equilibrium of the British constitution.[121]

Similarly, in the increasingly dynamic life of civil society, the meaning that civic virtue acquired in the language of civic republicanism was stretched out of shape to accommodate competing liberal and Christian conceptions of public and private morality. In the growing marketplace of ideas, Bolingbroke's conception of civic virtue had to compete, *inter alia*, with Christian campaigns demanding legal enforcement of their distinctive understanding of virtue. High Church Anglicans, for example, defined public virtue as conformity to the established church. For them, religious conformity was "the necessary and sufficient condition of good citizenship." Their low church brethren, however, were more preoccupied with promoting public virtue by combating "public licentiousness through the stricter enforcement of already existing moral legislation." Concerned to promulgate and enforce a more comprehensive code of behavior, they claimed that civil authorities had "a responsibility, indeed an obligation, to enforce religious standards of moral behavior."[122]

Meanwhile, Court Whigs and even many opposition figures busily promoted their own rival, privately-oriented conceptions of civic virtue. Still other conceptions of civic virtue simply sought to encourage morally acceptable patterns of behavior. These very different understandings of virtue upheld an ideal of conformity to a regularized and predictable way of life. Almost all of Bolingbroke's rivals in the struggle to define civic virtue denied that it required the revival of patriotism.

The Court Whigs, in particular, joined Hume in refusing to believe that liberty depended upon "preserving the fiction of a balanced constitution." Instead, "it was to be measured by concrete political achievements that improved the life of the individual citizen." Conversely, the individual

---

121 David Hume, "Of the Independency of Parliament," in David Hume, *Political Essays* edited by Knud Haakonssen (Cambridge: Cambridge University Press, 1994), 26.

122 Burtt, *Virtue*, 40, 49.

citizen need not subordinate his private interests to a public-spirited zeal in defence of the constitution. Citizens who devoted themselves to their own material well-being would never become dependent on government. Hence "the dispositions that contributed most importantly to the preservation of public liberty" were not found in love for the constitution but rather in qualities such as personal honesty, industry and frugality in one's private affairs.

Even the opposition figures, Trenchard and Gordon, entered the public arena not because of an "abstract public spirit" or love of country "but from the most visceral personal concern" for their "individual safety and happiness."[123] Their writing was concerned with the behavior of both rulers and ruled. In *Cato's Letters* Trenchard and Gordon acknowledged that the "virtues of the people and their magistrates differed significantly." But, in both cases, they looked to "personal interest rather than public-mindedness" to "produce the behavior that Cato and other republicans regard as civically virtuous." Enlightened self-interest on the part of magistrates could usually be depended upon to "produce the desired behavior" but if that failed costly punishments should be administered. For these writers, self-interest is a more dependable foundation for the civic virtues of the citizen because it is impossible to predict when an individual citizen might be moved by consideration of the public interest. But "vengeful behavior" can always be expected from citizens whose personal interests have been harmed by a public official. In the aftermath of the South Sea Bubble, Cato urges citizens who may have suffered financial losses to "make a virtue of their present Anger" and predicts that "[o]ur present Misfortunes will rouse up our Spirits, and as it were awaken us out of a deep Lethargy."[124]

In the political discourse of the eighteenth century, the self-interested behavior that Bolingbroke saw as a symptom of spreading corruption was encouraged by others as a necessary check against the abuse of public power. The Court Whigs, in particular, were quick to redefine the meaning of civic virtue "so as to make it a practical possibility among citizens that Bolingbroke would damn as corrupt." One Court Whig publicist insisted that "a well-lined pocketbook, protected by a frugal life-style, temperate tastes and industrious impulses" would provide the best protection against corruption by government. In Burtt's view, the "character traits linked to such behavior are properly denominated civic (as well as

---

123 *Ibid*, 89, 10, 11; see, John Trenchard and Thomas Gordon, *Cato's Letters or Essays on Liberty, Civil and Religious, and Other Important Subjects* 2 vols, edited by Ronald Hamowy (Indianapolis, IN: Liberty Fund, 1995).

124 *Ibid*, 77, 78, 79.

moral) virtues" because they were seen to be essential "to the preservation of a free, self-governing polity." Court Whigs saw such civically virtuous behavior arising out of the private concerns of Englishmen in their everyday lives. They maintained that as long as citizens "manifested such virtues England's governors could themselves return to more conventionally praiseworthy behavior."[125]

This widespread preoccupation with conformity to conventional codes of behavior was directly linked to the rise of the new political economy. The capacity of governments to achieve social purposes and to maintain social order was seen increasingly as a function of their capacity to promote regular and predictable patterns of behavior both within the internal political order of the state and in the life of modern civil society. Early arguments in favor of the emergent capitalist system "took the form of opposing the *interests* of men to their passions and contrasting the favorable effects" of interest-motivated behavior "with the calamitous state of affairs that prevails when men give free rein to their passions." Hirschman demonstrates that, "once money-making wore the label of 'interests' and reentered in this disguise the competition with the other passions, it was suddenly acclaimed and given the task of holding back" the more unruly passions. Once interest came to "be considered a dominant motive of human behavior", it was recognized to have certain specific assets. "The most general of these assets was predictability." Statesmen were attracted to the idea that men were "invariably guided by their interests" because it suggested that the world could, if properly managed, become a more predictable place.[126]

Interest-motivated behavior came to be seen as a virtue in its own right. There were advantages for others when someone single-mindedly pursues his interests because "his course of action becomes thereby transparent and predictable almost as though he were a wholly virtuous person." This was thought to be true in both politics and economics. But the benefits "to be derived from the predictability of human conduct based on interest" were most evident in the economic sphere where the "by-product of individuals acting predictably" was a more cohesive community rooted in "a strong web of inter-dependent relationships." As conformity to a regular and predictable pattern of interested behavior came to be understood as a social and political virtue, the meaning of corruption was drastically narrowed. Previously identified by civic humanist writers

125 *Ibid*, 112, 118.

126 Albert O Hirschman, *The Passions and the Interests: Political Arguments for Capitalism Before its Triumph*, (Princeton, NJ: Princeton University Press, 1977), 32, 41-42, 48, 49.

with the degeneration of governmental forms, the term could also denote the act of bribery. As the political system adapted itself to the economic imperatives of economic growth and development, corruption entered into a new "semantic trajectory" in which "the monetary meaning drove the nonmonetary one out almost completely."[127]

Eventually, as the systemic character of political and economic life became ever more pronounced, the language of civic republicanism lost its ready reference points in everyday experience. The concept of civic virtue fell into desuetude. One can speak, today, of corrupt public officials who are known to accept bribes but one cannot expect public figures, much less the vast body of ordinary citizens, to display the classical civic virtues of resolute courage in their actions or sound wisdom in their judgements. Instead, we demand only that politicians, bureaucrats and corporate managers remain "accountable" for their behavior. Concepts such as civic virtue and corruption are now the archaic and obsolescent residues of a bygone era, accessible only to those prepared to immerse themselves in the merely academic study of a dead language.

Liberty: Ancient and Modern

In Bolingbroke's day, the expanding system of mobile property was already subverting inter-generational solidarity in both the political community and the family. A more or less unrefined utilitarianism quickly came to occupy a prominent place in the propaganda produced in defence of the Walpole regime. Swarms of publicists proclaimed the legitimacy of the Court Whig administration, lavishing praise on its proven capacity to promote the prosperity proper to a happy and contented people.[128] As the bourgeois regime embarked on its long campaign to confuse "being" with "having," tradition was drained of substance. Englishmen at home and throughout the British diaspora focused frantically on the future; an authority of ends gradually displaced the authority of origins. Before long, the rising tide of material interests swept away residual classical ideals of republican virtue, leaving the past in ruins.

During the Anglo-Saxon and feudal eras, political obligation had been grounded in covenants sealed by oath. By the end of the eighteenth century, people were bound to their rulers not because they swore fealty on

---

127 *Ibid*, 50, 51, 52, 40.

128 Reed Browning, *Political and Constitutional Ideas of the Court Whigs* (Baton Rouge: Louisiana State University Press, 1982), 66.

the faith of their fathers but because obedience was in their interest. This did not happen overnight. In fact, a Hanoverian regime of uncertain legitimacy propped itself up by multiplying the number of oaths that office-holders in church and state and even ordinary subjects were required to swear. But in "an age of deism, even atheism, the binding force of an oath in the face of God was debatable." Oaths, critics claimed, in addition to encouraging insincerity and infidelity, "merely perpetuated strife." As the century wore on, opinion leaders began to carry the inner-directed character of possessive individualism to its logical conclusion, professing "fearlessly, a contempt for all tie but that of interest." Such attitudes "made nonsense of traditional views of the State as a moral force, an expression of communal values."[129]

Such a pronounced shift towards the *telos*—the purposive logic—of constitutional legitimacy linked the liberties of Englishmen to the capacity of governments to promote the collective welfare of the nation through a process of economic growth and development under their presumptively enlightened stewardship. Accordingly, Bolingbroke's contrary emphasis on the ethnohistorical *genesis* of constitutional liberty was castigated regularly as an obstacle to the progress of commerce and industry. Court Whig journalists flatly denied that their English ancestors had possessed a spirit of liberty that was then "unknown to all the world." On the contrary, they insisted that Old England "had been steeped in slavery" and only after the Whigs had triumphed in the Glorious Revolution did the English begin to enjoy their present freedoms. Bolingbroke's call for a return to the original principles of the constitution was therefore absurd. "To bring the government of England back to its first principles is to bring the people back to absolute slavery." In the dark days of the past, "the people had no share in the government;" they were merely the villeins, vassals, or bondsmen of their lords, "a sort of cattle bought and sold with the land."[130] Those slavish ancestors had submitted, more or less willingly, to the yoke fastened on their necks by those who prayed and those who fought. Such a servile mentality, it was said, had no rightful claim to a voice in the political community of the modern English commonwealth.

The view that the spirit of liberty had never been grounded in the original principles of the ancient constitution received support from some surprising sources. As far back as the civil war, James Harrington, a writer often identified with the English revival of classical republicanism, dismissed the "Gothic balance" of double majesty as little more than a

129 Langford, *Public Life*, 107-112.
130 Kramnick, *Bolingbroke*, 130-131.

perpetually unstable "wrestling match" between the king and nobility that had lasted from the Anglo-Saxon invasions until the advent of the Tudors. Neither party could adjust to the power of the other, nor could they achieve independence. Harrington rejected any return to the "ancient" or "balanced" constitution because its foundations had always been insecure and, in any case, they had been washed away by the Puritan Revolution.[131] His major work, *Oceana*, was written to persuade Cromwell to establish a popular government.[132]

Harrington's utopian blueprint for a remodelled English common-wealth was far removed from the thought of Edmund Burke, the late eighteenth century parliamentarian who became the patron saint of modern conservative thought. Nevertheless, Burke, too, rejected every call to reform the English constitution on the ground that it had degenerated from its original principles. According to Burke, the English constitution was immemorial and customary; its "sole authority is that it has existed time out of mind." Constitutional legitimacy was based on prescription not choice; a prescriptive government having been produced "by the peculiar circumstances, occasions, tempers, dispositions, and moral, civil, and social habitudes of the people, which disclose themselves only in a long period of time." The constitution was not the work of any legislator, it was not the product of any identifiable original principles; "consequently none can be alleged as a means of evaluating its workings."[133]

Burke affirmed the essential continuity of the immemorial constitution. True, the common law upon which it rested was always in flux and was constantly being restated but change emerged insensibly in response to immediate practical needs as the deliberate election of ages and generations.[134] Burke turned a blind eye to the revolutionary changes that had produced radical and abrupt changes in the character of the English people and their government since the Tudor and Puritan Revolutions, leaving his admirers ill-prepared for those to come in the future. Bolingbroke was much more sensitive to the discontinuity in constitutional practices that had been produced by the contemporary financial revolution. But even he failed to recognize a deeper and more profound discontinuity between the spirit of liberty known to the ancients and the liberty celebrated by the heirs of the Glorious Revolution. He was more percipient

131 Pocock, *Machiavellian Moment*, 385, 388.

132 See, James Harrington, *The Political Works of James Harrington* edited by JGA Pocock (Cambridge: Cambridge University Press, 1977).

133 Pocock, *Politics, Language and Time*, 226-228.

134 *Ibid*, 221, 226.

than either Burke or the Court Whigs in sensing the need to restore the original principles of the constitution. But Bolingbroke had no way of uncovering those original principles, either in the biocultural sediments of primordial European spirituality or in the Anglo-Saxon reception of their nation-building Christian faith.

Despite their differences, both ancient and modern liberty stem from a common root: the trifunctionality of the archaic Borean or Indo-European *Urkultur*. Much later, in its medieval Christian manifestations in England and northern France, the tripartite hierarchy united those who worked with those who prayed and those who fought to create embryonic forms of civic humanism bearing a strong family resemblance to the classical republicanism of the ancient Mediterranean world. But when it was brought down to earth that triadic social ideal could not contain the revolutionary energy generated by the third estate—as the producers of wealth came to be known in France. Their labor and industry supported the entire medieval social edifice, and thereby reinforced the theologically sanctified autonomy and integrity of the terrestrial sphere. Labor, undertaken by Puritan saints for the greater glory of God, also satisfied the desire for "commodious living" among the less pious people at large. Once labor was embedded in an autonomous system of production, distribution, and exchange, liberty took on a radically new meaning unknown to the ancients.

The ancient "*pólis* was not a conspiracy of self-seeking individuals joined for mutual profit and protection in a temporary legal partnership that would be dissolved when it ceased to suit their interests; it was a moral community of men permanently united as a people by a common way of life."[135] From a modernist perspective this carries a substantial downside. The nineteenth century French liberal, Benjamin Constant, acknowledged that citizens of the ancient republics exercised "collectively, but directly, several parts of the complete sovereignty" when they deliberated together in the public square on how best to achieve the common good. But this collective freedom was compatible with "the complete subjection of the individual to the community." All private activities were subject to "severe surveillance." Individual independence was of no importance, whether in relation to opinions or labor and certainly not in religious matters. Among the ancients, the individual was "almost always sovereign in public affairs" but "was a slave in all his private relations."[136]

135 Rahe, *Republics*, 30-31.

136 Benjamin Constant, "The Liberty of the Ancients Compared with that of the Moderns," in Benjamin Constant, *Political Writings* edited by Biancamaria Fontana (Cambridge: Cambridge University Press, 1988), 311.

By contrast, we moderns, according to Constant, enjoy the right to express our "opinion, choose a profession and practise it, to dispose of property, and even to abuse it; to come and go without permission...to associate with other individuals" or just to spend our time in accordance with our inclinations or whims. Of course, modern liberty, too, has a downside. Constant acknowledges that we no longer enjoy "an active and constant participation in collective power." Today, the individual is lost in the multitude and can almost never impress his will upon the whole. By way of compensation, however, the progress of commerce and communications "have infinitely multiplied and varied the means of personal happiness." Constant was in no doubt that the liberty of the moderns is much to be preferred to that of the ancients. Only a fool or a madman would advocate a return to the original principles of the ancient constitutions. Those who work should never again submit to those whose claim to civic virtue rests on their alleged wisdom or courage.[137]

In celebrating the virtues of bourgeois liberty, Constant exaggerates both the subordination of individuals to the social power in the ancient republics and their independence in the modern world. When Aristotle described man as a political animal, he highlighted the capacity for rational speech that made it possible for citizens "to perceive and make clear to others through reasoned discourse the difference between what is advantageous and what is harmful, between what is just and what is unjust, and between what is good and what is evil."[138] There is no doubt that the duties of the Athenian citizen to the commonwealth outweighed his individual rights. At the same time, it is equally clear that the citizen "experienced his social conformity as being determined from within." Athens, in particular, had developed a civic culture that endowed the individual's mind with "a specific structure...which enabled him to establish, or to create the organizing norms of his environment." For the Athenian citizen, "the external authority of the law had...become the inner authority of consciousness or reason."[139] Conversely, in our high intensity consumer culture, the individual liberty to spend one's life in the pursuit of private pleasures is contingent upon the perpetual growth of a mass-mediated and all-pervasive form of spiritual despotism.

137 *Ibid*, 310-311, 316, 323.

138 Rahe, *Republics*, 35.

139 Barbu, *Problems*, 121-122.

Conclusion

The classical language of civic republicanism always presupposed the separation of the private household and the political realm. In modern mass societies, the dividing line between the private and the public spheres of life has become blurred: "all matters pertaining formerly to the private sphere of the family have become a 'collective' concern." As political life assumed responsibility for the well-being of the economy, it was transformed into "a gigantic, nation-wide administration of housekeeping." In such circumstances, all members of the nation are equally subject to the despotic power of the social realm. After several centuries of development, "*society* expects from each of its members a certain kind of behavior." The *social* becomes a complex, interdependent system of needs that imposes "innumerable and various rules, all of which tend to 'normalize' its members," making them behave and excluding "spontaneous action or outstanding achievement."[140]

As the phenomenon of conformism spreads into every sphere of life, despotism appears in a new guise. The assumed one interest of the national household is no longer represented by one-man, monarchical rule. Instead, it has been transformed, in stages, "into a kind of no-man rule." Bolingbroke identified the first step in the process when he warned that the prerogative power was being replaced by the impersonal power of money. In our day, the rise of bureaucracy (described by Arendt as "the most social form of government") has made it clear that "the rule of nobody is not necessarily no-rule; it may, indeed, under certain circumstances, even turn out to be one of its cruellest and most tyrannical versions."[141]

Conformism has become an essential ingredient in the smooth management of the modern political economy. It was "only when men had become social beings and unanimously followed certain patterns of behavior" that economics "could achieve a scientific character." The perceived need to substitute regular and predictable patterns of behavior for spontaneous, erratic and fluctuating forms of action cannot be met by the science of economics alone. The shift away from personal rulership to the bureaucratic rule of nobody encouraged "the all-comprehensive pretension of the social sciences which, as 'behavioral sciences', aim to reduce man as a whole to the level of a conditioned and behaving animal." The very increase in the size of modern societies lends greater validity to the

---

140 Arendt, *Human Condition*, (italics added), 33, 28.
141 *Ibid*, 40.

laws of statistics by levelling out fluctuations and decreasing deviation. It turned out that "the more people there are, the more likely they are to behave and the less likely to tolerate non-behavior." As the rise of the social devoured both the private and the public realms, "those who did not keep the rules could be considered to be asocial or abnormal."[142]

Neither Arendt nor Bolingbroke expects the new social system to dictate the end of freedom by formal decree. Rather, it is the substantive *spirit* of liberty that fades away. Every individual remains "free" to behave as he chooses. But we are all submerged in the life-process of society which demands of its members "a sheer automatic functioning." We are not compelled to obey the decrees of any arbitrary, prerogative power. We are merely expected to acquiesce in a dazed, 'tranquillized', functional type of behavior which can usually be said to conform to our own best interests. In effect, it is a set of "statistical laws which … rule human behavior and make the multitude behave as it must, no matter how 'free' the individual particle may appear to be in its choices."[143]

But this does not mean that all forms of human behavior have been finally and completely subordinated to the laws of statistical probability. Like Bolingbroke, Arendt refused to give up hope that the spirit of liberty might be revived, even in the darkest of times. Anglo-Saxons, indeed, European peoples generally, must prepare themselves for dark times to come. Constant was right to draw a stark contrast between ancient and modern liberty; he erred in supposing that bourgeois liberalism could combine the best of both worlds. Conceding that, in modern representative states, there is a real danger that citizens preoccupied with the pursuit of private interests will surrender their "right to share in political power too easily," he remained optimistic that a "deep and sincere patriotism" would triumph in his country.[144] But without a civic culture that binds the members of a nation together into a moral community of memory, blood and tradition, there can be no civic patriotism. Indeed, patriotism of any description is becoming difficult to sustain in a globalized economy open to the free flow of capital, technology and labor.

If Constant were to be resurrected today, even he might doubt that the developments he heralded have served the "most sacred interests" of the French nation. In 1817, Constant was confident that modern political liberty would "enlarge" the spirit of his compatriots. Who could now believe that the commercialization of everyday life has "ennobled" the thoughts

---

142 *Ibid*, 42, 43, 45.

143 *Ibid*, 322-323.

144 Constant, "Liberty," 327.

of ordinary folk—much less their rulers? Transnational corporate capitalism is hopelessly incapable of fostering the "kind of intellectual quality which forms the glory and power of a people."[145] An officially orchestrated civic nationalism now substitutes the universalistic ideal of cosmopolitan democracy for patriotic traditions that affirmed the power and glory of a *particular* people rooted in the soil of their ancestral homeland. Contrived to breathe artificial life into multiracial "proposition nations," this transparently statist ideology feeds like a vampire on the reserves of mutual trust built up over millennia in north-western European societies that were accustomed to non-kinship based forms of reciprocal exchange.

Civic patriotism cannot be sustained in multiracial societies. Ethnic diversity imposed from on high accelerates the mutation of still comparatively benign forms of early modern possessive individualism into the virulent postmodern pathology known as civic privatism. In the racially homogeneous, overwhelmingly Protestant, society of seventeenth century England, trust between inner-directed co-ethnics who happened to be strangers built up a fund of social capital that contributed greatly to economic growth and development. The predisposition towards trust in Anglo-Saxon societies remains a precious resource that is being depleted rapidly by mass Third World immigration. Surrounded by aliens, people are mistrustful of their leaders, their professional colleagues, and their neighbors—even those belonging to their own race, religion, or ethnicity. The more ethnically diverse the area, the more likely people are to "pull in like a turtle," avoiding active involvement in their largely fictional "communities." Having few close friends, people in racially-mixed workplaces and neighbourhoods retreat into their homes, huddling unhappily in front of the television set.[146] Even without the added burden of ethnic diversity, anomic consumer cultures sap the vitality of established communities.

The doubly corrosive combination of ethnic heterogeneity and hedonistic consumerism leaves the legitimacy of the corporate welfare state dangerously dependent upon the cornucopian myth of endless economic growth and development. Should the regime fail to deliver on its promise of permanent prosperity, the consequences will be catastrophic. Individualistic WASPs will struggle to survive in competition with other, tightly-knit, often hostile, tribal groups. One hopes that such a state of emergency will trigger the need to return to the long-forgotten original

---

145 *Ibid*, 327.

146 Robert D Putnam, "*E Pluribus Unum*: Diversity and Community in the Twenty-first Century," (2007) 25(2) *Scandinavian Political Studies* 137-174.

principles of the tripartite social order, however "atavistic" such needs may seem to the modern managerial mind. The day may yet come when ineffectual WASPs give way to a new generation of Anglo-Saxon leaders possessed of both the sovereign wisdom to revive the communitarian ethos of the ancient republics and the selfless nobility to defend unto death the biocultural interests of their people.

To grasp the scale of the challenges facing us, we must understand the modernist revolution in which a compact and cohesive Anglo-American Protestant civilization united by a shared allegiance to the British Crown was split asunder in the late eighteenth century by the abrupt rise of *homo Americanus*. The story begins with a colonial struggle to vindicate the rights of Englishmen which actually establishes a *novus ordo seclorum* based on an appeal to the rights of mankind. We near the end of this tale in our own time as America's Constitutional Republic mutates into a borderless system of market-states. It remains to be seen whether transnational America will seek or find a final solution to the WASP Question.

Part Two

Pathogenesis: Anglo-Saxon Identity in the *Novus Ordo Seclorum*

4.

Homo Americanus: A Post-Mortem on the First "White Man's Country"

Introduction

We have reached the point where we need to reflect upon the character of the insular ethnonation that became the founding race of a newly independent American Republic. This chapter is a theoretical and methodological interlude which will set forth two closely related propositions: Recent developments in the fields of biology and theology justify the view that racial differences between Anglo-Saxons and other population are real and also that they should be received as a gift from God. Even on its own, each of those propositions is fiercely contested by secular humanist guardians of the conventional wisdom. Right-minded, educated WASPs are predisposed to deny the existence of both race and God. The spread of such attitudes presaged the spectacular decline and fall of *homo Americanus* in the late twentieth century. This chapter contends a synthesis of sociobiology and neo-orthodox Christian theology is essential if we are to understand why the first "white man's country" came to grief by the end of what had been billed as the American Century. Here, in a nutshell, is what sociobiology and neo-orthodox Christianity contribute to our post-mortem examination of the American Republic in this chapter:

Sociobiology: reveals that Anglo-Saxon Protestants are an ethnoracial group like any other in that they have been engaged in various forms of inter-ethnic competition which have definite impact on their relative fitness in the struggle for group survival. This discipline also provides strong evidence that "being religious" is a net positive in relation to group fitness.

Neo-orthodox Christianity: a strand of academic theology known as Radical Orthodoxy represents the first tentative steps taken by a few WASP intellectuals towards a movement to repair the rupture between

167

the secular and the spiritual realms that stems from the Papal Revolution of the eleventh century.

In Part One we studied the process of *ethnogenesis* through which the English nation came into being. In Part Two we examine the *pathogenesis* of Anglo-Saxon Anglophobia. This is no simple matter. The WASP disease affects both the spirit and the body of an entire people. But, since the Anglo-Saxon countries, generally, present themselves as the most successful products of the progressive Enlightenment, the fact that their core ethnocultural identity is wasting away is routinely ignored or denied by all concerned.

The English settlers who colonized the New World bequeathed to their descendants opportunities to amass material riches unparalleled in the history of mankind. For two centuries after the upstart British colonists declared their independence of the mother country, the new nation was the envy of the world. But prosperity and power poured forth from a poisoned chalice. Now, Americans are utterly dependent on a bloated, increasingly corrupt, corporate welfare state that shows unmistakable signs of imperial overreach. A "Christian," a "white man," an "American citizen," and, latterly, a tapped-out "consumer," *homo Americanus* has worn many hats; but with such a chameleon personality, he never managed to father an ethnonation. His national identity was grounded explicitly in constitutional forms not in blood and soil. As a consequence, *state* eventually replaced *nation* in the American nation-state. Paradoxically, American colonists, rebelling against a distant king who governed with a remarkably light touch, opened the constitutional door to a home-grown Leviathan endowed with the power and resources to produce a passive and pliable people incapable of recognizing much less resisting the all-pervasive despotism of modern mass society.

For more than two centuries, Americans were a people of plenty. They cast off the corruption of the Old World for a future of boundless abundance. That future is now receding into the past. The American Dream is fast becoming an air-conditioned nightmare complete with power outages. The long boom is over, America is browning, and the long emergency is unfolding. Dazed, disoriented, and increasingly despondent, *homo Americanus* now represents the senile face of defeat and decay. Americans who trace their bloodlines back to Britain now walk with the living dead, stranded in an alien nation far removed from their ancestral homeland.[1]

---

1 David M Potter, *People of Plenty: Economic Abundance and the American Character* (Chicago: University of Chicago Press, 1954); Peter Brimelow, *Alien Nation: Common*

The power and prestige once attached to old-stock Americans as the founding race of the Constitutional Republic ebbed away, leaving behind little more than an acronym conceived in acrimony, then sugar-coated and dressed as an empty Brooks Brothers suit—the WASP. Coined some-time in the 1950s as a snide epithet aimed at the patrician products of Ivy League colleges, the term can be stretched to include anyone anywhere descended from the indigenous peoples of Britain. As a collective noun, WASP refers to a mechanical aggregation of individuals rather than an organic social whole; ethnic solidarity is all but unknown among WASPs, especially those safely ensconced in the upper reaches of the managerial-professional class. Not even the most highly educated WASPs care that their own children remain ignorant of Anglo-Saxon ethnohistory. At best, an epigonal snobbery sustains the infant ethnoancestry industry track-ing Y-chromosomes and mitochondrial DNA back to the British Isles and beyond. Upper-class WASPs in America have presided "over the dissolu-tion of their own dominion,"[2] leaving their less privileged co-ethnics to face a future of public denigration and deliberate degradation. The lan-guage and institutions of the merely middle class WASP—his biocultural capital, indeed, the whole of what a biologist might call his extended phe-notype, a patriot his country, or a priest his faith—was socialized, com-mercialized and not infrequently vandalized by free riders of all colors and creeds.

By the late Sixties, American opinion leaders openly encouraged the wholesale expropriation of WASP culture. *Time* magazine, for example, pointedly unhooked WASP identity from any particular race, religion, or ethnicity. In fact, America's leading newsweekly issued, in its most mag-isterial manner, a journalistic dispensation authorizing collective identity theft on a mass scale. "Ultimately," its middle class readers were informed, "Waspism may be more a state of mind, a pattern of behavior, than a rigid ethnic type." Since some "non-Wasps display all the characteristics nor-mally associated with the most purebred Wasps," being "white, Anglo-Saxon and Protestant" is not enough to make someone "a Wasp in spirit." Signalling the final collapse of Anglo-Saxon Protestant hegemony, the magazine consigned the ethnoreligious signifier in an already "mildly offensive" ethnonym to lower-case orthography. "Waspism" was defined not as an ethnicity but as an upper-middle class lifestyle, the product not

---

Sense About America's Immigration Disaster (New York: HarperPerennial, 1996); James Howard Kunstler, *The Long Emergency: Surviving the Converging Catastrophes of the 21st Century* (London: Atlantic, 2005).

2   "Are the Wasps Coming Back? Have They Ever Been Away?" *Time* (January 17, 1969), available online at: http://www.time.com/time/magazine/article/0,9171,838862,00.html

of British blood but of "the right education, style, social position, genealogy, achievement, wealth, profession, influence or politics." From the commanding heights of the corporate media, *Time* extended its blessing to a rapidly expanding class of "Waspirants" altogether bereft of ancestral ties to England.[3]

The English colonists who settled America knew nothing of "racism" and had a healthy suspicion of the Other; but they, too, eventually lost touch with the spirit of God as it pulsed through the veins of their kinfolk. Looking for God with their minds rather than their hearts, the Puritans, in particular, regarded the multitude in both England and America as unregenerate sinners. They gave more weight to the voluntaristic obligations of covenant than to the customary claims of kindred. We found the origins of that cultural norm in the first sea-borne invasion of Britain by Germanic warriors sworn to follow the Saxon brothers Hengist and Horsa; it was given its highest philosophical expression when Hobbes and Locke declared that society is based upon contractual consent not the sacred bonds of blood. Yet another secular parody of ethnoreligious identity appeared in the political theology of white nationalism. Following the collapse of the White Republic, American WASPs stand in need of an ethnotheology capable of re-uniting the spiritual depth and moral vitality of orthodox Christianity with a realistic appreciation of the biological imperatives of group survival. Over the long haul, the Anglo-Saxon Protestantism bequeathed by the New England colonists left their descendants ill-equipped to defend the biocultural interests of their kith and kin.

Seventeenth century Englishmen believed that they were a nation blessed in the eyes of God. English colonists set sail for the New World as soldiers in the army of Christ. Far more than creatures of commercial interests and state power, the Massachusetts Bay and Jamestown colonies were part of a folk movement organized and inspired by Protestant churches in both England and America. The Bay Company "was an organized task force of Christians, executing a flank attack on the corruptions of Christendom." Shortly after landing in Virginia, Sir Thomas Dale wrote to a friend in London that he was waging "*religious* Warfare" with no expectation of reward "*but from him in whose* vineyard *I labor, whose* Church *with greedy appetite I desire to erect.*" In that colony, too, "the cosmological and religious premises of the epoch…governed the search

---

3   *Ibid.* This *Time* "think piece" used the Anglo-Saxon Anglophobe, E. Digby Baltzell, as a major source. See, *The Protestant Establishment: Aristocracy & Caste in America* (New York: Random House, 1964).

for wealth, and in that regard defined, even for investors, the errand" the colonists were "running in the wilderness." But *homo Americanus* was seduced by the enchantments of Mammon.[4] Despite reinventing itself in the mid-nineteenth century as a self-styled "redeemer nation," America effectively relegated the church to a supporting role in a secular society dedicated to life, liberty, and the pursuit of happiness. Bereft of an orthodox Christian ethnotheology, Anglo-Saxon Protestants eventually found themselves suffering substantial disadvantage in competition with rival racial, religious, and ethnic groups.

The Invisible Race and Its Rivals

The deracinated "Wasp" image is now the creature of corporate culture. From the mid-twentieth century onward, the "organization man" belonged not to an ethnonation but to a market demographic. The contemporary WASP is a hollow man devoted, above all else, to a lifetime of tasteful consumption. A man without a country to call his own, the pragmatic WASP thinks it a fair trade to receive, in return, the promise of consumer sovereignty in a borderless economy. But all is not yet lost. A sickness of the soul can be cured. Even the postmodern WASP, conditioned from birth to celebrate diversity and condemn Anglo-Saxon chauvinism, can be reborn as a patriot. The politics of identity in the United States would be utterly transformed by an ethnoreligious revival among WASPs praying to be reborn as Anglo-Saxons. Politics as usual, however, presumes that self-abnegating, ever-accommodating WASPs will assume guilt and take responsibility in perpetuity for the satisfaction of "minority" grievances. But browbeaten WASPs, after decades of direct experience with ethnic minority status, may yet reassert the manly Anglo-Saxon virtues of their ancestors, once again becoming part of an historic, transterritorial people sprung from English loins. If so, a postmodern archipelago of Anglo-Saxon tribes will foster the continuing evolution of an ancient race, in body and in soul, towards ends known only to God.

Only the ethnoreligious regeneration of Anglo-Saxon Christianity will sustain such a renaissance. The epic saga of *homo Americanus* teaches us that man cannot live by bread alone. The question is whether his WASP avatars can muster the spiritual strength to reconstitute themselves as an

---

economically self-sustaining and politically resilient network of ethnoreligious communities.

Such sudden, unexpected reversals of fortune have been a recurrent
theme in Jewish history. In medieval and early modern Europe, Jews were
a pariah people. Even after the French Revolution endowed them with
the rights of man and the citizen, they became embroiled in a series of
murderous ethnic conflicts that had horrendous consequences for all
concerned. Today, however, they are a physically secure, exceptionally
wealthy, and politically influential minority almost everywhere in the
Western world, most particularly in the United States.

Conversely, the founding race in every Anglo-Saxon country is the
new pariah people. Only in the parvenu guise of the contrite WASP are
representatives of this "demographic" welcome in the presence of the
Other.[5] Clustered in isolated colonies, surrounded by the rising tide of
color, WASPs everywhere are ill-prepared to cope with their increasingly
perilous geopolitical plight. Facing the challenges of survival as a despised
minority in a hostile world, WASPs can learn valuable lessons from the
Jewish experience.[6] Yet, still wallowing in "the world's highest standard of
living," American WASPs ignore the pressing need for such a primer in
collective survival strategies.

Certainly, in the brash self-confidence of his youth, *homo Americanus*
had no good reason to take the early modern Jewish diaspora as a role
model. Before the late nineteenth century, Jews were a marginal presence
in every Anglo-Saxon country. Jews were hardly unknown to the English
but they were at best outsiders. Having been expelled from England in
the High Middle Ages, Jews turned up again under Cromwell's regime
and even, in small numbers, in the American colonies. At that time, few
English colonists worried overmuch about the Jews in their midst. Other
races posed much more immediate problems. Bruising confrontations
with Indians and the need to control a growing Negro population were
matters of much greater concern, especially in the South which soon
developed a complex racial hierarchy. Indeed, race was the central theme
of Southern history.[7] White Southerners were confident that they could

5   cf., Hannah Arendt, *The Jew as Pariah: Jewish Identity and Politics in the Modern Age* (New
     York: Grove Press, 1978).

6   Kevin MacDonald, "Can the Jewish Model Help the West Survive?" (2004) 4(4) *The
     Occidental Quarterly* 5; the experience of other "market-dominant minorities" may become
     equally relevant, see eg, Amy Chua, *World on Fire: How Exporting Free Market Democracy
     Breeds Ethnic Hatred & Global Instability* (London: William Heinemann, 2003).

7   Ulrich B Phillips, "The Central Theme of Southern History," (1928) 34(1) *American
     Historical Review* 30.

teach Northerners everything they needed to know about interracial competition.

But now that Jews and Negroes have united successfully to erase every trace of the old White Republic from American public and corporate life, WASPs will need to learn anew the rules of inter-ethnic competition, this time from the bottom up.[8] Comparing the biocultural evolution of the Jewish and Anglo-Saxon peoples over the past two millenia provides considerable insight into the symbiotic relationship between race and religion. Such comparisons immediately throw up the question: How has such a tiny Jewish minority come to punch so far above its demographic weight?

For centuries, the strength of the Jewish diaspora lay not in numbers but in its fierce ethnocentrism, combined with the intellectual capacity to use infrastructures created by host populations to its own advantage. Jewish ethnotheology proclaims in-group altruism as its primary moral imperative. Ever since the Babylonian exile, Hannah Arendt remarked, "survival has been the single aim of Jewish political thought and action."[9] Perhaps because they often suffered persecution *as a group*, the group became paramount in both thought and behavior. In medieval and early modern Europe, Ashkenazi Jews lived in widely-scattered but close-knit ghettoes, dwelling separately and apart from the often hostile majorities surrounding them. Jews occupied specialized economic niches in fields, such as banking and finance, that required developed cognitive skills. A largely self-imposed isolation was a key element in the "evolutionary group strategy" pursued by the Jews of the diaspora. Under such circumstances, practical eugenics—the enhanced reproductive opportunities that were extended to the brightest offspring over many generations—combined with natural selection to accelerate the evolution of the high average intelligence central to the Jewish way of life.[10] Ethnic nepotism came easily to such a small and cohesive minority. The comparison with politically correct WASPs is startling: open advocacy of an Anglo-Saxon "evolutionary group strategy" is proof positive of poor breeding.

Stripped of the soul and substance marking a serious people, WASPs everywhere have become the invisible race. The collective invisibility of WASPs is built into the operating constitution of managerial

8   Cf Alexander Saxton, *The Rise and Fall of the White Republic: Class, Politics, and Mass Culture in Nineteenth Century America* (New York: Verso, 2003).

9   Arendt, *Jew as Pariah*, 22. See, generally, Kevin MacDonald, *Separation and its Discontents: Towards an Evolutionary Theory of Anti-Semitism* (Westport, CN: Praeger, 1998).

10 Gregory Cochran and Henry Harpending, *The 10,000 Year Explosion: How Civilization Accelerated Human Evolution* (New York: Basic Books, 2009), 187-224.

multiculturalism. In English Canada, governments and corporations are required by law to extend protection and preferences to rapidly proliferating "visible minorities." Everywhere other-directed WASPs pursue personal power, prestige, and material success within interlocking corporate and governmental bureaucracies. Group survival is simply not an issue.

In sharp contrast, New England Puritans were made of sterner stuff; they imposed real limits on the individual pursuit of wealth through powerful norms of in-group solidarity. The following vignette is illustrative: a Boston merchant was found guilty, by both the civil authorities and his own church, of "selling his wares at excessive rates." Denounced from the pulpit, he begged forgiveness from his congregation and "did with tears acknowledge and bewail his covetous and corrupt heart."[11] And yet such socially cohesive communities of intensely religious Puritans were the progenitors of today's secularist, individualist WASPs. Can secular reason explain that metamorphosis or did it flow instead from a fatal flaw in Puritan theology? Providing an answer to such questions requires analysis and evaluation of both the theological origins and the sociobiological consequences of the *novus ordo seclorum* created by *homo Americanus*.

Theology in Darwin's Cathedral

Nineteenth century writers bathed the American Adam in a carefully crafted aura of innocence. But, in fact, the idea of *homo Americanus* did not spring fully formed from the virgin soil of the New World; it drew heavily upon the cultural baggage carried over from the Old World by English colonists.[12] Indeed, even the crass materialism of American popular culture and its often cloying religiosity are rooted in a Christian heresy dating from the High Middle Ages. As we have seen, Protestant piety powered the eventual triumph of secular reason on American soil but it was the medieval Catholic deformation of Christian theology that first pried the sacred away from the secular realm.

In stark contrast to medieval Catholic scholasticism, the orthodox Christian *gens Anglorum* found God in every corner of the created world. Prior to the Papal Revolution, God revealed himself everywhere to the English people, not just in their churches but also in their homes and

---

11   David Hackett Fischer, *Albion's Seed: Four British Folkways in America* (New York: Oxford University Press, 1989), 156.

12   RWB Lewis, *The American Adam: Innocence, Tragedy, and Tradition in the Nineteenth Century* (Chicago: University of Chicago Press, 1958); Henry Nash Smith, *Virgin Land: The American West as Symbol and Myth* (Cambridge, MA: Harvard University Press, 1950).

hearths, their fields and forests, and, through their kith and kin, in the blood of their island race. The orthodox Christian faith of the Anglo-Saxon era was not defined by a set of beliefs but by a sense of belonging to the Body of Christ.[13] Certainly, it is hard to deny that life in Old England possessed a depth of meaning altogether absent from the "lifestyle choices" now available to today's cutting edge WASP. We can blame Western Christianity for "flattening" the world, separating faith from reason, body from spirit, and the sacred from the secular. Divine presence was drained out of everyday life and placed under the strict supervision of the clerical order. The medieval papal monarchy employed a highly refined philosophical reason to legitimate its role as the essential mediator between God and Man. Matters spiritual fell within the exclusive jurisdiction of the church. The Holy Spirit ceased to move, independently of the ecclesiastical hierarchy, in and through the body of lay Christians.

The effect, if not necessarily the intention, was to disenchant the secular realm, even if the arid rationalism of scholastic philosophy did not go unchallenged; the Eastern Orthodox tradition refused to sever blood and race from the Holy Spirit. On the other hand, in England both the natural sciences and Anglican theology followed in the footsteps of scholastic philosophy, collaborating in a long campaign to disincarnate God from this world by shifting Him to the realm of the infinite, somewhere beyond space and time. By the nineteenth century, secular reason was invoked routinely to explain the behavior of inorganic gases, liquids, and solids while Darwinian biology investigated the organic realm of "nature red in tooth and claw." Neither required reference to God. But a confluence of biology and theology might reveal that Darwin did not write the last word in the history of life. Recent developments in the biological sciences have plunged orthodox Darwinism into crisis. At the same time, WASP theology is rediscovering its orthodox Christian roots. These intellectual stirrings may breathe new life into the Old English cosmology buried under centuries of philosophical rationalism. Intellectually effete WASPs may find a new lease on life in a postmodern fusion of sociobiology and theology.

Sociobiology, a discipline largely invented by WASPs, suggests that group selection arising out of inter-ethnic competition helps to drive the evolutionary process. One must wonder whether we perceive intimations of the divine presence in the spirit driving us to defend our kith and kin. For far too long, WASPs have ignored the divine stirrings within, looking

---

13 Fr Andrew Phillips, *Orthodox Christianity and the English Tradition* (Frithgarth: English Orthodox Trust, 1995), 202-207.

to the mind alone as the measure of the true faith. In the orthodox traditions of the Old Faith, however, it was not unusual to understand both racial conflict and ethnic solidarity as manifestations of God's will.

Sociobiologists tell us that inter-group competition is part of the perennial struggle facing all organisms for space, resources, and life itself. In principle, therefore, sociobiology should be relevant to a study of *homo Americanus*, beginning with the English colonization of America. To the natural historian, the English of the colonial diaspora appear as the fittest of the several races thrown together in British North America, a victory enshrined in the constitutionalist tradition they impressed upon the "first new nation."[14] What, then, was this singular being, the American? How did Englishmen in America evolve into *homo Americanus*? When *homo Americanus* ceased to be a British subject, did he acquire a new ethnocultural identity? What role has religion played in shaping the American character? Has religion enhanced or diminished the relative fitness of the founding people, Americans of British ancestry, in between-group selection? In particular, did religion help or hinder the emergence of the self-loathing WASP?

Anglo-Saxon Anglophobia presents the sociobiologist with a peculiar puzzle. During the past half century, WASP elites joined in a concerted effort with rival racial, religious, and ethnic groups "to deconstruct the nation they governed," a project, "quite possibly without precedent in human history."[15] A famous scholar bearing the impeccably WASPish name of Samuel P Huntington, a man directly descended from one of the founding families of Puritan New England, recently asked his fellow Americans: "Who Are We?" There spake the voice of a lost soul. Watching his tribe plod down the road to extinction, Huntington feels no pain and certainly no remorse. Reporting the terminal decline of the WASP ethny with well-bred aplomb, he holds out hope that the emergent non-white majority will come to embrace the "Anglo-Protestant values" that made America great. How did an American "nation" possessed of unparalleled prestige, power, and wealth lose the will to survive as a "people," the ethnocultural entity that the Germans call a *Volk*? It seems unlikely that the *science* of sociobiology alone can account for the *spiritual* collapse of *homo Americanus*. One must wonder also whether Anglican theologians are any more likely to recognize, much less understand, the depths to which

---

14 Seymour Martin Lipset, *The First New Nation: The United States in Historical and Comparative Perspective* (New York: Doubleday Anchor, 1967).

15 Samuel P Huntington, *Who Are We? Challenges to America's National Identity* (New York: Simon & Schuster, 2004), 143.

WASPs have descended. Science and theology remain two solitudes, greeting the disaster unfolding around them in mutual incomprehension.

On the one hand, liberal theologians lift their skirts in horror whenever biological science broaches the sensitive subject of racial differences. Whether an unborn foetus has a right to life is an issue within the acceptable purview of theology; but threats to the survival of the Anglo-Saxon ethnonation are surrounded by a deafening silence from both churches and seminaries. On the other side of the disciplinary divide, sociobiologists claim jurisdiction over an allegedly objective realm of "facts," all the while remaining professionally aloof from theological issues, relegating them to the subjective domain of "values." For example, when Frank Salter offers an ethic of "adaptive utilitarianism" to justify the defence of ethnic genetic interests, he forswears any appeal to religion. Salter notes that while "genetic interests are as old as life, the scientific idea of inclusive fitness is not explicitly discussed in any religious tradition." In any case, even if the interest that every organism possesses in the reproduction of its own genes were to become a matter of religious concern, there are so many religions that only the single, objective standard of scientific rationality can hope to still the "incessant debates that characterized philosophical (let alone religious) differences before empirical and mathematical studies began their exponential growth." It is to "mature Enlightenment values," not Christian theology that Salter turns to ground his claim that all human beings have an ethical duty to nurture their ethny and a moral right to defend it.[16]

Salter contends that the duty to defend and nurture ethnic genetic interests is binding because it gives rise to a rule of "universal nationalism" which is adaptive for all ethnies, large and small. In developing this argument, Salter exposes the schizophrenic character of the WASP mentality. He accepts as a given the modern split between secular reason and the spiritual realm, as if that bifurcated consciousness is rooted in the nature of being. But neither the belief that there can be "only one standard of scientific rationality" nor the assumption that ethical principles must apply universally are simply given to us as facts of nature.[17] On the contrary, both are contingent products of Western Christian civilization. Anglo-Saxon Protestantism became the most fertile seedbed for the tradition of natural theology out of which orthodox Darwinism was to grow.

---

16 Frank Salter, *On Genetic Interests: Family, Ethny, and Humanity in an Age of Mass Migration* (Frankfurt am Main: Peter Lang, 2003), 284, 321.

17 *Ibid*, 316-317, 321.

Is There a Cure for the WASP Disease?

WASP intellectuals favor the head over the heart which yearns for an infusion of the Holy Spirit into the blood of a reinvigorated people. Hardly surprisingly then that ordinary WASPs display such morbid indifference to their collective health and well-being. Pathologists define a crisis as the point in the development of a disease at which a decisive change occurs, leading to either recovery or death. Anglo-Saxon civilization is now in crisis. The problem goes far beyond a passing bout of political instability or a downturn in the economic cycle; at bottom, WASPs are suffering from collective neurasthenia.

Unless the ancestral *Volksgeist* of the Anglo-Saxon race can be resuscitated, WASPs will not survive the crisis. Successful treatment is impossible as long as the schizophrenic split between WASP sociobiology and Anglican theology persists. A sociobiological analysis of WASP ethnopathologies cannot penetrate to the heart of the folk so long as it remains walled off from theological discourse. Secular reason errs when it banishes the sacred from the province of natural science. Nor can religion simply renounce the materialism of a fallen world. Splitting the body from the soul has damaged the WASP auto-immune system, dissolving the in-group solidarity necessary to constrain selfish behavior by opportunistic defectors. It is no accident that the core ethnocultural identity of the Anglo-Saxon countries crumbled while Anglicans around the world entered into an earnest debate as to whether they should deny or instead merely deplore the death of God.

There is a close connection between the deterioration of Anglo-Saxon Protestantism into a spiritual desert and the demographic decline of WASP populations. Sociobiologists recognize that religion plays a positive role in the process of between-group competition; it is well past time for theology to follow suit. But WASP theologians have played a double game, sometimes fostering, sometimes subverting in-group solidarity; their hostility to ethnic cooperation among their co-ethnics sits oddly beside the unqualified support lavished on other groups which compete with WASPs for territory, resources, and political power. Rowan Williams, the Archbishop of Canterbury, provides a particularly flagrant example of that double standard: he recently opined that only the introduction of Shari'a law can preserve "social cohesion" in Britain. Apparently, English Christians are duty-bound to accept the alien folkways of Muslim colonies proliferating throughout Britain.[18] More than a thousand years ago

---

18 Stephen Doughty and Michael Seamark "Sharia Law Row" *Daily Mail* 11 February 2008.

the ethnocultural core of the English nation was conceived in the womb of the church; today's Church of England piously proscribes political parties struggling to foster ethnic solidarity among the indigenous people of England.[19] Anglicans owe ostentatious displays of Christian charity to the Other, but not to their WASP brother. Among WASPs the norms of between-group selection have been turned inside-out; in-group solidarity is stigmatized while altruism directed toward out-groups is rewarded with power, prestige, and even wealth.

In evolutionary terms, Anglo-Saxon Anglophobia is profoundly maladaptive; it also reflects a perversion of Protestant piety. That much is clear from the experience of *homo Americanus*. Let me explain. Although the American experience has always been of central importance for religious historians, few recognized colonial America as a laboratory, the site of an unprecedented experiment in human evolutionary biology. There several major continental races, genetically distinct population groups that for ages had evolved separately and apart from each other, met head-on in no-holds-barred competition for space and resources. The comparative strengths and weaknesses of the biocultures contending for dominance were decisive factors in the outcome of between-group competition. During the colonial era, the rock-solid Protestant faith of small, ethnically homogeneous, local communities promoted high levels of in-group solidarity among English settlers, allowing them to prevail not just over hostile Indian tribes and potentially rebellious Negro slaves but over their French, Spanish, and Dutch rivals. Contemporary WASPs, however, shun explicit manifestations of ethnocultural solidarity.

Even on the micro-social level, people of English ancestry are not only more likely than members of other ethnic groups to "marry out" but the offspring of such exogamous unions are more likely to identify with their Irish, German, or Italian heritage than with their far less fashionable WASP roots. Many fewer Americans tell the US Census Bureau that they are of English ethnicity than one would expect to find as a result of the natural increase of the British colonists before and the British immigrants who came following the creation of an independent white republic.

In sharp contrast, 4.5 million Irish immigrants in between 1820 and 1920 somehow spawned a swarming multitude of 40 million descendants.

19 *Cf* Bede, *Ecclesiastical History of the English People* revised edition (London: Penguin, 1990); members of the clergy in the Church of England, trainees, and lay staff in the Church of England are forbidden membership in the British National Party. Martin Beckford, "Church of England votes to ban clergy from joining BNP" *Daily Telegraph*, 11 February 2009 http://www.telegraph.co.uk/news/newstopics/religion/4582683/Church-of-England-votes-to-ban-clergy-from-joining-BNP.html

This vast expansion of the Irish-American population clearly cannot be the product of natural increase. Rather, it reflects the "social increase" stemming "from the joint effects of a high rate of intermarriage and the high probability that someone will express a particular ethnic attachment." As it happens, WASPs taking spouses of Irish ancestry have produced descendants far more likely to feel an "unexplained subjective 'closeness' to Ireland" than with England. In other words, the development of Irish-American identity provides an illustration of the "social construction of race." The unexpectedly large numbers of Americans who claim German ancestry reflects a similar tendency among many descendants of America's founding race to disremember and disrespect the ethnic heritage of old-stock Americans who introduced English bloodlines into the families of later immigrant groups.[20]

It seems that "a British ethnicity is somehow less salient to those of British ancestry than an Irish or German ethnicity is to those of Irish and German ancestry." The declining prestige of English ancestry has thinned out the ethnic heritage of WASPs in the United States. The "social decrease" of the self-identified Anglo-American population as reflected in census data is a striking symptom of Anglo-Saxon Anglophobia. Simply projecting the natural increase of the colonial and immigrant populations forward to 1980 would predict 82.5 million Americans reporting British ancestry alongside 36 million Irish-Americans, 34 million German-Americans and 10 million Italians. In fact, "the 1980 Census counted 61 million British, 40 million Irish, 49 million Germans, and 12 million Italians."[21] By 1980 more than twenty-one million WASP souls had disappeared. Thirty years on, that deepening demographic drain signals the spread of a psychic poison that will cause slow-motion ethnocide unless some antidote is found. Whether the final fatal dose will have been self-administered or introduced by some hostile hand remains to be seen.

Wherever blame lies, the ongoing social deconstruction of the once-hegemonic Anglo-Saxon race is sapping the spiritual strength of WASPs, rendering them powerless to police exogamous relationships with outgroups. In effect, WASPs marry out; few outsiders marry in. Compared with hyphenated American ethnic groups, WASP families and churches rarely deploy ethnoreligious sanctions to discourage defectors or to recruit outsiders through intermarriage. American WASPs are, arguably,

---

20   Michael Hout and Joshua R Goldstein, "How 4.5 Million Irish Immigrants Became 40 Million Irish Americans: Demographic and Subjective Dimensions of the Ethnic Composition of White Americans," (1994) 59(1) *American Sociological Review* 64-82.

21   *Ibid.*, 68.

the world's least ethnocentric people. Judging by the explicit norms governing their public behavior and subjective preferences, few WASPs attach social, much less sacred, significance to their English ancestry. Can the sociobiology of between-group selection shed light on the role of religion in the rise and fall of *homo Americanus*? Sociobiologists have confirmed the secular utility of religion among a great many population groups; the evolutionary impact of a religion *of* secular utility is less clear.

Group Selection in Evolutionary Theory

Darwinism holds that mankind is subject to natural laws of evolutionary biology. Sociobiology tells us that natural selection turns on the relative fitness of groups as well as of individuals. Evolutionary development is sometimes said to be the product of an amoral struggle for survival among both men and beasts. But Darwin conceded that the natural world moves in mysterious ways, almost as if there were a God. In particular, he remarked on the important role played by morality in natural selection. While "a high standard of morality" might confer little if any "advantage to each individual man and his children over the other men of the same tribe," Darwin observed, any advance "in the standard of morality" within one group provides "an immense advantage" over its competitors. Within a social group, selfish individuals may well out-compete altruists, "but internally altruistic groups out-compete selfish groups." Natural "selection takes place at more than one level of the biological hierarchy." In any species, a social group functions as an adaptive unit only if its members do things for each other. Individuals whose behaviors are beneficial for a group seldom reap relative fitness benefits within the group; but if selfish behaviors become dominant within a group, the group itself will not survive. That rule applies not just to the Anglo-Saxon race but to every form of life, from the highest to the lowest, from the simple to the complex.[22]

The problem of achieving adaptive forms of "social cohesion" is an old one, appearing not just on the mean streets of modern English and American cities but in the earliest stages of life on earth. One graphic illustration of elementary social relationships has been provided by studies of the "wrinkly spreader (WS)" strain of the bacteria known as *Pseudomonas fluorescens*. In an unshaken broth culture, a population of ancestral smooth (SM) *P. fluorescens* rapidly diversifies through genetic

---

22 David Sloan Wilson and Edward O Wilson, "Rethinking the Theoretical Foundation of Sociobiology," (2007) 82(4) *Quarterly Review of Biology* 327, at 328-330.

mutation. WS creates a niche for itself by colonizing the air-liquid inter-
face, thereby avoiding the anoxic conditions that rapidly build up beneath
the surface. The key to the survival of WS is an adhesive polymer that
forms a mat on the surface. Cooperation between genetically related WS
cells in the production of the polymer secures their evolutionary success. But cooperation between individual WS cells comes at a cost since
the polymer is expensive to produce. The cost is distributed unequally
once mutant "defectors" hitch rides on the mat created by cooperating
WS, thereby gaining access to oxygen but not paying the price of polymer production. As a consequence, the non-producing "cheaters" reap
an unearned reproductive advantage. Because cheaters enjoy the highest
relative fitness within the group, their numbers increase. As the cheaters
spread, the mats become liable to a sudden, premature collapse, eventually sinking to the bottom. Within any given group, cooperative WS cells
are at a selective disadvantage in competition with free-riding defectors,
but WS survives within the total population as a consequence of between-
group selection. Groups containing relatively more cheaters are relatively
less fit than more cooperative clusters of WS. "Cooperation [is] costly to
individuals but beneficial to the group."[23] Similar conclusions have been
drawn from laboratory and field studies of other microbes as well as
plants, insects and vertebrates.

"Social cohesion" between individual organisms is a tangible reality in
the everyday life of the wrinkly spreader. But "sticking together" is little
more than an elusive metaphor for individualistic WASPs; no adhesive
polymers physically bind selfish WASP elites to their hapless co-ethnics.
Ordinary WASPs sink to the bottom as their ethnoculture disintegrates;
meanwhile, social climbers freed from the constraints of in-group solidarity soar upwards into the oxygen-rich atmosphere of political and plutocratic privilege.

Of course, the evolutionary path from mutant wrinkly spreaders to
modern Masters of the Universe spanned many major transitions in
the history of life. Sociobiologists maintain that group selection plays a
major role in such evolutionary leaps. Indeed, higher level selection often
allows groups *of* organisms to become groups *as* organisms. Symbiotic
associations of some creatures became "so integrated that the associations
qualified as single organisms in their own right." Within-group selection
is not always suppressed so completely that some higher-level units are
prevented "from functioning as organisms in the full and truest sense of

23   Paul B Rainey & Katrina Rainey, "Evolution of cooperation and conflict in experimental
      bacteria populations," (2007) 425 *Nature* 72-74, (4 September 2003).

the word." But the metamorphosis of cooperative groups into individual organisms has been cited as one example of a major transition *produced* by group selection.[24]

Another illustration of the role of group selection in the history of life is the appearance of eusociality among some species of insects. When members of insect colonies "are multigenerational, cooperate in brood care, and are separated into reproductive and nonreproductive castes," they can be described as "eusocial." Specialization of roles among biologically sterile worker insects appears to manifest the most extreme form of kin altruism, allowing colonies to function as adaptive units. Traits that suppress the reproduction of workers "seldom increase in frequency within the colony; they evolve only by causing the colony to out-compete other colonies...either directly or through the differential production of reproductives." Insects that specialize in nest defence, raiding other colonies, or provisioning the colony "provide public goods at private expense." Within any single colony, slackers "are more fit than solid citizens...but colonies with more solid citizens have the advantage at the group level." A greater propensity toward within-group altruism will foster functional interactions that suppress individual selfishness and even nepotism enables "the multifamily colony to be the primary unit of selection." Eusociality allows "an insect colony to make complex decisions comparable to the neuronal interactions that allow individual organisms to make decisions."[25]

But not even the most complex social interactions within an insect colony generate consciousness of the difference between altruistic and selfish behavior. More than a few major transitions in the history of life were required to produce the human "capacities for symbolic thought and the social transmission of information." Sociobiologists suggest that "a shift in the balance between levels of selection" was required before such "fundamentally communal activities...could evolve." Religion is a particularly significant adaptation to the biocultural imperatives of group selection. Primordial religions were egalitarian, rewarding in-group altruism and punishing selfishness.[26] They aimed to create a group mind within which individual personalities were subsumed. Some say that Hebrew monotheism reflects the higher stage of evolutionary psychology associated with the most important transition in the history of human life, the emergence of consciousness. On this view, the Old Testament helps us to understand the relationship between religion and evolutionary fitness.

---

24 Wilson & Wilson, "Sociobiology," 339.

25 *Ibid.*, 340-341.

26 *Ibid.*, 343.

The Secular Utility of Religion

On a Darwinian reading of the Book of Genesis, when Adam and Eve ate the forbidden fruit from the Tree of Knowledge, mankind experienced for the first time a state of self-consciousness. Richard Fausette argues that human brains developed in tandem with an expanding behavioral repertoire. At some point, "man found himself choosing from among a growing number of behavioral alternatives and his unique sense of self emerged, a consequence of having to juggle many behavioral alternatives in his struggle for survival." Behavior was no longer instinctive; individuals had to choose among possible futures. Their choices made a difference not just to their individual prospects for survival but to the relative fitness of their kith and kin. Unlike the wrinkly spreader or the honey bee, humans regularly *chose* between in-group altruism and selfishness. But men could not be sure whether they were making the right choice. Error was an inescapable consequence of freedom. Religion arose from "the natural desire of an evolved self-conscious mind to return to a time (the beginning) and a place (paradise) before men made tools and plotted the murder of other men."[27] In this fallen world, man pines for an earlier state of consciousness in which instinctive behavior preserved his primal union with God.

Before the dawn of self-consciousness, behavior was neither taught nor learned; man was neither alienated from nor feared God. According to Fausette, "man's fall from grace was a result of an evolutionary transition from instinct to learned behavior." After the fall, the freedom to make personal choices becomes "also the freedom to 'sin,' to make the wrong personal choices," thereby estranging man from God. Learning to make the right choices and passing on that knowledge strengthens oneself and one's progeny; survival enables man to return from the fall. Failure to pass on one's genes is the ultimate sin, the final irrevocable victory of death. Religion is a practical discipline, enabling men to avoid wrong choices. In other words, religion "evolves so as to enhance the persistence and influence of its practitioners." Religion endures by binding groups of men to common practical traditions of proven efficacy. On this interpretation, Jewish Law was a handbook of practical eugenics, teaching that man ought "to learn as much as he can for as long as he lives until learning becomes intuitive and a man can stand in the presence of God without fear."[28]

---

27 Richard Fausette, "The Book of Genesis from a Darwinian Perspective," (2007) 7(2) *The Occidental Quarterly* 37-40.

28 Ibid., 38-41, 43, 45, 54.

Sociobiologists such as David Sloan Wilson and Kevin MacDonald reject Richard Dawkin's characterization of religion as a "renegade meme." On the contrary, they point out that many, if not all, religions are adaptive. Fausette, too, concludes that "Genesis, the first book of the Hebrew Bible" sets out "the core elements" of a highly successful "evolutionary strategy of Judaism."[29] David Sloan Wilson's study of a wide variety of religions led him to advance "the organismic concept of religious groups as a serious scientific hypothesis." He reports that religious communities are often compared by their members "to a single organism or even to a social insect colony." Such biological metaphors capture the essence of religion as a group-level adaptation that prevents cheating while coordinating behavior. When practiced successfully, the ideals of in-group altruism allow members of religious groups to "prosper more than isolated individuals or members of less adaptively organized groups." While acknowledging that religion "may change some aspects of what people want," Wilson maintains that "it is built upon a foundation of providing what all people want through the coordinated action of groups." To the sociobiologist, religion needs no justification beyond the material benefits that it demonstrably delivers. According to Wilson, in particular, the case for "the secular utility of religion" has been established beyond reasonable doubt.[30] Unfortunately, the tragic career of *homo Americanus* suggests that this sociobiological understanding of religion is radically incomplete. Few would deny that American Protestantism produced material benefits for its adherents. But can Christianity survive as a formula for success in the worldly quest for wealth and power, health, and prestige?

Sociobiology takes a purely pragmatic approach to religion: if membership in a religious group has a measurable material pay-off, it must be adaptive. For the sociobiologist, the issue of whether a religion is "true" or "false" hardly arises; the relevant question is whether it possesses some degree of "secular utility." In principle, religion serves the same function whether one worships the Golden Calf or Balinese water gods, whether one is an Orthodox Jew preoccupied with the survival of his people or an Anglican clergyman horrified by the twin specters of "white racism" and "anti-Semitism." In the world of sociobiology, all religions are created equal. But not all religions are equally successful: *homo Americanus* made a religion *of* secular utility that is now demonstrably inimical to the biocultural interests of his WASP avatars. Individual fitness has been achieved at

---

29   *Ibid.*, 54.

30   David Sloan Wilson, *Darwin's Cathedral: Evolution, Religion, and the Nature of Society* (Chicago: University of Chicago Press, 2002) 1, 45-46, 162.

the expense of group interest; alternatively, between-group selection now operates *within* WASP populations stratified along class lines.

Sociobiologists inhabit an autonomous, secular realm of scientific discourse. Their "objective," allegedly "value-free" professional stance frees them of any need to concern themselves with "subjective" issues of spiritual meaning. Until recently, mainstream theology, too, acquiesced in that dualistic world-view, readily consigning faith and reason to separate compartments. But there are signs of change, even in the arid world of WASP theology. The fault line separating biology from theology is becoming blurred. Indeed, it is now possible to imagine a novel fusion of sociobiology and theology. The first faint glimmerings of such a synthesis are visible in the work of Radical Orthodoxy (RO), a loose grouping of mainly WASP theologians convinced that the dualistic opposition of the sacred and the secular is no longer tenable. Seeking to dissolve that artificial boundary, RO reveals, *inter alia*, the theological foundations of Darwinian biology. When writing his scientific classic, *The Origin of Species*, one RO scholar remarks, Darwin gave expression to "a secularized type of natural theology."[31] This suggests that the intellectual genealogy of both Darwin and *homo Americanus* stretches back to the great rupture in the life of medieval Christianity that gave birth to secular reason.

Orthodox Christianity and the *Saeculum*

Neither the Scientific Revolution of the seventeenth century nor the eighteenth century Enlightenment first deformed the Christian faith by severing the realm of the sacred from the secular domain. Much earlier, in the High Middle Ages, the rise of the papal monarchy set the West on the path towards its exit from the Old Faith. If the first millennium of the Christian era is the Age of Incarnation, the second can be styled the Age of Disincarnation. In the first thousand years of its history, the Church was "a Commonwealth of local Churches, a Community of unity in diversity...founded on the Orthodox Christian theology of the Holy Trinity." Unity within the Church was "the expression of the common Orthodox faith, which is itself the expression of the experience of the Holy Spirit common to Her members." The unity of the Church was spiritual, not secular or organizational. The clearest sign that the Church was "not a secular institution, but a divino-human one" was the fact that she had

---

31   Anthony D Baker, "Theology and the Crisis in Darwinism," (2002) 18(2) *Modern Theology* 183, at 193.

"no visible Head, but the invisible Head of the God-Man, present in the Church through the Holy Spirit." Early medieval Europe was also an Age of the Saints when monasteries and ascetics inspired a society guided by theology rather than "legalism or military dictatorship or rationalist philosophy as it had been in Pagan Rome." In stark contrast, the second millennium of Christian history was an "age of worldly greatness, but spiritual enfeeblement."[32]

No surprise, then, that the spectacular success of *homo Americanus* gave birth to the spiritually enervated figure of the other-directed WASP. At the beginning of the third millennium of Christian history, the question is whether a serious people can re-emerge from the Anglo-Saxon gene pool, re-infusing the true spirit of Christian communion into the blood of a regenerated ethnonation? In the early medieval era, Christian faith immeasurably strengthened the Anglo-Saxon bioculture. The Anglcynn of the first millennium nurtured their faith in monasteries and churches all over Britain. Theirs "was a mystical theology, the fruit of prayer." In the eleventh century, however, theology was rejected in favor of philosophy just as monasticism was rejected in favor of scholasticism.

One Orthodox Christian priest charges that scholasticism abandoned "the only real theology, the mystical theology of practical experience, for a rationalistic philosophy." From their seats in the new universities, Catholic scholars set out to conform faith to a fallen human reason. The scholastic reconciliation of Christianity with the pagan thought of classical antiquity underwrote the expansion of a proto-totalitarian imperial papacy. In the Age of Scholasticism, "learning was no longer obtained in the monastery through prayer, but in the university through the human mind and logical analysis."[33] Similarly, theology in the United States and the United Kingdom today remains an academic enterprise.

Because Radical Orthodoxy, too, remains cloistered in that academic cocoon, its adherents are somewhat disingenuous when they describe their work as "radical." Their attention remains firmly fixed on the celestial sphere of ideas. Identifying the most decisive shift in Western Christianity with the academic disputes which led to the late medieval displacement of theology by philosophy, RO confirms the continued self-absorption of the modern university. Orthodox Christian churches, by contrast, are more inclined to cite more mundane matters—in particular,

---

32 Phillips, *Orthodox Christianity*, 280-286, 225.

33 *Ibid.*, 283, 287-288. On the Papal Revolution, see, Harold J Berman, *Law and Revolution: The Formation of the Western Legal Tradition* (Cambridge, MA: Harvard University Press, 1983), 85-119.

the papal drive to centralize ecclesiastical authority—as the proximate cause of the Great Schism of 1054 that split the Eastern from Western churches. Unfortunately, one would be hard-pressed to find, anywhere in the Anglosphere, more than a few scattered priests with small congregations of WASPs who still follow the Orthodox way of life practiced by their ancestors in the Old English Church. Such neo-orthodox communities may harbor a decidedly more radical critique of modernity than the academic labors of many RO theologians. But both groups are critical of the WASP culture of secular humanism, long since severed from sacred space and time. When Henry VIII dissolved the monasteries and seized their lands in the name of the Crown, Anglo-Saxon Protestantism demonstrated the absolute autonomy of the secular realm.

Few academic theologians, of course, object to the "rejection of monasteries in favor of universities," much less to the scholastic elevation of pagan philosophers above the Gospel, a prominent feature of their own work. Indeed, the most prominent RO thinker, John Milbank, explicitly rejects efforts to restore "a pre-modern Christian position." One may well deplore RO's tendency to cultivate the intellect at the expense of the heart, but its exponents do provide an interesting and useful starting point for a self-critical, Christian history of Anglo-Saxon bioculture. [34] Milbank points in the right direction when he reminds us that "Once, there was no 'secular.'" In the orthodox Christian cosmology of the early Middle Age, the *saeculum* "was not a space, a domain, but a time—the interval between fall and *eschaton*."[35] If Milbank is right, the so-called "domain" of the secular is an imaginary social construct not a fact of nature.

No less mythical is the notion that a tyrannical and irrational Christian priesthood cruelly suppressed the autonomy of secular reason until the Enlightenment. He argues that, throughout the Middle Ages, both the church (*sacerdotium*) and the state (*regnum*) drew upon natural reason in a cooperative effort "to cope with the unredeemed effects of sinful humanity." Faith in the grandeur of reason was the distinguishing characteristic of Western Christendom in the High Middle Ages; modern social theory, therefore, wrongly supposes that religion is set in opposition to the universal dictates of human reason. Milbank draws our attention to the fact that the foundations of secular reason itself are found in "the modification or the rejection of orthodox Christian positions." And it is not just the "social sciences" that have evolved from medieval Christian roots;

---

34 Phillips, *Orthodox Christianity*, 134; and John Milbank, *Theology and Social Theory: Beyond Secular Reason* second edition (Oxford: Blackwell, 2006), 1-2.

35 Milbank, *Theology*, 9.

Darwinism and sociobiology share the same provenance. Moreover, Milbank dares to suggest, the "intellectual shifts" that split the "secular" from the "spiritual" realm are "no more rationally 'justifiable' than the Christian positions themselves."[36]

Sacred and Secular: Competing Mythologies

RO attacks both modern theology and secular humanism from a frankly postmodern perspective. Milbank concedes that theology is a "contingent historical construct" that emerged out of a particular way of life practiced by a particular people guided by a particular *mythos*.[37] In the case of orthodox Christianity, the *mythos* announced "nothing less than the eternal rule commencing here and now on earth of a dead, executed man, ostracized from the Jewish, Hellenistic and Roman communities." Christ founded a new polity on a wholly counterfactual metanarrative. In Milbank's account, the *sacerdotium* and the *regnum* were united in and through the Holy Spirit incarnate in the *ecclesia* (from the Greek for "governing assembly" or in Hellenic Judaism "the gathering of the elders of Israel"). The church gathered believers together in a multiplicity of local communities (each incarnating the Body of Christ in accordance with its own distinctive biocultural character) to create a decentralized but catholic polity that transcended worldly boundaries of time and space, class and gender, race and ethnicity.[38]

By contrast, politics as known to classical Greeks and ancient Romans was grounded in the will-to-power. Christians, of course, were not blind to the reality of death and suffering. They knew that men were governed by the base passions of the flesh, each condemned to struggle for "survival, self-satisfaction, erotic possession of, and military triumph over, others." Christ's victory over sin and death demonstrated, however, that the good is "more than a human illusion."

For Milbank, Christianity adopted a frankly counterfactual "ontology" (from Greek *on* + *logos*, "the study of being"). The "*ecclesia* as founded by Christ names the only polity, or at least possibility of a polity, which collectively lives, beyond death...because it replaces the political animal

---

36 *Ibid.*, 9, 1.

37 *Ibid.*, 1-2.

38 John Milbank, "Paul Against Biopolitics," unpublished paper, available online at: http://www.theologyphilosophycentre.co.uk/papers/Milbank_PaulAgainstBiopolitics.pdf,   54, 43-45; see also, William T Cavanaugh, *Theopolitical Imagination: Discovering the Liturgy as a Political Act in an Age of Global Consumerism* (London: T & T Clark, 2002), 89-94.

with the pneumatic body of grace-given mutual trust." Undying goodness and justice were conceived as "an ultimate reality, ontologically subsisting before evil, both human and natural, including the natural negativities of death and suffering."[39] Milbank openly acknowledges that the orthodox Christian *mythos* is grounded in nothing more than the persuasive power of the story it tells. For Christians, truth is not correspondence with an objective external reality "but *participation* of the beautiful in the beauty of God."[40] The Christian ontology of peace is based not on demonstration, in accordance with the canons of secular reason, but on a truth infused with the beauty and goodness of the God-given gift of life.

Taking the offensive, RO denies that natural science has privileged access to truth. "Its 'truth' is merely that of instrumental control," a highly refined expression of the will-to-power. Milbank insists that secular suspicion of religion is grounded in a *mythos* of its own, a metanarrative in which being is grounded in power and conflict, not peace and harmony. Although "scientific" social theories and Darwinian biology rest their claims on reason rather than faith, they "are themselves theologies or anti-theologies in disguise." In fact, "secular discourse…is actually *constituted* in its secularity by 'heresy' in relation to orthodox Christianity, or else a rejection of Christianity that is more 'neo-pagan' than simply anti-religious." Before the late medieval invention of the "secular," there was no possibility of projecting the "spiritual" to an unknowable realm beyond time and space. But the same movement that "reimagined nature, human action and society as a sphere of autonomous, sheerly formal power" concurrently "completely privatized, spiritualized and transcendentalized the sacred."[41] Paradoxically, the centralized *Kirchenstaat* produced multiple fractures in the *ecclesia*—between East and West, Church and State, sacred and secular—which undermined the *symphonia* characteristic of orthodox Christendom.[42] Uniformity imposed from on high by the Pope in Rome replaced a unity in diversity that arose from the bottom up.

Mutual trust rather than legal authority once bound together the parish priests and bishops, monks and abbots, sacred kings and powerful princes, local lords and pious peasants of orthodox Christendom. When, in the late eleventh century, the Pope in Old Rome became a universal bishop, he ceased to serve humbly, like other bishops, as the vicar of St Peter; instead he asserted a novel monarchical authority as the Vicar of Christ

---

39   Milbank, "Biopolitics," 43, 45, 53, 67, 69.

40   Milbank, *Theology*, 279, 260, 434.

41   *Ibid.*, 2-3, 9.

42   Phillips, *Orthodox Christianity*, 184.

himself. The papal monarchy thus followed the lead set by Charlemagne who sought to rival the Emperors of the New Rome in Constantinople. Claiming a spiritual monopoly over the salvation of souls, the papacy ceded to secular rulers responsibility for purely temporal matters. Endless legal wrangling ensued as the church pushed to expand its jurisdiction over the "spiritual" dimension of worldly affairs from the cradle to the grave. Not surprisingly, secular princes pushed back in defence of their novel prerogatives.[43]

The centuries-long crisis of church and state distanced Christians ever further from the divine. Western attitudes exhibited more worldliness, revealing "a lack of respect for Creation." In early Christendom, Nature "had been seen as a pattern or code of signs and symbols of God's presence among men on Earth." Some men and women, of course, were closer to God than others. The monastic movement within the eleventh century church divided the faithful of the *ecclesia* into three groups on the basis of sexual purity. On that scale, there were three degrees of merit: virgins, the continent, and married persons. As "the best, the purest, the most angel-like of men," the monastic orders stood closest to God, followed by clerks and laymen. Together, they worked to "bring Christ's *religio* under the plow." At least one monastic writer explicitly likened "the unity of the three parts of the social body...to the mystery of the Trinity."[44] The papal monarchy turned the monastic model of the *ecclesia* upside down; the "secular" clergy and its episcopal hierarchy were elevated over the "regular" clergy of independent monastic orders. These rival visions of the *ecclesia* reflected the theological tension between two incompatible understandings of the nature of God.

For orthodox Christians, "God was the source and the informing energy of that descending process by which being flows through all the levels of possibility down to the very lowest." As a practical ideal, the orthodox program "summoned men to participate, in some finite measure, in the creative passion of God, to collaborate consciously in the processes by which the diversity of things, the fullness of the universe, is achieved." By contrast, in the scholastic theology that served as the handmaiden of papal monarchy, God became "the goal of...that ascending process by which the finite soul, turning from all created things, took its way back to

---

43   Milbank, "Paul Against Biopolitics," 46; Phillips, *Orthodox Christianity*, 285-286; Berman, *Law and Revolution*, 85-119.

44   Phillips, *Orthodox Christianity*, 294; Georges Duby, *The Three Orders: Feudal Society Imagined* (Chicago: University of Chicago Press, 1980), 85-86.

the immutable Perfection in which alone it could find rest." Only through the intercession of the church could the believer be absolved of his sins.

The meaning of the incarnation was changed radically by decreeing that the "way up" was the only "direction in which man was to look for the good."[45] As a consequence, the Body of Christ was transformed into a *corpus mysticum* controlled by an ecclesiastical hierarchy that had perfected the secular "techniques of remote, secret and invasive clerical control."[46] When the famous *filioque* clause was added to the Nicene Creed somewhere around 800AD at the insistence of Charlemagne, the Holy Spirit became incarnate in the priestly caste. This doctrine declared that the Holy Spirit proceeds from the Son as well as the Father, a proposition that the papal monarchy, billing itself as the Vicar of Christ, invoked to affirm that man can enter into communion with God only through the intercession of the ecclesiastical hierarchy established by canon law. In the Old Faith, the authority of the *ecclesia* was undermined if the goodness of God, the Holy Spirit, was not incarnate in all of its members. "The faithful people of God, who should be organically one with the faithful clergy, are no longer able to speak by the Holy Spirit." If the people do not themselves embody the divine energy circulating within the *ecclesia*, then they are "obliged to submit to the exterior authority of the divine nature, represented by the clergy." Not only were the people and the clergy separated, so too were the church and the state, papal and royal authority. Since Christ was no longer incarnate in the hearts of the people, the Holy Spirit could only proceed from Him to secular rulers and their subjects through the mediation of his "Vicar." Not surprisingly, the "monolithic monarchism" of the papacy developed an insatiable appetite for power; whenever the opportunity arose ambitious Popes sought to absorb the embryonic states of Western Europe into the church.[47]

Toward a Flat Earth

The remote, monarchical image of the Pope as the unseen but all-powerful, spiritual Head of Christendom mirrored the removal of God from the world. Previously, "every sphere of reality and human life was understood as being suspended, as it were, from the transcendent." The material world was not simply "nature," it was creation, no part of which was "unhooked"

---

45   Arthur O Lovejoy, *The Great Chain of Being: A Study of the History of an Idea* (Cambridge, MA: Harvard University Press, 1964), 83-84.

46   John Milbank, *Being Reconciled: Ontology and Pardon* (London: Routledge, 2003), 125.

47   Phillips, *Orthodox Christianity*, 61-62, 65-66.

from participation in the divine.[48] The divorce of God from man was sealed when scholastic philosophy distanced "the Holy Spirit from the Earth, putting Him where the Gothic spires pointed, in the empty sky."[49] RO holds Duns Scotus (1266-1308), in particular, responsible for placing the Holy Spirit beyond man's reach, sundering the symphonic harmony that united reason and faith, philosophy and theology. In so doing, Scotus simultaneously reduced God and elevated man. According to Scotus, "both the Creator and the creature exist in the same way or in the same sense" in that they share the attribute of Being. In other words, Scotus conceived a metaphysical framework which "elevated being (*ens*) to a higher station over God, so that being could be distributed to both God and His creatures." Creator and creatures are distinguished only by their specific, qualitative properties: God is an infinite, man a finite, being. In the orthodox tradition, finite being exists only by and through the grace of God. But Scotus made man an object of idolatry by granting "to finite being its own subsistence and autonomy." In effect, the philosophical separation of God from man created a flat earth.[50]

The world was not flattened overnight; it took centuries to deliver philosophy from contamination by theology. Meanwhile, the natural sciences set about squeezing spirit out of the physical world of matter and energy. But there were countless ways in which spiritual and secular experience remained fused long after the Papal revolution. Bishops triumphed over abbots but only by imposing the monastic rule of celibacy on the "secular clergy." Conversely, the monastic order of merit was folded into the tripartition between "those who prayed" (*oratores*), "those who fought" (*bellatores*), and "those who worked" (*laboratores*). As a consequence, all those who prayed, whether they were monks or priests, resisted a sharp dualism of body and spirit.

Even episcopal efforts to extend clerical control helped to preserve the sacramental character of everyday life by exploiting the fuzzy distinction between spiritual and temporal realms. For example, "the papacy to some degree encouraged the submission of knightly anarchy to a code of Christian honour." Accordingly, knights developed "a fully-fledged lay priesthood, involving a kind of ordination rite that communicated a lineage at least as honorable as that of St Peter." Relationships between feudal lords and "those who worked" also were governed by a "theological code."

---

48 James KA Smith, *Introducing Radical Orthodoxy: Mapping a Post-Secular Theology* (Grand Rapids, MI: Baker Academic, 2004), 88-89.

49 Phillips, *Orthodox Christianity*, 135.

50 Smith, *Introducing Radical Orthodoxy*, 97-99.

Both lord and peasant upheld "a 'liturgical' rhythm of social practice and meaning." Both assented to a "sacralized gift-exchange" of services and obligations. The nobility built up prestige through "manifestations of glory and bestowals of gifts" falling "into socially recognized categories." Unlike modern plutocrats, they could not "do so by pursuing a 'pure wealth' that may become equivalent to anything whatsoever."[51] Medieval Christendom remained an enchanted land even as its wealth and power was displayed and secured by the growing autonomy of the secular realm.

Because all men, those who prayed as well as those who fought and those who worked, lived in ecclesial time, the sacred rhythm of seasons was spaced out in accordance with the cyclical recurrence of Advent, Incarnation, Lent, Resurrection, and Pentecost. Adopted by the Nicean Council in 325, the Julian calendar sought to hallow, Christianize, and purify time. The past, present, and future of the *saeclorum* dated from the intersection of solar and lunar calendars with the most important event in the life of Christ "and in the whole history of Creation—the Resurrection." In reckoning time, it was not "the stars, planets and satellites of the Fallen Cosmos" that mattered to early Christians. What was important was Christ's victory over death "which takes man across time into Eternity—Timelessness."[52] Ecclesial time was not formally separated from astronomical time until the adoption in Rome of the Gregorian calendar in 1582. Even so, the motions of heavenly bodies were seen to be under the sway of unseen powers. Partly for that reason, the old calendar remained in force in the Church of England until 1753. Was it pure coincidence that, shortly after the Anglican Church switched to astronomical time, *homo Americanus* was born?

Milbank associates the rise of *homo Americanus* with "a politico-religious culture which in classically Christian terms is perverse, because it tends to play down the centrality of the Trinity and of the Incarnation." Consider the hallmarks of the civic culture of the Constitutional Republic today. The Holy Spirit has been evacuated from American public space and time. There are "no real sacred centers, no spacing of the year by Advent, Incarnation, Lent, Resurrection and Pentecost, in keeping with the rhythm of the seasons." Moreover, the sectarianism of American Protestantism is far removed from the orthodox Christian recognition that "the visible unity of the Church [is] central to the work of salvation."

---

51 John Milbank, "Geopolitical Theology: Economy, Religion, and Empire after 9/11," unpublished paper, available online at: http://www.theologyphilosophycentre.co.uk/papers/Milbank_GeopoliticalTheology.pdf, 105-109.

52 Phillips, *Orthodox Christianity*, 50-52.

When combined with the unimportance of sacred space and time, Protestant sectarianism deprives religious experience of depth by confining it to the private realm where it is often reduced to a matter of therapeutic technique. Milbank observes that when American churches enter the public realm, they "tend to inculcate a civil religion and a trite and sentimental bourgeois moralism." In their pious patriotism, the churches acknowledge their due subordination to the secular authority of both the state and the corporation.[53]

But *homo Americanus* was not born into a spiritual and intellectual vacuum. Well before the advent of the American Adam on the world stage, English science had expunged all trace of both the trinity and the incarnation from mathematics and physics. Sir Isaac Newton's life (1643-1727) ran parallel with the colonial foundation of British North America. His scientific achievements endowed secular reason with overwhelming prestige in the American mind. By simplifying the motion of heavenly bodies in accordance with mathematical formulae, Newton expanded secular time to infinity. His formulation of the universal laws of physics pushed God outside time and space, rendering Anglo-American culture indifferent to the sacramental Julian calendar. But, in one vitally important sense, Newton was pushing on an open door. His revolutionary science had its metaphysical foundation in the scholastic rationalism that opened up the "possibility of considering being without God, as more fundamental (supposedly) than the alternative of finite versus infinite, or temporal versus eternal."[54] But the death of God in Anglo-American culture was to be a long drawn-out affair.

Many hold Charles Darwin responsible for pounding the last nail into His coffin. Such a harsh indictment seems somewhat premature given the contemporary crisis of Darwinism. There is little doubt, however, that Darwin's bleak and disenchanted vision helped to leach the last residues of religious space and time from the American mind, leaving *homo Americanus* unfit to survive in competition with other peoples still moved by the religious spirit of in-group solidarity. As we shall see, Darwinism was very much a product of the Anglo-American mind.

---

53 Milbank, "Geopolitical Theology," 70-71.

54 Catherine Pickstock, "Duns Scotus: His Historical and Contemporary Significance," (2005) 21(4) *Modern Theology* 543, at 548. Newton was no atheist; he remained convinced that the laws of nature had been promulgated by God the Creator. Both Newtonian science and Anglican theology were premised on the belief that "the universe of an infinite Being ought to be organized according to an equally infinite geometry." However remote He may have become, Newton still conceded God a place in His Heaven. See, Baker, "Crisis in Darwinism," 186

Darwinism and Divinity

For most of its history, the Darwinian theory of natural selection steeped in an ontology of power and violence was far removed from Christian visions of divine plenitude. All the more reason, therefore, for one to ponder the intellectual genealogy of Darwinism, a scientific research tradition directly descended from the medieval philosophical and theological movements sponsored by the papal monarchy. The "heresy" of scholastic rationalism did not flatten the earth in one fell swoop but it did launch secular humanism on an evolutionary path that eventually led tough-minded sociobiologists and pragmatic philosophers to equate the good with the survival of the fittest. English intellectual developments derived from the ostensibly Christian metaphysics pioneered by Duns Scotus profoundly influenced Darwin as he set out to explain the history of life. Indeed, Darwin's *Origin of the Species* presupposed a secularized tradition of natural theology that already had produced both Newtonian physics and the "dismal science" of economics.

Darwin conceived his theory of natural selection "as an analogue for Newton's universal law of gravity: selection pressure checks the inherent tendency of species to vary, just as gravity checks the inherent tendency of planets to wander off in a straight line." Before Darwin, few imagined that biology could be recreated on the model of Newtonian physics: "The study of life seemed certainly to be the single realm of the universe where God chose to act not through discernible and timeless laws but directly and unpredictably." Adam Smith's analysis of the "invisible hand" in political economy guided Darwin in his search for the "gravitational" force that controlled biological variation. The Scottish philosopher demonstrated that the selection of economic measures favorable to the population need not be left to a monarch: "individual agents working for the greatest possible private gain would in time balance each other out, so that the entire society would benefit." Thomas Malthus was equally influential in the intellectual genesis of Darwinism, showing that populations grow exponentially while their food supplies increase only arithmetically. In the competitive "struggle for existence," the "invisible hand" of natural selection ensures that beneficial variations are preserved in nature by organisms that "out-eat, and consequently...out-survive, and finally out-reproduce" their contemporaries.

But Darwin's natural selector "is still a kind of supernatural thing, a transcendental empty space" serving to fill the God-shaped hole in a natural world red in tooth and claw.[55] There might well be a "plan of creation" in Darwin's cosmology but it demands that all living creatures engage in an endless, ruthless, bloody, and destructive struggle to the death. Christians might agree that, in this fallen world, death, destruction, and decay await all. Darwin did not explicitly reject orthodox Christian narratives of the Fall and the Resurrection; instead, he radically reinterpreted the meaning of good and evil. Simply put, the lesson that orthodox Darwinists draw from the Fall is this: survival is everything. In the Darwinian imagination, Eden was a "paradise...because its population is in equilibrium and never reaches the carrying capacity of the land." In the fallen world, God no longer provides "the unlimited resources of a paradise and men must now contend with the selection pressures" produced when population exceeds carrying capacity.[56] To the orthodox Christian, Darwinism resembles a *natural (a)theology*. God is removed from the world to be replaced by "a force that cannot act otherwise than by constant destruction and starvation." In enabling progress towards complexity, "selection serves as a *biological* coronation of warfare." Bloody and destructive as the process may be, Darwin and his followers claim to discern "endless forms of beauty" in the evolution of higher forms of life.[57]

Certainly, in Fausette's Darwinian interpretation of the Book of Genesis, life is a *given*, not a *gift* as it is for the orthodox Christian. Life is not "suspended" from the Creator; it does not participate in God. Life is "unhooked" from the transcendent.[58] Creation has been flattened so that God is present only in the guise of the natural force that favors the genetic interests of human groups whose religion "contains a discipline for making learned behavior intuitive." Man is brought, psychologically at least, into the presence of God when he passes on survival skills, in and through both his genes and his ethnocultures, to successive generations. To fail the survivability test damns a race to extinction. After the Fall, Fausette tells us, successful adaptation could no longer depend on instinct. Adam was compelled to choose between good and evil, a choice governed by the felicific calculus of secular utility.[59] Radical Orthodoxy, on the other hand, regards the "notion that there is such a choice" as a fiction "invented by Adam at the Fall."[60]

---

55 *Ibid.*, 183, 188, 190-193.

56 Fausette, "Book of Genesis," 49.

57 Baker, "Crisis in Darwinism," 194-195.

58 Smith, *Introducing Radical Orthodoxy*, 87-89.

59 Fausette, "Book of Genesis," 45.

60 Milbank, *Being Reconciled*, 8.

In other words, Adam's fatal fantasy identified freedom with "a finite autonomy of the will." Radical Orthodoxy condemns the idea of an absolutely free choice between good and evil for two reasons, each grounded in biblical and patristic authority. First, if Creation is good, evil cannot be "lodged in any reality, power or being whatsoever." Evil is not *caused* by freedom; indeed, according to Augustine's privation theory of the good, evil "is radically without cause." Second, because freedom causes only the Good, the will is not autonomous.[61] Evil is the perversion, the absence, the privation, of the good. Evil has no positive existence. Prey to all the weaknesses of the flesh that impair our will to receive the grace of God, Adam was guilty of self-idolatry. All of us share in Adam's original sin when we "refuse the offer of grace and remain content with [our] deficient inheritance."[62] From an orthodox Christian perspective, Adam's assertion of autonomy foreshadows the hubris of modern secular humanism.

As we have seen, by the seventeenth century, God had retreated so far into his heaven that Hobbes imagined man's natural state as a war of each against all. In the absence of an absolute sovereign power, life would be brutish, nasty, and short; an ontology of power and violence that Darwin extended to the whole of creation. It now seems clear, however, that the intellectual hegemony of Darwin's theory of natural selection has fallen into doubt. Postmodernists have grown old exposing Christianity as an ungrounded metanarrative. It is ironic, then, that orthodox Darwinism may be less congruent with current developments in evolutionary theory than the incarnational *mythos* of orthodox Christianity.

Darwin identified natural selection as the "*necessarily* unequivocal force driving all speciation." It is "the generation by generation selection of organisms" in a process of constant gradual change that explains the emergence of new species. It seems, however, that biological "variation is *not* a constant, but comes and goes for unknown reasons and in largely unpredictable ways." *Selection might not explain everything, after all.* It is not just the missing fossil records of intermediate species that casts doubt on orthodox Darwinism. Important biological research now emphasizes the role of chance and experimentation, or some form of genetic drift, in accounting for much of the real change in species. A layman might ask: Was the wrinkly spreader mutation of *Pseudomonas fluorescens* already armed with the capacity to produce adhesive polymers? One might also wonder how group or individual selection can account for the phenomenon of vision? "Selection cannot make an eye see, but only give the reproductive

---

61 *Ibid.*, 17, 8.
62 *Ibid.*, 3, 6-10.

edge to an organism with better vision." The Darwinian metanarrative is helpful in understanding the microevolutionary development or *descent* of already existing species; it "is totally inadequate to indicate the *origin* of those species." In the struggle to explain that macroevolutionary process, the theory of natural selection faces serious competition.[63]

We can discern the outlines of an alternative narrative of evolutionary processes, one freed from the metaphysics of secular modernism. Orthodox Darwinism pictured evolution as a site where two or more competitors circulate around a static core set of resources. But the universe is in flux; the criteria for adaptive advantage are always in motion. Moreover, "individual organisms are not at one another's throats, competing for their own survival at any cost." They are, instead "irreducibly interdependent," surviving "by cooperation, by expenditure and intake." As selfish WS bacteria discover, maximizing the intake while minimizing the expenditure of energy "can only lead to isolation, and doom an organism to dilapidate and, finally, to die with a wealth of dormant energy."[64]

Energy, it seems, is the key to evolution. Every localized ecosystem is "a pocket of energy self-organized at the edge of chaos" and evolution is a process that circulates "energy among its various organisms." Everywhere in the universe, "energy is constantly circulating, forming pockets of intensities that just as quickly dissipate and move on." Natural systems as various as hurricanes, boiling water, and intracellular arrangements appear to organize themselves spontaneously into recognizable patterns "without any 'invisible hand' (whether that of a divine designer or a natural selector) reaching in from the outside." This is not unlike the orthodox Christian notion that we are pulled toward "the form of the divine beauty of which our soul has some recollection." Modern evolutionary theory finds another distant echo in Milbank's cryptic observation that "the mind's kinship to beauty" can be conceived "as the capacity of a particularly strong 'intensity' to become the fulcrum for events."[65] The question remains: Is it possible to bridge the gulf separating secular truth from the beauty and goodness of the divine?

---

63 Baker, "Crisis in Darwinism," 195-196, 198.

64 Ibid., 207-208.

65 Ibid., 207-208; Milbank, *Theology*, 434.

The Pacifist Theology of Anti-Racism

A history of life that focuses on the evolution of interdependent ecosystems can be accommodated within the incarnational *mythos* of orthodox Christianity. Indeed, a former Milbank student, Anthony Baker, believes that the new emphasis on self-organization in evolutionary theory restores a trinitarian depth to being. It seems that "an ecosystem can be guided intrinsically, drawn by a 'desire' to self-organize such that energy can be circulated." Complex systems theory, therefore, posits "a directionality that excludes directedness" very much like the triune relationship between each person of the Godhead: "the intermingling dance of Persons and energies in the eternal commerce of gifts within God." This is reminiscent of the evolution of the *ecclesia* as a complex network of localized ecosystems. Early Christians circulated wealth and property within local churches, engaging in a wide range of altruistic activities unknown to their pagan neighbours. They were, in reality, localized cells of a developing system, "perched contingently at the edge of chaos, stabilized by the constant exchange of energy within a universe otherwise tending toward destruction."[66] Races and ethnic groups, too, can be conceived as self-organizing pockets of energy participating, however imperfectly, in the divine plenitude of creation. Radical Orthodoxy remains strangely reluctant to recognize that possibility. The specter of race weighs like an incubus on the academic mind, conjuring up nightmare visions of a resurgent fascism.

At the same time, of course, sociobiologists put on a different pair of blinders in claiming that the truth claims of theology extend beyond the purview of scientific research. But sociobiology cannot escape at least one vitally important theological puzzle. A theory of group selection can read the Old Testament plausibly as a survival manual; it has more difficulty explaining Christ's preference for "the ones most *unfit* to survive in a world controlled by wealth and strength."[67] Orthodox Darwinism predicts that a religion securing the material well-being and reproductive success of its members will thrive. Orthodox Christianity, by contrast, learned long ago that "it is easier for a camel to pass through the eye of a needle than for a rich man to enter into the kingdom of heaven."[68]

The Church came into being bearing "witness to a good that is utterly divorced from stories of progress or complexity."[69] But the orthodox theol-

---

66   *Ibid.*, 209.

67   *Ibid.*, 209-210, 205; Wilson, *Darwin's Cathedral.*

68   *Matthew* 19:24.

69   Baker, "Crisis in Darwinism," 205-206.

ogy of incarnation cannot remain aloof from the history of life. Indeed, as we have seen, orthodox Christianity is premised on the organismic character of the Church. Within the orthodox *mythos*, believers are guided ceaselessly toward the ecclesiastical Body of Christ by the Holy Spirit. It is through self-organizing pockets of biocultural energy that the spirit becomes manifest in the here and now. The church is not a given; nor does it exist somewhere beyond space and time. It arrives endlessly in and through the bodies and souls of the faithful even as it passes away. The infinite of the divine *Logos* becomes incarnate in the biological finitude of particular human cultures.[70]

Here in the *saeculum*, of course, churches may drift away from God, becoming "objectified as mere human sovereignty." But, however deformed their desires, men are still drawn towards a superabundant good that, unlike gold, cannot be hoarded by individuals or monopolized by an institution. Like the sunlight showering the world with life-giving energy, grace must be received in common.[71] "Christ Himself becomes revealed as truth not *in* a community, but *as* a community."[72] Does it follow that the divine incarnates itself as a "local community" through the biocultural medium of race and ethnicity? Does the Gospel present the Jews as the first of many sacramental "local communities" to emerge in the secular history of the *ecclesia*? Can other peoples, the Anglo-Saxons in particular, choose or be chosen to receive the saving grace of God?

Radical Orthodoxy simply denies when it does not avoid the biocultural realities of race. Indeed, Baker gives Christians licence to dodge the racial issue at will by declaring that "we are free to believe *more* in the creed than in the modern scientific story of reality."[73] His affirmation of faith is orthodox enough, but begs the question: Who, exactly, are *we*? If race and ethnicity are observable biocultural phenomena, why should WASPs refuse that God-given gift? Nor is it clear why WASP theologians should remain wilfully blind to clear evidence that inter-ethnic competition is deeply implicated in the continuing contest between science and Christianity. One notices, first of all, that the debate has been conducted, first and foremost, in the Anglo-Saxon countries.[74] It appears as well that

70 Phillips, *Orthodox Christianity*, 65.

71 Milbank, *Being Reconciled*, 105.

72 John Zizioulas, quoted in Frederick Christian Bauerschmidt, "The Theological Sublime," in *Radical Orthodoxy*, 212.

73 Baker, "Crisis in Darwinism," 206.

74 The intellectual history of the Science versus Christianity debate is replete with Anglo-Saxon names; notable individual contributions aside, other ethnicities figure in the story mainly as onlookers and also-rans, see, eg, David J Depew and Bruce H Weber, *Darwinism*

Jewish intellectuals are far more likely to display ethnocentric attitudes than thoroughly deracinated WASP scholars. But both groups are equally likely to deny the reality of racial differences. There are those who wonder whether Jewish ethnic interests are served when WASPs accept the conventional wisdom that race is nothing more than a social construct. It is no accident that efforts by "secular humanists" to fold "anti-racism" into the "scientific story of reality" told by academe, the media, and government have been crucial to the social construction of the deracinated WASP in twentieth-century America. Surely, one is entitled to ask: *Cui bono?*[75]

The WASPs who populate the ranks of Radical Orthodoxy are loath to raise such issues. Milbank acknowledges that Christianity can "be adequately repeated in very diverse cultural settings, involving very different sets of cultural roles."[76] But one searches RO literature in vain for any discussion of Anglo-Saxon Christianity as a distinctive cultural adaptation worthy of recognition and support. RO scholars prefer to avert their eyes from the ethnoreligious roots of the Anglican Church. Rather than deal frankly with the evolutionary role of group selection in the history of the *ecclesia*, RO clings to a one-sided image of peace and harmony within the interdependent, self-organizing structures of localized ecosystems. Whether by design or by accident, this emphasis serves as an alibi for those disinclined to defend the biocultural interests of the descendants of the indigenous peoples of the British Isles.

RO obscures the ethnoreligious character of the orthodox Christian tradition prior to the Papal revolution. Milbank promotes instead a "liberal," Anglo-Catholic orthodoxy, a "generous, open-ended and all-inclusive" celebration of diversity. To that end, RO holds up the language and liturgy of the Latin Mass as "at once universal and particular." According to Catherine Pickstock, Catholic liturgical space incarnates the infinite divine "without suppressing regional difference." Approved "regional" differences most emphatically do not include European racial or ethnic identities. Milbank condemns the nation-state as "semi-racist, because it gathers around the notion of a people." In his view, the nation-state exists to "cream off" and "pile up...in the name of a people" a "pure power:

Evolving: Systems Dynamics and the Genealogy of Natural Selection (Cambridge, MA: MIT Press, 1996).

75   Vincent Sarich and Frank Miele, *Race: The Reality of Human Differences* (Boulder, CO: Westview Press, 2005), 89; Kevin MacDonald, *The Culture of Critique: An Evolutionary Analysis of Jewish Involvement in Twentieth-Century Intellectual and Political Movements* (Westport, CT: Praeger, 1998), 21-52.

76   Milbank, *Theology*, 422.

whose other name is evil." Milbank insists that the ethnonation must be submerged in an ecumenical vision of a world in which Christianity works with Judaism and Islam to serve the common good. RO is committed to social inclusion, a dangerous strategy as long as other faiths and peoples remain wedded to the ontology of power and violence.[77] As a high-minded Anglican, however, Milbank joins with his mentor, Rowan Williams, to forgive ethno-religious nepotism, but only when practiced by Jews or Muslims, Hindus or Buddhists, or, indeed, any other non-European people.

Milbank cuts no such slack for his co-ethnics, denouncing Tony Blair (of all people!) as a "racist" (of all things!) for floating the idea that "Britain should accept only 'skilled' immigrants and refugees who can increase the gross national product." An immigration policy that openly requires racial and ethnic compatibility with the English people would leave Milbank speechless, gasping in disbelief and horror. The merest hint that England belongs to the English deeply offends "the Christian principles of polity." Governments, he believes, should treat people not as "abstractions" but as they appear in "micro-social bodies" such as regions, local cultures, and religious bodies, all forming part of "the universal human cosmopolis." Milbank dreams of a "shared overarching global polity" in which "the North" will extend "benignly paternalist assistance" to "the South." His utopian ideal demands "the maximum possible dispersal and deflection of human power," thereby rendering European ethnonations powerless to preserve their homelands. Milbank worries that "We will not be able peaceably to accommodate Islam in Europe unless we treat Islam as a 'political' body rather than just a mass of individual believers." It never occurs to the good professor that Islamic colonization of England need not, indeed should not, be tolerated.[78]

Bloodless Theology and Unfaithful Science

RO theologians are WASPs whose disapproval of conflict and violence receives its most impassioned expression in a visceral distaste for in-group altruism—especially, if not exclusively, when practiced by their

---

77 See, Milbank, *Theology*, xxii-xxiii; John Milbank, "The Last of the Last: Theology, Authority, and Democracy," *Telos* 123 (Spring 2002), 18; Catherine Pickstock, "Liturgy and Modernity," *Telos* 113 (Fall 1998), 35; John Milbank, "Sovereignty, Empire, Capital, and Terror," *Telos* (Fall 2001), 147.

78 John Milbank, "Liberality versus Liberalism," *Telos* 134 (Spring 2006), 9-10; *id.*, "Sovereignty, Capital, Terror," 148, 158.

co-ethnics. RO recognizes that, in the nature of things, the eucharist must be performed in "local communities," but only on condition that "each local embodiment of the body of Christ" collapses spatial and temporal distinctions into "the universal *Catholica*." Within "the complex space of the body of Christ, attachment to the local" must not become "a fascist nostalgia for *gemeinschaft* in the face of globalisation."[79] Note that the German word for "community" is now a code word for fascism in liberal circles. Any suggestion that the *ecclesia* is or ought to be conceived as a *Volksgemeinschaft* triggers an automatic *reductio ad Hitlerum* in the minds of academic theologians. But the Church in Anglo-Saxon England mixed the Christian faith with the blood of a Germanic people. Such ethnoreligious communities were the norm in European Christendom.

Fr Andrew Phillips, an Orthodox Christian priest in England, likens the early medieval churches of Western Europe to "sovereign States joined together in a confederation or family of Faith."[80] From the beginning, the orthodox Christian *ecclesia* incarnated the ideal of universal nationalism. The evangelical mission of the church is to infuse the Holy Spirit into the blood of each and every *Volk*. At best, the "adaptive utilitarianism" advocated by secularist sociobiologists such as Frank Salter is but a pale, atheistic reflection of the saving faith that pulled the Angelcynn toward nationhood. The Western church ceased to be an extended family of ethnonations, however, when the papal monarchy became the prototype of the modern sovereign state. In the nature of things, the *Kirchenstaat* was bound to sacrifice the ethnic genetic interests of its subjects in every nation whenever they were perceived to conflict with the service of its own enhanced growth and vitality.[81] Milbank observes that the ecclesiastical hierarchy became a pyramid in which "clerical control over the laity increased," administration became more centralized and remote, and theology became the province of academic specialists. Of course, a hierarchy had existed in the Old English Church too, but "there was no clericalism; the average parish priest was a villager who was married, he was a family man" in a homely church to which everyone belonged and in which everyone participated. Orthodox Christianity united clergy and people in a

79   Cavanaugh, *Theopolitical Imagination*, 98-99.

80   Phillips, *Orthodox Christianity*, 277.

81   Frank Salter does not consider whether churches could provide a better vehicle for the defence of ethnic genetic interests than the State. He recognizes that states posing as nations sometimes "abrogate their tribal promise." But citizens faced with such a betrayal have only one option: namely, "to reform or tear down their states and build new ones whose ethnic composition and constitution better serve their genetic survival." Salter, *On Genetic Interests*, 317.

Commonwealth of Faith; the church was a way of life practiced in "a simple, hallowed England" which remains "this home of homes, this wooden-steepled land, rich in old beauty" for millions today. Unfortunately such reverence for the spirit of Old England is altogether absent from the work of RO scholars.[82]

One might think that theologians seeking to restore Christian orthodoxy would venerate "the England of the English saints" as an Anglo-Saxon Holy Land. They might even call for an Anglo-Saxon Law of Return restricting immigration to persons whose ancestors sprang from the British Isles.[83] But RO rejects a "retrograde" Anglo-Saxon Christian patriotism in favor of a rationalist theology designed to leach out the residual ethnoreligious character of Anglicanism. RO is thus trapped inside a contradiction. On the one hand, Milbank dismisses popular neo-orthodoxy, labelling it mere "fideism;" on the other, he wants to recover the depth of being that has been flattened under the weight of late medieval theology.

Unfortunately Radical Orthodoxy brings to the task of restoration little more than an arid intellectualism. RO sheds no tears for the passing of Old England; it regrets far more the loss of "the common Hellenistic legacy of Aristotle fused with neo-Platonism, and blended with allegorical readings of the Hebrew Bible, which it shared with Islam, Judaism, and Byzantium." Eschewing the parochial spirit of the Old English Church, Milbank embraces "the one final universal truth" of Catholic Christianity. Milbank locks up the theology of incarnation in the liturgical life of the church, safely sequestered from the biology of between-group selection. [84] Securely ensconced in the ivory tower, RO theologians remain as remote from the people as their scholastic forbears. Catholic pacifism prevails over patriotic populism, multiracial empire over the ethnonation, ecology over group selection, and mind over heart. RO recoils from any suggestion that the army of Christ might have to march yet again into battle in defence of their kith and kin, or that a terrible beauty will shine through the self-sacrificial heroism of those who fight.

Baker appropriates the evolutionary dynamics of complex systems to serve a theology of pacifism. His case relies heavily upon Depew and Weber's *Darwinism Evolving* but fails to heed the cautionary note sounded in the preface to the paperback edition of that monumental text. There the authors express regret at not having said loudly enough "that ecological systems cannot form and behave the way they do without a good deal

---

82   Milbank, *Being Reconciled*, 111; Phillips, *Orthodox Christianity*, 276-277, 27.

83   Phillips, *Orthodox Christianity*, 27.

84   Milbank, "Theology, Authority, and Democracy" 16; id., *Theology*, xxiii.

of (potentially conflicting) natural selection working both on individual organisms and on groups." They warn against any suggestion that ecological systems "run in sublime indifference to processes in which organisms and groups...play decisive roles."[85] If organisms themselves are "informed and integrated ecological systems," it follows that ecological communities *cannot* be as coherent as organisms. In the course of their struggle to survive, individual organisms and groups both become "key nodal points" in the self-organization of the system as a whole. Perched on the edge of chaos, even churches must demonstrate their inclusive fitness. Unfortunately, in his encounter with evolutionary theory Baker has not taken to heart Radical Orthodoxy's recognition that "our knowledge of God...is *always and only* given through a shift in our understanding of this world."[86] Sad to say, the most sustained reflection thus far on the relationship between theology and the crisis in Darwinism steers clear of the micro-evolutionary role of group selection in ecclesiastical history.

Orthodox Christians should not be shocked to discover that the mystery of the Holy Spirit appears to have been encrypted in the human genome, waxing and waning in and through the bioculture of every racial and ethnic group receptive to its call. One can only pray for a resurrection of the Anglo-Saxon *ecclesia* as a self-organizing network of local communities. Every parish church will become a localized pocket of intensity, allowing genes and culture to co-evolve into distinctive languages, liturgies, and ways of life. God became incarnate not as a generic human being but as a Judean; the ecclesiastical Body of Christ also "irradiated" the distinctively Anglo-Saxon bioculture of medieval England. It is therefore within the *ecclesia* that the Anglo-Saxon *Volksgeist* has its highest expression.[87] Conversely, outside and apart from the Old Faith, contemporary WASPs deviate through ignorance and weakness ever further from their appointed end. However conventional such a warning may once have been, few today pay it any heed. But, if religion is known to play a vital part in the relative fitness of population groups, why should WASPs be required to embrace a bloodless theology that sacrifices their biocultural interests to those of rival population groups? Anglo-Saxon Christians are in competition with other organismic religious communities, some of which, Jews and Muslims most notably, are locked in perpetual conflict

---

85   Depew and Weber, *Darwinism Evolving*, viii.

86   John Milbank, "Foreword" in Smith, *Introducing Radical Orthodoxy*, 13.

87   Phillips, *Orthodox Christianity*, 63; see also, Peter J Richerson and Robert Boyd, *Not By Genes Alone: How Culture Transformed Human Evolution* (Chicago: University of Chicago Press, 2006).

with the church. Unilateral moral disarmament transformed Anglo-Saxon Protestantism into a dying faith. RO's dogmatic pacifism will not reverse that trend.

Academic sociobiology and theology are united in indifference to the ethnopathology that afflicts WASPs. Theologians fear the intense pockets of energy that might emerge from the self-organizing tendencies of an Anglo-Saxon ethnonation. Sociobiologists are simply nonplussed by the spectacle of a religious people whose individual affluence masks their collective demoralization. Well before it was transplanted to America, Anglicanism and its dissenting offshoots were wedded to the secularized theologies of sovereignty and property. With the rise of America to world power, WASP churches became handmaidens to both the state and the corporate sector. While the Anglican Church struggles to escape "its Anglo-Saxon captivity,"[88] emasculated WASPs actively collaborate with a managerial regime hostile or indifferent to the future of the Anglo-Saxon race. In the late twentieth century Anglo-Saxon Anglophobia brought *homo Americanus* to his knees. Anglo-Saxon patriots everywhere know in their hearts that the American Adam betrayed God and his Anglcynn fore-fathers; he sold his soul to Caesar and Mammon for the proverbial mess of pottage.

Errands in the Wilderness

Even a thumbnail sketch of early American history brings theology face-to-face with sociobiology. On the American frontier, creation was unhooked from the Creator; the orthodox Christian "view of the necessary goodness of the universe became a compartmentalized creed that did not withstand the subversion of experience." Peace and harmony might reign in heaven but earth remained subject to the ontology of power and conflict. God often seemed a remote presence to colonists fighting desperately to clear an untamed wilderness peopled by bloodthirsty savages. Nature "in its purest and therefore most dangerous state was the central enemy whose defeat was usually thought to be essential to godliness, prosperity, and progress." For the Puritans, in particular, "the business of the Christian was relentless war against the forces of evil."[89] In such circum-

88 Kevin Ward, *A History of Global Anglicanism* (Cambridge: Cambridge University Press, 2006), chapter 15, "The Anglican Communion: Escaping the Anglo-Saxon Captivity of the Church?"

89 Loren Baritz, *City on a Hill: A History of Ideas and Myths in America* (New York: John Wiley, 1964), 100, 6.

stances, English settlers established village communities allied together on one side of the bright boundary separating them from Indian tribes with whom they were locked in often bloody, life-or-death conflict.

Military metaphors loomed large in the language of the colonists. Puritan preachers cast themselves as "the special intelligence branch of the Christian armies" waging "the eternal war with Satan." Their job was "to persuade their congregations to arm in time, to deploy effectively, and to close ranks."[90] Other colonies differed substantially from the Puritans in their manner of praying, as well as in the ways they worked and fought. But, whatever the regional differences in colonial folkways, they all bear a strong resemblance to what twentieth-century military writers call "mission-oriented warfare."

The first point of comparison relates to the form taken by orders in mission-oriented warfare. "A mission-type order tells the subordinate commander *what* his superior wants to have accomplished. It leaves *how* to accomplish it up to the subordinate." The superior does not prescribe in detail the steps the subordinate *must* take to achieve the objective. Rather the relationship between the two is contractual: "the subordinate agrees to make his actions support the mission in return for wide-ranging freedom in selecting the means." Mission-oriented warfare involves a decentralized pattern of command and control. Commanders must be guided by the reconnaissance undertaken by forward units not by preconceived plans. Operations are pulled by reconnaissance rather than pushed by the high command. All of these features were incorporated into the social structures and cultural practices of the English colonies, often as a consequence of bitter experience with more rigid forms of organization.[91]

English colonists were men and women on a mission, bound to carry out the will of God. The organized religious interest behind the Massachusetts Bay colony is obvious enough, but it was no less important in Virginia. Progressive historians once portrayed the Virginia settlement as "a mercantile adventure, a purely business proposition." Perry Miller led a revisionist assault on that view, showing that the Virginia Company, too, exhibited "a set of principles for guiding not a mercantile investment but a medieval pilgrimage." The principal concern in the literature of that enterprise "is neither the rate of interest nor the discovery of gold, but the will of God." The English migration to Virginia was undertaken as an

---

90 Ibid., 6.

91 Compare William S Lind, *Maneuver Warfare Handbook* (Boulder, CO: Westview, 1985), 9-24, with Douglas Edward Leach, *Flintlock and Tomahawk: New England in King Phillip's War* (New York: WW Norton, 1966).

explicit covenant with God under which both God and man were bound to respect certain reciprocal obligations. There was no conflict between commerce and Christian mission: "as they go forth to trade and colonize, Christians automatically carry the Gospel with them, and when mankind has been once more united by the merchants, it can be made one in profession by the preachers."[92]

Even in its role as a commercial enterprise, the Virginia Company soon abandoned the "command-push" form of organization for a "recon-pull" approach. At first, the Company was run from London by means of an autocratic military governor. When that centralized system of command and control failed to deliver profits, the colony was granted a local Assembly "not to defend the rights of man, but…in order that men on the spot might find out and execute those measures that would best tend to their own prosperity." Before long, "in spite of every restraint, tobacco was planted" because the "weed alone offered any return" to planters unable to turn a profit by adhering to the Company's original plan.[93] Waging war to push back Indians and domesticate the forest rendered traditional hierarchies obsolete, along with the functional differentiation between those who prayed, those who fought, and those who worked. Every English settler was expected to pray, to fight, and to work, for himself and for his community, as circumstances required. Tradition-directed patterns of character formation associated with feudalism gave way to a novel, inner-directed character type better adapted to the challenges of between-group competition faced by pioneering settlers in a new land.[94]

The centralized and deeply entrenched ecclesiastical and political hierarchies of the Old World were of little relevance in the New. Pursuing their divinely-ordained errands in the wilderness, English colonists left behind the old order of the *ecclesia* with its elaborate distribution of ranks, honours, and roles. Most rejected the Church of England as hopelessly corrupt. Until well into the nineteenth century, the church in America was local and homogeneous, unconsciously replicating the circumstances of Anglo-Saxon England. In both cases, the church aspired to, and partially realized, "a real harmony of differentiated persons by blending together a diversity of characters and roles" whose affinity manifested the incarnate Body of Christ.[95] Both Anglicans and dissenters in England retained "a

---

92 Miller, *Errand*, 100-101, 119, 117.

93 Ibid., 135.

94 David Riesman, *The Lonely Crowd: A Study of the Changing American Character* (New Haven: Yale University Press, 1961).

95 Milbank, *Being Reconciled*, 20.

notion of Church and nation," but in the early American republic, one
British minister remarked, "even Anglicans speak only of village and congregation." Typically, colonial towns were "ethically, religiously, and preferably ethnically one people." If "significant ethical or religious differences
developed between divergent groups," the only solution was separation.
"Harmony required homogeneity."[96] Decentralization was the norm; colonial society was permanently in flux and energy flowed rapidly towards
pockets of intense activity concentrated in local communities, energy
flows that just as quickly ebbed or moved onward. The patterns governing
the circulation of energy were shaped by pressures emerging from racial
conflicts over land and resources. It was "the existence of the Indians on
the frontier" that slowed "the advance westwards of the settlements" and
compelled "the backwoodsman to keep in touch with his countrymen in
the rear."[97]

The mission-oriented practice of granting religious freedom to local
communities did not, of course, emerge spontaneously from the American
forest. Well before the Mayflower set sail, religion in Europe had changed
its nature. In the late Renaissance, Europeans began to conceive *religio*
as a universal impulse planted in the heart of every individual. As such,
the idea of religion was detached from the liturgical space of the *ecclesia*
and relocated into the private, interior domain of individual conscience.
Another change, already well-advanced by the early seventeenth century,
was "toward religion as a system of beliefs. Religion moves from a virtue
to a set of propositions." Claims for religious liberty now followed from
"the construal of Christianity as a set of demonstrable moral truths, rather
than theological claims and practices which take a particular social form
called the Church." Orthodox Christianity had endowed "certain bodily
practices within the Body of Christ" with sacramental significance. But
the Protestant Reformation confined religion "to the realm of the 'soul'"
while the body was "handed over to the state." Secular states recognized
freedom of conscience but once the people embraced a form of religion,
the sovereign was free to "forbid any public dispute over religious matters
to break out and thereby threaten his authority."[98] Such precedents guided
public policy in the English colonies.

96   Barry Alan Shain, *The Myth of American Individualism: The Protestant Origins of American
     Political Thought* (Princeton, NJ: Princeton University Press, 1994), 52, 66-67.

97   Baker, "Crisis in Darwinism," 207; Madison Grant, *Conquest of a Continent*, (York, SC:
     Liberty Bell, 157.

98   Cavanaugh, *Theopolitical Imagination*, 33-34.

One must be wary of the myth of American individualism. It would be "a sin against history" to ascribe the English colonization of America to "an assertion of individualism" while "leaving out of account the cosmology of the colonists." Seventeenth century English colonists lived in "a world where every action found its rationale, not in politics or economics, but in religion." Colonial religious life was decentralized and "continued along largely local communal lines." Like small units in mission-oriented warfare, every community could find its own way to serve the will of God but only if its members were disciplined enough to cooperate in pursuit of a shared objective. Each community "sought to shape, in ethically intrusive ways the 'souls' of [its] residents;" the "good life demanded local corporate closure regarding essential ethical and religious issues, often along ethnic lines." Every village church became a "localized pocket of energy," the hub of a micro-ecosystem in which individuals were expected to restrain the demands of the self. The adult white male enjoyed the status of "a full citizen not because he was a rights-bearing individual human being… but because he was a landed head of household." As such, he enjoyed a substantial measure of personal liberty. That freedom was not to be construed as the liberty to do evil or detriment, however, even to himself. A locally "prescribed form of life" defined the "socially approved and communally directed (and, more indirectly, divinely commanded) ethical uses to be made of choice by the individual." Every community "was made up of a series of covenants, ascending from the basic and essential covenant between a man and God, to the family, church, and state." It was axiomatic that "an uncovenanted or otherwise exotic individual would be a threat to the entire structure."[99]

Covenant theology was most highly developed in New England. Religious life was based upon "the absolute theoretical autonomy of local congregations." But authority within each congregation was lodged, at first, in those who could offer testimony in public to their saving experience of faith. In the Puritan cosmos, the distance between God and man was infinite: His will was utterly inscrutable. Living a godly life provided no guarantee of salvation; the reward of eternal life came not through good works but through an unpredictable and essentially arbitrary "condescension on God's part which he hath been pleased to express by way of Covenant." As a practical matter, of course, the invisible church of the elect must be represented by visible saints. In a fallen world, the visible church was charged with the governance not only of large numbers of

---

99 Miller, *Errand*, 114; Shain, *Myth of American Individualism*, 65, 106, 98, 119; Baritz, *City on a Hill*, 19.

visibly wicked persons but also of the visibly good who had been denied the experience of saving grace. Unlike the Church of England, Puritan congregationalism "wholly neglected the church's evangelical mission to perishing sinners outside the families of its members." Instead, Puritan elders put pressure on civil authorities to compel the unregenerate multitude to attend church services.[100]

Puritan preaching was addressed more to saints than to sinners. But, over time, as fewer and fewer people could testify to an authentic saving experience, the visible church was in danger of dying out. The solution was a "halfway covenant" that extended full membership in the church to the children of the visible elect and then to their children's children, whether or not they had been saved. The half-way covenant was "a narrow tribal way of recruiting saints" that, according to some historians, reflected a decline in Puritan piety.[101] Sociobiologists might dispute that interpretation. Successive generations of godly New Englanders appear to have pursued their callings with customary diligence, seeing in their worldly success a sign that they had been touched by the finger of God. Thus was the religion *of* secular utility practiced among those for whom work was a form of heartfelt piety.

Regional Cultures on the Racial Frontier

The large landowners of Virginia were considerably more ambivalent in their attitudes to work. They were more apt to favor the aristocratic ethos of those who fight even though most "worked harder than they cared to admit." Their Anglican religious folkways emphasized a "devotional-liturgical style" of worship adapted to the needs of a hierarchical, slave-holding society. Although many of the Chesapeake planter families "were men and women of deep piety," Virginian folkways were vulnerable to the levelling impact of secular reason. Nominally, the Anglican Church was established in Virginia but there was little support for the creation of a colonial episcopacy; authority rested with local vestries made up of large landowners. In the absence of a bishop, the ritual forms of the church were substantially impaired; not even church buildings could be consecrated. The definition of sacred space was further confused when many Virginians insisted on transferring rites of passage from the church

---

100 Baritz, *City on a Hill*, 35; Edmund S Morgan, "The Halfway Covenant," in Cushing Strout, *Intellectual History in America: Contemporary Essays on Puritanism, the Enlightenment, & Romanticism* (New York: Harper & Row, 1968), 21-34.

101 Morgan, "Halfway Covenant," 33-34.

to the home; "specifically Christian ceremonies" came "to be closely surrounded, and even overshadowed, by social rituals and forms of celebration that persons in the Anglo-Virginian tradition would have defined (if
forced to distinguish) as secular rather than religious."[102]

The origins of the distinctive regional cultures of British America
"were highly complex, involving differences of British region, religion,
rank, and generation, as well as of the American environment, and the
process of migration."[103] Patterns of settlement reproduced in America
the cultural and political divisions that had existed previously in England.
Once across the Atlantic, British colonists settled in the areas most like
the part of England which they had left, among other people sharing the
same regional culture. Those transplanted regional cultures often generated substantial friction when they rubbed up against each other; it
was never a foregone conclusion that they would work together to build
a new nation. On the other hand, despite their differences, all colonial
Englishmen shared a common language, political unity, and Protestant
religion. They were bound together also by the expanding commercial
"empire of goods" that provided a solid material foundation for English
settlements in the New World.[104] Although each regional culture developed distinctive patterns of child-rearing and character development,
they were alike in producing numerous individuals capable of seizing the
opportunities offered by the emergent system of political economy driving colonial development.

Individuals and groups alike were locked in a competitive struggle to
conquer the American continent. The colonial system of political economy manifested, with a vengeance, the ontology of power and conflict.
"The fear of the forest led to a virtual apotheosis of the farmer who would
destroy the enemy and give birth to the garden." A *mythos* emerged in
which the American farmer became "the hero who was peculiarly blessed
in his land;" the farmer was to be "the savior of the nation that was to be
savior of the world." But he was no prince of peace. Madison Grant, never
one to denigrate the achievements of the Nordic race, saw the local communities of New Englanders and Virginians who leapfrogged across the
continent as a marauding army: "Probably no more destructive human

102 Fischer, *Albion's Seed*, 332-334; Rhys Isaac, *The Transformation of Virginia, 1740-1790*
    (Chapel Hill, NC: University of North Carolina Press, 1982), 68-70.

103 Fischer, *Albion's Seed*, 788.

104 TH Breen, "An Empire of Goods: The Anglicanization of Colonial America, 1690-1776,"
    (1986) 25(4) *Journal of British Studies* 467.

being has ever appeared on the world stage than the American pioneer with his axe and his rifle."[105]

Pioneering communities pushed westward like a series of tornadoes touching down in localized fits of creative destruction. East Anglian Puritans, Virginian cavaliers from southern England, Quakers from the Midlands and Scotch-Irish from the borderlands between England and Scotland coalesced into independent storm cells pushing across mountain passes and pouring through gaps in Indian defences. As each rival English tribe encountered radically alien races, group selection reached an often terrifying pitch of intensity. The Indians on the bloody edge of the racial frontier and the more or less ubiquitous everyday presence of Negroes in settled areas—especially but not only in the South—made a profound impression on English colonials. They saw the Indians either as savages by contrast to their own civilized state or as heathens outside the Christian fold. Understood as savages, Indians were not seen as fundamentally different from the civilized English; they were merely at a lower stage in a process of development that the English themselves had undergone. As heathens, they remained stubbornly resistant to the Christian faith. As a result, English identity emerged more or less intact from encounters with the Indians.[106] Contact with Negroes, on the other hand, worked a profound change in the collective identity of Anglo-American settlers.

English experience with Negroes was a function of the trans-oceanic market for slave labor. British North America was a crucial node in the emerging commercial networks of the modern world-system. Most Negroes there were slaves; although a population of free Negroes did emerge, some of whom owned slaves of their own race. Free labor was hard to come by and very expensive in a country with abundant land available for the taking. The institution of slavery in the American colonies marked a radical departure from involuntary servitude as it was known either in classical antiquity or in Anglo-Saxon England. Ancient and medieval slavery had been a form of personal domination connecting master and slave by obligations carrying an element of reciprocity. But, in the New World, the "peculiar institution" transformed Negroes into fungible units of labor power. Negro slavery made a significant contribution to the primitive accumulation of capital driving the explosive growth of British commerce and industry. With the expansion of the slave trade, masters could dispose of Negro labor power as if it were a commodity

---

105 Baritz, City on a Hill, 101; Grant, Conquest, 221.

106 Winthrop D Jordan, White over Black: American Attitudes Toward the Negro, 1550-1812 (Chapel Hill, NC: University of North Carolina Press, 1968), 94-95.

like any other. Negroes became living tools whose value was set by their relative utility when put to work in fields, factories, mines, and manor houses throughout the New World. The institution of Negro slavery in America was a prototype of the "proletarianization" associated with the rise of capitalism in every Anglo-Saxon country.[107]

Uprooted from all over West Africa and thrown together helter-skelter in America, Negroes had little by way of a common culture that compelled recognition or respect from English colonists. On the contrary, the racial character of slavery magnified the degradation that most of the free settler population came to associate with the commodification of labor power. For most colonial Americans, the dignity of labor was synonymous with the sturdy independence of the yeoman farmer, the self-employed artisan, and the small businessman. Drawing the line between the formal freedom of the wage-earner and the bondage of a Negro slave was not always an easy matter. Eighteenth century common lawyers knew well that the distinction was often little more than a legal technicality. Scottish jurists affirmed that colliers who bound themselves contractually to labor for life in mines and salt works still remained free men in the eyes of the law.[108] Wearing a collar that bore the name of his owner and liable to sale together with the mine, such a "free" worker was hardly less debased than a pampered Negro house slave on a Virginian plantation. But, because the colliers were the original proprietors of the labor power that they sold to the mine owners in return for an agreed wage, at law they were, formally at least, free men. There were differences, of course. The colliers enjoyed a civil status denied to the Negro slave; they could marry and their condition of indentured servitude was not hereditary.

Such formalities were overlooked often enough by the masters of the many thousands of free-born Englishmen who became indentured servants in the American colonies. Indeed, their situation was not unlike Negro slavery in the colonial era. White indentured servants were often sold on the block as soon as they arrived in colonial America from Britain. Their new masters put them to hard labor on plantations and farms where they were poorly fed and clothed and harshly punished for any disobedience. Some "owners" whipped and branded servants who attempted to run away. They were even forbidden to marry without their master's

107 Jean Baudrillard, *The Mirror of Production* tr Mark Poster (St Louis, MO: Telos Press, 1975), 94-95.

108 David Brion Davis, *The Problem of Slavery in the Age of Revolution, 1770-1823* (Ithaca, NY: Cornell University Press, 1975), 490-491.

permission.[109] On the other hand, white indentured servants were free of the indelible stigma attached to the most remarkable visible feature of the Negro slave: his *color*.

The more importance colonists attached to the *blackness* of the Negro, the more significant became the *whiteness* of Protestant Englishmen. As one historian put it: "From time immemorial Englishmen had been born to a status, to a cultural role: now they were being born to an appearance, to a physical condition as well."[110] British colonists were shocked to the core by the appearance and the behavior of the Negro. It was only when they encountered the alien blackness of Negroes, whether slave or free, that English colonists discovered their own whiteness. But both Negro slaves and their colonial masters were enmeshed in an expanding commercial empire; both had their identity flattened, each forevermore reduced to the lowest common denominator of a racial phenotype. Fate decreed that *homo Americanus* was to be a white man. In the first "white man's country," age-old ethnic differences between English, Scotch-Irish, Scots, Welsh, German and French Huguenot colonists literally paled into insignificance.

The Political Theology of White Nationalism

In popular mythology, *homo Americanus* was born on July 4, 1776. Once American independence was secure, powerful commercial and financial interests agitated in favor of an ambitious program of nation-building to be directed by a strong central government. Supporters of the federal constitution of 1787 set out deliberately to create a *novus ordo seclorum* in which traditional American localist institutions would be replaced by more modern economic, political, and social practices. The myth of the American Adam was an essential element in the legitimation of the Federalist regime. Postmodernists are right about at least one thing; *homo Americanus* was, indeed, a cultural construct. The American nation is truly an "imagined community." Mostly English colonists *chose* to renounce their allegiance to the British Crown to be reborn as republicans. Americans became "a people without a past."[111]

Both federal and state governments grew by usurping power from lesser communal bodies, a process pioneered by European states. Typically,

---

109 Don Jordan and Michael Walsh, *White Cargo: The Forgotten History of Britain's White Slaves in America* (New York: New York University Press, 2008).

110 Jordan, *White Over Black*, 164.

111 Shain, *Myth of American Individualism*, xvii, 54.

the modern sovereign state was constituted "in *opposition* to kinship and other local groupings." So, too, in America, powers and responsibilities formerly lodged in the villages and congregations of colonial society were absorbed into the state, "thereby freeing the individual from the caprice of local custom and sub-loyalties which would divide them from their fellow-citizens." Property and contract laws enforced by the state became the medium through which individuals in a free market society related to each other. This may be seen as "secularization" to the extent that churches ceased to be the hub around which autonomous local ecosystems revolved. Religion in the new secular order became "a universal essence detachable from particular ecclesial practices;" its role was to "provide the motivation necessary for citizens of whatever creed to regard the nation-state as their primary community, and thus produce peaceable consensus." Writing from the perspective of Radical Orthodoxy, William Cavanaugh points out that secularization is not simply "the progressive stripping away of the sacred from some profane remainder." The *novus ordo seclorum* established by the Founding Fathers substituted its own *mythos* of salvation for that of the churches and local communities. In other words, the political theology that justified the new regime was "actually the *repression or displacement of sacrament*." Unfortunately, the repressed and displaced returned "in a different but malignant form." Well before the Civil War revealed the extent of the malignancy, Abraham Lincoln articulated the political theology of American nationalism. "Let reverence for the laws" of the American republic, he intoned in January 1838, "become the *political religion* of the nation; and let the old and the young, the rich and the poor, the grave and the gay, of all sexes and tongues, and colors and conditions, sacrifice unceasingly upon its altars." In America, the state became a "secular parody" of the Church.[112]

From the beginning, the *religio* of the American republic created a communion of white men by excluding Negroes and Indians from citizenship. At both the national and state level, the process of state-building secured popular loyalty and legitimacy by limiting citizenship to "whites." In return for civic recognition, white men adopted the salvation *mythos* of the state as their own.[113] Most white Americans, Northerners and Southerners alike, shared a faith in the Manifest Destiny of their

---

112 *Ibid.*, 54-55; Cavanaugh, *Theopolitical Imagination*, 72-74, 82, 84-85; McCarraher, "Enchantments of Mammon," 450; Lincoln, quoted in John P Diggins, *The Lost Soul of American Politics: Virtue, Self-Interest and the Foundations of Liberalism* (New York: Basic Books, 1984), 306; William Cavanaugh, "Beyond Secular Parodies," in Milbank, *et al*, *Radical Orthodoxy*, 182-200.

113 Cavanaugh, *Theopolitical Imagination*, 52.

nation-state to rule over the entire North American continent and all its inhabitants. By extending "white-skin privilege" to those on the right side of the color line, both federal and state governments encouraged ordinary folk to identify themselves with the state-sponsored myth of *homo Americanus*.[114]

With the adoption of the federal Constitution, the sovereign people were said to have created their own government. As things turned out, American governments created their own people. At first, public policy ensured that citizens were of the white race but Americans of Anglo-Saxon ancestry, the overwhelming majority of the citizenry, had no formal constitutional standing as a founding people. In the eyes of the law and the Constitution, Anglo-Saxons were simply "white." Among the first statutes enacted by the federal Congress was a naturalization and immigration law which specified only that immigrants and citizens should be "white," not that they should be Anglo-Saxon. It followed, as was confirmed by the US Supreme Court in the *Dred Scott* case, that the Constitution excluded Negroes from American citizenship.[115] In other words, *homo Americanus* was a white nationalist by force of law enjoying what liberals would later call "white-skin privilege." But, because the meaning of "whiteness" was in the eye of the beholder, over the next century "white-skin privilege" was steadily diluted. It was finally abolished when a combination of *raison d'état* and the imperatives of capitalist development dictated the official embrace of racial egalitarianism. This should not have come as a surprise. Even in the slave South, more than a few wealthy planters ridiculed the notion that the "mere animal man, because he happens to wear a white skin" should be entitled to full and exclusive privileges of citizenship.[116]

Divisions among whites extended well beyond class antagonisms; *homo Americanus* did not emerge fully formed from the colonial womb. Until the 1860s it was uncertain whether *homo Americanus* was to be a Southern Cavalier or a Northern Yankee. A long and bitter sectional struggle was waged to secure control of the national government acting in his name. Militant nationalists, especially in the North, sought to construct the myth of *homo Americanus* on the foundation of a constitutional theory that located sovereignty in the American people and not in the several States of the Union. On that view, by creating "a more perfect

---

114 Reginald Horsman, *Race and Manifest Destiny: The Origins of American Racial Anglo-Saxonism* (Cambridge, MA: Harvard University Press, 1981); Lacy K Ford, "Making the 'White Man's Country' White: Race, Slavery, and State-Building in the Jacksonian South" (1999) 19(4) *Journal of the Early Republic* 713

115 *Dred Scott v Sandford* (1857) 19 How 393 (US Supreme Court).

116 Ford, "White Man's Country," 735.

Union," the Constitution of 1787 had established a sovereign authority to represent the common interests of *homo Americanus* in every State and Territory. The great Southern statesman, John C Calhoun, countered by arguing that the primary allegiance of every citizen was to his own state. He denied that a citizen of the United States was "a citizen at large," a perfectly nondescript sort of "citizen of the world" removed from the local attachments that alone gave citizenship substantive meaning. That confederal vision of the American republic was defeated utterly in the Civil War. White Southerners learned at great cost that war, for the national government, is "the primary mechanism for achieving social integration in a society with no shared ends." When the chips were down, the political theology of sovereignty trumped white racial solidarity. If any doubt remained, subsequent history confirmed that violence is the *religio* of the American state.[117]

The assault on white-skin privilege steadily expanded its beachhead following the Civil War. The Thirteenth, Fourteenth and Fifteenth Amendments to the Constitution extended the privileges of citizenship to Negroes thereby enabling black Reconstruction governments to lord it over white Southerners. Although white supremacy was restored in the South with the end of Reconstruction, the industrialization of America posed another, more serious, threat to the once unchallenged cultural and political hegemony of old-stock Americans in the North and the West. Faced with stiff resistance from *homo Americanus* to permanent wage labor, industrialists imported a ready-made proletariat, first from Ireland and later from central, eastern, and southern Europe. Nativist objections were met with the soothing observation that Italian or Polish Catholics, even remarkably alien Russian Jews, were just as "white" as Anglo-Saxon Protestants.

With the closing of the frontier and the consolidation of the corporate economy, however, *homo Americanus*, too, was compelled to abandon the dream of an independence secured by his own land or his own business; he, too, was forced to get a job. In the twentieth century, most native-born Americans of British ancestry, faced with a life-long struggle to keep a roof over their heads, freely sold themselves into wage-slavery. (In time, of course, a shiny new car in the garage would provide Americans of every color and creed with the illusion of freedom.) Increasingly brazen assaults on the hegemonic status and core ethnocultural identity of *homo Americanus* were beaten back temporarily in 1924 when Congress adopted a national origins quota system to regulate immigration. In

---

117 John C Calhoun, quoted in *Slaughter-House Cases* (1873) Wallace 36, at 94 (*per* Field, J); Cavanaugh, *Theopolitical Imagination*, 46.

retrospect, it is clear that the 1920s were the high-water mark in the life of *homo Americanus*.

It was in that decade, however, that women breached the age-old boundary between the public and domestic realms. The old-stock American woman was enlisted by the state in its continuing campaign to iron out the natural differences between the sexes, to flatten herself and her menfolk into the pliably plebeian form assumed by the androgynous zombies we see today thronging suburban shopping malls. Thanks to the twin challenges of Depression and World War II, WASP men were able to maintain their crumbling authority for a few decades following the adoption of women's suffrage. But the civil rights revolution marked the end of the road for the American Adam.

It was not just the forced integration of whites and Negroes and the rise of feminism that doomed white America. In 1965, the doors were thrown wide open to a rising tide of utterly unassimilable Third World immigration. When President Lyndon Johnson signed the Kennedy immigration bill into law, he issued the death warrant for *homo Americanus*.

The Neo-Communist Revolution

The upshot of this story can be summarized very briefly: the deliberate campaign to liquidate *homo Americanus* established *neo-communism* as the official religion of the USA and the other "Anglo-Saxon countries." Do not imagine that communism was defeated with the fall of the Soviet Union. Soviet communism was little more than a crude form of state capitalism. After all, as understood by Marx, communism was to be the highest stage of capitalism. It is now obvious that, having failed to conceive "a mode of social wealth other than that founded on labor and production, Marxism no longer furnishes in the long run an alternative to capitalism." In reality, Marxism merely generalized "the economic mode of rationality over the entire expanse of human history, as the generic mode of human becoming." But, by contrast with the Bolshevik model, neo-communism has no need, much less the desire, to establish a dictatorship of the proletariat. Indeed, it is under the auspices of the transnational market-state that contemporary neo-communism aims to realize Marx's deepest aspiration: "the *idea* of man *producing* himself in his infinite determination, and continually surpassing himself toward his own end."[118]

---

118 Baudrillard, *Mirror of Production*, 31-33. See also, Flora Montcorbier, *Le Communisme de Marche: De L'Utopie Marxiste A L'Utopie Mondialiste* (Lausanne: Editions L'Age d'Homme, 2000) *passim*.

Neo-communism is a materialist (a)theology that glorifies fallen man and the power of secular reason; it absorbs the individual into the inscrutable workings of the systemic labor power that transforms nature in accordance with human ends. "Lonely and lost in a meaningless universe," atheist or agnostic WASPs are especially receptive to the seductive appeal of neo-communism. The cornucopian *mythos* of the Divine Economy may be little more than another secular humanist parody of the *ecclesia* but it has eaten away the ethnoreligious core of WASP identity. Neo-communism allows man "to empty his mind and heart of God." Long since "locked in the bubble of his own egoistic godlessness, his own self-worship," the WASP has become "grace-proof." Invincibly complacent, neo-communist WASPs are sure that the salvation myth of universal human rights will clear up "the mystery of iniquity." The question is: Will WASPs resist the neo-communist tyranny of good intentions?[119] As a spiritual force, neo-communism "strives to incorporate itself into fallen man and change the world after its own patterns."[120] The religion of humanity finally flattens man, washing away his racial, religious, and ethnic differences in the universal solvent of the market. Everyone everywhere is absorbed into the corporate monoculture.

The colonization of the entire world by capital completes the process of proletarianization that began with Negro slavery. First, English colonists assimilated themselves to the pervasive presence of Negro labor, recasting their identity as a function of the merely chromatic category of "whiteness." Finally, well-meaning WASPs dissolve their bioculture into the "communism of the market" that washes away the gulf separating them from the Negro and the Chinese, the Hindu and the Muslim masses of the Third World.[121] For all his legendary parochialism, it seems that *homo Americanus* inadvertently helped to design the steamroller of universal human rights that flattened all the protective barriers that surrounded his unique way of life.

The rights that the nation-state settled exclusively on *homo Americanus* because he was "white" have been extended to non-whites simply because they are "human." Ironically, white nationalism turns out to have been the first fateful step down the path to a universalistic "civic nationalism." The American Adam, celebrated in song and story, was admired far and wide for the "inner-directed" independence and "rugged individualism" that set him apart from the backward English nation. Described as a

---

119 Phillips, *Orthodox Christianity*, 136-137.

120 *Ibid.*, 136.

121 Montcorbier, *Communisme de Marche*, 120-123.

white man, *homo Americanus* was genetically and culturally if not legally an Anglo-Saxon. He is dying as a WASP. The government of the United States long ago disowned the white nationalism of *homo Americanus* as the face of absolute evil. Only in the embrace of the Other may the WASP participate in the plenitude of humanity's self-productive power.

Like *homo Americanus*, WASPs in the British dominions have fallen under the sway of the Other. In none of the historic Anglo-Saxon countries will neo-communism be defeated by the politics of white nationalism. Whiteness is a biological concept, a statistical construct, and a dangerously over-inclusive racial phenotype. It has little ethnocultural or political—much less spiritual—significance. Those who share nothing more than their whiteness have little claim to the stockpile of biocultural capital—the *richesse* which distinguishes an advanced people—created by the Anglo-Saxon countries and now being eroded by the transnational market-state. Defined in opposition to a debased blackness, whiteness always implied the inherent equality of anyone passing for white. This has been a fatal source of weakness. The egalitarian logic of whiteness repelled both conservatives, who would rather rub shoulders with the talented tenth of any other race than pander to the riff-raff of their own, and capitalists concerned not with the color of their laborers but with their cost.

In the era of universal human rights, right-thinking WASPs ritually denounce the real and imagined crimes of "racist" white men. To aspire to the leadership of white people is to become a social pariah; the cost of "white pride" in terms of social exclusion and lost self-respect is exceedingly high. But WASPs are not forced to identify as whites. Indeed, WASPs have nothing to lose and much to gain by shrugging off their "white" badge of shame. Simply by re-asserting their ancestral identity as Anglo-Saxons, WASPs inherit a wealth of opportunities to play—and win—the postmodern game of identity politics. After all, people of Anglo-Saxon stock created the lion's share of the biocultural, social, and physical capital in Australia, Canada, New Zealand, and the United States, not to mention the United Kingdom. No ethnic group is better placed, in any of those countries, to launch claims for the protection of its cultural heritage and sacred sites than Anglo-Saxons—if only they could regenerate a sense of in-group solidarity.[122]

---

122 Consider the constitutional significance of the following set of circumstances in an "age of diversity":

Harvard College was founded in 1636 by and for English Puritan families estranged from the corrupt and imperfect Church of England. Traditionally, Harvard men were overwhelmingly Anglo-Saxon and Protestant. By the nineteenth century, Harvard was wedded to the religion of secular utility. The student body became more ethnically diverse

Conclusion

An orthodox Christian ethnotheology offers WASPs the divine gift of the *ecclesia* as a genuine alternative to the spiritually bankrupt market-state sucking dry the lifeblood of "white America." The rise and fall of *homo Americanus* is a case study in the perversion of Christian orthodoxy. WASPs are now reaping the deadly harvest sown by their British ancestors. *Pace* Samuel P Huntington, Anglo-Saxon Protestantism is not part of the solution; it has been a very large part of the problem. Thanks to the white man's religion of secular utility, neo-communist ideologues can proudly proclaim that *The World is Flat*.[123] Only when freed from whiteness and Protestantism—those shallow and shop-worn simulacra of ethnocultural identity—will WASPs rediscover the hidden depths of being in a risen world. The theopolitical struggle against both the corporate culture of concupiscence and the state *religio* of power has barely begun.

American history has been a battlefield upon which *homo Americanus* was pitted against other racial, religious, and ethnic groups, most notably Indians, Negroes, and Jews. More recently, other peoples such as Mexican

but remained *de facto* a bastion of WASP gentility well into the twentieth century. As late as the 1970s, Jewish students at Harvard College openly resented the WASP ascendancy they often derided as "the episcopacy." Since then, admissions and hiring policies allegedly premised on the mutually contradictory principles of "meritocracy" (favoring high IQ Jews and Asians) and "affirmative action" (favoring Negroes, Hispanics, and women) have reduced WASP men to a small minority of the faculty and student body. Does that outcome constitute a form of ethnic cleansing?

Did the Harvard College administration intend the natural and ordinary consequences of its admissions policies and hiring practices? If so, did the University's conduct constitute a breach of a fiduciary obligation owed to the founding generation and its descendants? Is Harvard College an important part of the Anglo-Saxon cultural heritage; indeed, could it be considered an Anglo-Saxon sacred site? If so, did the breach of trust by the College result in a misappropriation of cultural capital damaging to the biocultural interests of Anglo-Saxons generally? Should or could a regenerated Anglo-Saxon *ecclesia* move to resume stewardship of the College?

In practice, whether or how the Harvard Question, in particular, is resolved is not of decisive importance. Simply as exercises in consciousness-raising, such scenarios can be replicated in relation to a host of other institutions, historical sites, and cultural artefacts in every country settled by Anglo-Saxons. Merely asserting such custodial claims is simultaneously a form of Christian witness and of Anglo-Saxon identity politics. Whatever tactics are adopted, the goal of Anglo-Saxon identity politics must be to become a protected minority; protected not by governmental or corporate subsidies but by the carefully developed economic and cultural autonomy of a self-reliant ethnoreligious community. Does the political theology of white nationalism offer WASPs a more promising strategy to recover lost ground, politically, socially, economically, morally, or theologically? I think not.

123 Thomas L Friedman, *The World is Flat: A Brief History of the Twenty-first Century* (New York: Picador, 2007).

and Central American mestizoes, Muslims, along with South and East Asians have entered the postmodern American game of identity politics. Orthodox Judaism, Islam, and even black liberation theology all confer fitness benefits in between-group selection. In principle, a Christian eth-notheology should be no less "useful" to Anglo-Saxons. But, in the end, *whether* Anglo-Saxons survive is less important than *how* they participate in the divine gift of life. Who knows what sacrifices may be expected of Anglo-Saxons in the coming struggle to redeem the world their people have done so much to enrich but also to corrupt?

Orthodox Christian ethnotheologies recognize the unique character of every human bioculture but, while not unknown in Christian circles, ethnotheology has been conceived thus far mainly as an evangelical strat-egy for converting non-European peoples to Christianity. As such, the concept belongs to missiology not to ecclesiology. In accommodating the Christian message to the cultural practices and language of pagan peoples, modern ethnotheology recapitulates the experience of the early medieval missionaries who won over the *Angelcynn* by Germanizing Christianity.[124] So far at least, the leading lights of Radical Orthodoxy have shown no interest in developing an Anglo-Saxon ethnotheology to win converts among their own people. Such indifference to the fate of one's co-ethnics is simply sinful. From a sociobiological perspective there is little doubt that WASPs have developed a distinctive bioculture, one that has been subverted systematically by the highly successful neo-communist move-ment dominant within contemporary Anglo-Saxon Protestantism. WASP theologians must take a pastoral interest in the biocultural survival of their profoundly dispirited people. Gregory the Great sent Augustine to England in the hope that he could turn the pagan Angles into angels.[125] It is high time to renew that mission.

It will be the task of the postmodern Anglo-Saxon Christian renais-sance to "irradiate" sickly WASPs with the Holy Spirit. A rising religion was the driving force behind the Anglo-Saxon conquest of the American continent; an obsolescent and dysfunctional theology was an active ingre-dient in the subsequent collapse of the WASP ascendancy. The theology we need today is not a *radical* but an *Anglo-Saxon* orthodoxy. Both the socio-biological imperatives of group survival and elementary Christian char-ity presuppose the incorporation of in-group altruism into the normative

---

124 Charles H Kraft, *Christianity in Culture: A Study in Biblical Theologizing in Cross-Cultural Perspective* (Maryknoll, NY: Orbis, 2005); James C Russell, *The Germanization of Christianity: A Sociohistorical Approach to Religious Transformation* (New York: Oxford University Press, 1994).

125 Bede, *Ecclesiastical History*, 103-104.

structure of everyday life. Unfortunately, even pugnaciously postmodern Radical Orthodoxy clings to the aracial ethnotheology of seventeenth-century Protestantism.[126] Although modern geology long ago revised the biblical timeline for the history of life, the theory of evolution still has not dented the anti-racist orthodoxy of most Anglican thinkers. Anglicans are eager to toss overboard established verities on just about any other issue, but when it comes to the fundamentalist dogma of monogenesis and the biological unity, indeed equality, of all branches of the human species, Anglicans will not rock the doctrinal boat. In light of what we now know not only about the reality of racial differences but the mutual interplay of race and culture, that ancient metanarrative needs to be rewritten. Different races, indeed, different ethnicities, participate in the divine in quite different ways. A return to the ethnotheologies implicit in orthodox Christianity would restore ethnomasochistic WASPs to spiritual health.

Secular WASPs never invoke the ancient Israelites as a prototype of Christian nationhood. Still less do they believe that the Anglo-Saxon *Volksgeist* can or ever did manifest itself in and through the Body of Christ. Even religious WASPs direct their altruism toward out-groups, a favor which is rarely returned. In stark contrast, secular and religious Jews alike work assiduously and unashamedly to advance their own group interests in their long and concerted campaign to expunge every trace of Christianity from the judicially approved canons of American civil religion.[127] Sociobiology warns us that dissipation of religious faith can have disastrous consequences in the competitive process of between-group selection. Now that WASPs are just another, not very cohesive, ethnic minority, they need an ethnotheology grounded in the biocultural reality of racial differences. A postmodern Anglican Reformation is the essential precondition for the rebirth of an Anglo-Saxon ethnonation.

Jewish experience is instructive: religious Jews have known for millennia that a nation surrendering to self-indulgence and self-loathing will, sooner or later, destroy itself. Orthodox Judaism may be a minority faith, but rooted as it is in an organic synthesis of theology and sociobiological imperatives it remains a source of strength for all Jews. If WASPs hope to survive as anything more than a shadow of their historic ethnonation, they must restore the ethnoreligious integrity of the Anglican Church. Recalling the Anglican Church to its original mission as the Church of

126 Colin Kidd, *British Identities Before Nationalism: Ethnicity and Nationhood in the Atlantic World, 1600-1800* (New York: Cambridge University Press, 1999).

127 Gregg Ivers, *To Build a Wall: American Jews and the Separation of Church and State* (Charlottesville: University Press of Virginia, 1995).

the Anglo-Saxons is an urgent theopolitical imperative. Not all religions are created equal. Religions which promote in-group altruism are more adaptive than those which create a self-denying people programmed to channel altruism outward to other allegedly more deserving tribes.

The corporate welfare state established the worship of the Other as its official creed. For WASP men, in particular, the celebration of diversity has become a mandatory ritual of self-abasement; in public and in private; formal and informal mechanisms of social pricing discourage deviance through the loss of jobs and reputation. For all its ostentatious altruism, however, the disciplinary/therapeutic practices of managerial multiculturalism have perverted the biocultural foundations of Christian morality. Although sociobiology and orthodox Christianity may agree that charity begins at home, such an inward orientation is eschewed by Anglicans.

Orthodox believers are the socially cohesive core of the Jewish ethnonation. They make up what they lack in numbers in the intensity of their faith, recognizing that ethnoreligious communities depend for their survival upon such deeply committed minorities. By contrast, knowing that all men are drawn to an end beyond mere survival, Christians deplore the Jewish determination to survive, even at the expense of the golden rule. WASP religious leaders place selfless humanitarianism far above racial self-defence in the scale of theological virtues. WASP sociobiologists, of course, do recognize the utility of a survivalist ethic but only when packaged as a secular philosophy of universal nationalism. Faced with these countervailing forces, a new breed of manly Anglo-Saxons is needed to defend by all necessary means those of their own kind who work and pray. Otherwise Anglo-Saxon ethnohistory will crawl to a close, not with a bang but with a whimper. WASPs living in multiracial societies must learn that the practice of ethnic nepotism is both a theological and a civic virtue.

Once upon a time, the English nation understood itself as a Christian communion. In every country settled by the British, loyalty to the state became a surrogate for ethnic solidarity. Statehood as an expression of ethnocultural identity made some sense when the English Crown served as the vice-regent of God, in whose image the English people were made. Unfortunately, Old English Christianity was weakened following the Great Schism and the Papal revolution of the eleventh century. Even after the shackles of a corrupt papal monarchy had been cast aside in the sixteenth century, the English remained on the path to perdition. White Anglo-Saxon Protestants prostrated themselves before the false gods erected by the new system of political economy, greeting the Age of Mammon with loud hosannas. Finally, in the late twentieth century, the infection could be contained no longer and burst forth as a virulent ethnopathology. Pulled along in the wake of the American empire, Anglo-Saxon Protestantism morphed yet again into the neo-communist theology of global capitalism.

While an established church retains a residual role in the ideological state apparatus of the United Kingdom, the state in every other nominally Anglo-Saxon country stands at arm's length from formal religious affiliations. Nevertheless even those ostensibly secular regimes are shot through with pseudo-theological claims, recycled religious rituals, and a sham sacred symbolism. For WASPs otherwise bereft of a collective identity, the pious and public profession of allegiance to the sovereign state bears all the hallmarks of an idolatrous cult. Without the fusion of theology and political economy under the aegis of the nation-state, the rise of *homo Americanus* was unthinkable. With the apotheosis of the modern business corporation, his downfall was unavoidable.

5.

Divine Economy:
The Modern Business Corporation
and the Lost Soul of WASP America

Introduction

As we have seen, Anglo-Saxon Anglophobia is a spiritual malady in which deracinated WASPs discover "a new form of sacrament" in the worship of the Other. Now that the church has washed its hands of responsibility for the biocultural interests of the Anglo-Saxon peoples, Anglicanism has become just another brand of post-Christian rationalism, recoiling from "racism" as the last trace of original sin. Once upon a time in Old England, the hearts of simple country folk were set on fire by the epic tales recounting the incarnation, crucifixion, death, and resurrection of the Son of God. Sophisticated, postmodern Anglicans detect the divine elsewhere, in the mysterious movements of complex, transnational social and economic systems. The most exalted spirits among them sublimate their religious longings into neo-communist movements for peace, love, and universal human rights.

In the materialist universe of secular humanism, the theology of money mediates the dialectical relationship between communism and capitalism. In the older, bourgeois stage of capitalist development, when the gold standard reigned supreme, money became the God of commodities. We live in the era of fiat currency. Now that money can be created out of thin air, anyone with a gold card credit rating can enjoy the WASP lifestyle. But an authentic ethnoreligious community remains one of those things that money can't buy. In its place, the neo-communist regime provides the invisible race with a simulacrum of spiritual plenitude in the artificially enchanted image of the Other.

As "the trinkets of the market" came to "ape the delights of the heavenly city," the performance of sacrament was perverted by capitalists and communists alike—in active collaboration with Anglican theology. Weber and Tawney pioneered the study of the "repression, displacement, and renaming of the sacred" in Anglo-Saxon countries as they explored the intimate connection between the Anglo-Saxon Protestant ethic and the spirit of capitalism.[1] WASPs pioneered the organizational techniques which transformed the modern American business corporation into a secular parody of the *ecclesia*. Corporate culture created "the WASP lifestyle" as its hopelessly hollow avatar. Neo-communism is the highest stage of capitalism; it takes the form of a global system of managerial/therapeutic regimes terminally addicted to economic productivity, material wealth, and sensual gratification as the point and purpose of human striving. Even the most conformist WASPs are beset by a nameless longing for someone or something to fill the inner void left vacant by the disappearance of the living God-Man at the center of the Old Faith. Not surprisingly, WASPs are forever seeking a quick, supra-sensual "fix" for their psychic "diseases." In the late twentieth century the corporate welfare state annointed exotic "people of color" as the last reservoir of spiritual vitality available to "white" Americans. The American Negro became the first beneficiary of the new annunciation.

The predatory political economy of bourgeois capitalism brought Anglo-Saxon Protestants into close and regular contact with Negroes from sub-Saharan Africa. Slave labor on the plantations of the New World foreshadowed the widespread transformation of peasants into proletarians that Marx identified as the essential prerequisite of capitalist development. He claimed that the surplus value skimmed from slaves producing staple crops of sugar, tobacco, indigo, rice, and cotton made possible the primitive accumulation of capital financing the growth of commerce and industry in both Britain and the United States. Publicly pilloried as the principal beneficiaries of Negro slavery, contemporary WASPs are expected to pay perpetual penance for the sins of their forefathers. It is not just the shaming rituals devised by the diversity industry that drives WASPs to seek the well-springs of spiritual authenticity in the hot-blooded rhythms of Negro culture. In a world made flat, WASPs are one-dimensional proletarians. Altogether bereft of any other source of

1   Eugene McCarraher, "The Enchantments of Mammon: Notes Towards a Theological History of Capitalism," (2005) 21(3) *Modern Theology* 429, at 433, 447. See, generally, Max Weber, *The Protestant Ethic and the Spirit of Capitalism* (New York: Charles Scribner's Sons, 1958); and RH Tawney, *Religion and the Rise of Capitalism* (New York: Harcourt, Brace & Co, 1926).

meaning, value, and purpose, the system immerses everyone in the ubiquitous, mass-mediated cult of the Other. After four centuries, American Negroes still stand on the fringes of Western civilization; ironically, their obdurate otherness serves as a sacrosanct secular surrogate for the lost soul of WASP America.

Negro slaves were sea-lifted out of primitive, indeed pre-historic, African societies to be marketed in the New World as a sort of superior livestock. But, their transformation into fungible units of abstract labor-power was far from complete. At most, they became proto-proletarians. While tending tobacco and chopping cotton under the blazing southern sun or, even more obviously, peeling potatoes in the comparative comfort of a plantation kitchen, black slaves were bound to their white owners in "an organic relationship so complex and ambivalent that neither could express the simplest human feelings without reference to the other." According to conservative Marxist historian Eugene Genovese, "the slaveholders' own legal apparatus…discredited the essential philosophical ideas on which slavery rested and, simultaneously, bore witness to the slave's ability to register the claims of their humanity." In theory, slaveowners had full power over their chattels. In practice, the "moral, not to mention political needs of the ruling class as a whole required that [state power] interpose itself…between individual masters and their slaves."[2] Law and morality alike obliged masters to exercise a paternal dominion over their slaves in sickness and in health, from infancy to old age, weaving a thousand ties between the two peoples.

By comparison, the exploitation of free labor by capitalist employers was not constrained by the domestic bonds of mutual dependence—even affection—between master and slave. Southern planters were compelled to "guard their slaves' health and life as among the most vital of their own interests; for while crops were merely income, slaves were capital." As a consequence, whenever possible, free immigrant labor was employed in the most dangerous work. On one Louisiana plantation, Irish laborers were hired to do the heavy labor of draining swamplands and felling forests. The wage bill was high but as an observer noted, "It was much better to have Irish do it, who cost nothing to the planter if they died, than to use up good field-hands in such severe employment."[3] All things considered,

---

2   Eugene D Genovese, *Roll, Jordan, Roll: The World the Slaves Made* (New York: Pantheon, 1972), 3, 43-49.

3   Ulrich Bonnell Phillips, *American Negro Slavery: A Survey of the Supply, Control, and Employment of Negro Labor as Determined by the Plantation Regime* (New York: Appleton, 1918), 255-256.

emancipation must have seemed a mixed blessing to untutored Negro slaves exposed for the first time to a heartless market for free labor.

Apologists for slavery erred greatly, however, when they imagined that Yankee capitalism was producing a bleak, impoverished landscape of alienation and unrelieved desperation. In fact, late nineteenth century corporate capitalism generated a self-sustaining aura of religiosity that bound capital and labor together in the worship of abundance. Free workers were swept up into an unswerving faith in the magical mystery cult of mass-marketed consumerism. Marx was among the first to recognize that the secular "rationality" of the capitalist system bears vestiges of the enchantment associated with pre-modern religions. Throughout his career, "Marx framed his analysis of capitalism in religious terms." Indeed, in describing the capitalist as "a sorcerer who is no longer able to control the powers of the nether world whom he has called up with his spells," Marx offered "an oddly sacramental critique of commodity civilization."

Capitalism spawned new sources of enchantment; in the words of Norman O Brown, the "animating spirit of commodity fetishism" became "the heir to and substitute for the religious complex, an attempt to find God in things." For that reason, Eugene McCarraher argues that only theology can fully fathom the perversity of capitalism.[4] Unfortunately, most Anglo-Protestant theologians succumbed as easily to the siren call of Mammon as they have to the commands of Caesar. Equally disturbing is the fact that few mainstream American Christians recognize a spiritual scandal when they see one.

Capitalism and the Spirit of Anglo-Saxon Protestantism

The question arises: What can orthodox Christians do to redeem the church? In their theological challenge to capitalism, the champions of Radical Orthodoxy (RO) have set out to "rewrite and incorporate both the Marxist 'narrative of proletarianization' and its complementary account of commodity fetishism." While there can be little doubt that Marx was right to identify capitalism as a Christian heresy, John Milbank is dead wrong to urge acceptance of Marxism as "the ally of Christian orthodoxy." An ostensibly charitable commitment to Christian socialism draws theologians such as Milbank and McCarraher into a unitarian and universalist mindset hostile to the trinitarian social structure of orthodox

---

4   McCarraher, "Enchantments," 436-437, 443.

Christendom. They advocate resistance to "proletarianization" but only because, like Marx, they call "into question the sundering of the sphere of 'making' from the sphere of 'values,' and hence the separation of a 'technologically' conceived economics and politics from ethics, aesthetics and religion." Like Marx, Milbank and McCarraher treat all of these spheres as expressions of a single realm of human creativity. Unlike Marxist humanists, however, they "affirm the indissoluble unity of soul and body" relegated by Marx to the allegedly illusory realm of religious mythology. Otherwise, far from offering an alternative to the perversity of either capitalism or communism, RO joins them in embracing the apotheosis of Work as "the Messiah of the modern world."[5]

Christian socialism claims that its secular counterpart has "wrought a massive desecration of sacramental labor." Milbank insists that "only in the unity of thought and action could work afford 'a certain contact with reality, the truth and beauty of the universe and with the eternal wisdom which is the order in it.'" Seeking to consecrate labor within the Church understood as the Body of Christ, RO joins with Simone Weil in condemning the degradation of labor as a sacrilege "*in exactly the same sense* that it is sacrilege to trample upon the Eucharist."[6] On the contrary, Milbank declares, "God himself is fundamentally and primordially a worker." Far from being a curse suffered as a consequence of the Fall, "our work is pleasurable because it is the creative tending of God's universe." The proletarian in a capitalist society differs from the worker in a Christian community only because paid employment is necessary to his survival in a historically contingent economic order that imposes strict divisions between work and leisure. For the Christian, Milbank says, "work is always a form of play (as Creation is for God) whereas so called 'spare time' is the serious time of redemption, of our relation to others and to God."[7]

In this respect, Milbank's radical orthodoxy echoes Herbert Marcuse's Freudian revision of the orthodox Marxist gospel of work. Both writers reject the notion that work is a necessary evil that must be endured until a socialist society produces the necessities of life through "a totally communal and mechanized process" whereby the individual will be free to spend his spare time as he chooses. Marcuse portrays socialism as the

---

5   Jean Baudrillard, *The Mirror of Production* (St Louis, MO: Telos Press, 1975), 37.

6   *Ibid.*, 447-448; John Milbank, "The Body by Love Possessed: Christianity and Late Capitalism in Britain," (1986) 3(1) *Modern Theology* 35 at 61; *id.*, *Theology and Social Theory: Beyond Secular Reason* second edition (Oxford: Blackwell, 2006), 178.

7   Milbank, "By Love Possessed," 54.

breakdown of the rigid divisions between work and play characteristic of a capitalist economy. His goal is not "the transformation of labor but its complete subordination to the freely evolving potentialities of man and nature." For both the Frankfurt School and Radical Orthodoxy "The ideas of play and display reveal their full distance from the values of productiveness and performance." Because play "cancels the repressive and exploitative traits of labor and leisure," it becomes "*unproductive* and *useless.*"[8] Marx's utopian vision aimed at freedom *from* labor; Milbank and Marcuse seek freedom *within* the world of work.

On the other hand, as secular humanists, Marx and Marcuse contended that the alienated forms of wage labor and commodity fetishism reflect the power of religious illusions. Milbank's response is that if, indeed, capitalism is "somewhat like a religion," it can in consequence "only be questioned or replaced by 'another religion.'" Christianity may be "equally unfounded" but it is less prone to hubris than Marxism or critical theory, both of which remain firmly committed to the autonomy of the secular realm "where humanity defines itself as power, echoing God's self-definition in the Creation."[9]

While faulting Marx for failing fully to recognize "the historical particularity of the economic," Milbank himself turns a blind eye to the biocultural contingency of modern capitalism.[10] The close connection noted by Tawney and Weber between the system of political economy and peoples of British ancestry is not simply an historical fluke. The vanguard of the bourgeoisie if not of the proletariat was mainly English. Meanwhile, Scottish thinkers such as Adam Smith spelled out the principles of a market society. At about the same time, the still overwhelmingly Anglo-Saxon Protestant American republic launched itself on a path of spectacular economic development. Before long, the visible hand of the modern business corporation was at the tiller of Anglo-American capitalism, charting a course which would unite the whole of society in a cornucopian future of boundless prosperity for producers and consumers alike. Marx was wrong; even though the proletariat was estranged from its labor power and plunged into poverty, it did not become the vehicle for the universal interests of humanity. The peculiar character of Anglo-American capitalism, and particularly the rise of the modern business corporation in the United States confounded Marx's prediction.

---

8   Herbert Marcuse, *Eros and Civilization: A Philosophical Inquiry into Freud* (New York: Vintage, 1961), 178.

9   Milbank, " By Love Possessed," 53, 60; *id.*, *Theology and Social Theory*, 198.

10   Milbank, *Theology and Social Theory*, 192.

According to Arnold Toynbee, it is "neither poverty nor humble birth" which is the "true hallmark of the proletarian." Rather, the proletarian is someone with "a consciousness—and the resentment which this consciousness inspires—of being disinherited from his ancestral place in Society and being unwanted in a community which is his rightful home; and this subjective proletarianism is not incompatible with the possession of material assets." Applying that definition to American capitalism, Wilmot Robertson suggested that the WASP corporate manager may well be the quintessential proletarian. Proletarianization reaches high into the glass towers of American corporate management, where WASP executives, "caught up in an octopean mass of government regulations, labor contracts, taxes, affirmative action, and administrative red tape, have become as much the faceless cogs of a soulless economy as the lowliest workers on the production line." Not even wildly overgenerous levels of executive compensation can "compensate for the frustration of losing command, of giving fewer orders and taking more." American managers have been compelled endlessly to bow and scrape to bureaucrats, troublesome shareholders, and, in the bad old days before offshoring, bumptious union shop stewards. By the mid-twentieth century, WASP executives had become "a nomadic bureaucratic caste that moves from company to company in an unending, nonsensical circular migration."[11]

By comparison with Japanese, Chinese, or Russian corporate managers, rootless WASP executives were far removed from the possibility of occupying an ancestral niche in an organic society. Nevertheless, Adolf A Berle Jr once compared American corporate managers to a traditional priestly caste. Indeed, he breathlessly announced, the corporation will play "the role of conscience-carrier of twentieth-century American society." Berle was just one of many scholars to preach the theology of corporate redemption. He went a bit further than his academic peers, however, when he professed to see in the American corporation the makings of a modern City of God. While some social critics assailed corporate America as a corporate Babylon, Berle proclaimed that true justice could be realized in a corporate Zion. He denied that the corporate realm is "soulless," declaring instead that moral and intellectual leadership at the highest level was capable of compensating for corporate excesses.

Expressing confidence that the American corporate system could bring Augustine's heavenly city down to earth, Berle saw "some sort of consensus of mind emerging" which would act "by compulsion as it were...for

---

11 Wilmot Robertson, *The Dispossessed Majority* (Cape Canaveral, FL: Howard Allen, 1981), 374-375.

good or ill...surprisingly like a collective soul." Ever the optimist, he saw big business corporations moving "toward a greater rather than a lesser acceptance of the responsibility that goes with power." If the corporate manager is a proletarian, he is also a worker-priest, albeit one placed in the service of Mammon if not of Christ.[12] Needless to say, Berle was no more concerned than Marx or Milbank with the impact of the twentieth century corporate revolution on the biocultural health of the American WASP.

An orthodox Christian theological narrative of proletarianization would emphasize its destructive impact on the spiritual life of the Anglo-Saxon diaspora. In such an account, proletarianization appears as an evil, not because it establishes a rigid division between work and leisure time but rather because it flattens the social divisions once characteristic of an organic and hierarchical Anglo-Saxon Christian society. In the tripartite structure of Old England, the upper classes were honor-bound to defend the interests of the common folk who were subject to their authority. An Anglo-Saxon Christian ethnotheology will recognize that corporate capitalism, no less than socialism, is committed to the obliteration of traditional hierarchies based upon faith, honor, and blood. The socially corrosive principle of equality manifests itself most readily in the cash nexus: "My dollar is as good as your dollar!" Christian socialists, Marxist revolutionaries, and corporate managers alike hope that a re-ordering of the relations of production, distribution, and exchange will reshape the social character of the proletarian masses. Indeed, today's corporate neo-communism not only reduces class differences to the lowest common denominator, but aims also to transcend the particularities of race, religion, and ethnicity. Transnational corporate capitalism has revealed itself to be a Frankenstein monster bent on the destruction of the very people who brought it into being.

It is a mistake to conceive the modern business corporation as an inherently private economic unit of capital accumulation. Intimately involved in the aetiology of Anglo-Saxon Anglophobia, American corporate culture is a biocultural pathology not just an engine of wealth-creation. Corporate capitalism is also a religious phenomenon; in its origins the modern corporation owes just as much if not more to Anglo-Saxon Protestant theology than it does to the allegedly universal laws of economics. Indeed, the legal concept of the corporation has its deepest roots in the organizational history of Roman Catholicism. Medieval canon law

---

12   Adolph A Berle, Jr, *The 20th Century Capitalist Revolution* (New York: Harcourt, Brace & Co, 1954), 182.

identified the church itself as a corporation. In America, we can trace the ancestry of the corporation to the covenant theology of Puritan New England. Not surprisingly, therefore, the modern corporation not only claims credit for raising American living standards, it has also appropriated "the authority that once devolved on the priesthood."[13]

The New England Seedbed of the American Business Corporation

As we saw in Chapter One, the first sea-borne invasions of Britain disrupted kindred ties among the Germanic warriors who settled there. Covenants binding warriors to their lords contributed more to social cohesion in Anglo-Saxon England than in Germany where kinship networks remained relatively strong. We also saw that in medieval England contractual obligations between unrelated parties contributed greatly to the development of social and economic life. Covenants were even more important to the success of the second great sea-borne migration of the Anglo-Saxon peoples. Covenants were also more sophisticated, both in form and in substance; grounded in mutual trust, those non-kinship based forms of reciprocity provided English colonists with a valuable stock of social capital.

Drawn up aboard ship and signed upon landing, the Mayflower Compact is the most famous covenant in American colonial history. Under its terms, a congregation of Pilgrims joined together "in the Presence of God and one another" to found Plymouth colony as a "civil Body Politick" held together not by the bonds of blood but by mutual promises. The Massachusetts Bay Company was another such body politic and corporate; it, too, was a covenant community. Whatever the formal legalities surrounding the grant of its royal charter, its substantive foundation lay in a free contract among its members. Because the company owed its existence to its members, they were convinced that its charter belonged to them alone. Accordingly, in defiance of custom, they physically carried the company's charter to America, thereby removing it beyond the legal jurisdiction of either Crown or Parliament.[14]

---

13 Paul Edward Gottfried, *Multiculturalism and the Politics of Guilt: Toward a Secular Theocracy* (Columbia, MO: University of Missouri Press, 2002), 139.

14 Loren Baritz, *City on a Hill: A History of Ideas and Myths in America* (New York: John Wiley & Sons, 1964), 115-116.

Covenant was more important even than blood ties in ensuring social cohesion in New England. True, Pilgrims and Puritans sailed for the New World in family groups rather than as warrior bands. But the husbands and wives who, with their children and servants, undertook the hazardous voyage to the West were united by a shared Christian faith not by unconditional loyalty to an extended family. Certainly, "Puritans thought of the family as a concentric set of nuclear and extended rings" but "they gave central importance to the innermost nuclear ring." The nuclear family itself was a product of covenant. Marriage was conceived as a civil contract based on the free consent of the parties, a contract that could be dissolved should the terms of the covenant be broken. The "covenanted family became a complex web of mutual obligations between husbands and wives, parents and children, masters and servants."[15]

As the colony expanded, younger families and households were gathered together in new churches and civil bodies politic, themselves grounded in covenant. On several occasions, religious differences within a settlement led to separatist movements and the formation of new covenant communities. The Fundamental Orders of Connecticut provide one well-known example. Of course, colonial New Englanders gave formal recognition to the established authority of the king and the Church of England. In practical terms, however, the congregations of colonial churches and the civil governments of New England towns and villages remained for a long while more or less independent of the mother country. An unresolved tension built up between the ever-present power of covenant to draw individual persons into autonomous joint enterprises and the inter-generational, customary authority of throne and altar. Not surprisingly, the proclamation of the Declaration of Independence caused a seismic shift in the biocultural balance of power. Covenant finally triumphed over blood. The American Revolution was not just a political and a social movement; it was also a religious revolution. It suppressed the spirit of ethnoreligious loyalty owed by all British colonists to the blood and faith of Old England.

In the seventeenth and eighteenth centuries, New England colonists established healthy ethnoreligious communities. In their own minds, the Puritans were godly Protestants enlisted in the army of Christ, first, and Englishmen owing allegiance to earthly kings, second. And, of course, they had always refused any form of communion with Catholics. No doubt the Puritan was estranged from the Anglican *ecclesia*. It was also

---

15 David Hackett Fischer, *Albion's Seed: Four British Folkways in America* (New York: Oxford University Press, 1989), 70, 77-78.

true that the inner-directed conscience of most Puritans opened up a vast gulf between them and both God in his heaven and the king on his throne. Nevertheless, the covenants that Puritans made "in the Presence of God" were a classically English method of securing the reproductive fitness of the families clustering together in small villages in a hostile and threatening wilderness. The New England settlements were not alone in facing the ever-present threat of social disintegration in the New World. Yet no other European people organized themselves into civil bodies politic to cope with that danger; not the French in Canada, the Spanish in Latin America, not even the Swedes, the Germans, or the Dutch scattered along the eastern seaboard replicated that form of social organization. Only the Puritans embraced the covenant of grace as the essential foundation of a church polity that stood in for far-distant kings and bishops. It seems that the co-evolution of English blood and Protestant theology accounts for the persistent appeal of the covenant idea to enterprising Americans descended from the Puritans.

Hannah Arendt disagreed; she emphasized instead the classical republican roots of American covenant communities. Highlighting the cosmopolitan character of American constitutionalism, she gave little credit to either the English blood or the Christian spirit of the Puritan colonists. Arendt acknowledged, of course, that the Puritan's shining City on a Hill drew inspiration from the biblical language of the Old Testament and, especially, from "their rediscovery of the concept of the covenant of Israel." Clearly, the "federal theology" of Puritan divines looked to the biblical covenant as the "key to the history of the universe, the innermost meaning of divine revelation, the foundation of law in the apparent lawlessness of nature."[16]

Puritans were obviously inspired by the trials and tribulations of ancient Israel to plant a New Zion in the wilds of America. But Arendt denied that the Puritan settlers were the latter-day incarnation of a Hebrew tribe, a view taken by some intellectuals associated with the European New Right. Tomislav Sunic for example, contends that the Puritans introduced a "distilled version" of the "Jewish spirit…into the American mindset." Indeed, he holds that "alien 'anthropology'…directly responsible for the spread of an egalitarian mass society and the rise of a 'soft' liberal thought police." Sunic maintains that the "Judeo-Christian tradition" encapsulated in Puritan theology injected the Jewish spirit into *homo Americanus*—along with the anti-Semitic delusions which it provokes. The archaic traditions

---

16   Hannah Arendt, *On Revolution* (Harmondsworth: Penguin, 1973), 172; Perry Miller, *The New England Mind: The Seventeenth Century* (Boston: Beacon Press, 1961), 376.

of European paganism, he writes, provide the best antidote to both.[17] This argument, however, grossly overstates the influence of Old Testament tribalism on New England's covenant theology. It also ignores altogether the simultaneous influence on the development of the civil body politic in New England of the neo-pagan tradition of classical republicanism.

It is of course commonplace to assert that the biblical covenant idea exerted a continuing influence on American constitutional thought, mainly because it implied government by consent: "God gave the law and Israel consented to keep it." But the truly unique contribution of the covenant principle to colonial America was altogether unknown to the tribal peoples of ancient Israel. Arendt observes that the Old Testament "covenant implied government by consent," but ancient Israel never conceived "a political body in which rulers and ruled would be equal, that is, where actually the whole principle of rulership no longer applied."[18] She explains the civil bodies politic of colonial New England not as an expression of a transplanted Jewish tribalism but as a rediscovery of the elementary principles of politics first uncovered by the pagan city-states of ancient Greece.

Nonetheless, both Sunic and Arendt overlook the distinctively *English* character of the covenant communities established in New England. Arendt, in particular, treats the unique civil bodies politic of colonial America as the spontaneous product of experience, suggesting that the Puritan insight into the elementary structure of political action flowed more or less automatically from the experience of men transported into a state of nature. Freed from the cake of custom, communities can be held together only by the reciprocal force of mutual promises and these form the basis for a new power structure. In one important respect, Arendt was right: Puritan theology moved beyond the Old Testament by applying covenant to human affairs. In other words, covenant was no longer confined to the relationship between God and man. Somehow, Puritans came to understand that "we must not make God's Covenant with man, so far to differ from Covenants between man and man, as to make it no covenant at all."[19] By covenanting together into a rapidly expanding network of families, churches, and civil bodies politic, Puritan colonists ensured the intergenerational transmission of a novel cultural adaptation, a synthesis of old English folkways, Calvinist theology, and the elementary grammar of politics first known to the ancient Greeks. They were

---

17   Tomislav Sunic, *Homo Americanus: Child of the Postmodern Age* (Charleston, SC: BookSurge, 2007), 104-107.

18   Arendt, *On Revolution*, 172.

19   *Ibid.*, 167-172; Miller, *New England Mind*, 376.

not simply replicating the experience of biblical Israel, classical Greece, or even that of their Anglo-Saxon ancestors. Puritan settlers were an isolated gene pool, separated by three thousand miles of stormy ocean from a church and a king that they condemned, openly or covertly, as corrupt; they created a distinctive extended phenotype not found elsewhere, a way of life that proved to be enormously successful, whether judged in terms of reproductive fitness or of material wealth.

Families and corporate communities such as towns and churches, together with "the alliance of merchants, magistrates, and ministers known as the 'Standing Order'" remained the bases of New England society down to the 1780s.[20] With the rapid growth in population, property, and prosperity, covenant communities took their place as one element in the increasingly pluralistic and heterogeneous fabric of the system of political economy that underpinned the Atlantic world. No longer politically or economically isolated from the mercantilist framework governing the "empire of goods," the survival of the Standing Order of late colonial New England came to depend less on the saving grace showered upon the visible saints of the Puritan commonwealth than on the worldly interests and commercial ambitions of the Yankee merchant.[21]

Even before the American Revolution, the secular discourse of political economy challenged the intellectual hegemony of Calvinist theology. Scottish writers on political economy such as Sir James Stewart projected the model of the patriarchal household onto the national polity. Adam Smith believed that if perfect liberty was to become a social reality, "churchly interference in the free workings of the market" had to be substantially curtailed.[22] All agreed that it was the enlightened statesman-legislator who should fuse the "polity" and the "economy" into a single household in which all the objects of administration would be maintained in their rightful place. This no doubt was a form of secularization. But in New England the relative decline of Calvinist theology in favor of political economy reflected the *displacement* rather than the *decline* of religious feeling. The rise of the secular did not suppress the religious impulse; pushed out the front door, religion came back in through the window.

---

20   Peter Dobkin Hall, *The Organization of American Culture, 1700-1900: Private Institutions, Elites, and the Origins of American Nationality* (New York: New York University Press, 1982), 16.

21   TH Breen, "An Empire of Goods: The Anglicanization of Colonial America, 1690-1776," (1986) 25(4) *Journal of British Studies* 467.

22   D Stephen Long, *Divine Economy: Theology and the Market* (London: Routledge, 2000), 190.

Both the Standing Order in New England and the English ruling class succumbed readily to the worldly temptations of power and wealth held out by the leading lights of the new economic order. Seeking inner consistency and harmony within a polity divided "by sector (trade, manufacture, agriculture) or by consumption (productive versus unproductive populations)," statesmen-legislators unveiled a new secular aesthetic in which classical beauty could be joined with strength in the exercise of power. In that way, the secular discourse of political economy released a powerful current of neo-paganism within eighteenth century Anglo-American culture.[23] The Scottish Enlightment enlisted *en masse* in the cause of progress and prosperity despite concerns that such a trading society would ultimately sap the resources of noble strength required for warfare and political devotion." But, as Milbank points out, the new economic order offered an acceptable substitute in the form "of a 'playful' warfare, within limits, according to rules and permitting the testing and exercise of a constant ingenuity." Writers such as James Stewart and Adam Ferguson hoped that the ancient passion for glory could be sublimated into the desire for gain. This "clear-sighted vision" of capitalism as a new "Spartan republic" openly celebrated the will to domination rejected by Christian theology. "Here again," Milbank avers, "the 'autonomy' of secular reason involves as a condition of its very independence, the endorsement of a viewpoint which Christianity earlier presumed to call into question."[24]

While the neo-pagan doctrines of political economy gained influence within mercantile and political circles, the established clergy in New England upheld a profoundly elitist and conservative scheme of religion. In effect, their theology capitulated to the crypto-paganism of the governing class in both England and the colonies. Designed both to maintain a healthy discipline among congregations and to defend the corporate privileges of the established parish churches, the cold-blooded rationalism of "legal" Christianity provoked an evangelical revolt. The radicalism of evangelical revivalism did much to lay the spiritual foundation for the American Revolution; it also contributed directly to the development of the modern business corporation in the early American republic.

From the Great Awakening of the 1740s onward, evangelical preachers continually emphasized "the role of the affections in religion and in making virtue dependent on the reception of a vital indwelling principle from the Holy Spirit." In place of the orthodox Christian understanding

---

23 Keith Tribe, *Land, Labour and Economic Discourse* (London: Routledge & Kegan Paul, 1978), 85.

24 Milbank, *Theology and Social Theory*, 32-37.

of the *ecclesia* as the sacramental Body of Christ, revivalists looked to the "inward operation of the holy spirit in regeneration." It was the direct emotional intuition of divine love by every individual believer that held the "atoms of creation" together. On this view, "spiritual authority lay not in the church but in the individual's heart and conscience." Defenders of the Standing Order saw the "enthusiastic" approach to religion as "subversive of peace, *discipline*, and government." They were right to view evangelical revivalism as a real and serious threat to the vested interests of the established clergy. Stated in its simplest terms, the "goal of evangelical liberty was...the abolition of parish lines." Itinerant evangelical preachers insisted that only complete religious liberty—including freedom from inherited relationships—would enable men to sit down with their brethren "in good order and pleasure." Respectable men of learning and culture, however, looked upon roving evangelists "as an intrusion upon the covenant relationship of minister and people." Their worst fears proved to be well-founded.[25] During and after the American Revolution evangelical radicals did not limit themselves to the rejection of the spiritual authority institutionalized in the body corporate of the church. They were among the first to insist that the sovereign authority of government, once torn from the hands of the Crown, was seated in, rather than merely derived from, the people.

Corporations in a Democratic Republic

Let us see how such radically democratic theories affected the politics of the early republic. After years of turmoil, conservative propertied elites throughout the new nation saw the federal Constitution, drafted in Philadelphia in 1787, as the ideal means to establish a strong government ready, willing, and able to hold the licentious propensities of "the Many" in check. JGA Pocock argues that the Founding Fathers assumed "that the alternative to a hereditary, entrenched or artificial aristocracy was a natural aristocracy—an elite of persons distinguished by natural superiority of talent, but also by contingent material advantages such as property, leisure, and learning, as possessing the qualities of mind required by the classical Few."[26] The fundamental difficulty faced by Federalist statesmen-legislators was that the early republic was a house divided.

---

25 Alan Heimert, *Religion and the American Mind: From the Great Awakening to the Revolution* (Cambridge, MA: Harvard University Press, 1966), 1-15, 106-108, 119-121.

26 JGA Pocock, *The Machiavellian Moment: Florentine Political Thought and the Atlantic Republican Tradition* (Princeton, NJ: Princeton University Press, 1975), 515.

When Alexander Hamilton, the first Secretary of the Treasury, proposed a national bank, it at once became the subject of a prolonged and bitter political battle that "outstripped its economic importance." Hamilton's proposal was not received as the disinterested project of an enlightened statesman. On the contrary, the federal bank was condemned as "a plain defiance of agrarian interests and of the view that the powers of the federal government were definitely limited."[27] The battle over the bank and similar conflicts pitting backwoods farmers against urban merchants and bankers soon crystallized into the open party warfare that led finally to the "Revolution of 1800" that deprived "the Few" of their accustomed place at the head of the nation.

Having applied the enthusiastic spirit of evangelical revivalism to the populist art of electioneering, a new political party headed by Thomas Jefferson triumphed in the federal election of 1800. The propertied classes feared that the rise of Jeffersonian democracy would cause the rapid erosion of the "habit of subordination" among the people at large. Many Federalists genuinely hated the people for their new-found spirit of independence. "They are vicious," wrote one gentleman of the old school, "and love vicious men for their leaders." It seemed as if the entire natural order of hierarchy and authority was threatened with destruction now that "the herd have begun to walk on their hind legs." But despair and resignation were not the only responses to this crisis of authority. Although Federalist gentlemen of the founding generation looked upon public office as a right and a duty, even as a special kind of property, their sons of necessity developed a significantly different attitude toward politics and public life. Men of both generations were convinced that property ownership made for a special sort of civic virtue. But younger men knew that in a free and popular republic, gentlemen of property and standing no longer enjoyed an automatic right to govern.

With the rise of Jeffersonian democracy, the days of the old Standing Order of New England were numbered. The new national government, "which had been devised as an effort to limit and contain the popular will, became an instrument of the popular will" mediated through the novel organizational forms of the political party. Indeed, the "very existence of an organized political opposition challenged fundamental Federalist concepts of political, economic, and cultural authority." For nearly two centuries, the Standing Order "had seen itself as the steward of the common good—as the guardian of the church, of learning, of the state, and of

---

27 Bray Hammond, *Banks and Politics in America: From the Revolution to the Civil War* (Princeton, NJ: Princeton University Press, 1957), 118-120.

the world of commerce." It was "faced with an opposition that wanted not merely to occupy the seats of power, but to alter the institutions of power." Now that public power had passed out of their hands, it became absolutely imperative that "the best men in the country" take steps to reassert their cultural hegemony with the institutional life of American civil society. Recognizing that necessity, important elements within the old propertied elite developed a program of political, social, and economic activism that amounted to a "revolution of American conservatism."[28] Foremost among the battery of institutional devices employed in the conservative campaign to conquer and colonize American society was the civil body corporate and politic, what we now call "the corporation."

No longer able to expect unchallenged control over the state, the propertied elite in New England and, to a lesser extent, elsewhere invented the private corporation as an institutional expression of their renewed and reinvigorated claim to civic authority. Particularly in Massachusetts and other New England states, those who sought grants of corporate privileges from the legislature were moved at least as much by the evident *political* utility of a corporate charter as by its *economic* advantages. As part of a larger scheme to restore an encompassing hierarchy of order and authority in American civil society, Federalist elites sought to ensure private control over an expanding range of educational and charitable corporations. The decision of the US Supreme Court in the *Dartmouth College* case affirmed the constitutional autonomy of "private" corporations. In his landmark judgement, Justice Joseph Story rejected the view that the distinguishing feature of the private corporation was the pursuit of private profits. He affirmed that the distinction between private and public corporations depended not upon their object or purposes but upon the interests at stake in each. When private persons gathered together to promote public purposes such as education, charity, or public health, the private property dedicated to those goals did not become "instantaneously the property of the government;" nor could the trustees appointed by the donors "be compelled to yield up their rights to whomsoever the government might appoint to administer [such gifts.]"[29] Corporations that featured a stock of purely private capital were entitled to a constitutionally protected autonomy.

---

28   David Hackett Fischer, *The Revolution of American Conservatism: The Federalist Party in the Era of Jeffersonian Democracy* (New York: Harper Torchbooks, 1965), 23-24, 30; Hall, *American Culture*, 83.

29   *Trustees of Dartmouth College v Woodward* (1819) 17 US 518, at 668-72.

Paradoxically, such autonomy was vital precisely because profit-making, private business corporations were chartered to undertake projects that were clearly in the public interest. Most early charters went to private corporations willing to build turnpikes or canals at their own expense. Banks and insurance companies also served important public purposes. As a consequence, all private corporations, whatever their objects, were conceived as civil bodies politic. The legislative grant of a corporate charter established public spaces (such as general meetings) wherein individual shareholders could exercise the political prerogatives of citizenship (such as voting and speaking rights) within the joint enterprise. Across the entire range of the hundreds of corporations chartered in New England in the early nineteenth century, conservatives hoped to counter the intense anti-institutionalism that had been spawned by evangelical radicalism. They set out to erect "*new* institutions capable of dealing with an increasingly complex urban and industrial society and to restore social cohesion and public virtue."[30] Any enterprise endowed with a charter was thus lifted above the worldly pursuit of merely private interests by the common law conception of the corporation as an association of persons vested with certain powers necessary to promotion of some design of general utility and public benefit. Indistinguishable in principle from the ancient *polis* defined by Aristotle as "an association of persons formed with a view to some good purpose," the American business corporation was born as a little republic.

For several decades republican norms were applied more or less faithfully to the realm of corporate governance. In principle, each shareholder entered into a world common to all of them and distinguished from his privately owned place in it.[31] According to one judge, it followed that a corporation could not permit voting by proxy at corporate meetings without special authority from the state legislature. Voting by proxy, he declared, might suit the personal convenience of members but it could not "be for the good of the corporation." Both the interest of the company and "the good of the public, would be better promoted and more effectually secured by the personal attendance of, and mutual interchange of opinions among the members, than by actions of proxies." Another republican principle held that every owner of one share is a member of the company, enjoying the rights and privileges of membership which "cannot be greater or different in one member than they are in another." Such

30 John F Kasson, *Civilizing the Machine: Technology and Republican Values in America, 1776-1900* (Harmondsworth: Penguin, 1977), 63.

31 Hannah Arendt, *The Human Condition* (Chicago: University of Chicago Press, 1958), 52.

principles were not always observed in practice. The legal conception of
the corporation as a civil body politic ran directly counter to the interests
of large shareholders seeking to transform the enterprise into a purely private, profit-seeking unit of capital accumulation. The most obvious way of
bending to pressure from that quarter would be to allow voting by share
rather than by voice. In fact, the one-share, one-vote rule was incorporated into many corporate charters. Others put a cap on the voting power
of large shareholders. But hard-core republicans were in no doubt that in
the absence of a special legislative authorization "every corporator, every
individual member of a body politic, whether public or private, is *prima
facie*, entitled to equal rights."[32]

The importance of the corporate form to the maintenance of a stable
and well-ordered republican polity had been recognized as well in the
ecclesiastical law of post-revolutionary Massachusetts. Because Article III
of the Declaration of Rights appended to the Massachusetts constitution
of 1780 declared that "the good order and preservation of civil government, essentially depend upon piety, religion, and morality," the public
worship of God was not left to the individual conscience; it became a
public duty. The legislature was directed "to authorize and require the
several towns, parishes, precincts, and other bodies politic, or religious
societies" to provide for "the public worship of God, and for the support and maintenance of public Protestant teachers of piety, religion, and
morality."[33] With the support of the courts, the "better sort of men" set out
to ensure that the legal establishment of religion in Massachusetts worked
to ensure that their "invisible" authority remained effective. In *Barnes v
Falmouth*, Chief Justice Parsons held that the words "religious societies"
in the third article of the Declaration of Rights "must, from the nature of
the duty imposed upon them, necessarily mean societies having corporate
power." Without such corporate powers, no voluntary association would
have "legal authority to assess money on all the members, or to compel
payment, or to elect a teacher by the vote of the greater part." On this
understanding, the church as an ecclesiastical body could not "subsist but
in connection with some corporate parish or religious society."[34]

In the eyes of many, this regime smacked of secular neo-paganism.
Critics argued that this sort of religious establishment was aimed not

---

32 *Taylor v Griswold* 2 Green Rep (NJ) 223, at 229, 237.

33 The text of the *Declaration of Rights* can be found in Jacob C Meyer, *Church and State in
Massachusetts from 1740 to 1833: A Chapter in the History of the Development of Individual
Freedom* (Cleveland, OH: Western Reserve University Press, 1930).

34 *Barnes v Falmouth* 6 Mass Rep 400 at 412-413.

at the salvation of souls but at providing security for property by preventing crime and disorder. The goal was to maintain all the objects of
civil administration in their rightful place. In determining whether a
particular form of religious activity should be licensed and protected by
law, the test was one of benefit to the polity. Federalist politicians and
Congregational clergymen were alarmed by the erosion of habitual subordination and deference among a people emboldened by the twin experiences of revolution and independence. In clothing their religious, charitable, educational, and business activities in the corporate form, propertied
and professional elites were adapting the federal theology of covenanted
communities to a secular crisis of authority in a modern republican polity.
As a consequence, the common law model of the corporation as a civil
body politic became the focal point for a prolonged and often bitter political, social, and religious struggle. The deep-rooted and continuing contest
between "evangelical" and "legal" Christianity had its exact parallel in the
struggle between radical advocates of free and general incorporation and
conservative proponents of incorporation by special act of the state legislatures. The modern business corporation was conceived in a frenzy of
millenarian revivalism.[35]

Millenarian Capitalism

Even in its most conservative manifestations, the early American republic
was a revolutionary regime. Having tossed aside the ancestral authority
of throne and altar, most Americans chafed at "undemocratic" institutional restraints. Reaching its crescendo during the Jacksonian era, a wave
of evangelical enthusiasm and secular reformism swept aside the few
remaining conservative influences in religion, politics, and law. Radical
democrats were particularly incensed by the legal privileges and social
status that flowed from possession of a corporate charter. Evangelical
reformers were repelled by a religious establishment whose *raison d'être*
was limited to the prevention of crime and other threats to property and
social order. Reformers of all stripes were determined to strip both ecclesiastical and business corporations of their constitutional identity as civil
bodies politic. Evangelical religion burned with a passionate desire to save
souls. That same evangelical fervor inspired the campaign to eliminate the

---

35 See generally, Andrew Fraser, *The Spirit of the Laws: Republicanism and the Unfinished
    Project of Modernity* (Toronto: University of Toronto Press, 1990), chapter 4.

"aristocratic influences" and "special privileges" that attached to corporate charters.

Both movements were driven by a boundless faith in America's future as a "redeemer nation."[36] That faith amounted to a cult of revolution. The millenarian enthusiasm of evangelical Protestants could not be contained within the framework of institutionalized religion or confined to the received forms of theological debate. And that religious zeal was bound to spill over into the secular realm. Conversely, perhaps, American evangelicalism was firmly grounded in the *novus ordo seclorum* established by the American Revolution. Believing that America's unique role was to realize the Kingdom of God on earth, radical millenialists struggled to "overturn" obstacles on the road to the Kingdom wherever they appeared, in every area of American life; somnolent acceptance of things as they were was seen as "the principal device by which Satan now hopes to frustrate the divine plan." Thus, ante-bellum social reform movements were uprisings "directed at spiritual evil, not simple political wrongs, however little religion may seem at the time to be involved." Just such an apocalyptic spirit moved a writer in the *Presbyterian Quarterly Review* of 1853 to condemn the common law conception of the chartered corporation as a civil body politic:

> Whenever and wherever the rights secured by everlasting charter and sealed by the blood of the covenant, alike to every human being, are withheld and monopolized; wherever institutions, obviously distrusting general happiness are sustained by force and appeals to passions and interests; revolutions will occur as light increases marked with more or less violence, in proportion to the resistance offered, or the wisdom employed, till human rights are all properly guaranteed and wrong principles and institutions are swept away.[37]

Clearly, the dynamic expansion of American capitalism in the age of Jackson cannot be ascribed lightly to any narrowly "economic" impulse. Economic activity was not an end in itself. People were moved by a deep need to interpret prosperity and worldly success as visible signs that divine grace had been bestowed upon America and its righteous citizens. At the same time, evangelicals were convinced that the spirit of divine love could never be captured and frozen in any fixed and stable set of institutional arrangements. Acting on that conviction, evangelical reformers

---

36 Ernest Lee Tuveson, *Redeemer Nation: The Idea of America's Millennial Role* (Chicago: University of Chicago Press, 1968).

37 *Ibid.*, 76.

repeatedly urged their fellow Americans to dissolve their worldly ties with other men.

The spirit of evangelical Christianity was profoundly hostile to the civic humanist model of the corporation as a little republic. Indeed, the movement harbored a profoundly anti-institutional animus towards the established order in general; few of its members were receptive to the older view that "True Virtue" can be distilled from the civic experience of sharing in the ownership and control of a banking, insurance, or turnpike corporation; however worthy the public interests such a joint enterprise might serve. Evangelical preachers condemned both the neo-paganism of civic republicanism and the orthodox Christianity of their Old English ancestors. Instead, they offered every individual direct and unmediated access to God. The voice of the Holy Spirit, they claimed, could be heard only by a listener attentive to the innermost longing of his own heart. Those who heeded the evangelical call to turn inward hastened the progressive dissolution of both the worldly body politic and the ecclesiastical Body of Christ. The evangelical message was simple: "Overturn, and overturn, and overturn, till he come, whose right it is, is the great annunciation."[38]

In the hope of securing their personal salvation amidst such revolutionary changes, Americans were sorely tempted to find in worldly success the tangible evidence of their individual and collective redemption. Few were taken aback when the author of a *Practical Treatise on Business* insisted that it was a "religious duty…to get money." Among those who followed that injunction, "the theory of natural aristocracy was overshadowed by a philosophy of individual success and the concept of a republican community gave way to the image of a loose association of individuals each making his own way in the world."[39]

The revolutionary anti-institutionalism of the new regime was reflected in the legal changes associated with the emergence of the modern business corporation. In summary, the special charter regime was replaced by general incorporation laws. What had been an association of persons covenanting together with a view to some good purpose became a legal fiction created by the merely formal act of registration. Corporate law soon became a legal technology justified solely and simply by its economic rather than political or religious utility. But this should not be read as the

---

38 Id.

39 Louis Hartz, *Economic Policy and Democratic Thought: Pennsylvania, 1776-1860* (Cambridge, MA: Harvard University Press, 1948), 20; John G Cawelti, *Apostles of the Self-Made Man* (Chicago: University of Chicago Press, 1965), 43.

triumph of homespun American pragmatism over the confusions engendered by archaic English common law doctrines. The religious fervor of
evangelical Protestantism destroyed the chartered corporation just as it
had earlier overturned the authority of kings, nobles, and priests. Property
was no longer recognized as the material foundation of political authority, much less of civic or ecclesiastical virtue. Pooled within the business
corporation, private property was transformed into economic capital, the
utility and worth of which depended upon its efficient allocation within
an organized system of production, distribution, and exchange.[40]

Marx was among the first to recognize that once property takes on the
form of economic capital—once it is treated by owners as a mere commodity—it loses its political character and becomes a *social* relation. An
individual capitalist then appears as "the personification of this relation:
he is a function of his own capital, and direct expression of his private
property." Ownership has been separated from control in the modern
business corporation; the result is the abolition of private property in the
socialized capital stock of a joint enterprise. With the rise of social capital, "capital comes to represent all capitalists, and the individual capitalist
is reduced to an individual personification of this totality."[41] No longer
can the corporation function as a civil body politic. As each shareholder
becomes the "personification" of his individual capital, the republican
notion that every shareholder should have one vote whatever the size of
his investment in the joint enterprise becomes patently absurd. The capital stock of the corporation takes on a life of its own.

General incorporation laws elevated the property rights of shareholders above the associational rights attached to membership in a joint enterprise. It was no longer assumed, therefore, that all shareholders must stand
in the same relation to the enterprise or that they would enjoy an equality
of rights. New and different classes of shares, some of which might not
even carry voting rights, made their appearance. And, if the associational
rights of the shareholder were limited so too was his responsibility for the
conduct of corporate business. In chartered corporations limited liability was not an automatic and universal privilege of membership. General
incorporation laws soon limited shareholder liability for corporate debts
to the par value of their shares. Under the charter regime, the constitutional principle of *ultra vires* had recognized that all members of a body
corporate and politic belonged were engaged in a common enterprise: the
charter set out the specific objects of the business and thereby limited

40   Andrew Fraser, "The Corporation as a Body Politic," *Telos* 57 (Fall 1983), 29-30.

41   Mario Tronti, "Social Capital," *Telos* 17 (Fall 1973), 105.

the scope of corporate powers. By contrast, general incorporation laws allowed corporations to define and redefine the nature of their activities more or less at will. The common world of shareholders lost its concrete character as the objects and purposes of the joint enterprise were pitched at ever-higher levels of abstraction. The new governing assumption was that the primary goal of any business corporation is to maximize profits as, when, and how shareholders and managers saw fit. As a consequence, minority shareholders were powerless to protest should a railroad corporation, for example, choose to divert its capital to the purchase of a hotel chain. Under general incorporation laws, the corporation's only constant aim is to obtain a higher-than-average yield on its capital stock.

By the late nineteenth century, a national market in the shares of large industrial companies had replaced the original practice of "private" subscriptions. And, with the rise of investment banking, "even the marketing of original shares of corporate stock no longer entailed a formal relationship between the corporation and a subscriber."[42] Once the role of the shareholder was reduced to that of a mere "investor," corporate management came to play the role of the "collective capitalist." On the one hand, management becomes "the supreme mediation and composition of all particular bourgeois interests while on the other it is the direct representative of the general interest for capital." With the rise of the big business corporation, the socialization of capital eliminates shareholders as the controlling power. In fact, the separation of ownership and control amounts to "the abolition of capital as private property within the framework of capitalist production itself." Having taken on the corporate form, capital "raises itself to the level of a general social power, while the capitalist is reduced to the level of a simple agent, functionary, or emissary of this power."[43] In the standard Marxist narrative, corporate capitalism flattens pre-existing social and political hierarchies in an ongoing process of abstraction that is both necessary and irrational.

Corporate capitalism is said to be necessary because it is only through the socialization of production that labor reveals itself as the true measure of value. At the same time, the corporate system is irrational because the appropriation of surplus value generated by the productive power of labor remains in private hands. Economic man makes history, but he knows not what he hath wrought; the social being of workers and capitalists alike stands over against them as an alien, uncontrollable force. Milbank points

42 Morton J Horwitz, *The Transformation of American Law, 1870-1960: The Crisis of Legal Orthodoxy* (New York: Oxford University Press, 1992), 97.

43 Tronti, "Social Capital," 107-108.

out that "capitalism is not regarded by Marx merely as a particular historical conjuncture which has become so deeply sedimented as to appear unchangeable." In orthodox Marxist theory, "capitalism finally reveals the economic foundations of all societies and helps us to interpret all societies." Marx expected capitalism to have a profoundly corrosive influence on the bonds that united human beings in every particular local political and cultural community. As our relations with nature and each other come to be governed by the laws of the marketplace, all of us are deprived of a secure location in the world. Under the impact of money and commerce, even "the natural-ethnic tie of particularistic communities" dissolves: "the individuals which were enclosed therein are cast forth like free atoms; the localistic barriers fall away together with blood and lineage." In the money relation, "individuals *seem independent*...free to collide with one another and to engage in exchange within this freedom" but that freedom is an illusion. Only if one abstracts from the substantive conditions which govern the individual entering into a contract can that illusion be supported: "individuals are now ruled by *abstractions*, whereas earlier they depended on one another."[44] However irrational that process of abstraction might appear, Marx insisted that it was a necessary stage in mankind's progress toward the final emancipation of labor in a communist society.

Marx attached no particular significance to the uniquely European and, in particular, Anglo-Saxon provenance of modern capitalism even as he incorporated a quintessentially Anglo-Protestant natural theology into his own critique of political economy. It became an axiom of orthodox Marxism that "[c]apitalist production...is as truly cosmopolitan as Christianity...In both it is only man in the abstract who counts...In the one case all depends on whether or not he has faith, in the other, on whether or not he has credit." [45] Foremost among the illusions that Marx was determined to dispel was the Christian religion. Marx acknowledged that Christianity, like capitalism itself, was a necessary stage in a historical process. The end of history would arrive when mankind was emancipated from the self-estrangement which reaches its highest pitch in the realm of labor. Until then, he expected, Christianity and capitalism will persist in a symbiotic relationship of mutual dependence. Both will finally collapse, however, under the weight of their rapidly accumulating internal contradictions. For Marx, the historic function of Christianity was to reveal the

---

44   Milbank, *Theology and Social Theory*, 192; Lucio Colletti, *Marxism and Hegel* (London: NLB, 1979), 58-67; Karl Marx, *Grundrisse: Foundations of the Critique of Political Economy* (Harmondsworth: Penguin, 1973), 163-164.

45   Colletti, *Marxism and Hegel*, 271.

essential equality and universality of human nature. His perception of the kinship between Christianity and capitalism must have been strengthened by the successive waves of evangelical revivalism in ante-bellum America. It was well known that in America the spirit of Christian love acted as a kind of "gravity inherent in the atoms of creation" which alone could "hold the beings of the spiritual world together."[46] Marx, too, perceived that "what was in the ancient world the *worldly bond*" between citizens of the ancient *polis* "with Christianity presents itself not only as an *other-worldly bond*, situated *above and beyond men*, but also as a cohesive bond 'in heaven' that has its basis in the atomistic disintegration of the individuals 'on earth.'" He drew the sceptical conclusion that men, through Christianity, had come to represent as God that which "is nothing more than man's own alienated essence."[47] On that materialist view, evangelical Christianity was fated to become the special religion of American capitalism.

But Marxists are wrong to treat American-style corporate capitalism as either a necessary or an irrational expression of the dialectical movement of the historical process. Neither evangelical Christianity nor the spirit of American capitalism were predestined elements in a natural process working inexorably towards a state of harmony and equilibrium. Evangelical Christianity is better understood as a heresy spawned within a distinctively Anglo-Saxon Protestant bioculture in a particular time and place. Similarly, the modern business corporation is not an irrational phenomenon doomed to disappear into the dustbin of history. Corporate capitalism will most likely remain "viable so long as certain asymmetries of wealth and power can be sustained, and the losers can be either coerced or seduced into quiescence."[48] It will not be superseded simply because some higher-order rationality exposes its inner contradictions. A perversion of Christian theology permitted the modern business corporation to establish itself as a secular parody of the *ecclesia*. Whether that sin can be redeemed by returning to an orthodox Christian ecclesiology, only God knows. But we can be sure that, for better or for worse, the rise of the business corporation was a crucial turning point in the ethnoreligious history of Anglo-America. From a biocultural perspective, the most important consequence of the managerial revolution in corporate governance was the recasting of Anglo-American social character into a novel form, one particularly susceptible to Anglo-Saxon Anglophobia.

---

46 Heimert, *Religion and the American Mind*, 115-121.

47 Colletti, *Marxism and Hegel*, 261-265.

48 Milbank, *Theology and Social Theory*, 194.

The Corporate *Ecclesia*

Those who contemplate the early medieval history of the Church of England with the eye of faith will recognize in it the Body of Christ. Others examining the same institution with the eye of reason will discover the protective shell that encapsulated the extended phenotype of the Anglcynn people. In those days, the ecclesiastical corporation was merely the legal form of an organic religious community. In early nineteenth century New England, the corporate form had migrated from the church into civil society. There it became the extended phenotype of an Anglo-American bourgeoisie that sought to stabilize its customary standing within a dynamic system of political economy, all the while under relentless pressure from commercial and military rivals abroad and a rising democracy at home. At least for a time, the corporation served tolerably well as an instrument of in-group solidarity, both for Anglo-Saxons as an ethny and the bourgeoisie as a class.

In America, however, it was not long before big business corporations metastasized into a vastly *over*-extended phenotype incapable of preserving either the class boundaries of the bourgeoisie or the ethnic character of the Anglo-American nation as a whole. Indeed, it became impossible to distinguish between particular corporations and the complex transnational, politico-economic system in which they were embedded. The corporation lost its organic character; bourgeois class solidarity was breached by the emergence of a moderately meritocratic managerial class charged with control over the corporate system; ethnic solidarity was stretched to the breaking point by the vast tide of immigrant labor toiling in the factories, mines, canals, and railroads of corporate America. Eventually, even the hegemony of WASP executives in the upper reaches of the corporate hierarchy was challenged by ambitious professional peers from other ethnic groups.

Nowadays, an inbred lack of in-group solidarity among WASPs is reinforced by the dominant legal view of the corporation which regards it as little more than a "nexus of contracts" between managers, directors, shareholders, suppliers and creditors, employees and customers scattered across the face of the globe. It is doubtful, however, whether the "nexus of contracts" theory constrains the ethnic nepotism practiced by more cohesive groups such as Jews, Chinese, Indians, and Negroes. In fact, those who dissolve the corporate entity into "a set of implicit or explicit contracts" are transferring a direct analogue of the "proposition nation" idea from the realm of constitutional law into the realm of corporate governance.[49] Not surprisingly, the result has been to transform the ethnocultural character of both the state and the corporate sphere.

According to the conventional wisdom, the corporation is not now, if it ever was, an organic biocultural entity; it does not follow that corporations have been drained of their primordial religious significance. Having migrated from the church to the economy, the modern business corporation simply shifted the innate religiosity of Anglo-Saxon Protestants toward a more mundane creed. For most of the twentieth century, workers and consumers alike embraced the corporate system with religious zeal. "Belief in the old gods may be flickering," Wilmot Robertson noted, "but belief in the more worldly deities of the present is laser bright."[50] As the unholy trinity of the state, the market, and the modern business corporation successfully colonized virtually every facet of American life, traditional reservoirs of meaning have become an ever-scarcer resource. Capitalism took off in the early American republic when the man of the Protestant ethic was available to supply power on the runway. But, once in flight, the corporate "economy moved ahead not on character but on technique. Hence, if at the center of the nineteenth century social imagination there had stood a man, in the twentieth he was replaced by the vision of a system."

In desperation, Americans sought to find ways to spiritualize the system. Many such self-help techniques were unsuccessful.

> But there was one more alternative for sanctifying the system without doing anything about it, another way of thinking to make everything come out right. This was to regard the economy in a traditional religious fashion, as an object of worship rather than for imitation, an occasion for dependency rather than for belonging. Men know the hidden God, the God of Will, only in His works, not in His nature. In a downward spiral, men could return by way of dialectic to the position of early Protestants, between whom and God there opened an abyss, to be bridged not by insight, by knowledge, by intelligence, by courage, by politics, by tradition, but by faith alone. Awesome, inscrutable, self-impelling, the system invited adoration.[51]

---

49   Frank H Easterbrook and Daniel R Fischel, "The Corporate Contract," (1989) 89 *Columbia Law Review* 1416.

50   Robertson, *Dispossessed Majority*, 258.

51   Donald Meyer, *The Positive Thinkers: A Study of the American Quest for Health, Wealth and Personal Power from Mary Baker Eddy to Norman Vincent Peale* (New York: Anchor, 1966), 194-195.

The corporate system successfully harnessed the deep well-springs of religiosity carefully constructed by many generations of Anglo-Saxon Protestants. In the increasingly rationalized, impersonal, and one-dimensional world of corporate America, evangelical Christianity declined into a form of mind-cure that extolled the power of positive thinking. Managerial technique sought to fill the spiritual void by broadcasting the "lyric of plenty" incessantly in the hope that the desires of the perfect, passive consumer would become automated. The therapeutic aim of this consumerist faith was to eliminate the very need for meaning. As Donald Meyer put it, "the wish for plenty was the wish not to have to wish wishes of one's own at all."[52]

But the managerial revolution in corporate governance engendered a new "corporate humanism" that put a more positive spin on the "new gospel of therapeutic release." Managerial theory set out deliberately to fashion a new "social self" in place of the inner-directed, rugged individualism fostered by the early modern Protestant ethic. Prominent turn-of-the-century progressive intellectuals such as William James, John Dewey, and John R Commons hoped that "the change in social life from an individual to a corporate affair" would sanction new forms of subjectivity embedded within "the ensemble of social and emotive relations within the corporate workplace." The corporate intelligentsia expressed confidence that what we now recognize as "the demon of consumerist nihilism" could be held at bay. A new sense of corporate selfhood was needed to unite workers and employers in a "spirit of brotherhood." To realize that "great industrial vision," management would shift "from figures to feelings as instruments of control." Managers were now to be responsible for the "credentialed orchestration of the corporation's emotional and spiritual, as well as physical, life."[53]

Randolph Bourne hailed this new scientific manager as "a walking evangel" for a "new thing that is to dominate mankind." The "new gospel" of scientific knowledge and industrial peace "combined the zeal of religion, the subtlety of moral philosophy, and the precision of productive efficiency."[54] The result was the late "nineteenth century crisis of authority" experienced most acutely by members of the traditional, college-educated, professional, and gentry classes. According to Thomas Haskell,

---

52 Ibid., 207.

53 Eugene McCarraher, "'An Industrial Marcus Aurelius': Corporate Humanism, Management Theory, and Social Selfhood, 1908-1956," (2005) 5(1) *Journal of the Historical Society* 79 at 85, 97, 98.

54 Ibid., 79.

that crisis had its roots in the growth of a complex, interdependent society produced by the rise of the modern business corporation. Revolutions in transportation, communications, and marketing totally transformed the American economy. As society became more interdependent, the isolated "island communities" characteristic of the pre-industrial world came to be more heavily influenced, if not dominated, by events and persons at a distance from themselves. The search for the effective cause of events occurring in one's own immediate environment became more complex and shrouded in mystery. "One's personal milieu which is the source of the average man's entire conception of the larger society, was drained of vitality and made transparent, so to speak, to the play of influences originating far beyond the individual's range of vision." In such circumstances, "the realm of inquiry must expand and the conditions of satisfying explanation must change. Common sense fails and the claim of expertise gains plausibility." All of this had profound implications for the traditional Anglo-American bourgeoisie of merchants, professionals, and propertied gentlemen because their "traditional social function was to ascertain causation and to mediate between the island community and the outside world."[55] The visible hand of corporate management transformed both the image and the reality of American society as a widely-scattered archipelago of more or less self-sufficient local communities became a continental system of production, distribution, and exchange.

The Corporate Culture of Critical Discourse

Doctors, lawyers, and clergymen were forced to follow the example set by "scientific managers." The old bourgeoisie sought a way to re-establish its traditional authority in the fundamentally altered circumstances of corporate America. Because the problems of social order and authority in a complex industrial society were bound up with the issue of social causation, the movement to establish authority on a new footing "required that there be a science of society." Colleges and universities were re-made in the image of the business corporation. "Scholars" became "researchers" in communities of inquiry designed "to identify competence, cultivate it, and confer authority on those who possessed it in accordance with universalistic criteria, or, more realistically, criteria that were not in any obvious

---

55 Thomas L. Haskell, *The Emergence of Professional Social Science: The American Social Science Association and the Nineteenth Century Crisis of Authority* (Urbana, IL: University of Illinois Press, 1977), 32-46, 82-89, 221.

way personal, partisan, or particular."[56] As the new "culture of critical discourse" spread its influence, "the collapse of the nineteenth century's proprietary-Protestant order" was unavoidable. The older proprietary-Protestant "moral economy" had rested on "the omni-competent male proprietor" who exercised a sole and exclusive dominion over the external things of the world as well as his household, his farm, or his business. By contrast, the rising corporate intelligentsia pioneered the applied science of social relations. It also "articulated a new character ideal, combining moral and religious longing, a greater awareness of social interdependence, and modern, 'scientific' forms of technical and organizational prowess." By transforming "management theory into a course in character-building," the new managerial archetype transformed the inner-directed Anglo-American bourgeoisie into a New Class of other-directed WASPs.[57]

The New Class which came to dominate corporate America fused intellectuals and the technical intelligentsia into a structurally differentiated and autonomous social stratum. Its power and influence rests upon its possession and control of the specialized culture developed and transmitted within the educational system, and especially within the universities. Soon, the specialized knowledge and cultural skills acquired by members of the New Class became objectified in the form of educational credentials. Those credentials were a form of cultural capital. On the one hand, personal professional qualifications became the property of individual members of the New Class who could use them to generate a stream of income. On the other hand, the collective cultural capital vested in the New Class as a whole underpinned its revolutionary role in the corporate welfare state.

The culture of critical discourse united this New Class as a "speech community." Members of the managerial-professional classes learn to manipulate a linguistic code with its own "historically evolved set of rules, a grammar of discourse which (1) is concerned to *justify* its assertions, but (2) whose mode of justification does not proceed by invoking authorities, and (3) prefers to elicit the *voluntary* consent of those addressed solely on the basis of arguments adduced."[58] In other words, the managerial culture of critical discourse institutionalizes a mode of communication which forbids any reliance by a speaker upon his authority or status in society to justify his claims; it therefore has the effect of de-authorizing

56 *Ibid.*, 87-89.

57 McCarraher, "Industrial Marcus Aurelius," 81-82.

58 Alvin W Gouldner, *The Future of Intellectuals and the Rise of the New Class* (New York: Continuum, 1979), 18-28.

all speech grounded in traditional societal authority. Inherited patterns of social, political, and religious authority are flattened into a single register of critical speech: "persons and their social positions must not be visible in their speech. Speech becomes impersonal…disembodied, de-contextualized, and self-grounded."[59]

The dominance of those who master this distinctive linguistic code of critical speech presupposes the separation of ownership from control in the corporate system. No longer could legal proprietorship be fused with productive labor. "Corporate managers and technical professionals simultaneously divorced mental from manual labor by appropriating the craft knowledge and organizational prowess once possessed by artisan-proprietors." The independent male proprietor was transformed into a wage or salary earner; at the same time, women began to exit the household to join the ranks of the labor force. One major consequence was a "prolonged sexual revolution that unsettled the Protestant moral economy's conventions of gender, sexual conduct, and reproduction." It was not just husbands and fathers who were de-authorized by the new corporate system; the "old" middle class of bankers, tradesmen, small entrepreneurs, and technically oriented engineers was dispossessed to make way for a new system of organization based "neither on equality nor on arbitrary authority, but on functional unity." Managerial theory set out to orchestrate new forms of *social* selfhood. Their ideal of the well-adjusted individual was exemplified most effectively in the moral character of professional-managerial workers, men and women accustomed to the shifting, unstable character of personal relationships in complex organizations. There is little doubt that the corporate self was far more manipulable than the inner-directed, bourgeois character once associated with Anglo-Saxon Protestantism. The ideal corporate manager mastered the art of wielding power without appearing to issue orders or advice from on high, a "managerial ruse" couched in the "parlance of pragmatism and psychology" but which "depended upon the enlistment of religious desires."[60]

The corporate humanism of the early twentieth century was a "secular faith" that "embraced three tenets: the group is the source of creativity; 'belongingness' or 'togetherness' is the highest good; and social science modelled after management provides the way to the *summum bonum*."[61] A new clerisy of academic experts and progressive intellectuals laid claim

---

59 *Ibid.*, 84-85.

60 McCarraher, "Industrial Marcus Aurelius," 83, 87, 98, 103.

61 *Ibid.*, 110.

to a "cultural authority" that was borrowed from traditional religion." But the high priests of the new order such as William James "detached religious experience from its social context, delivered it to secular professional surveillance," and transformed it into "a privatized, denatured, purely therapeutic mode of moral discourse." Corporate humanism rested on a pragmatic philosophy that valued religion for its perceived contribution "to secularized modes of psychological and social utility." James believed that theology "would have to evolve from the expression of a particular tradition to a generalized 'science of religions." To that end, he hoped to "broker a 'consensus of opinion' among religious adherents," deauthorizing "the individual and local elements of religious beliefs" while distilling the essential nature common to every form of religious experience.[62] The "radical subjectivity" of his definition of religion was part and parcel of the corporate self. James denied that any "overriding philosophy or theology held the key to life's existence." Within a complex and interdependent corporate system "each individual would find the truth by combining a number of different worldviews."[63]

The combination of radical subjectivity and the social self created the cosmopolitan, other-directed character of the WASP, a social type that first appeared among upper crust scions of corporate America in the late nineteenth century. By the mid-twentieth century, sociologists noted that the other-directed character was typical of the "new" urban middle classes who held down white-collar jobs in corporate and governmental bureaucracies. At that time, other ethnic groups, most notably Negroes and Jews, mounted a concerted challenge to WASP hegemony in the economy, politics, and culture. Soon, the theological perversity as well as the biocultural risks associated with corporate humanism began to manifest themselves. Within an ethnically homogeneous society, managerial efforts to "lay down the law, not of coercion, but of goodwill" to harmonize "all the relationships of capital and labor" might have improved the reproductive fitness of the Anglo-American working and middle classes. But, by the mid-twentieth century, the corporate system had transformed the Anglo-American republic into a multi-racial, polyglot empire.

On the eve of the post-war civil rights revolution, the other-directed "social self" of the middle class WASP was well-primed to mutate into the profoundly maladaptive cult of the Other—soon to become the established

---

62 Eugene McCarraher, *Christian Critics: Religion and the Impasse in Modern American Social Thought* (Ithaca, NY: Cornell University Press, 2000), 14-15.

63 Eric P Kaufmann, *The Rise and Fall of Anglo-America* (Cambridge, MA: Harvard University Press, 2004), 101.

religion of the transnational corporate welfare state. The corporate culture of critical discourse was an intellectual pathogen; as it spread outward from the technical intelligentsia into the immigrant settlement houses and *avant-garde* circles in Chicago and New York, it increased in virulence. As it was marketed in the popular idiom of news, advertising, and entertainment, corporate humanism enervated the auto-immune system of Anglo-American bioculture as a whole. In the name of cosmopolitanism and pluralism, the rise of the corporate clerisy precluded WASPs from recourse to a vital ethnoreligious tradition of in-group solidarity comparable to those undergirding their ethnic rivals.

The Cosmopolitan Cult of the Other

One scholar suggests that WASPs were their own worst enemy. According to Eric P Kaufmann, the decline of Anglo-America was not due to external factors; in particular, it did not follow an organized campaign by commercial and ethnic minority groups to challenge WASP hegemony. He contends that the decisive "forces of dominant-ethnic decline" emerged instead "from *within* Anglo-Protestant America." Brian Gratton suggests that the most significant psychological and spiritual force driving WASPs to commit *hari-kari* was the other-directed nature of the "social self" fabricated by the corporate system.[64]

It might be argued that Americans always have been "gregarious and subservient to public opinion." But the conformity of the inner-directed person "was in most cases very much concerned with his good repute" as well as external details such as whether ones clothes, curtains, and bank credit matched the standard set by the "best people." By contrast, the other-directed person aims to "keep up with the Joneses...not so much in external details as in the quality of his inner experience." He is sensitive to signals emanating from a far wider social environment than that of his parents, family, neighborhood, or local community. He also strives to keep "in touch with others on many more levels than the externals of appearance and propriety." Unlike the inner-directed person, he lacks the "capacity to go it alone." Tradition-directed people, too, learned to live in a group milieu, but in medieval England clear boundaries separated in-groups from out-groups. Modern other-directed people, by contrast, pride themselves on the cosmopolitan ease with which they can navigate

---

64 Ibid., 4; Brian Gratton, "Hari-Kari of the Anglo Elite," (2006) 25(4) *Journal of American Ethnic History* 181.

the boundaries between the familiar and the strange. In a sense, the other-directed person is "at home everywhere and nowhere, capable of a rapid, if sometimes superficial intimacy with and response to everyone." In a traditional society the signals from others "come in a cultural monotone." There is no need for complex receiving equipment to pick up rapidly changing messages from many widely scattered sources. But the other-directed person must internalize "elaborate equipment" both "to attend to such messages and occasionally to participate in their circulation." If the inner-directed person internalizes a set of guilt-and-shame controls that act like a gyroscope to keep him on course, the other-directed person experiences "a diffuse *anxiety*" that works like radar, enabling him to change course in accordance with the dictates of expediency.[65] It was no coincidence that pragmatism became the official philosophy of corporate America.

No doubt the emergent other-directed character of the WASP middle class was a uniquely Anglo-American cultural adaptation to the organizational imperatives of corporate capitalism. But if the home-grown corporate self provided the seed-bed for the cosmopolitan spirit of the Progressive Era, the WASP clerisy had considerable help from other ethnic groups in nurturing a full-blown cult of the Other. The raw material for a novel transethnic view of America was readily available in the tenement houses of the New York and Chicago slums, teeming as they were with tightly packed masses of new immigrants. Inspired by a "romantic-humanitarian ethic' that "led them to interpret Protestant Christianity in a very peculiar, almost secular, way," middle-class reformers provided "settlement houses" to assist alien newcomers in adjusting to life in America. "Most Settlement workers were of WASP origin, and nearly all were active members of mainline Protestant denominations." Their aim was to "put the immigrants (as individuals) on an equal symbolic footing with the natives." In adapting "the tenets of egalitarian humanism to their polyglot, culturally charged context," Settlement leaders fashioned "a concept of the nation…that would not violate the human dignity of the immigrants by denigrating their culture." In Chicago, Jane Addams and John Dewey were especially important in the campaign to recognize and accept immigrant cultures "as a 'gift' to the American amalgam." They implored the American nation "to shed its Anglo-Saxon ethnic core and develop a culture of cosmopolitan humanism, a harbinger of impending global

---

65   David Riesman, *The Lonely Crowd: A Study of the Changing American Character* (New Haven, CN: Yale University Press, 1961), 22-25.

solidarity."[66] The WASP intelligentsia was not alone in the campaign to liberate Americans from their cultural parochialism. Indeed, Kaufmann credits a Jewish intellectual with a leading role in awakening American progressives to the possibilities inherent in this new, pluralist vision of American national identity.

Prior to "the arrival of a seer from outside the Protestant fold," not even the most advanced Anglo-Protestant reformers had gone beyond a "humanistic, experimental embrace of non-Christian religions." Certainly, they had not been ready to advocate "stripping the nation of its implicitly white, Anglo-Saxon, or Protestant heritage." But Felix Adler first made the leap from transcendental pluralism to cosmopolitan praxis. Adler was born into the German-Jewish "family whose patriarch Rabbi Samuel Adler, was a leading figure in American Reform Judaism." To ease their assimilation into American society, Reform Jews performed "an intellectual divorce between Jewish religion and its ethnic myths and symbols." Reformed rabbis taught that the "messianic mission of Israel was not to restore the old Jewish state...but rather to spread monotheism around the world and unite all people under God."[67]

Adler took his father's ecumenism beyond the Jewish community when founded the universalist Ethical Culture society. He believed himself to be on a mission to spread the universal faith of his people to the world at large. But he was careful to note that the Jewish race "will keep apart and will do well to do so" until that evangelical task had been accomplished. When mankind had become united in peace and harmony, the Jewish race, too, would die. But, Adler did not expect the ethnoreligious particularity of the Jewish people to fade away until the day individual Jews could "look about them and perceive that there is as great and perhaps greater liberty in religion beyond the pale of their race." Ethical Culture was premised therefore upon a fundamental asymmetry; it is only when every Gentile tribe has given up its "peculiar idiosyncracies" that Jews will be free to follow suit.[68] Until that eschatological moment arrives, the messianic mission of Jews may not be foresworn.

On Kaufmann's reading, Adler's "realist logic brusquely exposed the tension between Reform Judaism's manifest universalism and its latent ethnicism." In fact, in the passage just quoted, Adler's Jewish ethnocentrism, far from being "latent," is on open display. He certainly did not issue a forthright call for the "termination" of his own group. Indeed, he

66 Kaufmann, *Anglo-America*, 95-98.
67 Ibid., 92.
68 Ibid., 91-95.

envisaged that, for Jews alone, no sacrifice of ethnicity would be necessary prior to the arrival of a far-distant "post-ethnic Utopia."[69] By contrast, the Ethical Culture movement expected Anglo-Protestant reformers
to apply the "cast-iron logic" of cosmopolitanism to their own people at
once. William James, for one, urged his fellow Americans to look "beyond
the pale" of the Anglo-Saxon race in their search for a religious experience to remedy their "inner incompleteness" and heal their "inner dis-
cord." To Adler's cosmopolitanism, James added a radical subjectivity. He
converted religion "from a code or a community into a 'will to believe.'"
He also "heralded a shift from theology to psychology as the key therapeutic arbiter of moral selfhood." Anglo-Saxon Protestants were urged to
embrace a pragmatic approach to religious experience, choosing whichever "type of religion is going to work best in the long run." It did not
much matter whether God was dead, so long as "we form at any rate an
ethical republic here below."[70] The critical turn towards "the repudiation
of America's Anglo-Protestant ethnic heritage in the name of liberal-egal-
itarian radicalism" came in the 1890s when Adler and James transplanted
"cosmopolitan ideas out of their Jewish-messianic context" and re-rooted
"them in the American atmosphere."[71]

The cosmopolitan ideal found fertile soil in the university and settlement houses of Chicago. The towering prestige of Jane Addams and John
Dewey transmitted the new faith to *avant-garde* intellectuals and artists in
New York. This rising status group identified strongly with "the outsiders,
revolutionaries, and heretics of the past whose martyrdom in the service
of humanity had assured their immortality." In an effort "to fuse their
old religious faith with their newly acquired political beliefs," progressive writers "repeatedly cast Jesus in the role of revolutionary." Bohemian
intellectuals were particularly drawn "to the 'homeless mind' of the cosmopolitan Jewish experience." Randolph Bourne was one prominent
Anglo-Protestant modernist "who readily acknowledged the influence
of his Jewish peers." But, unlike Adler's Ethical Culture, Bourne's radical
modernism did not seek to dissolve the distinctive ethnocultural identities of other peoples into a common humanity. On the contrary, "Bourne
considered ethnicity a cultural good to be experienced by a modernist
cultural consumer." The paradox is that Bourne did embrace "ideas of ethnic determinism and communal authenticity," but "only insofar as these

69   *Ibid.*, 91-93.

70   McCarraher, *Christian Critics*, 15.

71   Kaufmann, *Anglo-America*, 231, 100.

attacked the Anglo-Saxon hegemonic culture he detested."[72] Bourne was, in fact, an early and particularly rabid Anglo-Saxon Anglophobe.

While lauding the traditions of the Jew "who sticks proudly to the faith of his fathers and boasts of the venerable culture of his" race, Bourne sought the "ethnic destruction" of his fellow Anglo-Saxons. He hoped to foster a ethnic revival for minority groups that would preserve their ethnocultural traditions while imploring Anglo-Saxons to become cosmopolitan.[73] It was not just Anglo-American provincialism that raised his ire. After a visit to England he declared that he was "just about ready to renounce the whole of Anglo-Saxon civilization." If the world was "ever to have any freedom or any life or honesty or sensitiveness of soul," it would be necessary to get rid of "the old English way of looking at the world."[74] America could realize its destiny as the first "international nation" only by ridding itself of its Anglo-Saxon character: "The Anglo-Saxon element is guilty of what every dominant race is guilty of in every European country: the imposition of its own culture upon the minority peoples." He expressed satisfaction at "the degree to which that purpose of 'Americanizing,' that is, 'Anglo-Saxonizing,' the immigrant failed," or so it seemed during the Great War.[75] In fact, for a generation or more after Bourne's premature death in the influenza epidemic of 1918, the ethnic minority struggle against WASP cultural and political hegemony continued to face an uphill battle. Even as the corporate system worked objectively to corrode the demographic and cultural foundations of Anglo-American dominance, WASP elites were subjectively appalled by the influx of aliens into their neighborhoods, businesses, and colleges. Such attitudes did not go unchallenged, either privately or publicly. "Advanced thinkers" encouraged the increasingly other-directed offspring of the upper crust to admonish parents who harbored such parochial prejudices. Until ethnic minorities mobilized local, state, and federal governments to enter the fray on their behalf, mainline Protestant churches made it their mission to convert corporate elites to the cosmopolitan cult of the Other. During the 1960s, the last hold-outs in the clubs and boardrooms of WASP America ran up the white flag.

---

72   Ibid., 149-159.

73   Ibid., 156-157.

74   Christopher Lasch, The New Radicalism in America, 1889-1963: The Intellectual as a Social Type (London: Chatto & Windus, 1966), 92-93.

75   Kaufmann, Anglo-American, 156-157.

America's Abdication Crisis

Collaboration between corporate America and radical modernists was nothing new of course. Modern artists had been deeply involved in the growth of the advertising industry and the expressive individualism of the bohemian fringe found outlets in fashion, architecture, publishing, movies, and product design. Between the wars, in the northern cities, well-to-do WASPs in the rising professional and managerial classes "tended to combine an endorsement of free enterprise with a cosmopolitan stance concerning matters cultural."[76] But, as late as the Sixties, the comparatively few diehards still resisting the outright surrender of WASP economic, cultural, and political hegemony remained a cause for concern among the cosmopolitan vanguard.

Writing in 1964, E Digby Baltzell lamented that even today, "when our steadily expanding postwar economy is demanding more and more leaders of ability and education, regardless of ethnic origins, an upper class which is still based on the caste criteria of old-stock Protestant origins is simply an unrepresentative anachronism." Baltzell believed that America's continued success as a nation depended upon its capacity to regenerate an "aristocracy." On his idiosyncratic understanding, aristocracy implied not the classical republican ideal of rule by the virtuous few but rather an upper-class establishment open to talents from any and all ethnoreligious backgrounds. Baltzell claimed that a closed establishment, open only to WASPs, would cause the upper class to degenerate into a "caste."[77]

It is more than a little ironic that the implementation of Baltzell's program of cosmopolitan democracy over the past half century has had the effect of accelerating the proletarianization of WASP managers and professionals. Simultaneously, the abdication of the Protestant establishment empowered an increasingly corrupt corporate plutocracy in which Ivy League Jews are now heavily over-represented. As a consequence, important sectors of the new-modelled American establishment are no longer bound by blood to the founding race of the nation over which it presides. Worse still, Jewish elites harbor a deep-seated animus toward the Christian faith professed by most Americans. An enthusiastic philo-Semite, Baltzell saw no downside to the growing ethnoreligious disconnect between rulers and ruled in the transnational republic of his dreams.

---

76 Ibid., 170, 185.

77 E Digby Baltzell, *The Protestant Establishment: Aristocracy & Caste in America* (New Haven, CN: Yale University Press, 1987), 15, 7-9.

Baltzell came down with an acute case of Anglo-Saxon Anglophobia, embracing the cosmopolitan cult of the Other with all the ideological fervor of bohemian radicals such as Randolph Bourne. Baltzell was unalterably convinced that corporate America could save its soul only by rushing "to assimilate new elite members, primarily because of their *racial or ethnic origins*." He was incensed, in particular, by upper class WASP efforts to bar Jews from their clubs and colleges, as well as their boardrooms and beachside resorts. Of course, he was not altogether off the mark when he remarked that the WASP establishment had reached its high-water mark in the 1920s. In the Jazz Age of easy money and Al Capone, Prohibition and bathtub gin, WASP elites abdicated their claim to moral, intellectual, and spiritual leadership. As one well-heeled banker later recalled, "During the twenties, my daughter said to me, 'You've always taught me to respect law and the Constitution, and here you are making your own gin,' and I had no answer."[78] Baltzell retells the anecdote in the sure conviction that such men were deservedly reaping the bitter harvest they had sown.

We know, of course, that the corporate culture of critical discourse had de-authorized the old-stock WASP bourgeoisie well before the 1920s. From the late nineteenth century onward, leading American intellectuals, artists, and writers made it clear that WASPs were an unwelcome presence in the nation founded by their ancestors. The drumbeat continued into the twentieth century as prominent theologians rebuked WASPs for "the sinful twins of Protestant racism and American nationalism." Only by using "every stratagem of education and every resource of religion" to abolish racism, could WASPs hope to redeem themselves. Like Baltzell a generation later, in 1942 Reinhold Niebuhr urged Americans to re-order relationships among "ethnic, religious, and economic groups" so that the "richness and harmony of the whole community will be enhanced and not destroyed."[79]

Significantly, the 1940s and 1950s witnessed "a wave of denominational mergers and coalitions in mainline Protestantism." This ecumenical consolidation amounted to a "managerial revolution" in American Protestanism. As the corporate reconstruction of their churches proceeded apace, the "managerial parsonage" was modelled on the dominant structures of "political, educational, and economic executive or managerial authority."[80] To the other-directed corporate self in churches and universities, no less than in the business world, it was self-evident that "a

---

78   *Ibid.*, 8, 218.

79   McCarraher, *Christian Critics*, 96.

80   *Ibid.*, 80, 96, 105.

sacred and caste-protected executive suite may be less conducive to creative thinking than one with more cosmopolitan and secular make-up." By
the mid-twentieth century, conventional wisdom held that the corporation had become "the conscience-carrier" of American society. Baltzell
expected the modern corporation to play "a vital and revolutionary role
in gradually creating a world community." In his view, the fact that "the
large corporation executive suite is still mainly composed of managers of
an Anglo-Protestant background" ought to have weighed heavily upon
the corporate conscience.[81]

So determined was Baltzell to export rabid xenophilia from bohemia
to the boardroom that he sometimes allowed himself to rise above well-
established facts of comparative ethnology. At one point, for example, he
declared confidently that "one does not have to be a sociological deter-
minist to see that continual ethnic inbreeding leads to mental stagnation." It evidently did not occur to Baltzell that an age-old commitment to
endogamy is much more deeply entrenched among Jews than it has ever
been in WASP families. Nor did he bother to defend the bigoted suggestion that WASPs are more prone to "mental stagnation" than Jews. Baltzell
simply adopted the double standard symptomatic of WASPs afflicted
by Anglo-Saxon Anglophobia. On the one hand, comparatively feeble
traces of ethnocentrism among Anglo-Saxons are roundly condemned;
on the other, Jewish ethnocentrism is interpreted as a defensive reaction
to American anti-Semitism. For Baltzell, anti-Semitism could not be
blamed "either on the nature of the Jewish community or on the qualities
or personal characteristics of Jews." Racism generally and anti-Semitism
in particular, he asserted confidently, were "largely due to the values and
attitudes held by members of the dominant group." It was no surprise that
WASPs were losing ground politically: "the corporate establishment has
failed in its aristocratic function of assimilating into its ranks new men of
power and ambition from the Jewish and other minority communities."
His message to fellow WASPs was blunt: Anglo-Saxons are a dying race;
it is our historic destiny—indeed our duty—to surrender leadership to
more vigorous ethnic, racial, and religious rivals waiting in the wings.[82]

---

81 Baltzell, *Protestant Establishment*, 324, 320-321.

82 Ibid., 321-324, 383-384.

Conclusion

Anglo-Saxon Anglophobia soon became pandemic among other-directed, upper-class WASPs. The anxious need to be seen taking the lead on issues of racial integration and anti-Semitism created an all-pervasive atmosphere of competitive altruism among top managers.[83] Baltzell issued his own stern warning: "if management waits until the state takes the initiative it will have the statism it deserves." In the end, the corporate establishment was unwilling or unable single-handedly to cleanse American society of its ingrained "racist" attitudes towards Jews, Negroes, and other minorities. When it came to challenging the Jim Crow laws of the American South, corporate bigwigs were more than willing to assign the role of principal "conscience-carrier" to the federal government. Eager to launch a civil rights revolution, state and federal governments replaced freedom of association with forced integration. Negroes and Jews, along with a bevy of other protected minorities, soon carved out a place for themselves in the upper reaches of political, economic, and cultural power. The old-stock WASP upper class was overthrown.

A number of questions remain: is our contemporary rainbow coalition of plutocratic, political, and publicity potentates really the "aristocratic" answer to the public prayers offered up by prominent WASP defectors in every generation from Bourne to Baltzell? If the caste system allegedly enforced by upper class WASPs stood in "direct denial of the teachings of Christianity," has the cosmopolitan, transnational overclass now presiding over the market-state brought us measurably closer to the Promised Land?[84] How did the cult of the Other became incarnate in the constitutional law of the American republic? Did that constitutional faith pervert the orthodox theology of Anglo-Saxon Christianity?

Such questions bring us to the threshold of American political theology. In search of answers, we must examine how the civil religion of the early federal republic was reshaped to sanctify the nation-state forged by fire and steel in the Civil War, only to be invoked in yet another guise by the managerial/therapeutic regime that was ushered in by the New Deal during the Great Depression.

---

83 Ian Jobling, "Competitive Altruism and White Self-Destruction," (2003) 14(10) *American Renaissance* 1.

84 Baltzell, *Protestant Establishment*, 387.

6.

Political Theology:
How America's Civil Religion Fosters
Anglo-Saxon Ethnomasochism

Introduction

Americans often contrast the supposed conservatism of their Revolution with the bloody reigns of terror associated with the French and the Bolshevik Revolutions. In the received narrative, American patriots fought to defend their historic constitutional rights against encroachments by a tyrannical British king. Even as the rebellious colonists threw off their ancestral allegiance to throne and altar, they preserved the fundamental constitution of English liberty. Such a complacent view is profoundly misleading: the American Revolution spawned a radical social contagion that found a receptive host in the body politic of the new Republic. American patriotism ceased to speak in the Old English language of the common law to preach instead the French revolutionary creed of liberty, equality, and fraternity. The American Adam possessed the power and believed it to be his duty to create a glorious, gleaming city upon a hill; his manifest destiny was to redeem mankind. Two centuries later, the Constitutional Republic has been transformed into a transnational empire in which the increasingly formal legal distinction between an American citizen and a citizen of the world is on the verge of extinction.

When American revolutionaries in the several colonies rejected kingship in favor of a republican form of government, they "were changing their society as well as their governments, and they knew it." Tories were not packed off in tumbrels to the guillotine, nor did the poor supplant the rich, but almost overnight the American Revolution transformed colonial patriots from "monarchical, hierarchy-ridden subjects on the margins of civilization" into "the most liberal, the most democratic, the most commercially-minded, and the most modern people in the world." Gordon Wood holds that "[b]y the time the Revolution had run its course in the early nineteenth century, American society had been radically and thoroughly transformed." In a wider context, Wood actually understates the continuing role of the American Republic in the revolutionary overthrow of Western Christendom. The subversive influence of *homo Americanus* was amplified industrially and extended militarily as the imperial Republic rose to world power in the twentieth century. Far from having "run its course in the early nineteenth century," the colonial bid to create an independent American empire inaugurated a permanent revolution.[1] The French and Bolshevik Revolutions are over; the American Revolution is still a work in progress.

Having transformed "a petty rebellion within the Empire into a symbol of liberation for all mankind,"[2] the Constitutional Republic set out to incorporate the aspirations of the revolutionary Enlightenment into the living constitution of the *novus ordo seclorum*. Then, soon after Washington became the first President of the United States, the French Revolution spiralled out of control; radicals manipulating the Parisian masses triggered a political earthquake of unparalleled destructive force. Standing outside society and the body politic, the crowd in the French Revolution demanded the natural rights of man to food, clothing, and the reproduction of the species. When faced with the choice between bread and liberty, most were prepared to sacrifice the constitutional rights of freedom and citizenship. Rhetorical appeals to liberty, equality, and fraternity did little to disguise either the nakedness of the selfish interests that shaped the *mentalité* of the *sans-culottes* or "the nakedness of their unbearable misery." Not long after the fall of the monarchy, the masses discovered that republican constitutions were no panacea for poverty.[3] Not for the last time in the history of modern revolutions from below, a renovated authoritarian order was imposed from on high in the form of the Bonapartist tyranny. In the Old World, revolutionaries who overturned traditional hierarchies regularly provoked resistance from reactionary forces that promised relief from the anomic freedom of post-Christian rationalism. Only in America has the millennialist vision of a

1   Gordon S Wood, *The Radicalism of the American Revolution* (New York: Vintage, 1991), 3-7.

2   Pauline Maier, *From Resistance to Revolution: Colonial Radicals and the Development of Resistance to Britain, 1765-1776* (New York: Random, 1974), 272.

3   Hannah Arendt, *On Revolution* (Harmondsworth: Penguin, 1973), 109.

new heaven here on earth swept aside all opposition, transmuting society into a revolutionary perpetual innovation machine.

Civil Religion in the Constitutional Republic

On paper, the American constitutional order has been remarkably stable but an irresistibly revolutionary dynamic drives the development of the American republic. Fewer than thirty amendments have been made to the text of the Constitution but that formal legal continuity masks the reality of a state and a society seized by a utopian faith in human perfectibility. Since the Philadephia Convention of 1787 which cast aside the revolutionary Articles of Confederation, there have been several incarnations of the Constitutional Republic. As successive models of the republic failed, successor regimes better adapted to the headlong rush of political and economic modernity stepped into their shoes. The First (Federal) Republic survived for seventy-odd years before the secession of the southern states precipitated a civil war; the result was the subsequent creation of the Second (Bourgeois) Republic. Seventy years later, still nursing a hangover from its excesses during the Gilded Age, the enervated WASP bourgeoisie of the Jazz Age was displaced, almost effortlessly, by a radically centralist administrative state. A judicial *coup d'état* provided the formal constitutional warrant that authorized the Third (Managerial/Therapeutic) Republic. The contemporary corporate welfare state far surpasses the worst fears of the Antifederalists who opposed ratification of the Constitution in 1787; it is, quite simply, a constitutional abomination. Finally, with the advent of the Obama administration, we may be witnessing the birth-pangs of a Fourth (Transnational) Republic which no longer pretends that the federal government is bound by the legalistic constraints of constitutional scripture.[4]

And yet, having survived several major regime changes, for many Anglo-Americans the Constitution remains an object of religious

---

4   Prior to Barack Hussein Obama's Presidential inauguration, several federal and state courts rejected challenges to his constitutional eligibility to hold that office. Plaintiffs in those suits sought to establish whether the putative President is a "natural-born citizen" of the United States *as per* Article II of the Constitution. More such suits were filed after he was sworn into office. To date the constitutional issue still awaits formal resolution. If Obama is not, in fact or in law, a natural born citizen of the United States, the political reality of his electoral triumph must be taken to have rendered an explicit constitutional requirement null and void.

veneration "too sacred to be touched."[5] That constitutional faith survived the secession crisis in 1861; the founding instrument of the Confederate States of America made manifest the unshakable fidelity of Southerners to the spirit and, in large part, the letter of the Constitution of the United States. Today, WASPs, in particular, remain fervent constitutional loyalists even though the founding document has become—as Jefferson warned— "a mere thing of wax" which designing men (and now women too) "may twist and shape into any form they please."[6]

The most fundamental change wrought by the American Revolution occurred in the spiritual realm. Anglo-Saxon Christianity was perverted in the service of an avowedly secular state. John Adams, the second President of the United States once observed that the deepest meaning of "the Revolution" was "the change that took place 'in the minds and hearts of the people' which he described as 'a change in their religious sentiments of their duties and obligations.'" As churches became mere voluntary associations "within the commonwealth, in competition with perhaps hundreds of others," the Constitution was received as the sacred ark of a national covenant.[7] The new civil religion affirmed the miraculous nature of the American Revolution. Independence from Great Britain was received as the unmistakable revelation of the providential mission that the Republic was destined to fulfil. If the Declaration of Independence was the Annunciation of the Constitutional Republic, its Advent was marked by the inauguration of the truly messianic figure of George Washington as its first President. There is no doubt that the Constitution was, at one and the same time, a theological, a legal, and a political construct.

Accordingly, the Federalist framers of the Constitution of 1787 conceived their handiwork as a vital contribution to the sacred cause of liberty. The Antifederalist opposition feared that the political and civil liberties secured by independence would be surrendered to a strong central government serving the interests of a selfish few. In the Old World, clashes between the immovable object of aristocratic privilege and the irresistible force of raw popular power tore the body politic asunder. But the American Revolution had taught the governing classes how to bend with the breeze. The relationship between government and people in America

---

5 Thomas Jefferson, quoted in Sanford Levinson, *Constitutional Faith* (Princeton, NJ: Princeton University Press, 1988), 9.

6 Thomas Jefferson, Letter to Judge Spencer Roane, 6 September 1819, in Merrill D Peterson, *The Portable Thomas Jefferson* (Harmondsworth: Penguin, 1977), 563.

7 Sidney E Mead, *The Old Religion in the Brave New World: Reflections on the Relationship between Christendom and the Republic* (Berkeley, CA: University of California Press, 1977), 76.

was transformed utterly when the traditional English concept of representation was abandoned in the Constitution of 1787.

The eighteenth century British constitution was a mixed and balanced government; King, Lords, and Commons, the three estates of the realm, shared in the exercise of sovereign authority, each in its own fashion. The people participated in government vicariously, through their representatives in the lower house of Parliament. Political power was heterogeneous in nature. The power wielded by the King was different in kind from that vested in the Lords and both had their genesis in sources distinct from the rights to representation enjoyed by the constituencies sending members to the House of Commons. In revolutionary America, the transferral of sovereignty to the people at large had the effect of homogenizing political power.[8] The constitution of the American polity no longer merely *described* the qualitative difference between the powers vested in the rulers and those of the ruled. Rather the constitutional discourse of the American Republic *prescribed* the norms that governed the distribution of functions between the executive, legislative, and judicial agents of the sovereign people.

Once independence from Britain had been secured, the undifferentiated sovereignty of the revolutionary people at large fostered popular mistrust of all constituted authority, driving a wedge between the people and those who claimed to govern on their behalf. The push for a powerful central government was led by wealthy and powerful men worried by the radical populism of state legislatures that favored debtors over creditors, farmers over merchants, the many over the few. But the wealthy and the educated soon learned how to manipulate the radical rhetoric of popular sovereignty to their own advantage. They proposed that the Constitution be ratified by popularly-elected conventions in each state. In other words, they appealed over the heads of state governments to the sovereign people. Some state legislatures were thus prevented from mounting effective opposition to the Philadelphia Constitution. The Federalist strategy was a manifestly unconstitutional usurpation of states' rights under the Articles of Confederation, a legal technicality that was soon forgotten as soon as the Constitution was duly ratified.[9]

In the convention debates, the rising religion of the Constitutional Republic successfully repelled the rustic resistance of backwoods

---

8   Gordon S Wood, *The Creation of the American Republic, 1776-1787* (New York: WW Norton, 1969), 372-382.

9   Bruce Ackerman, *We the People: Foundations* (Cambridge, MA: Belknap Press, 1993), 165-171.

Antifederalists. Following the adoption in 1789 of the Bill of Rights, however, the Constitution won grudging acceptance from its erstwhile opponents. Even so, the political theology of the First (Federal) Republic could not contain recurrent conflict over the nature and scope of the liberties constitutionally guaranteed to the states and the people respectively. A bitter sectional struggle swirled around the peculiar institution of slavery as the sacred cause of liberty mutated into the no less sacred cause of equality. A crisis of constitutional faith turned Northern determination to suppress Southern secessionists into a bloody war of conquest; the smoldering ruins of the Old South turned out to be the *sine qua non* for the feverish rush into a new world of cities and factories, steel mills and railroads, overseen and facilitated by the Second (Bourgeois) Republic.

The constitutional faith of the Second Republic reinforced the revolutionary momentum of capitalist expansion. Overseeing the rapid industrialization of what had become a continental empire, the bourgeois regime turned an agrarian people into a nation of city-dwellers. In the process, the mushrooming masses of polyglot proletarians were infiltrated by subversive squads of socialist and anarchist agitators, aided and abetted by a younger generation of old-stock Americans. Disaffected intellectuals and alienated feminists sought redemption from the squalid materialism of their parents in a "progressive" campaign to turn the Fourteenth Amendment guarantee of equal protection into a sweeping charter of social justice. In response, "conservatives" defended a formal and legalistic definition of equality against radical demands for equality in every area of social, political, and economic life.

Faced with the twin challenges of war and depression in the early twentieth century, the Bourgeois Republic was plunged into constitutional crisis by Franklin D Roosevelt's New Deal. Roosevelt routed the opposition forces and his comparatively peaceful revolution marked the advent of a Third Republic. Under this new regime, private property rights ceased to be the bulwark of constitutional liberty. In the course of the movement to place all citizens on an equal footing the boundary between the state and the corporate sector became steadily more porous. The class struggle was suspended as the managerial revolution opened America up to the free flow of capital, technology and labor in a borderless world. The revolutionary creed of liberty, equality, and fraternity was finally to be consummated in and through the transnational market-state.

Over the past half-century the social capital invested by WASPs in their American citizenship has been confiscated in the campaign to open America's borders to the peoples of the Third World. The contemporary corporate welfare state has grown steadily more hostile to the founding race of the First Constitutional Republic. Yet Anglo-Americans appear almost indifferent to the blatant and unapologetic theft of their historic claim to independent nationhood. Something more is at work here than the merely mundane calculus of economic interests. Arguably, the spirit of corporatist neo-communism no less than the spirit of bourgeois capitalism derives its force from a secularized religious impulse. Managerial schemes to promote diversity are but the latest expression of a political theology with roots stretching back to the colonial period of American history.

But the Old Faith must stand opposed to the religion of the Republic as a false, heretical, even sinful, perversion of Christian theology. The revolutionary faith of the Enlightenment in the universal brotherhood of man now occupies the place once reserved for the heavenly Kingdom of God. The American Dream of endless economic growth and development has become a secular parody of the Christian pilgrim's progress toward salvation. Christendom once strove to achieve a *symphonia* among throne, altar, and people in the family of nations united in the Body of Christ. When the American Republic projected itself into history as "a nation with the soul of a church," Christendom became anachronistic and obsolescent. Since "*the* Church as such does not exist in visible institutional form" in the United States, the Constitutional Republic stepped into its shoes as a surrogate *ecclesia*.[10] Needless to say, the substitution of the Republic for the church is difficult to reconcile with an orthodox Christian theology.

A Bloodless Nation

Those who preach the religion of the Republic point out that, as far back as the colonial era, the proliferation of Protestant sects along with steadily growing numbers of Catholic settlers made religious pluralism a ubiquitous fact of life. In England the established constitutional order rested on the identification of religious and national society. In the United States, the breakdown of religious uniformity ruled out any hope that a single established church could infuse the Holy Spirit into an embryonic American *Volksgeist*. Instead, the Republic established a rule of strict neutrality to govern relationships between the civil authority and competing religious denominations. But if the Republic refused to embrace any

---

10   Sidney E Mead, "The 'Nation with the Soul of a Church,'" (1967) 36(3) *Church History* 262, at 266.

particular sect, it was neither irreligious nor anti-religious. Rather, the Constitutional Republic reflected the post-Christian rationalist religion of the Enlightenment. Proclaiming the liberty of individual conscience in matters of religious belief, the enlightened mind rejected the orthodox doctrine of any church. Calls to unite all Christians in the mystical Body of Christ struck both rationalists and Protestants as a coercive desire "to drown heresy in the blood of the heretic." As a consequence, "every ardent defence of sectarian Christianity, no matter how unintentional, was by implication an attack on the mainspring of the Republic."[11]

In the Enlightenment cult of the Constitution, religion was a matter of the spirit not of blood. An anti-sectarian refusal to countenance bloodshed produced by internecine religious feuds was paired with a cosmopolitan disdain for the atavistic familial and tribal allegiances so ingrained in the untutored instincts of common folk. While the orthodox Christianity of the Anglo-Saxon era had fused blood and spirit through the institutional medium of the church, the theology of the Republic segregated "religiosity as feeling, experience, and ideas from the institutional forms in and by which it was made tangible in society." From its rationalistic perspective, the "substance and essence of Christianity" can be found in other major religions, such as Judaism, Buddhism, or Islam. Thus, men of the American Enlightenment had little interest in the distinctive dogmas of the Baptists, the Methodists, or the Presbyterians, much less the superstitious scholasticism of the Catholics.[12]

Having distilled the essence of religion through the crystalline retort of reason, they were left with the lowest common denominator, a deistic faith that dispensed with both the revealed truth of biblical authority and the divinity of Christ. Faith in the American civil religion required commitment only "to an ideal world beyond the present world and to the incarnating of that ideal world in…our Republic." It was not "the theology of the denominations" that legitimated "the political and legal structure of the commonwealth." On the contrary, the sectarian notion that "only Christians could be morally upright and trustworthy" tended to drive a wedge "into the citizen's mind between his being as an overt Christian (which necessitated joining one of the sects) and his being as a citizen." By and large, the framers of the Constitution were free of such tensions; they

---

11 *Ibid.*, 270; id., *Old Religion*, 79; id., "The Theology of the Republic and the Orthodox Mind," (1976) 44(1) *Journal of the American Academy of Religion* 105, at 106.

12 Mead, *Old Religion*, 86, 69, 29.

had been converted to a new religion, one representing a clear departure from orthodox Christianity.[13]

The rationalist deism of the Enlightenment was the most powerful influence on the founding generation. The framers of the Constitution believed that the Creator and Governor of the Universe had endowed men with "Reason" and "Understanding," thus enabling "them to read and understand the revelation in His creation." But, because imperfections of human understanding meant that all knowledge was more or less uncertain, neither church nor state should impose religious beliefs by coercion. This was a genuinely revolutionary stance: "for the first time in Christendom the people of a commonwealth were offered an authentically religious alternative to orthodox Christianity." The Constitution set in motion "the struggle between sectarian Christianity and 'Americanism' which is commonly confused by calling it a struggle between Church and State." According to Sidney Mead, "the contest between what is commonly called 'church and state' is actually between the one coherent, institutionalized civil authority and about three hundred collectively incoherent religious institutions whose claims tend to cancel each other out."[14] Reason can prevail only when civil authority defends the freedom of each and every denomination to practice and propagate its private and particularistic beliefs. For the post-Christian rationalist, because sectarian passions sometimes pose a threat to public order, it is axiomatic that neutral public authorities must adjudicate conflicts between competing denominations.

The Constitution set up a permanent tension between two sources of cultural meaning: "the particularistic theological notions of the sects and the cosmopolitan, universal theology of the Republic." For those who embraced the theology of the Republic, "the nation…came to occupy the place in their lives that traditionally had been occupied by the church." With its own claim to be ordained of God, the Republic became "the ark of God's redemptive work in the world." Sovereignty in the religion of the Republic was conceived as "the power of God for the creation of ordered communities." Although radicals insisted that sovereignty was actually seated in "the people," the contrary view, as embodied in the federal Constitution, was that sovereign authority had been delegated by the people at large to rulers responsible to them. On either view, once religious freedom became the established norm in American popular culture, "no denomination could plausibly claim to be, or to function as 'the church' in the new nation." One of the foremost contemporary theologians of the

---

13 Mead, "Nation with Soul of a Church," 274; id., "Theology of the Republic," 109.

14 Mead, *Old Religion*, 84, 29; id., "Nation with Soul of a Church," 277.

Republic tells us that it was *"the nation"* itself that *"came more and more so to function"* as a church.[15] Note the effortless elision of the American "nation" into a federal Leviathan that absorbed both the states and the people into a single consolidated state apparatus.

The cosmopolitanism of the founding generation points to a crucial ambiguity at the heart of American civil religion. Was the constitutional faith of the Republic compatible with the biocultural interests of the historical American "nation"? To put the question more plainly still: Has the revolutionary religion of the Constitutional Republic been good for the Anglo-Saxons? The founding generation were cultural revolutionaries; they easily convinced each other that the cult of the Constitution would protect the interests of "our Posterity." Perhaps their urbane ways and polished refinement were highly-prized status markers, making them unduly anxious to avoid the appearance of parochialism, bigotry, or narrowness of outlook. Certainly, the revolutionary "generation was the most cosmopolitan of any in American history." American revolutionaries declared that too "intense a local attachment was a symptom of narrow-mindedness, and indeed of disease." The measure of one's enlightenment "was determined by the distance one was able to extend one's love outward." The ideal state for every enlightened gentleman, George Washington believed, was to become "a citizen of the great republic of humanity at large."[16]

The enlightened statesmen-legislators of the early Republic gave no formal constitutional standing to the Christian faith of Old England; Federalist spokesmen were even coy about the core ethnocultural identity of the new nation. In a passage much-beloved of contemporary white nationalists, John Jay noted that: "Providence has been pleased to give this one connected country to one united people—a people descended from the same ancestors, speaking the same language, professing the same religion, attached to the same principles of government." Significantly, Jay declines to give a name to the dominant ethny in the new Republic or even to the "same religion" allegedly professed by its citizens. Jay's evasiveness set the tone for succeeding generations in the highest echelons of Anglo-American society.[17]

It was left to a powerfully percipient Negro nationalist intellectual of the 1960s to expose that persistent pattern of prevarication. For Harold

---

15 Mead, "Nation with Soul of a Church," 277-279, 267.

16 Wood, *Radicalism*, 220-222.

17 John Jay, "The Federalist, No 2," in Alexander Hamilton, *et al The Federalist: A Commentary on the Constitution of the United States* intro Edward Mead Earle (New York: Modern Library, 1937), 9.

Cruse, "the American Constitution was written, conceived, defended and glorified for the *implied* social benefits of a group—the white Protestant, Anglo-Saxon, North European American." But the hegemony of the Anglo-Protestant ethnonation was never codified in the public law and Constitution of the new regime. In other words, Cruse draws attention to the fact that the white Anglo-Saxon Protestant character of the Constitutional Republic was merely *implicit*. In the eyes of the Constitution, Anglo-Saxons Protestants were legally invisible.[18]

John Jay made no explicit reference to either Anglo-Saxons or Christians in his cautious celebration of America's cryptonomous national identity. The son of a French Huguenot refugee, Jay did not belong to the dominant ethny of the early Republic. Perhaps that made him more sensitive to hidden fissures in the constitutional façade of national unity. In any case, he papered over the ethnoreligious and racial diversity of the early Republic. While Protestants of British ancestry clearly enjoyed *de facto* unchallenged cultural and political hegemony, the Constitutional Republic did not derive its legitimacy *de jure* from a single, legally entrenched ethnocultural "nation." Jay's assurance that Providence had decreed that the Republic "should never be split into a number of unsocial, jealous, and alien sovereignties" was decidedly premature.[19] In sharp contrast, to the Founders, Harold Cruse refused to shrink from the unvarnished truth, charging that "America is a nation that lies to itself about who and what it is." It has done so from the beginning; the founding generation was quick to confuse political enthusiasm for the sacred cause of liberty with spiritual devotion to the Christian faith of their fathers.

The First (Federal) Republic: Liberty

America's constitutional faith was conceived within the secularist tradition of civic humanism shared by the educated classes in the British colonies across the Atlantic. Indeed, between 1740 and 1776 colonial elites, particularly in New England, became more, not less, anglicized. Every patrician gentleman of property and standing owed a cosmopolitan allegiance to both the commercial empire of goods and the spiritual

---

18 Harold Cruse, *The Crisis of the Negro Intellectual: From its Origins to the Present* (New York: William Morrow, 1967). Kevin MacDonald uses the concept of "implicit whiteness" but even he appears reluctant to make explicit the core, Anglo-Saxon ethnoculture that gave birth to the Constitutional Republic, see, eg, "Psychology and White Ethnocentrism," (2006-2007) 6(4) *The Occidental Quarterly* 7.

19 Jay, "Federalist No 2," 9.

republic of letters. Black-clad ministers of the gospel joined with worldly merchants, planters, lawyers, and the political class, generally to create a novel intellectual constellation in which they began to re-imagine the character of Christian community. One scholar writes that "[b]y 1760 New England clergymen appear to have lost a clear distinction between the Kingdom of God and the goals of their own political community." The meaning of the American Revolution itself was framed by a "republican eschatology" that heavily influenced by the early modern English political thinkers whose neo-pagan civic republicanism endowed "the function of man as a citizen" with "a profoundly new religious significance." Republican liberty became "a cardinal principle of Christian belief once "the principles governing the civil order" were assigned a key role in the scheme of providential history. In colonial times, the chief threat to liberty was associated with French popery. During the French and Indian War, "New Englanders grounded their collective identity solidly in the ideals of British Protestantism and the British constitution. In fact, "the religious patriotism that animated the Revolution had intellectual roots that were far more British than American."[20]

The seeds of post-Christian infidelity already latent in civic humanism sprouted treasonous tendrils in the fertile soil of prosperous English colonies nurturing imperial pretensions of their own. Colonial Whigs rebadged as Patriots invoked the sacred cause of liberty to justify their struggle for independence from the mother country. Soon they conjured up apocalyptic visions of terminally corrupt British ministers suppressing liberties at home while plotting to enslave the colonies. "America as never before became the asylum of liberty and the seat of Christ's advancing kingdom." Following independence, the progressive transformation of churches into private voluntary associations reinforced those calling for the direct application of religious morality to the realm of politics, law, and government. Before long, the religion of the Republic "aligned national purpose so closely with religious conviction" that "the nation" replaced the church "as the primary agent of God's meaningful activity in history." It became second nature for Americans to treat their "political values as religious priorities." American civil millennialism readily associated the revolutionary trinity of liberty, equality, and fraternity with providential history. Sharing the political ideals of the American Revolution with all

---

20 Nathan O Hatch, *The Sacred Cause of Liberty: Republican Thought and the Millennium in Revolutionary New England* (New Haven, CN: Yale University Press, 1977), 43, 11-12, 48.

mankind came to be seen as "a necessary prerequisite for spreading the Christian message."[21]

But the early history of the American Republic sent mixed messages to the Christian faithful. From the start, many Revolutionary leaders were suspicious of traditional Christianity and looked to Freemasonry for a surrogate religion. As a consequence, the orthodox Christian fusion of blood and spirit, faith and kinship had little resonance in a revolutionary society which often appeared to be coming apart at the seams. Freemasonry was attractive to some because it created an "artificial consanguinity" which operated "with as much force and effect, as the natural relationship of blood." But hopes that the Revolution would usher in a new era of cosmopolitan benevolence under the enlightened leadership of a natural aristocracy were to be disappointed. In reality, "the Revolution had set loose forces in American society that few realized existed." By the turn of the nineteenth century, the Enlightenment tradition of neo-classical republicanism had been swept out to sea by the flood tide of democratic revolution, along with what remained of orthodox Anglo-Saxon Christianity.[22]

"Within decades," according to Gordon Wood, "the United States became the most egalitarian nation in the history of the world." A deepening humanitarian sensibility "in effect secularized the Christian belief in the equality of all souls before God." The principle of popular sovereignty revealed that all men were equal not just in the celestial sphere but also in the eyes of the law in this world. Republicanism and Christian theism were fused in the fiery heat of revolutionary change. Only the elect few among the Puritans were predestined to walk with God; the revivalist movements in the early Republic extended the promise of redemption to every sinner, rich or poor. Relaxed Arminian teachings on the personal attainment of grace were "a religious parallel to the secular emphasis on equality of opportunity and achievement."[23]

Republican liberty could no longer be monopolized by "the better sort" in politics, religion or in society at large. In ante-bellum America, "common ordinary men stripped the northern gentry of their pretensions, charged them at every turn with being fakes and shams, and relentlessly undermined their capacity to rule."[24] Religious and secular activities were inextricably intertwined; "voluntarism" in both spheres became the mutually reinforcing norm. Accordingly, hard work and economic ambi-

---

21   *Ibid.*, 53-54, 85, 141, 146.

22   Wood, *Radicalism*, 222-225.

23   *Ibid.*, 233-235.

24   *Ibid.*, 276.

tion were "perceived as the proper activity of a devout man."[25] In a free society, every man enjoyed an equal right to the blessings of liberty and was as good as his neighbour. Social status was a matter of money; an individual "was "weighed by his purse, not by his mind, and according to the preponderance of that, he sinks or rises in the scale on individual opinion."" But "more money did not justify any feelings of superiority on the one side or inferiority on the other." The wealthy could make no claim to special privileges.[26]

Democratic Decentralization in a Commercial Republic

The most significant social and political fault line in the First Republic lay "between the commercial and non-commercial elements in the population." Federalists who favored ratification of the Constitution were over-represented among "merchants and the other town-dwellers, farmers depending upon the major cities, and those who produced a surplus for export." Their Antifederalist opponents "were often isolated from the major paths of commerce and usually were less well-to-do because they produced only enough for their own purposes." The battle over ratification reflected an ongoing clash between the centralizing imperatives of economic modernization and the decentralizing pressures inherent in the rush towards political democracy.[27]

For Federalists, the Union was an object of religious veneration not least of all because it promised a cornucopian torrent of economic growth and territorial expansion. In the secularized theology of the Constitutional Republic the omnipotent God of the Old Testament assumed the guise of an enlightened and vigorous national government armed with an open-ended mandate to promote the general welfare. Alexander Hamilton declared that in order to secure "their own happiness," the people at large had delegated a "part of their Majesty and their political omnipotence" to those who held public office in the federal government.[28] He believed that enlightened statesmen such as himself could provide centralized direction in the development of a fully integrated national economy. But even the most fervent nationalists were soon forced to recognize that the

---

25 Seymour Martin Lipset, *The First New Nation: The United States in Historical and Comparative Perspective* (New York: Doubleday Anchor, 1967), 186-188.

26 Wood, *Radicalism*, 243, 341.

27 Jackson Turner Main, *The Anti-Federalists: Critics of the Constitution, 1781-1788* (Chicago: Quadrangle, 1964), 280-281.

28 Wood, *Creation*, 547.

formal homogenization of political power in the name of the sovereign people marked the beginning rather than the end of the process of building a strong national state. Constitutional forms had to be adapted to the economic, social, and political realities of a society which was governed mainly at the local level. Not until the early twentieth century did most Americans accept the political need for a national administrative apparatus on the European model to provide enlightened direction and support to the process of capitalist modernization.

In the ante-bellum era, rapid "economic growth continued to expand and multiply interests seeking national action, and the early Whig [ie the "conservative" successor to the failed Federalist Party] proposals for central action reflected these pressures." At the same time, "however, the democratic thrust extending the vote and increasing participation, shifted influence away from business elites aware of the nationalizing trends and towards farmers and working men whose economic position made them less directly implicated in the nationalizing economy." Until the late nineteenth century, most Americans lived in relatively undifferentiated, small-scale "segmented societies" whose interests could be more or less effectively represented and served within the already existing "confederated republics."[29] As a consequence, the democratization of American politics caused a substantial loss of political capacity in the national government. Unfortunately for Federalist elites the "politics of deference" appropriate to a traditional hierarchy of dependence ill-suited the independent temperament of the freeholding American farmer or the upwardly mobile urban artisan or small businessman. The unifying figure of the enlightened statesman-legislator was rejected in favor of lawyers, party politicians, and clergymen who possessed a sound understanding of their local communities.[30]

The decentralization of power in the early Republic was so pronounced that it generated an "illusion of statelessness" in the eyes of foreign observers such as Alexis de Tocqueville. "Nothing is more striking to a European traveller in the United States," Tocqueville wrote, "than the absence of what we term the government or the administration." Certainly laws were made and executed, "everything moves regularly," but "the mover can nowhere be discovered. The hand that directs the social machine is invisible." The federal nature of the constitutional order had diffused sovereign

---

29   Samuel H Beer, "The Modernization of American Federalism," (1973) 3 *Publius* 49, at 62;
     Robert H Wiebe, *The Segmented Society: An Historical Preface to the Meaning of America*
     (New York: Oxford University Press, 1975).

30   David Hackett Fischer, *The Revolution of American Conservatism: The Federalist Party in
     the Era of Jeffersonian Democracy* (New York: Harper Torchbooks, 1965).

authority among numerous widely spread and various agents and trustees of the people at large in local, state, and national governments "each of whom is given the degree of power necessary for him to perform his duty." The chief beneficiaries of "the peculiar appearance of statelessness in early America" were lawyers and professional party politicians. Before the Civil War, federalism meant that the primary loyalty of the citizens of each state was to their own "little republic."[31] The Constitutional Republic remained a relatively remote political deity.

The Federalist Chief Justice of the Supreme Court consistently maintained that the central government derived its authority from the sovereign people of the United States as a whole; but his constitutional theory was dependent in practice upon a notoriously meagre and imperfectly organized concentration of governmental controls at the national level.[32] Lawyers and courts played a crucial role in accommodating juridical theory to the everyday political realities of this segmented society. Along with lawyers, professional politicians helped to reconcile the potentially contradictory forces of political democratization and economic modernization through the specialized art of log-rolling the particularistic interests of their own regional constituencies within the legislative corridors of state and national governments. Additionally, shifting pork-barrel coalitions brokered by the federal party system held together a "nation" and a "government" disconnected by Constitution.[33]

A State of Courts, Parties, and Churches

Stephen Skowronek describes the First (Federal) Republic as "the state of courts and parties."[34] Examined through a wider frame, it looks more like a state of courts, parties, and evangelical churches. Practical politicians and practicing lawyers were in a better position than most to appreciate the limitations associated with the stoical, rational deism of the Founding Fathers. While it conformed to the limits of pure reason, the official religion of the early Republic warmed few hearts. Appeals to civic virtue failed to provide "the imaginative basis of a national consciousness

---

31 Alexis de Tocqueville, *Democracy in America* Vol I Henry Reeve trans (New York: Vintage, 1945), 72-74; Stephen Skowronek, *Building a New American State: The Expansion of National Administrative Capacities, 1877-1920* (Cambridge, MA: Harvard University Press, 1982), 5-14.

32 *M'Culloch v Maryland* (1819) 4 *Wheat* 316.

33 Skowronek, *New American State*, 23-25.

34 *Id.*

without which the new nation could easily have shattered into the divisions and fragments that continually threatened it." It was the burgeoning revivalism of evangelical Protestantism that filled the cold, external forms of the constitutional faith "with a warm inner life, appropriated and impressed into the imaginative life of the people." In the first decades of the nineteenth century, fears that sectarian orthodoxies would weaken the mainspring of the Republic were belied.

In fact, when evangelical preachers set out to justify the transfer of loyalty from the Crown to the Republic, the result was often mass "conversions" bearing all the hallmarks of religious experience. "Revolution, like conversion, is an act of liberation, a leaving of old structures, a movement away from constraint." The American Revolution avoided descent into anarchy when Protestant churches helped individuals and communities to crystallize conversion into a constitutional covenant. Given the denominational diversity of American Protestantism, there could be no authoritative interpretation of the Manifest Destiny of the Constitutional Republic; its inner meaning was left to private interpretations shaped by any and all men gifted with the power of persuasion. As Robert Bellah explains, it became "the role of the evangelists in the Second Great Awakening after 1800 not only to convert individuals but to inspire communities so that they might establish and transform institutions."[35]

Americans freely informed Tocqueville that religion was vital to the maintenance of their republican institutions. Concerned citizens knew that "out of the flotsam and jetsam of the pious and the reprobate who filled the towns and cities of the [American] West there had to be woven an entire associational life capable of carrying on the daily social functions, and social institutions had not merely to be established but uplifted and improved." Revivalists elaborated techniques to reach "into the deepest level of unconscious motivation in the common man." The aim was not just "to open him to the infusion of divine grace, but to make him a citizen." Revivalism was crucial to the religion of the Republic "in its operation as a controlling, purifying power in the consciences of the people." Individuals were left free to look out for themselves but they were not quite the rational maximizers envisaged by liberal theory. For most people, material self-interest was intertwined with religious idealism in deep and complex ways. The millennialism of the American Protestant tradition

---

35   Robert N Bellah, *The Broken Covenant: American Civil Religion in Time of Trial* second edition (Chicago: University of Chicago Press, 1992), 34-35, 44-47.

repeatedly threw up movements for social change and social reform; it was forever overturning "any simple commitment to the status quo."[36]

It must not be forgotten, however, that during this period the business of America was business. Some concluded "that this unruly society could tie itself together only by bonds that were in accordance with the realities" of self-interest—the "most powerful impulse of the human breast." Tocqueville, too, was convinced that it was interest and money that held a diverse and rootless people together. Commerce sometimes seemed to be "the major source of cohesion in the society." But those who stressed the social benefits of business and commerce did so knowing that they were simultaneously championing the sacred cause of liberty. After all, the expanding web of commerce enhanced the prestige of artisans, small businessmen, and farmers, indeed, all those most likely to join with radical democrats in their all-out assault on "aristocratic" privilege. The most visible sign of the gentleman was the leisure which gave him "both the time and the responsibility for public service." In the decades following the Revolution, that leisure was denigrated mercilessly as shameful idleness. Such attacks were "coupled with a heightened appreciation of the significance and dignity of labor." Soon, "there was nobody left, in the northern states at least, who dared publicly and proudly to claim that he did not work for a living."[37]

A natural social order dating from time out of mind had been levelled. The egalitarian sense that every free man must participate in labor now outlawed "invidious" social distinctions between those who worked, those who prayed, and those who fought. It also aggravated the growing sectional split between North and South. Both the celebration of work and the disparagement of idleness made "the South with its leisured aristocracy supported by slavery even more anomalous than it had been at the time of the Revolution." Combined with the anti-institutional fervor of evangelical revivalism, the democratic ideology of free labor eventually lent its mass appeal to a multi-pronged crusade against Negro slavery.[38] The French and Bolshevik Revolutions had devoured their own children almost immediately. But it was the grand- and great-grandchildren of the first American Revolution who perished in their hundreds of thousands on the industrial-scale killing fields of the Civil War. The conquest and destruction of the Old South marked the second phase of the permanent

---

36 Lipset, *First New Nation*, 180; Bellah, *Broken Covenant*, 47-49.

37 Wood, *Radicalism*, 277.

38 *Ibid.*, 336-337, 286; see also, Eric Foner, *Free Soil, Free Labor, Free Men: The Ideology of the Republican Party Before the Civil War* (New York: Oxford University Press, 1970).

American Revolution. Along with the Puritan Revolution in England and the American War of Independence, the War for Southern Independence counts as the third civil war within modern Anglo-Saxon civilization.

The Political Theology of Disunion

The abolitionist crusade against slavery perverted the profoundly religious sensibility that animated the Republic. Abolitionists spent decades manipulating the symbolism and rhetoric of America's constitutional faith to advance a revolutionary program of immediate and unconditional emancipation. Some denounced the Constitution itself because it condoned the evil of slavery. William Lloyd Garrison publicly tore to shreds a copy of what he condemned as "a covenant with death and an agreement with hell." Others believed that emancipation was implicit in the Constitution. Finally Christian holiness and republican liberty were fused together in the fires of war. "The Battle Hymn of the Republic" sanctified those taking up arms to trample "out the vintage where the grapes of wrath are stored." Loyal Unionists were adjured to "die to make men free" just as Christ died "to make men holy." At war's end, the religion of the victorious Republic, "One and Indivisible" elevated the personal martyrdom of Abraham Lincoln as "the spiritual center of American history."[39] But those who saw the Union as the Ark of the Covenant were mistaken; its triumph ensured that the revolutionary religion of the Republic would stand in even deeper contradiction to the orthodox traditions of Anglo-Saxon Christianity.

Arguably, the First Republic split along the seam between Protestant covenant theology and republican liberty. Those who feared that ardent "sectarian" defence of Christianity might subvert the religion of the Constitutional Republic were right. But orthodox Christianity, southern style, was in no position to replace America's civil religion. Some paleoconservatives credit the Confederacy with a courageous defence of orthodox Christianity against "the hollow men of modernity" in the North who had confused their own humanitarian hubris with the Spirit of God.[40] The truth is that America spawned not one but two mutually antagonistic civil religions in the space of seventy years. But the northern and the southern

---

39 Bellah, *Broken Covenant*, 50-54.

40 James Michael Hill and Thomas Fleming, quoted in Edward H Sebesta and Euan Hague, "The US Civil War as a Theological War: Neo-Confederacy, Christian Nationalism, and Theology," in Euan Hague, *et al.*, *Neo-Confederacy: A Critical Introduction* (Austin TX: University of Texas Press, 2008), 50.

versions of American political theology were essentially different denominations of a common constitutional faith; each condemned the other for deviating from the path of constitutional fidelity. Significantly, the black-letter text of the Confederate Constitution is all but indistinguishable from the US Constitution, using, in particular, the same language to prohibit the establishment of any religion and to guarantee the free exercise of all. The Union and the Confederacy were separated not by the cold, outward forms of their respective Constitutions but by the sectarian spirit spewed forth by fire-eating, fanatics on both sides of the Mason-Dixon line.

Both regimes invoked the sacred cause of liberty, but republican liberty acquired a radically different meaning on each side of the sectional divide. In the northern and western states, the defence of liberty justified demands that ranged from immediate and uncompensated emancipation to a halt in the territorial expansion of slavery; but neither abolitionists nor free-soilers would brook further compromise with the "Slave Power." For the southern gentlemen who seceded from the Union, the freedom of Negro slaves threatened not just their material interests but also, and more importantly, their standing as men of honor. The political theology of the Confederate Republic understood slavery's absolute deprivation of liberty as a divinely ordained badge of dishonour. Men of honor In the Old South distinguished themselves from slaves in three important ways: "they would never allow anyone to call them liars; they gave gifts; and they did not fear death." Each of those themes was intertwined with the rituals associated with duelling.[41]

The South reacted to Lincoln's election as if the North had pulled its nose, the ultimate insult to planters ready to take offence at the slightest provocation. Lincoln's partisans had a tin ear when it came to questions of honor. They scoffed when slaveholders emphasized their generous concern for the well-being of the Negro slaves in their charge on southern farms and plantations. In the North, it became a self-evident axiom of republican morality that slavery was an evil that must be eradicated forthwith from the soil of every free society. Abolitionists refused to treat slaveholders as men of honor, reviling them instead as monstrous throwbacks to the dark ages of superstition and tyranny. In the South, slavery went from being a "necessary evil" to a "positive good." Southern churches invoked biblical authority to defend slavery, upholding the letter as well as the spirit of Christian orthodoxy. Northern churches turned instead to theological liberalism, abandoning "the Word for a Spirit increasingly

---

41   Kenneth S Greenberg, *Honor & Slavery* (Princeton, NJ: Princeton University Press, 1996), xiii.

reduced to personal subjectivity."[42] Meanwhile, the planter aristocracy of the South was steeling itself to face death in defence of their liberties under the Constitution.

Not only could a strong scriptural case be made in favor of slavery but a strict construction of the Constitution also favored the pro-slavery argument. Unfortunately, close reading of the Bible does not by itself an orthodox Christian nation make; nor could constitutional faith unaided guarantee the survival of republican liberty. Because both the Old and the New Testaments appeared to sanction slavery, southern preachers confidently "denounced abolitionists as infidels abandoning the plain words of the Bible."[43] On the one hand, the master class cited Scripture in support of slavery; on the other, they acquiesced in the impotence of their churches. Both in the governance of slaves and in the defence of the southern way of life against Northern aggression, slaveholders readily subsumed Christian morality within their overarching faith in the Constitutional Republic. For southerners, no less than for northerners, the Republic served as the national *ecclesia*.

But Southern divines insisted that hierarchy was an essential feature of natural and social order that all men of honor were bound to preserve. They believed that republican freedom was part of God's plan for America, but, like the ancient Greeks, they saw in slavery the indispensable foundation of a free society. In this sense, the Confederacy, no less than the Union, remained a creature of the revolutionary Enlightenment; it, too, regarded itself as a nation with "the soul of a church." Southerners looked to the state not the church to articulate and to protect their vital interests. In particular, southerners expected the state rather than the church to uphold the institution of Negro slavery while defending the sacred cause of liberty for the white citizens of the Confederate states. On both counts, they doomed themselves to failure and defeat.

Had the church played the pedagogic and disciplinary roles assigned to the orthodox Christian *ecclesia*, the War for Southern Independence might have been avoided, perhaps even won. In Latin American slave societies, the church was able to reform Negro slavery, helping to ensure

---

42 Eugene D Genovese, *The Southern Front: History and Politics in the Cultural War* (Columbia, MO: University of Missouri Press, 1995), 12.

43 Eugene D Genovese, *A Consuming Fire: The Fall of the Confederacy in the Mind of the White Christian South* (Athens, GA: University of Georgia Press, 1998), 4. Perhaps the most powerful Scriptural defence of slavery was published shortly after the Civil War: see Robert L Dabney, *Defence of Virginia (and Through Her of the South) in Recent and Pending Contests against the Sectional Party* (New York: EJ Hale, 1867) [available in the Michigan Historical Reprint Series].

not just that the institution survived longer but also that it was abolished peacefully. In countries such as Brazil and Cuba, the presence of a powerful church with needs of its own was a factor that weighed on both the civil authorities and slaveholding planters. As a matter of course, the church insisted "on a dominant role in the formulation of all policy which might bear on the morality of the slave system and have consequences for the Faith." In the American south, "the church could do nothing. Its rural congregations were full of humane and decent Christians, but as an institution of authority and power it had no real existence." The governance of relationships between masters and slaves was a matter for courts, legislatures, and masters, not for churches. Not surprisingly, "the hegemonic function of the law" was performed in a manner much more sensitive to the interests of masters than to the needs of their Negro slaves. Suggestions that the operation of the slave system in the southern states was influenced solely by "the dynamics of unopposed capitalism" may overstate the harshness of American slavery; but there is no doubt, as southern divines knew only too well, that the morality of the slave system did not live up to Biblical standards. The abject failure of southern churches to reform and to be seen to be reforming the perceived cruelty and injustice of American slavery was no less important a factor in the drift towards an irrepressible conflict than the moralistic intransigence of radical abolitionists.[44] In the final analysis, the weakness of southern churches made it both possible and necessary for the Confederate state to assume sole carriage of the national defence effort.

One historian suggests that, in seeking the key to the failure of the Confederacy, one must search "in the depths of the Southern spirit, and particularly in the minds and hearts of the planter aristocrats and old army generals who led the South to disaster." It appears that the American civil religion that Confederate leaders took with them as they left the Union had much to do with that failure. Robert L Kerby points out that the southern leadership proclaimed secession "in the name of states' rights, local democracy, and individual liberty" but then "immediately reinstituted the forms, habits, traditions, symbols and customs of an established nation-state, saddling the South with the same complex of ideas and institutions against which Southerners were ostensibly protesting." As early as September 1861, one disaffected southern patriot complained that the military professionalism associated with the established

---

44 Stanley M Elkins, *Slavery: A Problem in American Institutional & Intellectual Life* (New York: Grossett & Dunlap, 1963), 68, 61, 37; Eugene D Genovese, *Roll, Jordan, Roll: The World the Slaves Made* (New York: Pantheon, 1972), 25-49; id., *A Consuming Fire*, 5-9.

religion of the Republic was destroying the capacity of local communities to defend themselves. As the army lay dying, Robert Toombs proposed an epitaph: "*died of West Point.*"[45]

Was there an alternative strategy? Kerby argues that it was futile for Robert E Lee to try to turn Johnny Reb into a soldier "when he continued to think like a militiaman or a guerrilla." He suggests that local irregular units could have conducted a war of national liberation in the American south, offering what the regular army conspicuously failed to provide: a defence in depth. Very early on, the centralist strategy pursued by Confederate leaders caused a collapse in popular morale.[46] But the Confederate Constitutional Republic had no military remedy for that spiritual problem. And unfortunately, given the institutional weakness of southern churches, there was no practical alternative to the established religion of the Republic. "The church had fallen into a thousand parts. The shadow of an Anglican church, disestablished in the wake of the Revolution and its doom forever sealed by the yearly anarchy of the camp meeting, was all that remained in the South of vested ecclesiastical authority."[47]

Everywhere in the South, religious vitality "was overwhelming, but that vitality lay primarily in demands for individual satisfaction which took inevitable and repeated priority over institutional needs." With new churches springing up everywhere in the wake of evangelical revivalism, "both the ideal of a learned ministry and the role of the individual minister as a powerful leader in the community could hardly avoid being drastically undermined."[48] The fragmentation of the church helped to ensure the crushing defeat of the Confederacy, thereby permitting the abolitionist interpretation of republican liberty to entrench itself in the Constitution. The alternative view, that America was meant to be a "white man's country," never enjoyed similar status. It was 1857—late in the day, far too late in fact—before that view received explicit constitutional recognition in Chief Justice Roger Taney's bitterly contested judgement in the *Dred Scott* case.[49] Lee's surrender at the Appomattox courthouse finally put paid to that constitutional conceit.

---

45 Robert L Kerby, "Why the Confederacy Lost," (1973) 35(3) *Review of Politics* 326, at 340-342, 338.

46 *Ibid.*, 339, 341-342.

47 Elkins, *Slavery*, 28.

48 *Ibid.*, 29.

49 *Dred Scott v Sandford* (1857) 19 How 393.

The Second (Bourgeois) Republic: Equality

A Second (Bourgeois) Republic planted itself astride the prostrate body politic of the slave South. American political theology was reformed by marrying the sacred cause of liberty to the constitutional guarantees of due process and equal protection extended to all American citizens by the newly ratified Fourteenth Amendment. In the reconstructed Union, citizenship was the gift of the federal government rather than the states. Negroes became the principal beneficiaries of the new regime in the South when they were granted formal political and legality equality with whites. But political pressure to flatten out several other deeply-entrenched differences of class, race, and sex steadily mounted. Then, when the economic depression of the 1930s too obviously belied the bourgeois gospel of wealth, the perpetual American Revolution went into overdrive once again. The Second (Bourgeois) Republic was overthrown and its successor regime launched another secular reformation. Under the Third (Managerial) Republic America's constitutional faith subsumed the revolutionary promise of liberty and equality into the fraternal ideal of universal human brotherhood.

But even in the heyday of the Second Republic, as might be expected, Anglo-Saxon Protestants were heavily over-represented in the ranks of the middle-class progressives drafting the agenda for the third major episode in America's endless revolution. Many knew, even hoped, that campaigns for "social justice" would damage the economic interests and weaken the political power of their working class co-ethnics. Weaving a tangled web of lies, evasions, and self-deception, courts and lawyers, preachers and congregations, politicians and businessmen, college professors and bohemian writers, radicals and conservatives, indeed, the entire priesthood of the Second Republic saddled the historically dominant Anglo-Saxon Protestant ethny with a dangerously confused and contradictory conception of just what America was, where it had come from, and where it was going.

Lincoln's war did not preserve the Union; on the contrary, the character of the Constitutional Republic was utterly transformed. The original meaning of the Constitution focused on federalism and the separation of powers. The states and the people retained important powers, thereby imposing limits on Hamiltonian schemes to create an "energetic government." During the Civil War, those limits were swept aside by executive decree and military might. By crushing the southern states, Lincoln fatally weakened the federal principle; his arbitrary exercise of emergency powers laid the foundations for executive dictatorship whenever exceptional circumstances justify the suspension of constitutional liberties. The war was an exercise in constitutional duplicity; the ratification of the Fourteenth Amendment in 1868 was accomplished only by means of blatant fraud and military coercion. Nonetheless, once securely enshrined in the Constitution, the amendment provided both the Second and the Third Republics with their formal constitutional warrant.

In effect, the Fourteenth Amendment transformed the Constitutional Republic from a federal union of sovereign states into a unitary "Nation." It did so by establishing the primacy in law "of United States citizenship and with it the primacy of Congress's authority to secure the rights of American citizens." Prior to the Civil War, individuals had been citizens of the United States by virtue of their citizenship in a state. Each state defined the status and enforced the rights of the individuals within their borders to life, liberty, and property. In proposing the Fourteenth Amendment, "Congress knowingly and purposely acted to revolutionize the structure of the federal union." In addition to defining United States citizenship, the amendment denied states the power to infringe upon the immunities and privileges granted to United States citizens; nor could they deny any persons due process and equal protection of the laws.[50]

It is clear, however, that Congress knowingly and purposely denied constitutional due process and equal protection of the laws to the southern states when it compelled them to ratify the amendment. Article V of the Constitution provides that proposed amendments submitted by Congress to the states for ratification must be approved by three-quarters of the states. Radical Republicans maintained that the southern states could not be re-admitted to the Union until redeemed from the sin of rebellion by Congress. Other politicians blanched at any suggestion that only northern states be counted in calculating the three-fourths majority on the grounds that such exclusionary tactics would be tantamount, legally speaking, to an admission that the secession of the southern states from the Union had been successful. Treating the South as a conquered province at the mercy of the Union was hardly consistent with the official line that the war had been waged "to preserve the Union with all the dignity, equality, and rights of the several states unimpaired." When required to pay lip-service to Article V, Radicals "were driven to the absurd conclusion that the states could not qualify as members of the Union until after they had performed a function which only members could perform,

---

50   Robert J Kaczorowski, "Revolutionary Constitutionalism in the Era of Civil War and Reconstruction," (1986) 61 *New York University Law Review* 863.

i.e. ratify a Federal constitutional amendment." Compounding the constitutional fraud, Congress changed the process after the amendment had been rejected by more than a quarter of the states. Under the new rules, ratification was to "be effected by a specified type of legislature, elected in a manner provided by Congress, a legislature chosen on the basis of Negro suffrage (though this was prior to the adoption of the Fifteenth Amendment, designed to force such suffrage.)"[51]

The southern states were not the only flies in the Radical ointment. Members of the executive and judicial branches of the federal government who objected to the Radical agenda became the targets of undue influence and varying degrees of duress. When the amendment met resistance from President Johnson, impeachment proceedings were set in motion. Every effort was made as well to ward off any judicial challenge. Eventually, by fair means and foul, the southern states were brought to heel; submission was preferable to continued military government and loss of representation in Congress.

By the standards of the First (Federal) Republic, the Fourteenth Amendment was unconstitutional. But, despite some initial resistance, the legal priesthood of the Republic soon elevated the amendment to the status of sacred writ. It retains that position today despite dramatic twists and turns in the meaning attached to the text of the amendment by the courts. The US Supreme Court has never cast the legitimacy of the Fourteenth Amendment into doubt. In 1872, in the *Slaughter-House Cases*, a majority of the Supreme Court did restrict the scope of the amendment, conceiving it merely as "a negative prohibition against racially discriminatory state action." But a dissenting judgement by Justice Stephen Field laid the foundation for what later became the ruling orthodoxy. Field vindicated the Radical view that the Fourteenth Amendment was "an affirmative exercise of constitutional authority." Indeed, he interpreted it as "a self-executing guarantee of civil rights." In other words, Field conceived the amendment as a tool enabling the federal judiciary to nationalize citizenship by securing the constitutionally guaranteed natural rights of all free persons.[52]

Before the Civil War, the anti-slavery crusade had taught Americans to defend the rights of free labor against the aggressive designs of the slave-owning southerners. Field deftly wove the egalitarian free labor ideology into the fabric of America's constitutional faith. Field was in the legal vanguard of America's bourgeois revolution. The Thirteenth, Fourteenth,

---

51 Bruce Ackerman, *We the People: Transformations* (Cambridge, MA: Belknap Press, 2000), 110-118.

52 *Slaughterhouse Cases* (1872) 83 US 36.

and Fifteenth Amendments to the Constitution were grist for Field's ideological mill. In Field's jurisprudence, the point of the Second American Revolution was to secure the privileges and immunities belonging to any citizen "against abridgement in any form by any State. The Fourteenth Amendment places them under the guardianship of the National authority." An "equality of right...in the lawful pursuits of life, throughout the whole country, is the distinguishing privilege of citizens of the United States. To them, everywhere, all pursuits, all professions, all avocations are open without other restrictions than such as are imposed equally upon all others of the same age, sex, and condition."[53] The remorseless, irresistible logic of the bourgeois revolution was revealed as well in an 1886 Supreme Court judgement which affirmed that business corporations, too, were "legal persons" equally entitled to protection under the Fourteenth Amendment.[54]

The rise of the big business corporation transformed the meaning of free labor in law and in fact. Prior to the Civil War, wage labor for most Americans had been a temporary expedient rather than a permanent condition. Most free workers expected eventually to quit the wage-earning class and own a farm or small shop. By the turn of the twentieth century, however, the middle-class goal of economic independence had become unattainable for a large and growing class of permanent wage earners. In this period, the religion of the Republic was presented with a formidable challenge: Could an "equality of right" be established between the vast concentrations of corporate wealth and the tired and huddled masses herded into urban slums? Did such formal legalisms provide any more protection to debt-ridden farmers in the South and West driven to the wall by monopolistic manufacturers, banks, and railroads?

Bourgeois Equality

In matters of law and social policy, the Second Republic sought, unsuccessfully, to balance an old concern—private rights and individual freedom—with the pressing desire to foster the development of a national economy. The post-Civil War period was an "epoch of industrial pioneering," a

---

53 Ibid., 98, 110.

54 The court's decision consisted of one short paragraph: "The court does not wish to hear argument on the question whether the provision in the Fourteenth Amendment to the Constitution, which forbids a State to deny to any person within its jurisdiction the equal protection of the laws, applies to these corporations. We are all of the opinion that it does." Santa Clara v Southern Pacific Railroad (1886) 118 US 394.

Gilded Age in which "the whole psychic energy of the American people was absorbed in the exploitation and organization of the material resources of the continent." For bourgeois gentlemen of property and standing, "business enterprise was virtually the only recognized sphere of action." America no longer "offered a career open to all the talents. It offered only one career, that of sharing in the material development of the continent. Into this one channel passed all the religious fervor of the race." Wealth came to mean something more than mere material possession to the best men; "the pursuit of it was nothing less than a sacred duty."[55] The gospel of wealth found authoritative expression not just in the jurisprudential language of laissez-faire constitutionalism but also in the social science pioneered by men such as William Graham Sumner.

Under the Second Republic, the sacred cause of equality was the *leitmotif* of American civil religion. Sumner's inner-directed mission was to demonstrate that escalating demands for social equality in a highly organized corporate system were a mortal danger to constitutional liberty. He argued that private property "produces inequalities between men;" at the same time, it is an essential bulwark of liberty. Sumner was a social Darwinist for whom competition "is a law of nature," a "niggardly" goddess who "grants her rewards to the fittest." Blessed with "liberty, men get from her just in proportion to their works." If we "take the rewards from those who have done better and give them to those who have done worse," we will, of course, lessen inequalities; we will also reward the unfit. Sumner warned "that we cannot go outside of this alternative: liberty, inequality, survival of the fittest; not-liberty, equality, survival of the unfittest." Liberty "carries society forward and favors all its best members;" equality "carries society downwards and favors all its worst members."[56]

But Sumner was no libertarian. He recognized that the advance of industrial organization necessarily imposes stricter subordination and higher discipline on workers who are solely dependent on their wages for survival. "All organization implies restriction of liberty." Increased comfort and abundance are made possible only through the industrial power generated by a "combination of force under discipline and strict coordination."[57] But the need for order and coordination must be confined within strict constitutional limits; the rule of law was the indispensable foundation of both liberty and property. A zone of individual liberty must

55 Van Wyck Brooks, *The Ordeal of Mark Twain* (New York: EP Dutton, 1970), 77-78, 80-81.

56 William Graham Sumner, *On Liberty, Society, and Politics: The Essential Essays of William Graham Sumner* (Indianapolis, IN: Liberty Fund, 1992), 164-165.

57 Ibid., 252-253.

be secured by private property rights. Similarly, the state must remain neutral as between different categories of citizens. If it educates or taxes one, it must educate and tax all—whether white or black, yellow or red; Jew or Christian; alien or native.

In this period, proponents of laissez-faire constitutionalism such as Sumner and Field were not the pliant tool of vested interests; on the contrary, they attacked every form of what they called "class legislation." Resolutely committed to the fundamental constitutional principle of equality before the law, they consistently rejected laws that used "government power to improve the condition of one group in society at the expense of others." In their eyes, protective tariffs favoring the interests of manufacturers over those of consumers were just as objectionable as minimum wage and maximum hour legislation. They opposed monopolies and special privileges of any sort. By contrast, socialists pushed the idea of equality to its limits. They denounced private property itself as a species of class legislation. At the same time, socialists advocated extreme forms of class legislation on behalf of the proletarian masses. Sumner strongly resisted demands for substantive equality of possession. He was no less determined in his defence of formal equality before the law as "one of the cardinal principles of civil liberty." He argued that as long as the state preserves a neutral stance towards every special interest, each man is left "to run the race of life for himself as best he can."[58]

Sumner has been characterized as a "conservative,"[59] a highly misleading label in his case. Despite Sumner's evident distaste for the socialist utopia brewing in Marx's imagination, he was no reactionary guardian of an entrenched ruling class. On the contrary, Sumner stood in the intellectual vanguard of the bourgeois revolution in America; he had no interest in preserving traditional folkways or hereditary privilege in American society. Unlike bloody-minded Bolshevik agitators, however, Sumner pondered the prospect of unrestricted class warfare from the cautiously realistic perspective of a social Darwinist. Competition may be the law of life but no society can survive a state of perpetual warfare. Every successful society requires mechanisms of peace and cooperation to constrain the destructive effects of competition. Christianity was one such "peace-group;" the "medieval church constructed Christendom as a cult-group reaching over all the disintegration and war of the feudal period." The Constitutional Republic was a more modern social mechanism to

---

58   Ibid., 177-178.

59   Robert Green McCloskey, *American Conservatism in the Age of Enterprise, 1865-1910* (New York: Harper Torchbooks, 1964).

promote civil peace. Nevertheless Sumner rued the failure of the American Republic to take proper advantage of its isolation from the Old World; it might have made a new start in peace and simplicity. Americans had fallen into the old ways of "war and glory, alternate victory and calamity, adventurous enterprises, grand finance, powerful government, and great social contrasts of splendor and misery." Sumner was no less realistic in his understanding of race relations in the Second Republic.[60]

Racial Realism

Following the Civil War, the Republic tried to absorb Negroes within its "peace-bond" but Sumner held out little hope of success. Negroes, Sumner declared were in the Republic but "not of it." Writing in 1903, he judged that "the two races live more independently of each other now than they did" in the days of slavery. That division between in-group and out-group was likely to persist far into the future. "No one has yet found any way in which two races, far apart in blood and culture, can be amalgamated into one society with satisfaction to both." Among natural and social scientists who discussed race in the Second Republic, the vast majority "accepted the concept of racial differences;" few doubted that "the evidence for nearly permanent Negro inferiority was conclusive."[61]

As ever, the Radical cutting edge of Anglo-Saxon Protestant opinion resisted such conclusions; cutting across the grain of class, caste, and custom, self-styled "progressives" labored ceaselessly to promote the egalitarian myth of the color-blind constitution. Justice John Harlan of the US Supreme Court gave the egalitarian credo legal currency when he famously asserted that "Our Constitution is color-blind." In a series of dissenting judgements stretching over decades, Justice Harlan inveighed against Jim Crow laws designed to entrench whites as the dominant race in southern states of the Constitutional Republic. Harlan's progressive interpretation of the Constitution foreshadowed the civil rights revolution of the mid-twentieth century.

But the majority of the Supreme Court in the Second Republic confined the Fourteenth Amendment to action by the states, leaving private persons and businesses free to discriminate against Negroes in their social and economic activities. Had Harlan's view prevailed, the "state action" doctrine would catch any and all private activities or enterprises licensed

60   Sumner, *On Liberty*, 312-313.

61   *Ibid.*, 312-313, 318; Charles A Lofgren, *The Plessy Case: A Legal-Historical Interpretation* (New York: Oxford University Press, 1987), 104-110.

or regulated in any way by the state, from marriage to managing a railroad, hotel, bar, restaurant, or theater. Harlan deemed racial classifications of any kind to be "inconsistent with the personal liberty of citizens, white or black." The states, therefore, were not at liberty "to regulate civil rights, common to all citizens, upon the basis of race; and to place in a condition of legal inferiority a large body of American citizens, now constituting a part of the political community called the People of the United States."[62] But not even Harlan dared to call for fraternal social intercourse between white and black races.

In retrospect, Anglo-Saxon Protestants of the Second Republic seem surprisingly realistic in their attitudes towards race. Nonetheless, despite their now much-maligned openness to "scientific racism," they often lapsed into self-deception, complacency, and jingoistic hubris. As the American colossus bestrode the world, political and religious leaders concocted comforting fantasies celebrating the Anglo-Saxon century to come. Meanwhile, aliens from the most distant and dangerous corners of Europe utterly transformed the demographic face of the nation. Race, language, and culture lost their currency as the defining features of a shared American nationality. Leading social scientists decried the "antipathies of sects" that threatened "to tear society to pieces." American society was "drawing apart into opposing camps of poor and rich, capitalist and worker, functionary and citizen, civilian and soldier, as well as the race enmity of white and black, or yellow and white, or Christian and Jew." Fearing that such demographic diversity would destroy America's core Anglo-Saxon identity, Edward A Ross summoned his "society to act or perish."[63]

Many patriotic Anglo-Americans rallied around the banner of racial solidarity. Indeed, mainly Anglo-Saxon Protestant populists in the southern and western states united with patrician New England elites to organize a successful immigration restriction movement. The introduction of the national origins quota system in the 1920s combined with depression and world war to stem the flow of immigration for forty years. But immigration reformers won what turned out in the long run to be a Pyrrhic victory. Without any constitutional assurance that the immigration floodgates would remain closed, they had conceded an uncontrollable plenary power over immigration to the federal government. In this period, racial

---

62 *Plessy v Ferguson* (1896) 163 US 537. See also, *Civil Rights Cases* (1883) 109 US 3; and *Berea College v Commonwealth of Kentucky* (1908) 211 US 45.

63 R Jackson Wilson, *In Quest of Community: Social Philosophy in the United States, 1860-1920* (New York: Wiley, 1968), 109.

realists adopted an uncritical stance toward the religion of the revolutionary American Republic; their constitutional faith revealed the spiritual
void at the heart of American racial realism.

Like Sumner, writers such as Madison Grant, Lothrop Stoddard,
Charles Conant Josey, and Edward Ross reflected the Darwinian turn
in Anglo-American social theory.[64] The lesson of biological evolution
appeared to be that there was no "moral law implanted in man's conscience" that would fit him for life in a modern industrial society. The
modern social state was conceived as an artificial construct bending "its
members into new kinds of conformity, substituting its collective will
for the private wills of its constituents." Social cohesion could not be
taken for granted; racial solidarity, in particular, was under threat from
"the constant pouring in of immigrants from progressively lower social
grades and from peoples more remote from the orbit of our civilization."
But in this account, Anglo-Saxon identity was flattened into an abstract
scientific classification which denoted a sub-group of what was variously
described as the white, Caucasian, or Nordic race. Lost altogether was the
primordial understanding that Anglo-Saxon identity is inseparable from
the blood faith of a Christian people. Once American political theology
fell under the influence of scientific modernism, racial realists lost interest in the ethnoreligous traditions of Anglo-Saxon Christendom. By the
late nineteenth century, Anglo-Saxon Protestantism had "lost much of its
power as an independent source of moral authority," becoming instead "a
handmaiden of the positivist world view."[65] Indeed, as science gained in
prestige, theology fell into disuse.

Scientific racism reflected the post-Christian rationalism of a rising
industrial civilization; as such it bore the stamp of a soulless and self-
defeating materialism. Racial realism was too cold and aloof to regenerate
a sense of ethnoreligious solidarity among Anglo-Saxon Protestants. It
left middle-class Americans unable to decide whether they were simply
whites, or one of several more exotic breeds such as the Nordics, Aryans,
or Caucasians. Lacking firm roots in the historical literature and popular culture of a folk religion, in ancestral myths of heroism, chivalry, and

64   Madison Grant, *The Passing of the Great Race* (New York: Charles Scribner's Sons, 1916;
     Lothrop Stoddard, *The Rising Tide of Color* (New York: Charles Scribner's Sons, 1920);
     Charles Conant Josey, *Race and National Solidarity* (New York: Charles Scribner's Sons,
     1923); Edward Alsworth Ross, *Social Control: A Survey of the Foundations of Order* (New
     York: Macmillan, 1904).

65   Wilson, *In Quest of Community*, 89, 92, 112; TJ Jackson Lears, *No Place of Grace:
     Antimodernism and the Transformation of American Culture, 1880-1920* (New York:
     Pantheon, 1981), 23.

romantic love, Anglo-Saxon racial solidarity had little purchase within the collective machinery of social control that increasingly governed industrial America.

Progressive Women and Other Aliens

Anglo-Saxon men of the Old Faith knew they were honor-bound to protect their women and children, to shelter the helpless and care for the sick and dependent. The incarnational theology of Old England had taught Anglo-Saxon Christians to sense a divine presence in the highly charged interplay between the polarities of masculinity and femininity. As a consequence, the English people learned how to generate bonds of spiritual solidarity between individuals of different sexes and from unrelated families. Norms of in-group altruism bound relative strangers together in comparative harmony generating results that enhanced the reproductive fitness of the Anglo-Saxon race. But, in a mechanized, industrial society, the same rationalism that deepened awareness of racial differences flattened the differences between the sexes.

American feminists invoked the egalitarian religion of the Second Republic to justify the proletarianization of housewives. Progressive women also encouraged their husbands and sons to abdicate headship of the family and to give up the hitherto exclusive prerogative of men to exercise leadership in politics and war, commerce and industry. While racial realists pointed to enemies gathering at the gates of the citadel, feminists employed the post-Christian rationalism of Anglo-Saxon Protestant social science to sow the seeds of subversion behind the lines, among America's womenfolk.

Anti-suffragists predicted that once women ceased to be good and obedient to their husbands by remaining "discreet, chaste, keepers at home," Christian civilization in America faced certain destruction.[66] Orthodox Anglo-Saxon Christians steeped in Scripture warned "that the theory of 'Women's Rights' is sheer infidelity." Biblical authority and the traditions of the church consigned women "to a social subordination, and expressly excluded [them] from ruling offices, on grounds of their sex." But Anglo-Saxon Protestant men eventually abandoned the traditional Christian model of family life. Their womenfolk became ever-more corrupted by "all the baleful influences of political life," further deepening the spiritual crisis engendered by American civil religion. Robert Lewis

---

66 Titus 2:5.

Dabney was on solid ground when he forecast that: "The politicating woman, unsexed and denaturalized, shorn of the true glory of her feminity, will appear to men as a feeble hybrid manikin, with all the defects and none of the strength of the male. Instead of being the dear object of his chivalrous affection, she becomes his importunate rival, despised without being feared." Dabney fully expected "women's rights" advocates "to win the day, because the premises from which they argue their revolution have been irrevocably admitted by the bulk of the people."[67]

The false principles of American civil religion ensnared racial realists, in particular, in a multitude of contradictions. Feminists were not above wooing ardent believers in Negro inferiority. In fact, realist appeals to racial solidarity were a common refrain in the campaign for women's suffrage. Once all Negro men had been endowed with a constitutional right to vote, it was but a short step to argue that "a Yankee white woman with her 'smartness' and education" has as good a claim to the suffrage "as a stupid, ignorant, Southern black."[68]

American civil religion preached the revolutionary doctrine that government must be based upon the consent of the governed. It followed that suffrage ought to be coextensive with allegiance. Women's suffrage turned out to be the most revolutionary achievement of the Second Republic. With the ratification of the Nineteenth Amendment, the divinely-ordained natural order of the Anglo-Saxon Christian family was placed in permanent opposition to the Constitutional Republic. Portraying themselves as "prisoners of their sex," otherwise well-heeled wives and daughters resisted the lawful authority of husbands and fathers. Calling upon the *state* to set them free, chronically captious women fatally compromised the ethnoreligious cohesion of America's WASP bourgeoisie.

Charlotte Perkins Gilman's short novel *Herland* provides a telling commentary on relations between the sexes in late nineteenth century America. Less a story than a utopian fantasy, the book describes a long-lost tribe of women living and working together in an advanced society of peace and plenty, altogether free of men, thanks to their evolved powers of parthenogenesis.[69] Meanwhile, back in bourgeois America where men were still a fact of life, the cult of equality formally inaugurated by the Fourteenth Amendment offered feminists a potent ideological weapon

---

67 Robert Lewis Dabney, "Women's Rights Women,":
    http://www.amprpress.com/women%27s_rights_women.htm

68 Id.

69 Charlotte Perkins Gilman, *Herland, The Yellow Wall-Paper, and Selected Writings* (New York: Penguin, 1999).

in their permanent cultural war against the "patriarchal" traditions of Anglo-Saxon Christianity. In the end, feminist identity politics ripped the heart out of Anglo-Saxon racialism.

The overpowering material success of American capitalism alienated many of America's most sensitive, intelligent, and educated Anglo-Saxon Protestant women. Feminists presented "the problem of the modern woman as essentially a labor problem; a problem, that is, created by the sudden superabundance of leisure." Women had been turned into parasites living on the labor of others as the family "gradually surrendered its functions to institutions outside the home—manufacturing to the factory, control over property to the state, the education of children to the public schools." For middle-class women "conscious of their intellectual gifts but unable, it seemed, to make use of them within the sphere of women's traditional duties, life, experience, 'growth' were always *out there*." That sense of superfluity lay behind the prevalent image of the "woman as alien."[70] Feeling that life was passing them by, Anglo-Saxon Protestant feminists directed powerful feelings of envy, suspicion, and resentment towards their menfolk. They barely noticed that their fathers, brothers, and husbands suffered from an equally debilitating spiritual malaise. Indeed, militant feminism neutered generations of WASP men; traditions of heroism and chivalry once central to Christian manhood shrivelled away into anachronistic irrelevance.

Leading Anglo-Saxon Protestant intellectuals were sensitive to the disappearance of the sacred from their society; they desperately sought a surrogate religion. Edward A Ross "reserved his most passionate encomium for the form of social control he called 'social religion.'" Ross emphasized the need for a "social affirmation of Jesus" that would foster "the essential and ideal unity of all men in a common life, the brotherhood of man, under the fatherhood of God." Josiah Royce refigured the religion of the Republic to accommodate the social realities of a rapidly developing industrial society. "It is the State, the Social Order, that is divine. We are all but dust, save as this Social Order gives us life." John Dewey offered a pragmatic substitute for the Christian practices and discourses that traditionally had communicated the goals and purposes of social order. The liberating potential of modern society, he believed, could be realized only through the commitment and devotion of a "great community," an "inclusive and fraternally associated public" in which reciprocal ties of gratitude and obligation would bind individuals one to another. In the name

---

70   Christopher Lasch, *The New Radicalism in America, 1889-1963: The Intellectual as a Social Type* (London: Chatto & Windus, 1966), 46-47, 62.

of fraternity, social religion absorbed all authority in the Constitutional Republic; churches were just another socializing agent alongside many others.[71]

During the Progressive Era, American society was "sucked into" a project aiming at the enhanced growth and vitality of the state. One important Anglo-Saxon intellectual warned against the uncritical sanctification of the State. Randolph Bourne pointed out that American entry into the First World War was the logical outcome of Dewey's religion of pragmatism. "War," he wrote, "is essentially the health of the state." Bourne saw the state as "a jealous God" that "will brook no rivals." Dewey's support for the war effort suggested to Bourne that a merely pragmatic philosophy privileges technique over vision. Bourne's alternative, "poetic vision" of a "transnational America" aimed to fuse the aesthetic and the scientific possibilities latent in the free, creative spirit of American youth.[72]

Aligning himself with the "malcontents" demanding a new orientation of the national spirit, Bourne denounced those who sought to preserve and protect Anglo-Saxon hegemony. He denied that Anglo-Saxons had provided the Republic with its core ethnocultural identity. "The Anglo-Saxon was merely the first immigrant, the first to found a colony." The founding race had no right to impose its culture on the swelling population of immigrants who were in the process of establishing their own colonies in the New World. Bourne was the first Anglo-Saxon Anglophobe to set forth a comprehensive vision of America as a "world-federation in miniature," a cosmopolitan federation of national colonies uniting "the most heterogeneous peoples under the sun."[73] His vision offered a sort of mind-cure to neurotic proto-WASPs in the expanding managerial-professional class. Women's rights women envied men; the other-directed opinion leaders of a de-sexed WASP citizenry were no less envious of the primitive vitality and earthy sensuality widely imputed to proletarians, immigrants, and Negroes. Accordingly, Bourne prescribed the worship of the Other as a substitute for the collectivist, coercive cult of the state.

Progressive hopes that transnational America would reinvigorate the spiritual life of the Second Republic were dashed when immigration restrictionists achieved their resounding legislative victory after the First

---

71 Wilson, *In Quest of Community*, 107, 146; Wilson Carey McWilliams, *The Idea of Fraternity in America* (Berkeley, CA: University of California, 1973), 533; AJ Conyers, *The Long Truce: How Toleration Made the World Safe for Power and Profit* (Dallas, TX: Spence, 2001), 181, 191-194.

72 Randolph S Bourne, *War and the Intellectuals: Collected Essays, 1915-1919* (Indianapolis, IN: Hackett, 1999), 69.

73 Bourne, *War and the Intellectuals*, 77, 63-64, 52, 107-123.

World War. Radical appeals to the ideal of a fraternal social order designed to tear down barriers dividing the people along lines of class, gender, and race continued to meet stiff resistance. Rooting out such retrograde recalcitrance required a third constitutional revolution. The Great Depression of the 1930s was a boon to social reformers; they rushed to join the ranks of the New Deal ushered in by Franklin D Roosevelt. Cultural progressives of an earlier generation such as Randolph Bourne had mistrusted the state; but it was the alliance of big government with big business and big labor that finally brought down the curtain on WASP cultural, political, and economic hegemony. The rise of the federal Leviathan empowered rival racial, religious, and ethnic groups to exploit the demoralized condition of old-stock Americans. The Third (Managerial/Therapeutic) Republic squandered what remained of the social capital that had been accumulated by America's founding people, the implicitly white, Anglo-Saxon Protestants soon to be left without an ethnonation to call their own. Heedless of the consequences, the managerial regime imported millions of Third World immigrants, admitting this welter of ever-more alien nations to full communion in the national *ecclesia*. Exploiting the weakness of their WASP rivals, Jews and Negroes spearheaded the revolutionary struggle to bring transnational America into being.

The Third (Managerial/Therapeutic) Republic: Fraternity

Writing in the *Harvard Law Review* in 1994, Gary Lawson declared flatly that the "post-New Deal administrative state is unconstitutional, and its validation by the legal system amounts to nothing less than a bloodless constitutional revolution."[74] Appealing to the federalism of the first republic and the laissez-faire liberalism of the second, Lawson argues that constitutional legitimacy depends upon fidelity to the text of the Constitution (as validly amended.) He holds that it was the original intent of the framers to create a federal government whose powers were few and defined, leaving responsibility for other matters to the states and the people respectively. The New Deal vastly expanded the powers of the executive branch *within* the federal government and *of* the federal government over the states and the people. An alphabet soup of federal administrative agencies reimagined the economy as a vast, seamless system of needs with a life

---

74 Gary Lawson, "The Rise and Rise of the Administrative State," (1994) 107 *Harvard Law Review* 1231.

of its own. In such circumstances, the Constitution no longer *prescribes* the rules and standards governing economic activity. In the hands of a profoundly politicized legal priesthood, the living Constitution no longer even *describes* the systemic imperatives that drive the divine economy. Rather, the established constitutional faith *normalizes* the irresponsible, unaccountable, corrupt, and uncontrollably interlocking apparatus of corporate and state power.

Since the New Deal Revolution, formal legal distinctions between federal jurisdiction over "commerce among the states" and state regulation of "mining" and "manufacturing" have lost all meaning and force. The point of distinguishing between "inter-state" and "intra-state" commerce was to reserve an autonomous zone of legislative rights and responsibilities to the states and the people respectively. In the Second (Bourgeois) Republic, Supreme Court justices took it to be axiomatic that "[a]ctivities local in their immediacy do not become national because of distant repercussions." But the newly consolidated managerial regime launched by the Roosevelt administration soon received judicial permission to dissolve important constitutional boundaries that protected the autonomy of local communities and state governments. *Wickard v Filburn* provides a striking example of a compliant Supreme Court ruling that a farmer in Ohio growing grain on his own farm to feed his own cows had entered into interstate commerce simply because his animal fodder was physically "available for marketing."[75] To find immediacy or directness in such cases was to allow federal power to intrude itself everywhere. Indeed, Lawson remarks that "the post-New Deal Supreme Court has never invalidated a congressional intrusion into private affairs on ultra vires grounds." The judiciary's continuing refusal, for over seventy years, to set effective constitutional limits to the powers of the federal government sends a clear and inescapable message: "The actual structure and operation of the national government today [have] virtually nothing to do with the Constitution." Not surprisingly, even professors of constitutional law now find it difficult to maintain their faith in "the utility of constitutional discourse."[76]

Radical historians deplore the "conservative" character of the New Deal. But appearances can deceive. Because the post-Civil War amendments to the Constitution were adopted at the point of a bayonet, Reconstruction seems more revolutionary than the New Deal era. The New Deal revolution did not entail "the shattering use of the national army to destroy

---

75 Compare, *Schecter Poultry Corporation v US* (1935) 295 US 495; with *Wickard v Filburn* (1942) 317 US 111.

76 Lawson, "Administrative State," 1249-1254.

dissenting state governments."[77] Instead, the profound constitutional transformation of the Roosevelt years was accomplished overnight as federal judges turned a blind eye to the amendment procedure set out in Article V of the Constitution. Southern states had been compelled to ratify the Fourteenth Amendment; but such duress amounted to a formal acknowledgment of the states as necessary actors in the constitutional drama of Reconstruction. By contrast, Roosevelt obviated the need for formal constitutional amendments. He left the states on the side-lines and chose instead to place the Supreme Court under intolerable political pressure until a majority of justices reversed their early opposition to the New Deal program. The Court was offered a stark choice: either the justices upheld the constitutionality of New Deal measures such as the pro-union *Wagner Act* and the *Social Security Act*, or the President would cause membership of the Court to be enlarged and packed with his hand-picked supporters. When the Supreme Court executed its famous "switch in time" in 1937, Article V of the Constitution was rendered irrelevant if not killed outright.

The judicial *coup d'état* engineered by Roosevelt was peaceful and non-violent. For that very reason; it provides a useful illustration of the recurrent role played by "conservatives" in the perpetual American Revolution. Robert Lewis Dabney, the rock-ribbed Confederate Christian who in his old age remained in the trenches to oppose women's suffrage, would not have been surprised to learn that ostensibly conservative judicial opponents of the New Deal were induced to switch their votes without recourse to force or violence. Dabney's contempt for conservative opponents of Radical causes from abolitionism to women's rights was unbounded. American conservatism, he charged, "is a party which never conserves anything." Having announced its opposition "to each aggression of the progressive party," conservatism "aims to save its credit by a respectable amount of growling but always acquiesces at last in the innovation." The accepted principle of today's conservatism is yesterday's resisted novelty. Within the broad church of America's constitutional faith, "conservatism is merely the shadow that follows Radicalism as it moves forward toward perdition. It remains behind it, but never retards it, and always advances near its leader."[78] The judicial conservatism of the Supreme Court followed this long-established pattern in its response to the New Deal. There is a price to be paid however. Sooner or later, the weight of cognitive

---

77   Bruce Ackerman, "Constitutional Politics/Constitutional Law," (1989) *Yale Law Journal* 453.

78   Dabney, "Women's Rights Women."

dissonance can undermine the constitutional faith of those charged with the task of interpreting the sacred texts of American civil religion.

The People's Republic of America

Recognizing the potential for a crisis of legitimacy, one prominent constitutional scholar recently seized the bull by the horns, openly acknowledging the revolutionary character of the Constitutional Republic. Indeed, Bruce Ackerman contends that all three revolutions in the constitutional history of the American Republic (ie the Founding, Reconstruction, and the New Deal) simply made manifest the higher lawmaking role of "the People." In his view, Roosevelt's triumph over the Old Court made a "profound contribution to the sense that Americans still live under government *by the People*." He contends that the Court was "wise" to adopt "new constitutional solutions that had gained the sustained and considered support of mobilized national majorities...without insisting upon Article V." America was a nation in the 1930s, not a confederation of sovereign states; the Court was merely adapting constitutional law to "the nationalist spirit of the New Deal's popular mandate."[79]

Not everyone's constitutional faith will be restored by glib assertions that President Roosevelt enthroned "the People" in a remodelled Constitutional Republic. Paleoconservatives such as Samuel Francis and James Burnham have drawn on Marxist class theory to offer a more realistic view. For Burnham, the New Deal represented a major shift in the locus of sovereignty, away from the bourgeois class represented by members of Congress to a new managerial class located in the executive branch of government as well as in the corporate sector. The legislative branch "was the sovereign body of the limited state of capitalism. The bureaus are the sovereign bodies of the unlimited state of managerial society."[80] Francis adds that "egalitarianism has been used as the political formula or ideological rationalization" enabling an emerging, managerial elite to displace established bourgeois elites. The managerial class rejected the formalist legalism of the bourgeois revolution. New Class ideologues were determined to extend the reach of equality beyond the courtroom. University law schools obligingly proclaimed the novel doctrine of legal realism; it was the "law in action" not the "law in the books" that mattered in the quest for social justice. In this new dispensation, egalitarianism became an environmentalist

---

79 Ackerman, *Transformations*, 344-350.

80 James Burnham, *The Managerial Revolution* (London: Putnam, 1942) chapter 2.

ideology. Differences and inequalities of all sorts, whether between classes, sexes, or races, were explained "as the products of their social and historical environment, rather than of their innate mental or physical natures."[81] It followed that science and rational technique would equip managers with the tools to eliminate inequality by manipulating the environment, thus eliminating artificial obstacles to social justice.

Burnham and Francis treat egalitarian ideologies as instruments of class rule. They contend that managerial elites adopt egalitarianism because it is in their interest to do so. Others, notably Paul Gottfried, contend that managerial elites are driven by a dysfunctional ideology. In this view, managerial multiculturalism has its roots not in the material interests of dominant elites but "in a progressively deformed but recognizable Protestant culture" in which racial discrimination is treated as a form of illness. The managerial regime of the Third Republic has acquired a therapeutic role in "sniffing out social sickness." For Gottfried, it has become a "secular theocracy" which fuses a liberal Protestant religious consciousness with the politics of guilt. This accounts for ambitious programs of socialization that require all members of the majority culture to seek public expiation of wrongs that they or their ancestors are alleged to have done to the protected minorities of an ever more "diverse" multicultural and multiracial society. According to Gottfried, it is a "liberal Christianity dressed up selectively with New Testament teachings about self-denial and sin" that "provides the suitable theological framework for multicultural politics."[82] Both Gottfried and Francis miss the mark. The willingness of WASPs to sacrifice their biocultural interests on the altar of diversity and social justice cannot be attributed to either the superstructural ideology of "liberal Christianity" or to the underlying structure of "managerial class interests."

Gottfried rightly insists that managerial elites tap into the rich vein of religiosity deeply entrenched in Protestant culture; Francis is equally correct when he replies that "liberal Protestantism" is far from the only religious and theological movement that the regime has enlisted in its war on traditional Western institutions and values.[83] But neither Francis nor Gottfried fully comprehends the revolutionary dynamic that reshaped the political theology of the Constitutional Republic in the aftermath of

---

81   Samuel Francis, *Beautiful Losers: Essays on the Failure of American Conservatism* (Columbia, MO: University of Missouri Press, 1993, 208-221.

82   Paul Edward Gottfried, *Multiculturalism and the Politics of Guilt: Toward a Secular Theocracy* (Columbia, MO: University of Missouri Press, 2002), 16, 72-73, 142.

83   Samuel Francis, "Power Trip," (2003) 3(2) *The Occidental Quarterly* 69, at 73-74.

Depression and another world war. The official creed of the multiracial-ist managerial revolution is an explicitly post-Christian civil religion; a free-floating *Constitutionalism* has displaced the implicitly Anglo-Saxon *Protestantism* of the first "white man's country." Even the post-bellum bourgeois republic had anchored American constitutional discourse in the common law tradition of Old England.[84] Since the New Deal, however, the myth of the Constitution has been severed from its biocultural roots in Anglo-Saxon Christendom.

The managerial/therapeutic regime treats the Constitution as a force multiplier which enhances rather than limits the power of the *state* to shape American civil society in its own image. Endowing the idea of "fraternity" with all the symbolic and physical force of constitutional law, the federal government, in alliance with increasingly militant racial, religious, and ethnic minority groups, undermined the hitherto unchallenged hegem-onic status of American WASPs. As loyal Americans anxious to ward off the accusations of "snobbishness" and "bigotry" that emanated from Jews and Catholics,[85] WASP theologians abjured the ethnoreligious core of the Old Faith. Deprived of leadership, American Protestants meekly submitted to the fraudulent fraternalism peddled to parishioners under the soothingly ecumenical label of "Judeo-Christianity." The successful campaign to market that patently ideological nostrum marked a major milestone on the road to managerial multiculturalism.

Rainbow Republicanism

Many competing population groups now share responsibility for the doctrinal development of America's constitutional faith; whites, Anglo-Saxons, and Protestants are far from being the most influential sects within the renovated national *ecclesia*. Leading roles in the political the-ology of "rainbow republicanism" are played by a highly ethnocentric Jewish civil religion; black liberation theology; Irish, Italian, and Polish

---

84 The most obvious example: Oliver Wendell Holmes, Jr, *The Common Law* (Boston: Little, Brown &Company, 1881); see also, *The Pollock-Holmes Letters: Correspondence of Sir Frederick Pollock and Mr Justice Holmes, 1874-1932* Mark DeWolfe Howe ed. 2 vols (Cambridge: Cambridge University Press, 1942).

85 One Catholic writer, Michael Novak, contends that the challenge to Anglo-American hegemony was spearheaded by "the great unwasped." He identifies "Poles, Italians, Greeks, and Slovaks—'PIGS' as Novak fondly, if infelicitously, dubbed them—as well as blacks, Hispanics, and Jews" not to mention the women's movement, as the major players in the "unwasped" movement, see Eugene McCarraher, *Christian Critics: Religion and the Impasse in Modern American Social Thought* (Ithaca, NY: Cornell University Press, 2000), 175.

Catholicism, even feminist and homosexual theologies. Ethnic minorities have an obvious interest in giving WASPs a guilty conscience, but one wonders why members of the "majority group" so readily assume responsibility for the real and imagined sins of their ancestors. When *Americans* offer to make amends for the crimes against humanity allegedly committed by the Constitutional Republic, the burden of guilt rests lightly on hyphenated-Americans who need not and, generally speaking, do not derive their primary ethnocultural identity from citizenship in the Constitutional Republic.

Jews and Negroes, for example, *happen* to be American. By contrast, the WASP *is* an American who merely happens to be of British ancestry. Having abandoned the Anglo-Saxon *ecclesia* of their forefathers, America's founding generation sought salvation instead in a "nation with the soul of a church." Thus, from its very conception, the Constitutional Republic carried the toxic spores of Anglo-Saxon ethnomasochism along with the revolutionary ideals of liberty, equality, and fraternity. The distinctive contribution of the Third (Managerial/Therapeutic) Republic to American civil religion has been to create the legal, administrative, and cultural means to compel all but the wealthiest and most powerful WASPs to fraternize with every racial, religious, ethnic, or deviant group known to man. In the name of diversity, the managerial regime empowers protected minorities to feast upon the vast stocks of biocultural capital accumulated by earlier generations of (Anglo-Saxon Protestant) Americans committed heart and soul to the cause of constitutional patriotism.

In the aftermath of the New Deal Revolution, courts routinely hold that intrastate transactions are so commingled with or related to interstate commerce that the entire economy must be subject to federal regulation.[86] In 1938, the Supreme Court signalled that the reformation of race relations was to be a major item in the agenda of the managerial revolution: commingling was to become the law of life in the sphere of social relations as well as in the realm of economic regulation. In other words, the constitutional peace-bond of the Republic was expanded to protect minority groups such as Negroes and Jews against majoritarian prejudice. Under the auspices of the federal courts, the revolutionary idea of fraternity spread from the urban enclaves of an educated elite into every home, school, and workplace in America. Because Supreme Court justices have been installed as the high priests of America's constitutional faith, it is no longer necessary to approve fundamental economic, social, and political changes through the formal amendments procedures set out

---

86 *US v Darby* (1941) 312 US 100 (US Supreme Court).

in Article V; it has been left "to the Justices themselves to codify the New Deal revolution in a series of transformative judicial opinions." Having placed every facet of national economic life within the legislative purview of Congress, judges reserved a leading role for themselves in the remaking of American society. Casting itself as *fidei defensor* in America's civil religion, the Court resolved to uphold "the higher law traditions handed down from the Founding and Reconstruction." In the hands of its judicial guardians, the Constitution was to become a sword not just a shield in the sacred cause of fraternity.[87]

Even as it allowed Congress to subordinate the free market principles of the Second Republic to social welfare programs invoking countervailing ideals of equality and fraternity, the Court sought to reconnect the new regime with the constitutional faith of the old. In *Carolene Products*, the Court announced that it would challenge the constitutionality of legislation affecting ordinary commercial transactions only if regulatory measures were clearly devoid of any rational basis. But, in the famous footnote four of that judgement, the Court reserved the right to determine whether similar leeway would be permitted in cases that involved "statutes directed at particular religious, or national, or racial minorities" or "whether prejudice against discrete and insular minorities may be a special condition, which tends seriously to curtail the operation of those political processes to be relied upon to protect minorities, and which may call for a correspondingly more searching judicial inquiry."[88] In rejecting the property-oriented ideals of laissez-faire constitutionalism, the Court "left the rich to take care of themselves." At the same time, it "suggested that the Fourteenth Amendment's concern with equality must take on a deeper meaning in the redistributional politics of the modern regulatory state."[89] In effect, the Court declared that the idea of fraternity would expand older notions of liberty and equality in a revised version of American political theology.

The Jewish Face of American Civil Religion

Minority groups such as Negroes and Jews were major beneficiaries of the New Deal Revolution. They mobilized to defeat conservative opposition to the new constitutional order. It is worth noting that women, too, were

---

87 Ackerman, *Foundations*, 119-129.

88 *United States v Carolene Products* (1938) 304 US 144;

89 Ackerman, *Foundations*, 129.

predisposed to favor the growth of an American welfare state.[90] Not surprisingly, newly enfranchised women switched their political allegiance during the revolutionary decade of the 1930s from a massively lop-sided preference for the Republicans in 1928 to an equally unbalanced support for Roosevelt in 1936. Negroes, too, were drawn into the New Deal coalition, abandoning their previous allegiance to the party of Lincoln. As a numerically insignificant minority, Jews contributed little to the tidal wave of votes that propelled FDR into his second term but they were major players in the design and execution of the new constitutional order. According to Benjamin Ginsberg, more than a few Jewish New Dealers harbored a deep animus towards still-established WASP elites. Such hostility was reciprocated in upper-class circles where dark imprecations against the "Jew Deal" were common. But such remarks were just as often disparaged as "unseemly" by more sensitive WASPs who supported the revolutionary ideal of fraternity.[91]

Ginsberg reveals as well that "Jews found the Roosevelt administration and New Deal programs to be a major route to power, status, and employment in a society that otherwise subjected them to severe discrimination in virtually every occupational realm." In return for the offer of protection and opportunity, "Jews provided the administration of Franklin D Roosevelt with a vitally important pool of talent and expertise." Jewish lawyers, economists, and other talented professionals provided an especially critical resource for the New Deal because most well-to-do WASPs despised Roosevelt and all his works. As "members of a state-building and governing coalition" promoting the massive expansion of the federal government, "Jews were able to achieve a lasting position of power and prominence."[92] While individual Jews enjoyed rising political influence and sometimes spectacular economic success, it was in their collective capacity as an ethnoreligious group that American Jews began to wield a disproportionate influence on the American body politic.

Many Jewish groups launched campaigns of legal and social action against discrimination primarily "as a means for creating a distinct group identity for American Jews." According to Jonathan Woocher, Jewish civil religion "synthesizes ethnicity and religiosity and places both firmly within the embrace of American pluralism." His study concludes that civil

---

90   John R Lott, Jr and Lawrence W Kenny, "Did Women's Suffrage Change the Size and Scope of Government?" (1999) 107(6) *Journal of Political Economy* 1163.

91   Benjamin Ginsberg, *The Fatal Embrace: Jews and the State* (Chicago: University of Chicago Press, 1998), 113.

92   *Ibid.*, 104-114.

Judaism rests upon a "constellation of beliefs and practices, myths and rituals" that animate "a sophisticated political system, with hundreds of local and national organizations." Operating "through a complex network of linkages," such organizations "raise and expend hundreds of millions of dollars to carry out the 'public' business of American Jewry."[93] Inspired by a powerfully evocative, ideologically multi-faceted ethnotheology, American Jews are now a nation within the nation. More precisely, Jews have become an ethnonation with the socially cohesive soul of a synagogue within a bloodless proposition nation with the innocently inclusive soul of an evangelical church. As soon as the opportunity arose, Jewish activists invoked the Jewish civil religion to rally their co-ethnics in a concerted campaign to displace WASPs from their historical role in the vanguard of the perpetual American Revolution.

Depression, war, and the pragmatic, expansive liberalism of the New Deal (and, later, Kennedy's New Frontier and Johnson's Great Society) provided Jewish lawyers, in particular, with a golden opportunity to re-imagine America's (*implicitly* Anglo-Saxon Protestant) constitutional faith. Through years of litigation sponsored by organizations such as the Commission on Law and Social Action (CLSA) established by the American Jewish Congress, Jews sought to remove Christianity from the public square. Simultaneously, every effort was made to place Judaism on an equal footing with Protestantism and Catholicism. Rabbi Arthur Hertzberg wrote that the presence of a rabbi at Presidential inaugurations, "the most sacred moment of American civic life," provides Jews with "*visual* proof that they are indeed equal, in every sense, and that they do belong as full *co-owners* of American culture." Jews quickly exercised the prerogatives of ownership to refashion the religion of the Constitutional Republic to accommodate their messianic faith in cultural pluralism and political liberalism. Jewish lawyers convinced themselves and others that they owed "a duty to mankind" to transform a backward and parochial, ostensibly Christian, Republic into an enlightened and secular liberal state.[94]

In its judicial campaigns to enforce a strict separation of church and state, the CLSA was "strongly guided by the belief that Jews would never be able to consider themselves equals in the scheme of American pluralism if they continued to view themselves as guests in a Christian nation."

93   Stuart Svonkin, *Jews Against Prejudice: American Jews and the Fight for Civil Liberties* (New York: Columbia University Press, 1997), 81; Jonathan S Woocher, *Sacred Survival: The Civil Religion of American Jews* (Bloomington, IN: Indiana University Press, 1986), 20.

94   John Murray Cuddihy, *No Offense: Civil Religion and Protestant Taste* (New York: Seabury Press, 1978), 114; Svonkin, *Jews Against Prejudice*, 80.

As it happened, Jewish lawyers met little resistance in the Supreme Court
when they sought to outlaw prayers and Bible readings in American public schools. In the landmark *Engel* judgement of 1962, only one justice
supported the recital of the following vapid, inoffensively ecumenical
prayer in the schools of New York state: "Almighty God, we acknowledge
our dependence upon Thee, as we beg Thy blessings upon us, our parents,
our teachers and our Country." In the following year, the *Schempp* decision proscribed daily Bible readings, giving full credence to expert witnesses who testified that readings from the New Testament would be not
just "offensive" but "psychologically harmful" to Jewish students.[95]

Several decades later, militantly Jewish legal academics still detect
an implicitly Christian bias in the conventional liberal understanding
of the First Amendment. Stephen Feldman, for example, contends that
the Supreme Court reveals a persistent (however subliminal) affinity for
Christian folkways and an insensitivity towards non-Christian religious
groups. His evidence: a Jewish air force officer was denied the right to
wear a yarmulke on duty even as Amish Christian children were exempted
from compulsory school attendance laws. His professional judgement:
"So long as this nation remains pervasively Christian, legal discourse…
cannot eradicate Christian domination." Such a compelling personal need
to expunge even residual traces of a merely implicit Christian identity
from the Constitutional Republic bespeaks the powerful influence of an
explicitly Jewish civil religion. Because "Christian domination" is perceived as a perennial threat to the survival and well-being of the Jewish
people, every good Jew falls under a religious duty to promote the de-
Christianization of American civil religion. Jewish ethnotheology "is a
religion of ethnic survival, which became its highest good." It is a primary tenet of civil Judaism that "there is nothing incompatible in being a
good Jew and a good American." To avoid any possibility of contradiction
between Americanism and Judaism, America's constitutional faith had to
be made safe for the Jews.[96]

The ethnotheology of American Judaism identifies in-group solidarity
as the highest religious duty of every Jew. Accordingly, the "appropriate
goal for Jewish communal endeavor" became "the strengthening of all

95 Gregg Ivers, *To Build a Wall: American Jews and the Separation of Church and State*
(Charlottesville, VA: University Press of Virginia, 1995), 56; *Engel v Vitale* (1962) 370 US
421; *School District of Abington County v Schempp* (1963) 374 US 203.

96 Stephen M Feldman, "A Christian America and the Separation of Church and State," in
id., Law and Religion: A Critical Anthology (New York: New York University Press, 2000),
268-277; E Michael Jones, *The Jewish Revolutionary Spirit and its Impact on World History*
(South Bend, IN: Fidelity Press, 2008), 54; Woocher, *Sacred Survival*, 95-103.

Jewish communities—in Israel and wherever Jews live—as ends in their own right." The maintenance of Jewish identity is central. As one community leader put it: "We *want* our children to conceive themselves as Jews who *happen* to be Americans—not Americans who happen to be Jews." The distinctive Jewish contribution to America's constitutional faith has been to promote a pluralistic society which encourages and accepts difference. But the Jewish celebration of diversity in America lacks an essential element of moral reciprocity. Jewish civil religion explicitly disallows the desire of both Anglo-Saxon Protestants and ethnic Catholics to live in predominantly European Christian societies. At the same time, organized Jewry loudly insists that Israel's character as an explicitly Jewish state must be preserved and protected.

When Rabbi Hertzberg contends that the "deepest and most messianic need" of the American Jew is for "*a truly equal status in American culture*," he implies that some cultures are more equal than others. The doctrine of the chosen people—and the correlative ethnic ingredient in Judaism—can be neither concealed nor foresworn. Judaism is not just another religious denomination; ethnicity and chosenness cannot be locked away in the closet.[97] Civil Judaism is an ethnocentric religion of Jewish destiny; references to God or any other form of transcendent reality are all but irrelevant to most American Jews. Jews are on a secular mission to institutionalize the revolutionary idea of fraternity in a just and orderly society that will supposedly be "enriched by the interaction of many groups, many cultures, many faiths." Jews and Jewishness will remain securely at the center of that pluralistic world. Indeed, the obsessive preoccupation of Jews with their own sacred survival raises the question of whether civil Judaism "advocates a collective Jewish self-deification."[98]

Orthodox Christianity long recognized Judaism as an ethnotheology dedicated to waging a perpetual propaganda war against Christianity. The Talmud provides its own narrative of the life of Christ, turning it into "a powerful anti-Christian weapon with the declared goal to discredit the new sect now and forever." Jewishness, therefore, is not a genetically determined biological or racial phenomenon codified in an individual's DNA. Rather, it is an ethnoreligious community of memory and tradition set in permanent opposition to Christianity. The Talmud flatly denies the divinity of Christ. According to Princeton Professor Peter Schäfer, rabbis steeped in Talmudic lore fight against Christianity by "means of parody, inversion, deliberate distortion, and not least with the proud

---

97 Woocher, *Sacred Survival*, 76; Cuddihy, *No Offense*, 114-119.

98 Woocher, *Sacred Survival*, 79, 88, 91-93.

proclamation that what their fellow Jews did to this Jesus was right." In other words, Christ "deserved to be executed because of his blasphemy." The Talmud teaches "that he will sit in hell forever, and that those who follow his example up until today will not, as he has promised, gain eternal life but will share his horrible fate."[99] A congenital anti-Christian animus with biocultural roots tapping into a rich reservoir of real and imagined grievances accumulated over two millenia of ethnoreligious rivalry is the defining feature of American Jewish identity. For most Jews, such inveterate hostility to Christianity is more important to their collective identity than "solidarity with Israel." Indeed, according to Michael Medved, the "rejection of Christianity" by Jews "remains the sole unifying element in an increasingly fractious and secularized community."[100]

E Michael Jones argues that because the Jewish people have deliberately and persistently turned their backs on Christ the Redeemer, they have "condemned themselves to worship one false Messiah after another—most recently communism and Zionism—and each has led to violent reaction or equally violent disappointment." Espousing a political philosophy antithetical to what Jews perceive as Christian other-worldliness, the Talmud committed "the Jews to Messianic politics," looking "forward to heaven on earth when a political Messiah would reign over a universal political system." Jones suggests that the most seductive false Messiah of them all turned out to be the Jewish Race, the idea that "the Jewish people taken collectively shall be its own Messias." American Jews have not been able to "shake themselves loose from the notion" that "they were God's chosen people, not even after they stopped believing in God."[101] Few WASPs now profess a belief in God; fewer still believe that people of British ancestry have a providential mission in this world. Clinging to the deracinated constitutional faith of their rebel ancestors, American WASPs know little and care less for the folk religion of their Anglo-Saxon forefathers. Blind to their own biocultural interests, WASPs have applauded the infusion of the Jewish revolutionary spirit into the official religion of the Constitutional Republic.

Traditionalist Catholic writers, however, warn that, like the Jewish colonies scattered throughout the Roman Empire after the fall of the Temple, every Jewish communal organization in America's Third Republic should

99 Peter Schäfer, *Jesus in the Talmud* (Princeton, NJ: Princeton University Press, 2007), 102, 129.

100 Michael Medved, "Why Are Jews So Liberal—A Symposium," September 2009 *Commentary.com* at: https://www.commentarymagazine.com/printarticle.cfm/why-are-jews-liberals-a-symposium-15223

101 Jones, *Jewish Revolutionary Spirit*, 51, 1066-1068.

be regarded as "a potentially revolutionary cell, emboldening Jews not only to revolt, but urging other subjugated ethnic groups to revolt too." According to Jones, the Jewish revolutionary vision has always been "both ethnocentric and altruistic. As God's chosen people, they bore revolutionary liberation to the nations." Under the Roman Empire, "Jewish revolutionaries saw themselves as the little stone that would shatter the Roman colossus." In the American Third Republic, Jewish liberals and leftists forged an alliance with Negro activists struggling to throw off the weight of the Jim Crow regime in the white South. Jews "allied themselves with blacks, at least in part, to eliminate discrimination against themselves;" but inspired by an age-old sense of mission they acted as well for the benefit of benighted gentiles, white and black, "who would seek their liberation under Jewish auspices."[102] Jewish liberals set out to do good and, as the old saying goes, they did right well. There remains a reasonable doubt, however, whether Negroes profited in equal measure from Jewish advice and leadership in the civil rights revolution.

The Dark Heart of Black America

Reflecting upon his experience of the Jewish/Negro alliance, Harold Cruse concluded that "the great default of the Negro intellectuals" was to allow "Jewish leaders who came out of the Jewish Federation to become experts on the Negro problem in America." Even Negro Communists failed to provide their people with alternatives to rage, resentment, and perpetual dependence upon the corporate welfare state. Cruse argues that Negro revolutionaries never understood that the historic role of the black underclass in the political economy of American capitalism, that only they, unlike Jewish Communists just emerging from the immigrant ghettoes, "possessed the remotest potential for Americanizing Marxism." Having accepted Jewish leadership, Negro intellectuals never managed to articulate a social creed committed to the economic, political, and cultural unification of their own people, to the autonomy of a self-sufficient Negro nation within the American nation. Instead, Negroes were led to identify "freedom" with the promise of racial integration. Jews insisted that Negroes must "be integrated as fast as possible and by any means." Most Negro leaders fell in with that strategy. Every Negro "knows he wants 'freedom,' but actually not one knows what he *really* wants out of

---

102 Jones, *Jewish Revolutionary Spirit*, 44; Ginsberg, *Fatal Embrace*, 226.

present-day America." In stark contrast, Cruse was convinced that Jews *"do know exactly what they want in America."*[103]

Cruse was struck by the fact that although Jews advocated integration for Negroes, for their own part "Jews can take integration, or leave it." Leftwing Jews of his acquaintance "were able to drop their Jewishness and pick it up whenever it suited them." Even as assimilated Jewish-American Communists vigorously opposed Negro efforts to organize as a national group within the Party, "unassimilated Communist Jews were upholding the historical purity of Jewish cultural identity in the *same* Communist Party." The consequence was clear and unmistakeable: "today Negroes truly have a Jewish problem." Cruse advised Negro intellectuals to pay attention not to what Jewish liberals say but to what they do. Above all, Negroes must learn that "[i]ntegration and assimilation have all to do with individuals, but very little to do with ethnic groups." To foster their own group identity, Negro intellectuals have to declare independence from Jewish influence while equipping themselves "with the latest research and propaganda techniques to move into control and guidance of every branch of the Negro movement."[104]

Cruse's message is clear: knowledge is power. Cruse hoped that Negro intellectuals would acquire both by committing themselves to "cultural nationalism—an ideology that has made Jewish intellectuals a force to be reckoned with in America." But Cruse missed the essential ingredient in the kosher brand of ethnocultural nationalism. Jewish leaders well understood that "the popular substructure of American Jewish belief and practice" is grounded in an ancient folk religion.[105] Because Cruse remained in thrall to the historical materialism preached by the Jewish left, he sought salvation through the Communist Party rather than the Christian church. As a secular humanist, Cruse was ill-prepared to recognize that the crisis of the Negro intellectual was not rooted in politics, economics, or culture. WASPs, too, refuse to see either the abject public failure of Negro leadership or the deepening darkness at the heart of an increasingly dysfunctional and degenerate, corrupt and criminal, American Negro culture. Most American Negroes are said to be Christians but the most disciplined and best known black nationalist movement today is the Nation of Islam. But even that successful ethnoreligious sect shows little interest in the creation of an autonomous Negro nation; it prefers to wrap itself in the plastic religion of the rainbow Republic.

103 Cruse, *Negro Intellectual*, 158, 482, 497.

104 *Ibid.*, 57, 381, 397, 351, 477-497.

105 *Ibid.*, 497; Woocher, *Sacred Survival*, 95.

Apostasy among Negro Christians was not a sociological accident. Long before the civil rights movement rose to prominence in the Fifties, Jewish activists set out to subvert the folk Christianity supported by well-known Negro leaders such as Booker T Washington. Negro preachers, especially in the New South, held to a strict Protestant ethic; they told their people to "cast down your buckets where you are" rather than chase the chimera of racial integration. In opposition to Washington's conservative accommodationism, the largely Jewish leadership of the National Association for the Advancement of Colored People enlisted WEB Du Bois, a light-skinned Negro radical, born and bred in New England, to promote its integrationist strategy. Du Bois studied at Fisk University in Nashville, Tennessee but, alienated by its fundamentalist ethos, he soon went back north to Harvard College. There he fell under the potent influence of the post-Christian rationalism that radiated from teachers such as William James.

Although Du Bois was not deeply religious, in writing *The Souls of Black Folk* he revealed an acute sensitivity to the spiritual dimension of Negro life. Throughout his long career, Du Bois oscillated between integrationism and Negro nationalism, ending his life as a Communist. In the course of his intellectual and political journey, he acquired considerable insight into the "double consciousness" of being both a Negro and an American. "Conscious of his impotence, and pessimistic," Du Bois wrote, the Negro "often becomes bitter and vindictive." His "religion, instead of a worship, is a complaint and a curse, a wail rather than a hope, a sneer rather than a faith." Cruse, too, noticed that resentment towards and dependence upon whites produces "a poisonous brew of hate, hopelessness, racial envy, and class inferiority complexes" in Negro life. Negroes seemed unable to break free of whites without expressing a paranoid "*hatred* of whiteness."[106]

Today, "black liberation theology" perpetuates the "racial drama of love and hate between slave and master, bound together in the purgatory of the plantation,"[107] a narrative imported into the constitutional faith of the Third Republic by countless Negro politicians, preachers, lawyers, and activists. Asserting that "divine truth is God's liberation of the weak from oppression," James Cone, the best-known black liberation theologian, does not shrink from the charge that he allows theology to be determined by social interest. The only important question for him is: "*whose* social

---

106 WEB Du Bois, *Dusk of Dawn* (New Brunswick, NJ: Transaction, 1984), 33; *id.*, *Souls of Black Folks* Henry Louis Gates Jr and Terri Hume Oliver eds (New York: WW Norton, 1999), 11, 127; Cruse, *Negro Intellectual*, 364.

107 Cruse, *Negro Intellectual*, 364.

interest, the oppressed or the oppressors?" Because, Cone insists, "white theology" remains fixed in "the axiological perspective" of an oppressive white culture, "that white theology is an ideological distortion of the gospel of Jesus." Indeed, he alleges that all white "communities and theologies are formed by the will of white people to oppress others not of their genetic origin." As a result, it is "impossible to be white (culturally speaking) and also think biblically" because "the oppressed are the only true Christians."[108] Needless to say, Anglo-Saxon Protestants need not apply for membership in that fraternity.

Under the auspices of the Third Republic, race became a religion for American Negroes. Accordingly, the political theology of race has been incorporated into America's constitutional faith. Practitioners of the critical race theory taught in American law schools suggest that Supreme Court decisions "promoting the free exercise of religion and preventing the establishment of any one religion" now provide the best model for constitutional adjudication in the field of race relations. In other words, the courts are encouraged to support the "free exercise of positive aspects of race" by mandating, in particular, "open discussion and implementation of governmental remedies to address the historical legacy of racial discrimination." On this logic, governments must dismantle completely the historical "establishment" of "racial subordination and white supremacy." But the goal of this movement extends far beyond racial equality. Critical race theory flatly rejects the color-blind constitutionalism favored by Justice Harlan in the late nineteenth century. Like white theology which transcends race in theory while continuing to underwrite white oppression in practice, "color-blind constitutionalists" would allow the Supreme Court to perpetuate the ubiquitous reality of white racial privilege. Critical race theorists insist that lawyers and judges must be alive to the danger of "white domination;" whenever necessary, courts must "interfere with the free exercise of race" by whites bent on re-establishing the racial subordination of non-whites.[109]

As such attitudes and practices become normative among rival ethnic and religious groups, WASPs appear doomed to become a shrinking and despised minority. But, even as post-America moves inexorably toward a Fourth (Transnational) Republic beholden to a hostile non-white majority, WASPs refuse to renounce the slyly satanic religion of their apostate

108 James H Cone, *God of the Oppressed* (Maryknoll, NY: Orbis, 1997), 87-88, 92, 136.

109 Neil Gotanda, "A Critique of 'Our Constitution is Color-Blind,'" in Kimberlé Crenshaw, et al., *Critical Race Theory: The Key Writings that Formed the Movement* (New York: New Press, 1995), 257-275.

Republic. Mired in a racial spoils system, the greed and corruption of the transnational corporate welfare state is matched only by the overweening imperial hubris of its renegade elites. Continued attachment to such a regime is not just pathologically maladaptive; it must also provoke the wrath of God.

Conclusion

America's constitutional faith is the proximate cause of Anglo-Saxon Anglophobia. That dis-ease cannot be cured by another application of the same post-Christian rationalism that gave birth to the Constitutional Republic. Nor will a one-sided science of sociobiology remedy this peculiarly Anglo-Saxon ethnopathology. We are told that religion can be adaptive; a strong religious faith can enhance the reproductive fitness of individuals and groups. But, whatever it may mean for Negroes and Jews, American civil religion has had a detrimental impact on the collective political, economic, and biocultural interests of Americans of British ancestry. And, adding insult to injury, the Third Republic has permitted opportunistic WASP defectors to prosper.

The religion of the Republic cannot be reconciled with the restoration of Anglo-Saxon Christendom. If WASPs are to survive the challenges of the twenty-first century, they must rediscover an authentically Christian folk religion firmly rooted in a regenerated Anglo-Saxon bioculture. Both Negroes and Jews have out-played WASPs in the postmodern game of identity politics. Black liberation theology and Jewish civil religion made crucial contributions to that outcome. Confronted with naked aggression couched in the evocative language of other folk religions, agnostic and other-directed WASPs typically turn aside. Others, Frank Salter for instance, seek an alternative strategy. Salter invokes the post-Christian rationalist philosophy of adaptive utilitarianism in the hope that WASPs can persuade their racial, religious, and ethnic rivals to adopt the principle of universal nationalism.[110] But even such sophisticated and disinterested appeals to the philosophy of biology constitute a flaccid response to the *theological* challenge posed by ethnoreligious pluralism in a "nation with the soul of a church." Sooner or later, WASPs will be compelled to abandon the spiritually debilitating *ecclesia* of the Constitutional Republic for the old-time religion of Anglo-Saxon Christendom.

---

110 Frank Salter, *On Genetic Interests: Family, Ethny and Humanity in an Age of Mass Migration* (Frankfurt am Main: Peter Lang, 2003), chapter 9.

Even its most sympathetic historian, Robert Bellah, recognizes that American civil religion today "is an empty and broken shell." But he, too, lacks faith in the ethnoreligious traditions of orthodox Christianity, arguing that "[o]ur lives are largely ruled by an insistent commercial culture that is a parody of any tradition." Not even the venerable religion of the Republic still inspires devotion. Bellah concedes that the external covenant of the Constitution remains intact but he worries that the constitutional faith has lost its inner meaning. The materialist ethic of adaptive utilitarianism is unlikely to satisfy Bellah's spiritual hunger. Like most post-Christian rationalist WASPs, Bellah believes in universal nationalism for every nation but his own. Bellah is an Anglo-Saxon Anglophobe. He notes with approval the "highly critical stance of Anglo-American intellectuals to much of the outlook of their own ethnic group." In his judgement, the "double crime" at the beginning of the nation—the expropriation of the Indian and the enslavement of the Negro—left an indelible stain on American society.[111]

Displaying the ethnomasochism peculiar to WASPs, Bellah wonders whether America has been punished for its sins by becoming "the most developed, progressive, and modern society in the world," all adjectives pointing to the "utter devastation of the natural world in which we live, of the ties that bind us to others, of the innerness of spiritually sensitive personality." Seeking absolution in an expansive openness to cultural diversity, he pays obligatory obeisance to the "struggle of oppressed racial groups to improve their position in America." He counsels passive acceptance of the never-ending attacks on his own people which have become "a major aspect" of this "time of trial." Predictably, he locates the path to restored spiritual health in the search for communion with the Other, in "experimentation with symbols and ways of experiencing reality from cultures once very alien to us." He revels in the "transvaluation of roles that turns the despised and the oppressed into symbols of salvation and rebirth."[112] Unfortunately, Bellah seems utterly oblivious to the harsh realities of inter-racial conflicts. He seems not to care that rival ethnoreligious groups routinely manipulate the Other-directed WASP mentality by casting themselves in the Christ-like role of victim and redeemer.

Jewish civil religion provides the most telling example of the use of Christian imagery to advance the hostile agenda of a non-Christian group. It is difficult to miss the parallels between the story of Christ's crucifixion and resurrection and the central myth of contemporary civil Judaism.

111 Bellah, *Broken Covenant*, 143, 151.
112 *Ibid.*, 98, 37, 88, 110, 106.

Every WASP, adult and child alike, is required to know by heart "the story of 'Holocaust to Rebirth,' the retelling by American Jews of the two most significant Jewish events of the twentieth century—the murder of six million Jews by the Nazis and the establishment of the State of Israel."[113] The Holocaust myth—whatever its status as historical fact—has been a potent ideological weapon in the inter-ethnic rivalry between American Jews and WASPs. Jews regularly call upon all European Christians to account for their complicity, if only by acts of omission, in what is allegedly the greatest crime known to man. Indeed, the validity of Christianity itself is open to question: "What does it mean to be a Christian when Christian understandings and actions issued in the death camps of Nazi Germany?" All Christians must "ask forgiveness of the Jewish people" as well as "from Jesus, himself a Jew, whose essential message of love was betrayed."[114] The tables have been turned: it is no longer the Jews who are to be condemned for crucifying Christ but the Christians who bear the guilt for allowing innocent Jews to be gassed.

Such guilt-tripping deliberately overlooks the orthodox Christian teaching that the coming of Christ changed the meaning of Jewishness. Scripture and tradition both confirm that Christians, having accepted Christ as the Messiah, became the true Jews; it is they who remained faithful to the spirit of the covenant between God and Abraham. Those who now call themselves Jews rejected Christ's message of love to the people of all nations, insisting that they alone were God's chosen people. It was Christ who first preached the gospel of universal nationalism. In refusing to recognize Christ, Talmudic Judaism constituted itself as the "synagogue of Satan," the very antithesis of the holy, catholic, and apostolic church.[115] For that reason, orthodox Christianity made Jews special targets for conversion. Conversion requires Jews to accept Jesus Christ as the one and only Messiah but it "also means an equally firm rejection of all forms of Talmudic deception, including sexual liberation, racism, Messianic politics, and deconstruction."[116] Only a return to orthodox Christianity will equip WASPs to meet the intellectual and political, moral and spiritual challenges thrown up by Jewish (and Negro) ethnotheology.

A decisive moment in the onset of Anglo-Saxon Anglophobia in America came when perhaps the most prominent theologian in the WASP

---

113 Woocher, *Sacred Survival*, 130.

114 Marc H Ellis, *Toward a Jewish Theology of Liberation* 3rd expanded edition (Waco, TX: Baylor University Press, 2004), 29.

115 Revelation: 2:9; 3:9.

116 Jones, *Jewish Revolutionary Spirit*, 1071.

intellectual firmament, Reinhold Niebuhr, declared in 1958 "that there is no need for Christians to try to convert the Jews." Niebuhr was the son of an immigrant, German-speaking Lutheran minister; he married into an upper-crust WASP family. He used all his influence to exhort American Christians to "come to terms with the stubborn will to live of the Jews as a peculiar people, both religiously and ethnically." Insisting that Christians must *assume* "the *continued* refusal of the Jew to be assimilated," Niebuhr sacrificed the militant truth of the Christian faith to the ecumenical ideal of fraternity. Missionary activity among Jews was simply "wrong." Because Christianity, in Jewish eyes, is "an oppressive majority culture," Niebuhr concluded that practically nothing "can purify the symbol of Christ as the image of God in the imagination of the Jew."[117] Only within the religion of the Republic could Jews and Christians find common spiritual ground, and then only if Christians checked the truth claims of their faith at the door to the national *ecclesia*.

James Cone writes that "whites" can undergo "the true experience of conversion" to the black liberation struggle only when "they die to whiteness and are reborn anew to struggle *against* white oppression and *for* the liberation of the oppressed."[118] Similarly, the political theologians of the Constitutional Republic counsel Anglo-Saxon Protestants to die to Christianity in the hope that they will be reborn as good Americans. The religion of the Republic is now openly in league with the synagogue of Satan. How, then, are ethnomasochistic WASPs to be "saved," above all from themselves?

---

117 Cuddihy, *No Offense*, 31-43.

118 Cone, *God of the Oppressed*, 222.

Part Three

Prognosis: The Return of the Repressed

7.

Archeofuturism:
Of Patriot Kings and Anglo-Saxon
Tribalism in the Twenty-First Century

Introduction

The First, Second, and Third Republics were variations on the secular humanist theme of constitutional modernity; America, the last best hope of mankind, was to be a universal nation bringing the revolutionary ideals of liberty, equality and fraternity down to earth. But, just when a triumphant liberalism declared the obsolescence of class, race, and gender distinctions, "fraternity" morphed, almost overnight it seemed, into the non-stop celebration of "diversity." The "imperial biopower" of the transnational corporate welfare state has extended its rule over "social life in its entirety." Under the auspices of the neo-communist Empire celebrated by Michael Hardt and Antonio Negri, the American People looks set to dissolve into the mobile mass of the global multitude. The Fourth (Transnational) Republic will be integrated into a trans-territorial system of imperial power "distributed in networks, through mobile and articulated mechanisms of control." The coming Empire will regulate human interactions; it will also seek "directly to rule over human nature." This postmodern system of biopolitical production will not be under exclusively American control nor will the United States be its center.[1]

According to the theoreticians of postmodern neo-communism, "the concept of the People no longer functions as the organized subject of the system of command, and consequently the identity of the People is replaced by the mobility, flexibility, and perpetual differentiation of the

---

1   Michael Hardt and Antonio Negri, *Empire* (Cambridge, MA: Harvard University Press, 2000), xiv-xv, 384.

multitude." In the neo-communist imagination, "the constituted power of Empire" is in perpetual conflict with "the activity beyond measure of the multitude and its virtual powers." For them, the rise of Empire does not bring the revolutionary project to an end. On the contrary, "the biopolitical existence of the multitude has the potential to be transformed into an autonomous mass of intelligent productivity, into an absolute democratic power." But, if its virtual power is to become real, "the mobile multitude must achieve global citizenship." Thus, neo-communism greets transnational corporate capitalism as an indispensable ally in "the struggle against the slavery of belonging to a nation, an identity, and a people." Both aim to break down "the walls that surround nation, ethnicity, race, people, and the like."[2]

But, linking the local to the universal is a long-term objective. In the meantime, the all-pervasive official and corporate celebration of diversity revokes the God-given right of the People to a homeland of their own from which the Other may legitimately be excluded. Michael Hardt and Antonio Negri proudly promote nomadism and miscegenation "as figures of virtue, as the first ethical practices on the terrain of Empire." In their view, the irrepressible movement (legal or clandestine) of individuals and groups across national and ethnoreligious boundaries is a revolutionary act; every step in such journeys makes an indispensable contribution towards the biopolitical production of a common species.[3] In my view, it is more realistic to expect the unholy alliance of neo-communism and transnational corporate capitalism to produce rising levels of social and political conflict in every multiracial society.

To keep the lid on a simmering stew of racial, ethnic, and religious resentments, managerial multiculturalism depends entirely upon steady economic growth. But the complex, interlocking political and economic systems of global capitalism are highly vulnerable to deliberate or accidental disruption. Whenever the social and physical networks that support the system fail to function normally, inter-ethnic competition is sure to escalate. Weakly ethnocentric WASPs will provide soft targets to tough-minded racial, religious, and ethnic rivals ready, willing, and able to seize more than their fair share of a shrinking pie.

The religion of the Republic leaves WASPs ill-equipped to resist ruthless exploitation in a collapsing Empire hopelessly addicted to the enchantments of Mammon. There is still hope, however, that born-again Anglo-Saxon Christians will put up a fight against their forecast doom;

2   Ibid., 344, 361-362.

3   Ibid., 380.

their unique bioculture will not disappear altogether without trace into the mixed bodies of a browning multitude speaking a common tongue.[4] There is still time to rebuild the ancient walls behind which Anglo-Saxon Christian commonwealths can find shelter from the coming storm. The spiritual reconstruction of strong and healthy Anglo-Saxon biocultures will be guided by the theory and practice of what the French writer Guillaume Faye calls "archeofuturism."[5] For WASPs, the Anglo-Saxon past holds the key to their future as an ethnonation.

The adjective "archaic" commonly carries a pejorative connotation. Such modernist prejudices are belied by the Greek noun from which the English adjective is derived. Originally the root *archaeo* denoted a "foundation" or "beginning." It also referred to the fundamental creative force underlying the immutable natural order of things. The convergence of catastrophes that confront Anglo-American civilization heralds not just the crisis of modern constitutionalism but the return of the archaic.[6] Old ghosts long thought to have been exorcized are returning to haunt the post-Christian rationalist imagination. Among those challenges are the rise in militant Islam, moral decline, financial collapse, and economic depression, ills for which ethnocentric Jewish elites bear a large, unacknowledged (but glaringly obvious, to those with eyes to see) share of responsibility. The growing disconnect between the cornucopian ideology of infinite growth and the inescapable reality of finite limits is revealed as well in intractable geopolitical conflicts; shrinking stocks of oil, minerals, food, water, and fish in an over-populated world co-exist with the deepening domestic disorder produced by the Third World colonization of the West and the pollution of an already over-stretched natural environment. We will confront anew the immemorial questions that our much-maligned Christian ancestors were similarly powerless to ignore.

A century from now, the constitutional history of revolutionary republicanism in America will appear as a comparatively brief interlude in Anglo-Saxon history. The mass hallucinations parading under the slogans of liberty, equality, and fraternity will founder upon the cascading catastrophes of the early twenty-first century. Indeed, mankind will revert to the archaic forms of biocultural life from which secular humanism promised to liberate us. With the collapse of self-perpetuating socio-economic

---

4   *Ibid.*, 362.

5   Guillaume Faye, *Archeofuturism: European Visions of the Post-Catastrophic Age* (Arktos Media, 2010).

6   *Ibid.*, 68-73; Guillaume Corvus, *La Convergence des Catastrophes* (Paris: Diffusion International Edition, nd).

systems that operate on a planetary scale, the household will recover much of its significance as a survival mechanism; accordingly, men and women can expect to reinvent the sexual division of labor that our ancestors accepted as part of God's plan for mankind. Likewise, the inter-generational transmission of ethnoreligious traditions will become an essential ingredient in the biocultural fitness of every successful people. Spirituality and ecclesiastical organization will be highly visible dimensions of hierarchical societies in which rites of initiation into ancestral cults are commonplace. Marriage will be de-individualized, becoming a matter of as much importance to extended families and communities as it is to the spouses. Even Anglo-Saxon Christian tribes will re-appear, reincarnating the archaic trifunctionality of Old England, restoring the manly prestige of a warrior caste sworn to protect those who pray and those who work. And, it will also be necessary, possible, and desirable for Anglo-Saxons to restore the archaic forms of the ancient British constitution.

The return of the repressed spirit of British liberty will transform the atomistic mass of individual WASPs into Anglo-Saxon Christian communities of blood and faith. To reclaim deservedly the name of their illustrious Anglo-Saxon ancestors, WASPs will be required to abjure their secular constitutional faith in the modern nation-state. In this chapter, I consider whether in principle the ancient constitution of Anglo-Saxon Christendom can and should be reinvented in a form adaptable to the biopolitical realities of life in the twenty-first century. In dealing with that issue I enter into an extended conversation with two thinkers that we have encountered in earlier chapters; namely the eighteenth century opposition thinker, Viscount Bolingbroke, and the twentieth century Jewish political philosopher, Hannah Arendt. Both lend support to the hope that new forms of action in political, social, economic, and religious life can work to regenerate the spirit of liberty among a corrupt and dispirited people. How such a goal might be incorporated into durable institutional practices is the subject of the next chapter. But first let us compare and contrast the ancient constitution with the theory and practice of modern constitutionalism.

Constitutionalism in an Age of Diversity

Modern constitutionalism presupposed the norm of a culturally homogeneous and sovereign people no longer subject to the tyranny of tradition. James Tully suggests that it was the English radical Tom Paine who best "articulated a distinctively modern picture of a constitution in the era of the American and French Revolutions." In this picture, the fundamental law embodied in a modern constitution is created by the deliberate and self-conscious act of a sovereign people. By that act "a people frees itself (or themselves) from custom and imposes a new form of association on itself by an act of will, reason and agreement." Once the people are enshrined as the sole locus of authority, a uniform system of government can be established in which all citizens are equal before the law and must therefore be treated identically. Tully contrasts the uniformity of modern constitutionalism with the plurality and irregularity of the ancient constitution. By incorporating a variety of local customs, the ancient constitution became "a motley of overlapping legal and political jurisdictions, a kind of *jus gentium* 'common' to many customary jurisdictions, as in the Roman republic or the common law of England."[7] The differential treatment of individuals and localities inherent in the ancient constitution becomes intolerable once a set of uniform manners and institutions comes to define the goal of historical development.

Thus, according to Tully, modern constitutionalism justified "the extinction or assimilation of different cultures." Based on a theory of progress from primitive to advanced stages of development, modern constitutionalism was a central element in the ideology of European imperialism. Not only did it authorize "imperial rule of former colonies over Indigenous peoples," but, even today, it underwrites "cultural imperialism over the diverse citizens of contemporary societies." Tully traces the imperial drive inherent in modern constitutionalism to Locke's theory that Europeans had a natural right to "appropriate land in America without the consent of the peoples who have lived there for thousands of years." Kant, too, denied that there was any need to recognize the non-European peoples of the world as equals until they "abandoned their lawless ways and submitted to European markets and republican constitutions." Within European societies, the drive to create a centralized and uniform system of legal and political authority made it difficult to recognize and accommodate "cultural diversity by arrangements of legal and political pluralism so that citizens can relate to government in culturally different ways or participate in different political institutions." Tully recognizes, however, that modern constitutionalism has been more than a tool of Western imperialism. Indeed, by fostering the idea of the nation-state, it has "also developed in opposition to imperialism."[8]

---

7   James Tully, *Strange Multiplicity: Constitutionalism in an Age of Diversity* (Cambridge: Cambridge University Press, 1995), 59-60, 66.

8   *Ibid.*, 70, 96, 73, 81, 83, 15.

Just as the modern constitution is premised on the equality of individual citizens, "each constitutional nation is equal in authority to any other." In Europe, the equality of independent, self-governing nation-states could not co-exist with the *imperium* of the papacy and the Holy Roman Empire. The same principle justified the global anti-imperialist movement against European hegemony which began with the revolt of the American colonies in 1776. For Tully, the politics of cultural recognition is a third movement of anti-imperialism in modern constitutional thought. Political life and constitutional development are now shaped by the struggles of aboriginal peoples, women, linguistic and ethnic minorities, suppressed nations and supranational associations to overthrow the imperial yoke imposed over their particular cultures by the constitutions of modern nation-states. Tully claims that the suppressed legacy of ancient constitutionalism will provide a powerful ideological weapon to all these oppressed groups.[9]

To do justice to demands for cultural recognition, Tully re-conceives the language of modern constitutionalism. He observes that, in an effort to accommodate cultural diversity, contemporary constitutionalism has already become "a composite of two dissimilar languages." On one level, constitutionalism still speaks the dominant "modern" language in which individual liberty and equality are the primary goods it aims to realize. At the same time, the vocabulary of ancient constitutionalism invokes a law common to different cultures to secure the experience of belonging for all elements of a heterogeneous population. In this composite language, the constitution becomes "a form of activity, an intercultural dialogue in which the culturally diverse sovereign citizens of contemporary societies negotiate agreements on their forms of association over time." According to Tully, justice requires that such agreements be formed in accordance with what he calls "the three conventions of the common language of constitutionalism:" namely, mutual recognition, consent, and continuity.[10] Tully's thesis implies that the operating constitution of the contemporary corporate welfare state endows "insular and discrete minorities" with the capacity to demand recognition by other groups. The state itself retains the power to give or withhold consent to measures, public and private, that adversely affect the biocultural continuity of every group that contributes to the multicultural mosaic of a constitutional order grounded in the politics of identity. Tully characterizes this explosion of multiracial and ethnoreligious diversity as a return to an archaic model of constitutionalism.

9   *Ibid.*, 15, 68, 16.
10   *Ibid.*, 30-31.

The convention of mutual recognition, for example, was embodied in the ancient constitution of France but was swept away by the Revolution of 1789. Before the revolution, Montesquieu upheld the authority of the diverse customs of a highly irregular realm. But the revolutionary regime located the foundations of government in "an act of the sovereign will and reason of the people, without any reference to the customs and ways in which the people are constituted." Those who argued that France was a confederation of regions and that any "written constitution had to recognize and accommodate itself to this ancient constitutional diversity" were branded as enemies of the people. There was no question of gaining the consent of the regions to their abolition; the imperial language of modern constitutionalism justified the decision to discontinue and extinguish the distinctive ways of the provinces. In England, by contrast, the idea of the ancient constitution upheld the conventions of consent and continuity. Even though William the Bastard "conquered England and imposed the Norman yoke of feudal law, he could not discontinue the pre-existing ancient constitution of Anglo-Saxon local government, trial by jury, independent property and individual liberties."[11]

According to Tully, these ancient constitutional conventions are recovering their suppressed normative force as "contemporary societies begin to enter a post-imperial age." As European imperialism loses its global hegemony, constitutional law and theory have begun to acknowledge "a vast undergrowth of cultural diversity," particularly "in the common law of Commonwealth countries and international law." Even after three hundred years of constitutional reform, "[n]either Kant's nor Paine's republican constitution determines every aspect of the whole." The composite language of contemporary constitutionalism "is a labyrinth of terms and their uses from various periods." Tully likens constitutionalism to an ancient city that has grown up in a variety of forms over the ages. In the heart of the city we still find a strange multiplicity of little streets and squares while the modern craving for generality has produced a regular pattern of straight and uniform streets in the outlying areas. The "newer uniformity and regularity of modern constitutions forms a surrounding multitude of boroughs around a maze of old and new formations and patchwork arrangements from many periods."[12]

Clearly, the "empire of uniformity" created by the modern constitution was never an end in itself; it was designed to facilitate and promote the political economy of perpetual growth. Modern constitutionalism became

---

11 *Ibid.*, 83, 85, 149.

12 *Ibid.*, 99-100, 103-104.

oppressive not because it created a common citizenship among all manner of men and women but because it diminished the personal meaning and constitutional significance of citizenship. Paradoxically, the modern constitution created governments that have more in common with the absolutist monarchies of eighteenth century Europe than they do with the ancient republics. Much vaunted theories of social contract and the practice of electoral politics turn out to be tools to "enlighten" the legally despotic will of the sovereign state. In fact, it is a fundamental maxim of modern constitutionalism that "despotism must be enlightened or not be at all."[13] Popular input helps a bureaucratic state to allocate the resources in its gift; this is the stuff of old-fashioned pork-barrel politics. But once the capitalist system of needs develops to the point where it requires the state to produce and inject its own inputs into the accumulation process, electoral politics is supplemented by new policy-production rules and procedures that no longer rest upon the social contract or the polite fictions of popular sovereignty.[14]

Deconstructing the Modernist "Empire of Uniformity"

The modernist language of uniformity now serves mainly to disguise a neo-feudal, corporatist process of interest intermediation. But, contrary to Tully's fondest hopes, the neo-feudal realities of the transnational market-state have much more to do with the systemic imperatives of perpetual economic growth than with the constitutional recognition of many diverse cultures. Tully confuses the interpenetration of private and public power characteristic of contemporary corporatism with the parcellized sovereignty of the ancient constitution. In every Anglo-Saxon country, territorial representation through electoral politics has been superseded by novel forms of functional representation. "In a developed corporatist system, a second circuit is added to the machinery of the democratic representative polity."[15] Alongside periodic elections, political parties and parliamentary government new decision-making procedures appear in

---

13   Leonard Krieger, *An Essay on the Theory of Enlightened Despotism* (Chicago: University of Chicago Press, 1975), 39.

14   Claus Offe, "The Theory of the Capitalist State and the Problem of Policy Formation," in Leon Lindberg, *Stress and Contradiction in Modern Capitalism: Public Policy and the Theory of the State* (Lexington, KY: Lexington, 1975).

15   Claus Offe, *Disorganized Capitalism: Contemporary Transformations of Work and Politics* (Cambridge: Polity Press, 1985), 242.

which organized interest groups and bodies of consultation and reconciliation play the major role. At most, Tully's vision of multicultural or "intercultural" constitutionalism expands the corporatist process of public policy-making to encompass the identitarian politics of cultural recognition. He claims that such a project will restore the essential principles of the ancient constitution to the heart of the modern constitutional order. Unfortunately, the managerial practice of intercultural negotiation merely reinforces a corporatist system of group representation highly sensitive to the absolute imperatives of capitalist growth and development.

Moreover, there is one ethnoculture that implicitly contradicts the multicultural conventions of mutual recognition: namely, the deracinated civic culture developed by and for Anglo-Saxon Protestant societies. Cynthia Ward argues that, faced with the reality of cultural diversity, the response of Anglo-American civic republicanism is typically *expansive* in nature; it is "geared toward the assimilation of difference." Corporatist constitutionalism, by contrast, is *separatist* or *exclusive* in that it is "geared toward the magnification and encouragement of difference."[16] These two, very different, constitutional cultures cannot co-exist; one must destroy the other.

In Ward's argument, Anglo-American civic cultures developed "a strong momentum toward political connectedness" in order to "overcome the separatist pull of diversity and disagreement." That fraternal ideal encouraged the "development of imaginative empathy" among citizens. We are all required to imagine ourselves "in the position of a person whose starting point is radically different" from our own. But the logic underpinning the corporatist politics of cultural recognition provides few incentives to direct altruism and empathy towards the members of out-groups. Indeed, in Ward's view, the system actively "encourages the citizenry to divide itself into groups in order to win politically controlled benefits." And experience shows that, once interest groups succeed in "winning special benefits, the separatist pull grows stronger." Inevitably, therefore, multicultural constitutionalism fragments the civic culture once shared by all citizens.[17]

Over the twenty years since Ward wrote her prescient piece, the momentum towards separatism has grown exponentially. Group representation creates elites with a vested interest in thickening the boundaries between citizens. For that reason, Ward described multicultural

---

16 Cynthia Ward, "The Limits of 'Liberal Republicanism': Why Group-based Remedies and Republican Citizenship Don't Mix," (1991) 91 *Columbia Law Review* 581 at 583.

17 *Ibid.*, 593.

constitutionalism as "communo-pathic." Among the pathologies proliferating since "rainbow republicanism" became a political religion "is the
denial of connectedness, manifesting itself politically in the championing
of a view of diversity that refuses to recognize the possibility of general
agreement on political goods."[18] Tully's constitutional prescriptions for
intercultural negotiation and dialogue are already breeding rising levels of
ethnic chauvinism. It has become all-too-obvious that substantial rewards
flow to minority groups organized to exploit self-serving WASP politicians and corporate executives ever ready to betray their co-ethnics in
conspicuous displays of Anglophobic ethnomasochism.

In practice, a comprehensive system of intercultural negotiation
means "that diversity can be acknowledged and empowered only through
constant political battle pitting the races and genders against each other in
a never-ending contest for recognition and public benefits."[19] Tully hopes
that every group will be able to stand on an equal footing in the contest
over recognition and the political rewards that flow from it. He seems
unaware that the parties to a process of corporatist interest intermediation must "share basic assumptions concerning the primacy of systemic
considerations (growth, economic performance, industry restructur-
ing etc.) so that policy formation within the framework of such bodies
both presupposes and generates consensus."[20] The effective production
of a consensus among elite players, however, presupposes a functional
differentiation between the constituent elements of the corporatist process; all the more so when corporatism degenerates into a racial spoils
system. In such a complex and dynamic political economy, not all groups
will possess or preserve equal procedural status in bargaining for power,
prestige, and resources. Groups that lack or lose functional relevance (or
which are perceived to be *dys*functional) will be shunted aside unless they
have access to some other resource or attribute that gives them a strategic
capacity to generate conflict.

Because corporatist politics reflects an unspoken understanding that
not all economic interest groups are created equal, this principle has particular application to inter-ethnic competition in a capitalist economy.
According to William H McNeill, polyethnicity is the rule rather than
the exception in the life of advanced civilizations. But he adds the companion caveat that such ethnic intermingling produces a "complex ethnic

---

18 *Ibid.*, 593.

19 *Ibid.*, 606.

20 Julian Triado, "Corporatism and Democracy," (1984) *Thesis Eleven* 33.

hierarchy" wherever it occurs.[21] A constitutional order that openly and deliberately grants special privileges to some and not other ethnic groups will produce an especially complex ethnic hierarchy along with increased risks of inter-ethnic conflict. The relative standing of particular groups now depends significantly upon their performance within the global system of needs. In such a dynamic system, there can be no automatic right to consent or cultural continuity or even recognition of group rights. A minority group whose members are functionally relevant or possesses a significant conflict potential today may find itself on the scrap heap of history tomorrow. The lesson for Anglo-Saxon Christians is clear: their idolatrous faith in modern constitutionalism is now nothing more or less than a hopelessly dysfunctional ethnomasochism. The American Constitution is another god which has failed. WASPs will bear a vastly disproportionate share of the costs associated with the spiritual (and fiscal) bankruptcy of the Constitutional Republic.

And yet it will still be difficult for the invisible race to wrench itself away from the modernist religion of the Republic. Even Tully's scheme of intercultural negotiation is a stretch since it requires WASPs to acquire a novel collective entity, to become an ethnonation *comme les autres*. To begin that task will require American WASPs to rediscover their ethnohistory; it is not inconceivable that the rediscovery of the archaic roots of Anglo-Saxon identity will lead many to renew their ancestral allegiance to the Crown and Church of Old England. The British monarchy and the Anglican Church are the last living links to the archetypical forms of Anglo-Saxon bioculture. And the dilemma facing WASP citizens of Australia, Canada, New Zealand, and the United Kingdom is no less poignant. In each of these countries, too, the managerial regime is eager to distance itself from its Anglo-Saxon origins. Resistance to that trend is probably futile; it may be unwise as well. Paradoxically, it may become necessary to abandon the "constitutional monarchy" throughout the old "white Commonwealth" in order to save Anglo-Saxon Christian kingship. As things stand now, the British monarchy and the Church of England are bound in constitutional chains that forbid formal recognition of their Christian character and their Anglo-Saxon provenance. Long ago, Anglo-Saxon loyalists warned rebellious American colonists that it would be a sin to abjure their allegiance to the Crown; contemporary monarchists err when they cling to the form while betraying the spirit of Anglo-Saxon kingship. WASPs in Australia, Canada, New Zealanders, and even

21 William H McNeill, *Polyethnicity and National Identity in World History* (Toronto: University of Toronto Press, 1986), 76.

in England stand idly by while flagrantly godless states hold the Crown
hostage. Modern British monarchs are little more than bureaucratic hood
ornaments, incapable of speaking and acting in defence of their kith and
kin; the seemingly endless, disastrous, reign of Elizabeth the Useless is the
most obvious case in point.

Recovering Lost Treasures

Is it possible or even desirable for a postmodern Anglo-Saxon king to
recover the regal powers of speech and action? Can the Crown ever again
speak on behalf of dead and unborn generations of Anglo-Saxons? Those
who live in the here and now, along with their posterity and ancestors,
have vital interests in the unbroken historical continuity of their biocultural ties not just to the ancient British constitution but to their co-ethnics
around the world. There is, of course, no shortage of academics, politicians, journalists and businessmen, especially in Australia, who urge their
fellow citizens to abandon their historic identity as a British people and
surrender to the allegedly irresistible forces of geography and economics.
Must the Crown remain silent in the face of this deadly challenge to the
authority of history, culture and tradition? It seems likely that Australian
republicans will continue their assault upon the historic allegiance of
Australians to the British Crown, mounting a series of plebiscites and
referenda until they grind down opposition and achieve the final victory allegedly written in the stars. Allegiance to the monarchy, they
believe, is restricted to a hard-core minority, a parochial party of the past
which is no match for the progressive party of the future. The Australian
republican movement bespeaks modernity's relentless war on tradition.
Precisely because the allegiance of many Australians, Canadians and New
Zealanders to the British Crown is a tradition of long standing, it remains
vulnerable to the corrosive influences that are causing the breakdown of
moral authority and social cohesion in every sphere of modern social,
economic and political life.

    As an institution, the monarchy is a conduit or carrier of traditions; it
is not itself a tradition. The allegiance of the subject and the obligations
of kingship, alike, entail "a set of observances, a collection of doctrines
or teachings, a particular type of behavior," as well as "a way of thinking about the world." The existence of hereditary monarchy embodies the
sense of trusteeship inherent in the meaning of tradition. Implicit in tradition is the notion "that (a) something precious or valuable is (b) given
to someone in trust after which (c) the person who receives the 'gift' is

expected to keep it intact and unharmed out of a *sense of obligation* to the giver."[22] A king's sense of obligation extends not just to God from whom his authority descends but to the people who are the beneficiaries of the royal trust. As Thomas Hughes pointed out one-hundred and fifty years ago, kings must have a real sympathy with the masses they are sworn to serve. "Our biblical training surely would seem to teach" that if "all people are to bow before the king, all nations to do him service, it is *because* 'he shall deliver the poor when he crieth, the needy also, and him that hath no helper.'" A "king prays for the judgements and righteousness of God… in order 'that he may judge Thy people according unto right, and defend the poor.'"[23] The Christian idea of kingship has been embedded in Anglo-Saxon bioculture from time out of mind.

But it is not just the British Crown that is under threat. It is not just this or that tradition that now teeters on the edge of extinction. Instead, as David Gross has shown, "*tradition itself* is disappearing." Before the modern era, tradition "provided the order that helped stabilize social existence. It set one right with ancestors whose heritage had to be preserved." Tradition gave people a sense of belonging and created respect for an authority going back to ancient times. But, in the modern world, "tradition as social cement gradually lost a good deal of its integrative power." The emergence of a complex, highly differentiated modern society produced "a multitude of different traditions operating simultaneously in different spheres." The appearance of rival traditions left people "freer to select the traditions they wanted, even to the point of leaving one tradition and attaching themselves to another."[24] New ways of thinking, particularly those linked to the Enlightenment encouraged a negative attitude to tradition. Enlightenment philosophes insisted that the dead weight of the past was crushing the human spirit of creativity and innovation. Capitalism, the industrial revolution, the growth of centralized, bureaucratic states and mass urbanization all contributed further to the breakdown and disappearance of traditional folkways.

The seemingly irresistible momentum of capitalist modernity encourages republicans everywhere to adopt a flatly dismissive attitude towards monarchist traditions which, in their view, should simply be laid to rest and forgotten. They often ridicule those who retain a sentimental allegiance to the old traditions and long to return to them. Gross suggests a third

---

22 David Gross, *The Past in Ruins: Tradition and the Critique of Modernity* (Amherst: University of Massachusetts Press, 1992), 8-9

23 Thomas Hughes, *Alfred the Great* (London: Macmillan, 1869), 11-12.

24 Gross, *Past in Ruins*, 3,20,21,23.

possible attitude to bygone traditions, "one that remains firmly grounded in the present but finds value in bringing traditions into a modern setting." This third way seeks neither to obliterate the past nor to escape back into it, but, rather, "to perform what might be called a 'rescue operation.'" The goal of the rescue mission is "to salvage certain outmoded traditions by asking what they can contribute to solving contemporary problems."[25]

In the context of the ongoing debate, at least in Australia, over the future of the British monarchy, this idea raises at least two important issues. First, can Anglo-Saxon Protestants throughout the diaspora advance their biocultural interests by rescuing the ancestral tradition of allegiance to the British Crown? Second, even if there is something of value to be salvaged out of an historic allegiance to what seems to be an outmoded and obsolescent institution, who is going to perform that heroic rescue operation?

In relation to the first issue, it must be acknowledged that the Anglo-Saxon monarchy, simply by retaining its obstinately and irredeemably premodern character, helps Anglo-Saxon Protestants to understand the problems and dangers peculiar to the politics of diversity. Because modernity is a world unto itself with its own self-propelling dynamic, it is exceedingly difficult to achieve any sort of critical distance from the social pathologies that are generated within the contemporary world-system. Gross maintains that even the most searching critiques of modern life "seem unable to provide a perspective from beyond the boundaries of the present." Having dismissed traditions as "backward-oriented forms of community," the most advanced thinkers such as Jürgen Habermas offer "at most a modern critique of modernity." Such immanent critiques of modernity "place in question what is given only from within the confines of the given." Gross contends that if we pay attention instead to the critical possibilities of past traditions we gain not only "a better understanding of modernity" but also the basis for "a critique of modernity from *outside* modernity." What seems "historically passé often contains the very otherness we most require to broaden and deepen our perspective on modern life."[26]

In the eighteenth century, Enlightenment thinkers waged a cultural war of liberation against tradition. For the philosophes, "it was only after the authority of the past had been abolished that an era of freedom could begin." But now that the authority of tradition has been effectively destroyed, renewed contact with the profound difference between tradition and the "deadly sameness" of everyday life in a relentlessly commercialized culture may serve as a source of spiritual renewal. Because

---

25   *Ibid.*, 77, 78.

26   *Ibid.*, 87-88.

tradition can never again provide a natural and accustomed sense of security, rootedness, and continuity in social life, the "same traditions our predecessors knew intimately now represent strange and alien forms of life which are strikingly different from those we are acquainted with in the present." For that reason, encounters with surpassed traditions can have a salutary shock effect on the modern mind, sending it "backwards, provoking memory and reflection." Our overly synchronous consciousness can acquire a novel diachronic dimension that might "jar or unsettle present-day securities, disturb complacencies, and perhaps put our certainties into question, since what is taken-for-granted would be seen anew in light of the past."[27]

The shock effect of a renewed encounter with traditions of allegiance to the Crown would be all the more profound were a modern Anglo-Saxon prince to lead the necessary rescue mission. For that to become even a remote possibility, the British monarchy will have to resurrect some trace or fragment of earlier traditions of independent royal action. To speak as the voice of history to his people, an Anglo-Saxon king must be free to defend Crown, Church, and Country. A "constitutional monarch," by contrast, is bound to speak and act on the advice of godless ministers hostile to the very existence of the Crown and indifferent to the fate of the Anglo-Saxon race. Clearly, the conventional norms constraining the behavior of modern princes must be unsettled. How can that be done?

The recovery of tradition requires something in the nature of what Hannah Arendt calls a "pearl-diving" expedition. We must descend deep into the past, seeking out fragments of now submerged traditions in the hope that, once exposed to the present, they will take on new meanings, quite different from those associated with times past. Anglo-Saxons need to recover not the petrified corpse of absolute monarchy but the archaic essence of the ancient British constitution. Arendt suggests that our chief aim in the critical interrogation of the past should be "to discover the real origins of traditional concepts in order to distil from them anew their original spirit which has so sadly evaporated...leaving behind empty shells." We need a way of thinking that seeks to wrest "thought fragments" from the past.[28]

Like a pearl diver who descends to the bottom of the sea, not to excavate the bottom and bring it to light but to pry loose the rich and the strange, the pearls and the coral in the depths and to carry them to the

27 Ibid., 83, 99.

28 Hannah Arendt, *Between Past and Future: Six Exercises in Political Thought* (New York: Meridian, 1963), 15.

surface, this thinking delves into the depths of the past—but not in order to resuscitate it the way it was and to contribute to the renewal of extinct ages. What guides this thinking is the conviction that although the living is subject to the ruin of time, the process of decay is at the same time a process of crystallisation, that in the depths of the sea into which sinks and is dissolved what once was alive, some things "suffer a sea-change" and survive in new crystallized forms and shapes that remain immune to the elements, as though they waited only for the pearl diver who one day will come to them and bring them up into the world of the living—as "thought fragments", as something "rich and strange", and perhaps even as everlasting *Urphänomene*.[29]

One such lost treasure of constitutional theory can be found in a short book by the eighteenth century English opposition thinker, Henry St John, Viscount Bolingbroke. Entitled *The Idea of a Patriot King*, written in 1738, and first published in 1749, this work has been examined and discarded by many historians who found little of lasting value therein.[30] Professionally interested in what they perceive to be the book's original meaning for Bolingbroke and his contemporaries, historians have generally been oblivious to the possibility that this little gem could be cleaned and polished in a way that allows it to shed light on the problems and realities of our own time. Brought to the surface in an historical dredging operation designed merely to excavate the past, *The Idea of a Patriot King* has been tossed aside as just another empty shell by one historian after another. Having concluded that the book contributes little to our understanding of constitutional politics and problems in Bolingbroke's day, historians generally miss the point of Bolingbroke's idea of a Patriot King.

The real significance of *The Idea of a Patriot King* lies not in what it meant for Bolingbroke or even in what it might tell us about political problems, social conditions or intellectual life in eighteenth century England. Instead, the importance of this text lies in the way it can help us reshape and inject new meaning into the role of the monarchy while we build a global network of postmodern Anglo-Saxon Christian tribes. Bolingbroke's ideas have a practical significance for us, today, that they could never have had either for him or his contemporaries. He gave expression to an intuition concerning the unfolding logic of political and economic modernity that was dismissed as absurd in his own time, when

---

29 Hannah Arendt, *Men in Dark Times* (New York: Harcourt Brace Jovanovich, 1968), 205-206.

30 *The Idea of a Patriot King* in David Armitage, ed *Bolingbroke: Political Writings* (Cambridge: Cambridge University Press, 1997), 217-294.

the process had barely begun. Indeed, the force of his insight is not immediately obvious, even to readers today as demonstrated by the failure of generations of mainly WASP historians to reach a consensus on the significance of Bolingbroke's work. By revealing why the historiographical imagination has found coming to terms with Bolingbroke's image of the Patriot King so difficult, we can appreciate his achievement and begin to build on his insights.

Some students of eighteenth century politics suggest that Bolingbroke's idea of a Patriot King encouraged George III to set himself up as a royal tyrant.[31] Whether real or imagined, such a threat could only arise within a political culture that took for granted the existence of a monarch who remained the active, not merely symbolic, head of the body politic. For those of us now standing on the far shore of constitutional modernity, where hierocratic traditions of kingship and royal government have been swept away by the inexorable advance of democratic republicanism, the idea of a patriot prince conjures up no such fears. Nevertheless, if we can recover its original spirit, we may be shocked to discover that Bolingbroke's striking image of the royal redeemer of a fallen world reveals unexpected possibilities for political action.

Deciphering the Idea of a Patriot King

The stated object of Bolingbroke's oppositional politics was to mobilize country gentlemen and their independent representatives in Parliament to counter the corrupt designs of the ministries headed by Robert Walpole from 1721 to 1742. In the days when the royal prerogative had been seen as the primary threat to the constitutional balance, the Crown had been attacked "for usurping a jurisdiction not properly its own." But, in the eighteenth century, when patronage and corruption became the issue, those who took a "Country" view denounced the executive "less for exceeding its constitutional powers than for bringing the individuals composing the legislature into a personal and demoralizing dependence on the Crown and the financial resources it controlled."[32] But the Country party never managed either to root out corruption or to supplant conventional partisan loyalties, and finally even Bolingbroke was compelled to recognize that his campaign had been a failure. Unable to win

31 Armitage, "Introduction," in *Bolingbroke: Political Writings*, xxiii.

32 JGA Pocock, *The Machiavellian Moment: Florentine Political Thought and the Atlantic Republican Tradition* (Princeton, NJ: Princeton University Press, 1975), 479.

over country gentlemen and their representatives in the Commons to his
patriotic opposition platform, Bolingbroke's later writings addressed the
natural leaders of society. When the nobility, too, failed to act, he called
for a Patriot King, hoping that a revolution from above would restore the
constitution to its original principles.

Contemporary historians are not impressed. By indulging himself in
fantasy, Bolingbroke is seen to have confirmed the irrelevance of his political philosophy. Some historians, particularly those associated with the
once-dominant Namierite school of English historiography, simply refuse
to take Bolingbroke's ideas seriously (admittedly the Namierites have
been loath to accept anyone's political ideas at face value). In their view,
eighteenth century opposition politics was simply a scramble for power
in which ideas were valued only for their capacity to help one achieve
political ambitions.[33] John Brooke raises this proposition to the level of
a general law of politics, claiming that "in politics the struggle for power
is dignified as a conflict between opposing political ideas." For him, the
"game of pure politics" cannot be played "in an ideological void." While
opposition politics is framed today in the language of economics because
mass electorates are preoccupied with their material interests, the far
more restricted electorate of the eighteenth century cared far more "for its
constitutional rights."[34] As a consequence, the "stock opposition program"
in those days sought "to evoke the Briton's immemorial dread of standing
armies "and other manifestations of a menacing executive power."[35]

Because Walpole's Whigs were entrenched in power, the opposition
strategy, according to Lucy Sutherland, came down to a matter of "out-
whigging the Whigs." The opposition program "expressed an archaic academic whiggism, by incorporating the demands for a Places and Pensions
Bill, the return to triennial parliaments and the reduction of the standing
army." Sutherland argues that the wide popular appeal of such measures
"made them embarrassing" to Whig governments even "though everyone
with inside knowledge of politics knew that no group or party intended
to implement these doubtful political principles."[36] On this interpretation of eighteenth century politics, the Country party program rested on

33   See, eg, Lewis B Namier, *The Structure of Politics at the Accession of George III* (London:
     Macmillan, 1929).

34   John Brooke, "Party in Eighteenth-Century Politics" in *Silver Renaissance: Essays in
     Eighteenth-Century English History* (London, 1961), 22.

35   Herbert Butterfield, quoted in *ibid.*, 25; Archibald Foord, *His Majesty's Opposition* (Oxford:
     Clarendon Press, 1964), 78.

36   Lucy Sutherland, "The City of London in Eighteenth-Century Politics," in Richard Pares
     and AJP Taylor, *Essays Presented to Sir Lewis Namier* (London: Macmillan, 1956), 58.

nothing more than a myth of patriotism more or less cynically cooked up by Bolingbroke to suit his personal political purposes. He was, so the story goes, trying to create a patriot party out of whole cloth. According to JCD Clark, "No 'Court' and 'Country' parties .. existed in the sense of groups of members voting together consistently." The language of "Court" and "Country" parties "was a sort of polemic" that did not accurately describe the party structure.[37] Linda Colley supports that view, suggesting that Bolingbroke faced a fundamental problem: "Patriot Whigs were anti-Walpolean but still partisan, independent Whigs were unmanageable, and the Tories felt their distinction from both groups." The suspicions that many Tories harbored toward Bolingbroke as well as their continuing partisan bias prevented them from accepting Bolingbroke's analysis. In the end, only Bolingbroke believed that his "jerry-built opposition was a coherent and durable political alignment."[38]

Basic to the Namierite argument is the assumption that the categories of ideological rhetoric cannot provide "either reliable description or reliable evaluation of the way the institutions of high politics worked" in Augustan England.[39] If one accepts that Bolingbroke's ideas were indeed devoid of any significance beyond their role as ideological drapery in an otherwise sordid struggle for power in his time, it is difficult to see how they could possibly be of any value in the understanding or resolution of our own constitutional quandaries. But the major premise of this sceptical stance has not gone unchallenged within the historical profession.

Namier and his disciples focus on high politics in and around the parliament. They are relatively indifferent to the large-scale social and economic developments that were to transform the political world over the next two centuries and therefore miss an important dimension of Bolingbroke's political thought. Other historians have shown that political thought in Bolingbroke's time and specifically in his work "became engrossed with the conscious recognition of change in the economic and social foundations of politics and the political personality." As a consequence, the modern citizen—the epigonal heir of Aristotle's agonistic *zōon politikon*—"took on his modern character as participant observer in processes of material and historical change fundamentally affecting

37 JCD Clark, "A General Theory of Party, Opposition and Government, 1688-1832" (1980) 23 *The Historical Journal* 295-325.

38 Linda Colley, *In Defiance of Oligarchy: The Tory Party, 1714-60* (Cambridge: Cambridge University Press, 1982), 97.

39 JGA Pocock, *Virtue, Commerce and History* (Cambridge: Cambridge University Press, 1985), 244

his nature."[40] Those intellectual developments are particularly interesting because Bolingbroke's contribution to them belongs to a neo-Machiavellian, or classical republican, challenge to the onrushing forces of political and economic modernity.

Bolingbroke was not simply waging a campaign to acquire power and the spoils of office. He was trying to understand and describe the lineaments of a new political economy that seemed certain to transform the constitutional order. That new political economy had its origins in the Glorious Revolution of 1688-9 which put William of Orange on the throne in place of the last Stuart king, James II, and "had to be paid for with intensive English involvement in the Franco-Dutch wars of the continent." Significantly, those military adventures were financed through a new structure of public credit centered on the Bank of England and the national debt. The novelty of such arrangements cannot be overemphasized. The landed and mercantile classes "were now encouraged to lend money to the government and live off the returns to their capital." Massive government borrowing funded the huge growth of the army, the navy and the civilian bureaucracies that supported them. The increasing burden of debt also caused a steady rise in land taxes. Meanwhile shares in the government debts themselves became a commodity, the price of which rose or fell according to the state of public confidence in the government's capacity to repay.[41]

Given such an enormous expansion of mobile and fluid property in stocks and bonds, the monied interest seemed set to displace the landed classes in terms of power and influence, if not authority. In those days, landed property was understood, in classical republican terms, as the material foundation of civic virtue. Bolingbroke was influenced by James Harrington, a seventeenth century contemporary of Hobbes who made a major contribution to English civic humanism. Harrington attributed the growth of the landed gentry to the Tudor confiscation and sale of church lands to the highest bidder. A newly landed class heavily larded with wealthy merchants and professionals was created almost overnight; its political weight enabled the Commons to counterbalance the weight of the peerage and the Crown. Because, according to Harrington, power followed property, the growth of the monied interest tilted the constitutional balance of forces. But many mistrusted the mobile property of the mon-eyed man since "the foundations of his civic personality were constantly

40   Pocock, *Machiavellian Moment*, 423.

41   JGA Pocock, "Early Modern Capitalism: The Augustan Perception," in Eugene Kamenka and RS Neale, *Feudalism, Capitalism and Beyond* (Canberra: ANU Press, 1975), 63-83.

shifting and tended to involve him in too fluid a nexus of relationships with others." Moneyed wealth, unlike land, was embedded in a vast, developing system of fluctuating values. The power of money was bound to detach the constitution from its original principles. As long as the new "system of economy" greatly expanded the financial resources available to government ministers, "a vast number of new dependents on the crown are created in every part of the kingdom."[42] Bolingbroke worried that "this change in the state and property of the public revenue hath made a change in our constitution...since it gives a power, unknown in former times, to one of the three estates," thereby rendering unachievable a harmonious balance of power between King, Lords, and Commons.[43]

Bolingbroke's attacks on the new men of power can be read differently, however; not as a cynical, hackneyed rhetorical device employed by an ambitious outsider to win power for himself but instead as the sincere expression of a "style of thought" characteristic of the nobility and gentry in Augustan England. This approach is taken by Isaac Kramnick in his study of Bolingbroke and his circle. On Kramnick's reading, Bolingbroke's ideas "illuminate more than partisan political preferences." They aimed to defend "an aristocratic social and political order being undermined by money and new financial institutions." In other words, Bolingbroke's world really was being turned upside down by a corrupt Whig oligarchy which he judged to be the enemy of his class.[44]

But, while Kramnick purports to take Bolingbroke at face value, he emphatically denies that the opposition leader's ideas, particularly his idea of a Patriot King, were a sure guide to political action, either in his time or in our own. Situating Bolingbroke's ideological campaign in its social context, Kramnick portrays him as the "political philosopher of the declining gentry."[45] As such, Bolingbroke led a "reactionary" and "populist" resistance movement against the mysterious new phenomena associated with early modern finance capitalism. Nailing his own progressive colors to the mast, Kramnick pointedly refuses to join Bolingbroke in mourning the passing of the old way of life. Indeed, he dismisses the relevance of Bolingbroke's ideas even for Englishmen in the eighteenth century, declaring that the "old order sought by Bolingbroke in his nostalgic

---

42 Bolingbroke, *Dissertation upon Parties*, in Armitage, *Bolingbroke: Political Writings*, 156, 175.

43 *Ibid.*, 176.

44 Isaac Kramnick, *Bolingbroke and His Circle: The Politics of Nostalgia in the Age of Walpole* (Ithaca, NY: Cornell University Press, 1992), 3-4.

45 *Ibid.*, 60.

flight from the political and economic innovations of his day was a dream which could not suffice for this new age." Walpole, by contrast, is hailed as the far-sighted harbinger of the brave new world of political and economic modernity. His ministry "represented an essential step on the path to a stable and modern British economy and polity." Kramnick endorses the standard defence made at the time by Walpole's forces to the charge of corruption, explaining that "without corruption, the constitution would not function properly." Precisely because power had followed property, "the balance of power had come to rest strongly on the side of the Commons, which now possessed some seventeen-twentieths of the land." Moreover, the Commons retained the "sole ability to give public money" upon which the Crown depended. In these circumstances, it was only because the King had the power to dispose of places of profit that the Crown retained its constitutional independence. Walpole's supporters regarded Bolingbroke's anti-corruption place bills as the real threat to the mixed constitution. For them, it was precisely because the King had the means to build a party prepared to support his ministers that England still enjoyed a truly balanced constitution not totally beholden to the parochial interests of the landed gentry who dominated the Commons. Accordingly, Kramnick dismisses Bolingbroke's desire for a Patriot King who would govern without a party as "a hopeless anachronism in the England of 1749."[46]

For an academic Marxist such as Kramnick, Bolingbroke's idea of a Patriot King remains an anomaly that defies explanation. Kramnick began his study of Bolingbroke's ideas with the promise that he would take them seriously. In practice, Kramnick recognizes Bolingbroke as an historically significant political thinker only when his thought appears to reflect the movement of the large social and economic processes shaping historical development. So, for Kramnick, Bolingbroke is most significant when he displays real insight into the structural changes that affected the balance of property in English society, particularly the institutional changes that produced the "corruption" of the constitutional order. Whenever Bolingbroke calls for moral and spiritual, rather than institutional and structural, changes to the English body politic to reverse the decline in virtue, Kramnick loses interest. Kramnick notes that Bolingbroke "suggests that the only way to reestablish the ideal order is the moral example and theatrical deportment of a humanist prince," curtly condemning the idea as pointless.[47] *The Idea of a Patriot King* retains significance only as

---

46 *Ibid.*, 5,6, 122-123, 152, 169.

47 *Ibid.*, 168.

a means of explaining and bearing witness to the failure of Bolingbroke's opposition movement. At the very least, Armitage suggests, this creates "unbalanced account of Bolingbroke's political thought: in effect, *Hamlet* without the prince."[48]

Kramnick reduces Bolingbroke's ideas to an expression of their social context. Unless the ideas espoused by those opposed to the Whig oligarchy reflects or promises effective resistance to the social and economic changes sweeping over Augustan England, Kramnick is at a loss in deciding how to interpret that ideology. It is an essential part of Kramnick's argument that Bolingbroke's position reflected the "nostalgia" of the landed gentry for an ordered, hierarchical society. But, JGA Pocock counters that this putatively "reactionary" and "Tory" position "which ought to have been and often was High Church and Jacobite, ought not to have been but often was radical and republican, Commonwealth as well as country." The fact was that Bolingbroke's oppositional rhetoric not only appealed to "elements of the country gentry", it also "gave a voice to those city and borough populations who found that the great financiers and the parliamentary oligarchs were depriving them of power."[49] Given such confused and contradictory circumstances, Pocock suggests that the social context of the idea of a Patriot King cannot be understood fully without first grasping Bolingbroke's intentions in writing that text. What, then, was Bolingbroke trying to do? To value tradition and to resist its disintegration is not necessarily to indulge oneself in sentimental nostalgia. It is not obvious that the idea of a Patriot King should be dismissed as a reactionary fantasy. Indeed, Bolingbroke's ideology may have been "radical precisely because it was backward-looking."[50] To grasp that paradox, our reading of Bolingbroke's work must consider not just the interplay between an author's intentions and the social context of the long-vanished era in which he wrote but also the wider problem of meaning in history.

Meaning in History

Thinking about the relationship between authorial intentions and the context of political writing raises questions about the point and value of historical understanding itself. The dominant tendency in intellectual history today is one which aims at the contextual reconstruction of political

---

48 David Armitage, "A Patriot for Whom? The Afterlives of Bolingbroke's Patriot King" (1997) 36 *Journal of British Studies* 400.

49 Pocock, *Virtue, Commerce, and History*, 245.

50 Armitage, "A Patriot for Whom," 399-400.

ideas coming to us from the past. Historians such as JGA Pocock are interested in what Bolingbroke had to say to Britons living in the eighteenth century, not what he might communicate to the twenty-first century subjects of the British Crown. Pocock does not expect Kramnick to endow the idea of a Patriot King with new life in the present. Instead, he charges Kramnick with a present-minded dereliction of his responsibility to the people of the past; it is *their* experience which the historian should understand and reproduce in its own terms, not ours.

Both Pocock and Quentin Skinner insist that the classic texts in the history of political thought "cannot be concerned with our questions and answers but only with their own."[51] The task of the historian, in other words, is to reconstruct the thought of dead political thinkers as a service to them, not to resurrect it for our purposes in the here and now. Unfortunately, the effect of this approach has been to turn the history of political thought into a matter of interest only to professional historians. Following the methodology prescribed by Pocock and Skinner, historians will read Bolingbroke's political writing with an open mind, as free as possible from prejudice, in order "to understand the text on its terms" rather than in terms of his own situation. The object of historical reconstruction then is to transpose ourselves "into the culture and into the mind of the author."[52] Unfortunately, this reconstructive methodology proves to be of doubtful validity and little worth when Pocock and Skinner examine *The Idea of a Patriot King*.

Skinner's reading of Bolingbroke's work assumes that it can be understood as an act of communication akin to speech. On that premise, *The Idea of a Patriot King* or any other text appears to us as "a sort of frozen speech, speech fixed in script." To recover Bolingbroke's authorial intention, the historian must strip the text of meanings imposed on it by subsequent generations of readers and then reconstruct "the historical situation in which it was originally written." Once the text is reinserted "in its reconstructed context", it becomes possible to "discern its indigenous, prenatal meaning." In recovering and describing the languages of patriotism and civic humanism in Augustan England, Skinner and Pocock claim to have gained "access to the menu of meanings those languages made available (or denied) to writers and readers living in that culture." But that

51   Quentin Skinner, "Meaning and Understanding in the History of Ideas" (1969) 8 *History and Theory* 50.

52   David Harlan, *The Degradation of American History* (Chicago: University of Chicago Press, 1997), 7.

claim overlooks the fact that "writers are not the same as speakers, and readers are not the same as listeners."[53]

Because the written text of the *Patriot King* was not a speech act, Bolingbroke's readers have never been in the same position as those who once listened to him speak. After all, Bolingbroke's listeners could interrogate him and he, in return, could respond to their questions and comments. We, as readers of the *Patriot King*, were absent during its creation as a text. Bolingbroke is similarly absent when we come to read his work. For that reason, "the common reality shared by speaker and hearer cannot be transferred to writer and reader". As a writer, Bolingbroke cannot invoke or refer to our common context to clarify his intentions and the meaning he attempts to represent through language. Once Bolingbroke vanishes from the reader's view, his intentions disappear as well "and the text begins suggesting possibilities its author may never have imagined."[54]

Skinner and Pocock claim to be able to tell us what Bolingbroke "really meant," to reveal what the *Patriot King* "really says." They believe "that historical texts convey fixed meanings and that those meanings are accessible and ultimately determinable, if the critic or historian will simply cut through the layers of interpretation that stand between the naked text" and their understanding of it. But this quest for authentic meaning is based "on the illusion of the text as a "congealed intentionality waiting to be reexperienced." By conceiving understanding as the reconstruction of authorial intention, David Harlan remarks, this brand of hermeneutics aims at nothing "more than the recovery of a dead meaning." [55] One need not deny that "the historian bears a responsibility to those who lived in the past" to recognize that his "*primary* responsibility must be to those who live in the present." It is for that reason that Harlan declares that "we need an interpretative tradition erected … on the recognition that every text, at the very moment of its conception, has already been cast upon the waters, that no text can ever hope to rejoin its father, that it is the fate of every text to take up the wanderings of a prodigal son who does not return." The task of the historian then is not so much to recover a definitive understanding of what the *Patriot King* might have meant to Bolingbroke as to help that text "generate new meanings in the present—that is, in helping us discover what a historical text might say to us when we place it in a textual complex of *our* devising."[56]

---

53   *Ibid.*, 7-11.

54   *Ibid.*, 7.

55   Hans-Georg Gadamer, quoted in *ibid.*, 10.

56   *Ibid.*, 21-25.

But few professional historians see much of lasting interest in Bolingbroke's idea of a Patriot King. Even Pocock, who generally treats the classical republican challenge to the early modern political economy as something more than reactionary nostalgia, dismisses Bolingbroke's later writings on the idea of patriotism as "mere moral exhortations" of no relevance to his time much less our own.[57] Must we accept the testimony of this virtually unanimous body of expert witnesses? Is it possible that the ostensibly objective and putatively disinterested weight of historiographical opinion about Bolingbroke conceals the hidden agenda of winner's history? Does Bolingbroke's continuing bad press within the historical guild reflect the ideological hegemony of a now mature managerial regime foreshadowed by the Whig ascendancy in Augustan England? Can it be that modern historians play the role once assigned to the political writers employed in defence of the Walpole regime against Bolingbroke's ideological assault? If so, the Court Whig historians of the present are part of a persistent problem which Bolingbroke helps us to understand, perhaps even to solve. Academic historians, morally crippled by a pragmatic professionalism obsessed with methodology, speak only to each other; they cannot converse with Bolingbroke. The professional mask of ideological neutrality prevents them from exposing the constitutional corruption of the twenty-first century corporate welfare state by evoking Bolingbroke's radically oppositional spirit of liberty.

In Harlan's view, our own cultural values and "prejudices" are not simply "obstacles to understanding," they "are in fact what make understanding possible." T S Eliot drew attention to the presence of the past when he wrote that "the historical sense compels a man to write not merely with his own generation in his bones, but with a feeling that the whole of the literature of … his culture has a simultaneous existence and composes a simultaneous order." If so, to recover the meaning of the *Patriot King* we must pay as much attention to its afterlives and the possibility of a resurrection to come as to an "original meaning" that died with Bolingbroke and his circle. Harlan says as much when he points out that "the interpretations that have gradually accumulated around a particular text" form "the medium in which the text lives in the only medium in which it can live."[58] The meaning of the *Patriot King* has not been fixed once and for all.

Kramnick's image of Bolingbroke as "the threnodist of a lost organic agrarian polity, and the proponent of the rule of a natural aristocracy remains the prevalent account of the social philosopher as nostalgic,

---

57   Pocock, *Machiavellian Moment*, 484.

58   Harlan, *Degradation of American History*, 22.

antidemocratic, and reactionary—in short as everything one might expect of a Tory and a viscount." But there is also Skinner's opportunistic spin doctor masquerading as a patriot. Not to mention Armitage's Bolingbroke who would have been recognized by "the American rebels of the 1770s, the petitioners of 1775, the English radicals of the 1780s, or the supporters of Reform in the 1830s…not least because it is Bolingbroke without the Patriot King."[59] Because each generation approaches the *Patriot King* with its own needs, its own conflicts and its own prejudices, the meaning of that text will remain "in a state of perpetual flux."[60]

A Conversation with Bolingbroke

Namier and his followers set out to *expose* the naked lust for power underlying Bolingbroke's high-sounding platitudes. Kramnick sought instead to *explain* the political ideology of a declining gentry. Skinner and Pocock want us to *understand* what Bolingbroke was doing when he engaged in political discourse. The argument presented here demurs from all of these approaches. It sets out instead to *re-educate* Bolingbroke and his *Patriot King* by "anachronistically imposing enough of our problems and vocabulary on the dead to make them conversational partners." By engaging Bolingbroke in such a conversation, we can reactivate and recontextualize the *Patriot King* so that, as Harlan suggests, it might be "put to new and important uses." To make that possible we need a new sort of intellectual history: "a history concerned not with dead authors but with living books." That history would not return Bolingbroke to his historical context. Instead, it would read the *Patriot King* in a new and unexpected context. The object would not be to reconstruct the past but to provide a "natural medium in which valuable works from the past might survive their past—might *survive* the past in order to tell us about our present."[61]

In our imaginary conversation with Bolingbroke, we can point to several pearls that he overlooked in casting about for models of a Patriot King. Bolingbroke extolled the golden age inaugurated by the first Queen Elizabeth but made nary a mention of Alfred the Great. Bolingbroke was not the first nor was he the last Englishman to slight the importance of "England's greatest king, remembered solely for a fable that almost certainly never happened." As the only English king ever to have been

59   Armitage, "Patriot for Whom," 417-418.

60   Pocock, quoted in Harlan, *Degradation of American History*, 23.

61   *Ibid.*, 25-26, 31.

granted the title 'Great,' Alfred seems an obvious candidate for recognition as an early patriot prince. But "if he is remembered at all today as anything more than a name, it is for the legend of the burning of the cakes."[62]

The story concerns Alfred's sojourn, while travelling incognito among his subjects, in a swineherd's hut where the good wife left Alfred to watch over her baking. Unfortunately he allowed the cakes to burn. Upon her return, the wife gave the disguised king a dressing down. In Bolingbroke's time, the story portrayed a virtuous monarch required "to bear with decorum the indignity of being thought an ordinary citizen." Unhappily, such humility hardly projects the heroic image of a Patriot King capable of inspiring opposition to the spreading tentacles of Old Corruption in eighteenth century England. In Anglo-Saxon England, the tale acquired a providential meaning that, in a curious twist of fate, carries a clear message to the heirs and successors of the British Crown who will be consigned to constitutional oblivion by the creation of republics in Commonwealth countries sometime this century.[63]

In his recent biography of Alfred the Great, Justin Pollard notes that the king's strange sojourn in the wilderness took place after he was overthrown on Twelfth Night 878 by the churchmen and nobles of his own witan, acting in cooperation with Viking invaders. The story of the burning cakes was received by Alfred's subjects as an allegory highlighting "the dangers of failing to tend to the needs of the kingdom." Recently, Alfred had enjoyed four years of peace which gave him "the opportunity to prepare better defences for Wessex and to secure his position, but he had wasted this." He even failed to notice the growing disaffection from his rule produced by that inattention. Vice and corruption spread throughout the land. "Politically, his cakes were burning, and only a severe scolding by his people would awaken him to the impending disaster." Alfred's humiliation was complete when Viking chieftain Guthrum met no resistance when he set upon the royal camp at Chippenham. But Alfred showed his mettle as a patriot prince; he accepted the rebuke and, although abandoned by most of his subjects, decided to fight back. With his few remaining followers, the deposed king found refuge on a small island known as Athelney set in the trackless wastes of the Somerset swamps. From that isolated base, he planned his successful campaign to regain the loyalty of his people and throw back the Viking invaders. After his extraordinary

---

62 Justin Pollard, *Alfred the Great: The Man Who Made England* (London: John Murray, 2006), 2.

63 David Horspool, *Why Alfred Burned the Cakes: A King and His Eleven-hundred Year Afterlife* (London: Profile, 2006), 83.

comeback, Alfred set out to realize his "vision of a new type of kingdom, where protection and prosperity resulted not from physical force alone, but from education, public building, commerce and law." In Bede's *History of the English Church and People*, Alfred found a model of the Anglo-Saxon Christian commonwealth he hoped to create. Church and Crown would work hand-in-hand to lead a people grown corrupt back onto the path of righteousness blazed by the King of Kings.[64]

Should the republican cause triumph as forecast, Alfred's story can inspire postmodern Anglo-Saxon Christians with the iconic image of a Patriot King come to deliver them from evil, seizing victory from the jaws of defeat. The idea of a Patriot King is not at all fanciful; the "strange multiplicity" that is pushing the transnational market-state to resurrect ancient constitutional conventions grounded in ethnoreligious diversity must encourage a revival of Anglo-Saxon identity politics. A patriot prince of the blood royal need not forsake his people merely because the political class has no further use for the constitutional monarchy; pretenders will find one, two, and, indeed, many, Athelneys in a world-wide archipelago of Anglo-Saxon communities loyal to both God and King. A vapid, neo-pagan republicanism is no match for the archaic, muscular appeal of an Anglo-Saxon Christian commonwealth.

The spiritual void at the center of America's constitutional faith is clearly the withered harvest of imperial hubris. Nor will an Australian or British religion of the Republic be any more worthy of devotion. Paradoxically, therefore, Anglo-Saxon patriots should greet contemporary republican movements as golden opportunities rather than as existential threats.

Who's Afraid of the Republic?

Sooner or later, self-respecting Anglo-Saxons who take pride in the blood of Alfred the Great running in their veins, must wake up to smell the smoke of biocultural bread left burning by the really existing British monarchy. Surely, the royal family stands sorely in need of a severe scolding. Indeed, both the British monarchy and the Church of England deserve to be publicly shamed. Yet, for all their failings as subservient creatures of the vampire state, both institutions remain the mystic incarnation of their ancient ethnonation; as such, they will retain their place in the hearts of Anglo-Saxon patriots. Throne and altar stand for the "pre-political 'we' assumed in the social contract, and in every democratic choice" in every

---

64 Pollard, *Alfred the Great*, 2, 159-161, 266.

nation founded by the Anglo-Saxon peoples.[65] The monarchy and the
Anglican Church are the two most venerable Anglo-Saxon institutions;
both the Anglo-Saxon Body of Christ and the royal stirpes will survive
the official proclamation of republican constitutions throughout the old
white Commonwealth.

Post-republican Anglo-Saxon kings will be well-placed to invoke
the three foundational conventions of postmodern constitutionalism;
namely, consent, continuity, and mutual recognition.[66] Their throne
will be grounded, first and foremost, in the allegiance of loyalist Anglo-
Saxon Christians around the world. Justice requires that the Anglo-
Saxon diaspora in every state be accorded constitutional recognition as
a "community-through-time." The Crown is the medium through which
Anglo-Saxons everywhere maintain continuity both with the ancient constitution of their ancestors and the generations yet to come. Accordingly,
the Anglo-Saxon Christian monarchy of the future will be indispensable
to success in intercultural negotiations with the state and other politically
significant population groups. It is in that context that we should understand Bolingbroke when he writes that "[t]he true image of a free people,
governed by a Patriot King, is that of a patriarchal family, where the head
and all the members are united by one common interest, and animated by
one common spirit."[67]

A postmodern Patriot King will occupy a place similar to that of the
popular monarchy in orthodox Christian societies in early medieval
England and Old Russia. Medieval communal tradition rested upon three
ideas, that of the popular monarchy, the ancient faith, and the free people working in their guilds and villages. "Each estate exists for the other,
and none can exist without the other." In Old England, as in Old Russia,
the "state, if it can be called such, was represented by a monarch with a
tiny retinue of supporters." Holy Scripture warned kings not to "overstep
their bounds and begin to worship their own power." Henry Tudor defied
that injunction; the Crown State he created has come, in our time, to represent "the worst of civilization: the crystallization of elite authority and
tradition into a series of coercive agencies." God's anger having been thus
provoked, the British royal family has been condemned to the strangely
disconnected life of the celebrity figurehead, presiding over the cancerous
growth of vast, soulless bureaucracies honeycombed with special interests

65 Scruton, "Democracy is not Enough," Herbert Spencer Lecture, 2 March 1999, Oxford
    University, 8.

66 Tully, Strange Multiplicity, 30-31.

67 Bolingbroke, "Patriot King", 257-258.

of unimaginable diversity, indeed perversity. By contrast, drawing inspiration from orthodox Christian monarchs of earlier ages, an Anglo-Saxon Patriot King of the twenty-first century will become "a symbol of God's power, and the unity of the law." He will not dominate but will act "in a mystic capacity rather than in a bureaucratic one." The king will be "a living icon rather than a politician, a charismatic personality rather than a tax collector." And, as an icon of the Trinity, the job of the popular monarch is to defend Anglo-Saxon Christians "from the heretics and schismatics from within and without."[68]

In Bolingbroke's day, the spirit of party divided the people of England; in modern times, the disembodied spirit of civic nationalism allowed governments to carve up the Anglo-Saxon gene pool into a set of selfishly independent bureaucratic fiefdoms. Majoritarian democracy extinguished our constitutional links and our moral obligations to an ancient ethnoreligious community. Republican constitutions aim to break up, once and for all, the already enfeebled biocultural bonds between WASP population groups throughout the old white Commonwealth. WASPs can and should resist further biocultural degeneration and demographic dispossession. The monarchy must return to its original and still legitimate role as the voice of Anglo-Saxon history and Christian traditions; recovering WASPs around the world must pray for a Patriot King who, instead "of abetting the divisions of his people...will endeavor to unite them, and to be himself the centre of this union."[69] A modern patriot prince will not stand idly by while multiracialist states, indifferent to Anglo-Saxon ethnocultural interests, flout their self-proclaimed conventions of mutual recognition, consent, and continuity.

In sharp contrast, the British monarch today is forbidden to speak in defence of Anglo-Saxon interests. Down under, the monarchy is granted legitimacy only to the extent that it presents itself as an indisputably "Australian" institution. For that reason, the present Queen lays low in debates over a republican constitution, ever so politely leaving it to "the Australian people" to decide the future of the monarchy. But should republicans succeed in their campaign to rid Australia of its "foreign" monarch, a patriotic Anglo-Saxon king should not "despair of reconciling, and reuniting his subjects to himself, and to one another." A patriot prince will work to wean his people away from the heretical religion of the Republic in Australia, in England, and, even more assiduously, in the United States;

---

68 Matthew Raphael Johnson, *Sobornost: Essays on the Old Faith* (np: Deipara Press, 2008), 154-194; http://www.rusjournal.com/sobornost.html

69 Bolingbroke, "Patriot King," 258.

he "may be obliged, perhaps, as Henry the Fourth of France was, to conquer his own; but then, like that great prince, if he is the conqueror, he will be the father too, of his people." Such a conquest would depend, not upon force of arms, but upon the powers of reason and imagination. He must speak against those who presume to speak against him; "but he will pursue them like rebellious children whom he seeks to reclaim, and not like irreconcilable enemies whom he endeavors to exterminate."[70]

Defending the Anglo-Saxon community of blood and faith of which he remains the head, a patriot prince will not provoke a civil war. On the contrary, he "will act with another spirit, and entertain nobler and wiser views." Certainly, a modern patriot prince will never aim to subjugate the Anglo-Australian much less the Anglo-American people. Instead, he will remind them that they owe their historic rights and freedoms to the ancient spirit of liberty that their British ancestors—even those who came in chains—carried with them to Massachusetts and Botany Bay. Neither a merely formal nor a coerced allegiance to the Crown is sufficient to secure its future. "Nothing less than the hearts of his people will content such a prince; nor will he think his throne established, till it is established there."[71] Bolingbroke recognized that the very conditions that create the need for a Patriot King also make the appearance of such a leader unlikely in the extreme. But it was in the traditional institution of monarchy that he saw the last glimmer of hope.

Kings are bound to serve their kingdoms, not the other way around. Accordingly, Bolingbroke declined to base the monarchy upon "a pretended divine right;" royal legitimacy depends entirely upon a king's determination to preserve and defend the liberty of his subjects. Because "majesty is not an inherent, but a reflected light," only "a good king… can derive his right to govern from God." In other words, Bolingbroke defended the principle of limited, not absolute, monarchy. And, just as he thought of a limited monarchy as "the best of governments," so he considered "an hereditary monarchy the best of monarchies." He acknowledged that nothing would "be more absurd, in pure speculation, than an hereditary right in any mortal to govern other men: and yet, in practice, nothing can be more absurd than to have a king to choose at every vacancy of a throne." Elections could become occasions for tumult and instability. In the end, he believed, "the multitude would do at least as well to trust to chance as choice, and to their fortune as to their judgement."[72] But the

70   *Ibid.*, 264.

71   *Ibid.*, 265.

72   *Ibid.*, 228, 229, 230.

most important ground for preferring an hereditary to an elective king turned upon his superior ability to defend and maintain the spirit of liberty.

Rekindling the Spirit of Liberty

Kings "are under the most sacred obligations that human law can create, and divine law authorize, to defend and maintain, in the first place, and preferably to every other consideration, the freedom" of the British constitution. In the end, it was because an hereditary monarchy was better placed than an elective king to discharge such an obligation that Bolingbroke was prepared to defend the institution. Whether hereditary or elective, every king is bound to defend the freedom of the constitution. An hereditary claim to the throne is subject to forfeiture were that obligation not respected. "[E]very prince who comes to a crown in the course of succession, were he the last of five hundred, comes to it under the same conditions under which the first took it, whether express or implied."[73] An hereditary like an elective king can be deposed if he threatens the liberties of a free and virtuous citizenry. It is only when the people themselves lose their commitment to the spirit of liberty that the decisive advantage of hereditary over elective monarchy reveals itself.

Only a Patriot King can save British peoples which have been corrupted. In making this claim Bolingbroke repeats a question first posed by Machiavelli. That is, "whether, when the people has grown corrupt, a free government can be maintained, if they enjoy it; or established, if they enjoy it not?" Machiavelli was pessimistic about the chances of success in either case. Both Bolingbroke and Machiavelli agreed that freedom under any constitution depends upon two elements. The first Machiavelli called the orders of the constitution, by which he meant "not only the forms and customs, but the different classes and assemblies of men, with different powers and privileges attributed to them, which are established in the state." The second element is the "spirit and character of the people." So long as that spirit retains its original purity and vigor, the orders of the constitution cannot be destroyed. But once the spirit ebbs away, Machiavelli predicted, the orders will have to be changed and "adapted to the depraved manners of the people." But this can never be achieved except possibly through the intervention of a strong king. Bolingbroke accepted the idea that a king can redeem a fallen people but not "by new

---

73 *Ibid.*, 244-245.

laws and new schemes of government." Liberty cannot be preserved by such means so long as "the corruption of people continues and grows." Instead, he claimed that "to restore and preserve [liberty] under old laws, and an old constitution, by reinfusing into the minds of men the spirit of this constitution, is not only possible, but is, in a particular manner, easy to a king."[74]

Machiavelli and Bolingbroke conceived corruption as the spiritual degeneration of a constitutional order. An elective king chosen by a corrupt people is unlikely ever to rekindle the spirit of liberty. By contrast, a hereditary monarch, the product of chance rather than choice, of education rather than election, can be moved by the spirits of the dead and the unborn to resist the general tide of corruption among the living. In a corrupt commonwealth, the orders and forms of the constitution "are indeed nothing more than the dead letter of freedom, or masks of liberty." But, an hereditary king, speaking as the voice of history, "can, easily to himself and without violence to his people, renew the spirit of liberty in their minds, quicken this dead letter, and pull off this mask."[75] An hereditary monarchy can serve as the last refuge for the spirit of freedom in a corrupt constitutional order.

Bolingbroke was convinced that modern forms of corruption are very different from the tyranny and oppression earlier associated with the arbitrary exercise by the Crown of the prerogative power. Corruption is a form of self-imposed tyranny. Those who sink into spiritual servitude will "outlive the shame of losing liberty, and young men will arise who know not that it ever existed." Unless the process of corruption can be arrested, a "spirit of slavery will oppose and oppress the spirit of liberty, and seem at least to be the genius of the nation." As soon as people perversely pride themselves on a slavish devotion to the absolute imperatives of the new political economy, the "way of salvation will not be opened to us, without the concurrence, and the influence of a Patriot King, the most uncommon of all phenomena in the physical or moral world."[76]

In Augustan England, Bolingbroke's call for a Patriot King was premature. As the eighteenth century wore on, the spirit of liberty revived sufficiently to mount an active defence of the ancient constitution against the contagion of radicalism spreading from America and France. The Court Whigs criticized by the Country party were simply the vanguard of a revolutionary movement that has yet to run its course. In the past century,

---

74 *Ibid.*, 249, 247, 250.

75 *Ibid.*, 250-251.

76 *Ibid.*, 249, 221.

however, the Anglo-Saxon spirit of liberty has been ground down to the vanishing point, leaving in its place abject submission to the assertedly omnipotent force of the capitalist world-system. The secular myth of the ancient constitution disappeared from the vocabulary of lawyers and politicians alike. The "nation," whether in Australia, America, or the United Kingdom, is no longer defined by consanguinity of blood and solidarity of spirit. In such circumstances, constitutional legitimacy can no longer be a matter of origins. Instead the political and economic system depends upon its proven capacity of to deliver material prosperity through an endless process of economic growth and development. Bolingbroke emphasized the genetic legitimacy of the constitution, its representation in the here and now of ancient spiritual bonds between people, throne, and altar. But constitutional discourse in the contemporary corporate welfare state reflects a secular shift towards telic standards of political efficacy and economic efficiency. Bolingbroke believed that the historical spirit of the constitution endowed members of the political nation with the freedom to act as responsible citizens. Modern managerial elites are much more conscious of the systemic need to ensure that the population subject to its control behaves in a regular and predictable manner.

It is striking that Australian republicans, for example, rarely exult in the freedom of action vested in the citizens of a future republic. Instead, they identify their movement with *impersonal* forces of geography and economics which brook no opposition. In republican rhetoric, continued loyalty to the British Crown is simply archaic and anachronistic. Such attachments are routinely dismissed as sentimental nostalgia, the symptom of a national immaturity that must be outgrown. For them, because the monarchy belongs to a period of constitutional tutelage, a sort of national adolescence, the republic will be the final stage in the nation's passage to constitutional maturity. This is not a matter of choice; because the republic is inevitable, the Australian people are free to determine *when* but not *whether* the residual constitutional ties between the Australian market-state and the British monarchy are to be severed.

Republicans will be surprised and dismayed should Anglo-Saxon patriots beat them to the punch by declaring the independence of both the king and his church from the godless and deracinated state apparatus. Once reconstituted as an ethnonation in and for itself, Anglo-Saxon Christians will not behave in the regular and predictable manner that their rulers expect of them. By force of example, a patriot prince will help to regenerate the freedom to act differently.

The Patriot King as a Man of Action

Bolingbroke portrayed the Patriot King as a man of action. Such an idea runs counter to the conventions now governing royal behavior. Bolingbroke knew that his call for royal activism "will pass among some for the reveries of a distempered brain." Kinder souls dismissed the idea of a Patriot King as merely impracticable. Bolingbroke admitted that "nothing can be more uncommon than a Patriot King." But, while acknowledging that the idea must "appear improbable or impossible to many," Bolingbroke's work demonstrates the philosophical depth of his insight into the nature of action.[77]

Action is distinguished from behavior by "its inherent unpredictability." Arendt maintains that because man is capable of action, we can expect the unexpected from him. To start something new is to act "against the odds of statistical laws and their probability, which for all practical, everyday purposes amounts to certainty." For that reason, there is something miraculous about action. The automatic historical and political processes that depend upon regular, predictable patterns of behavior can be interrupted by human initiative. History is full of such events. "Hence it is not in the least superstitious, it is even a counsel of realism, to look for the unforeseeable and unpredictable, to be prepared for and to expect 'miracles' in the political realm." Indeed, "the more heavily the scales are weighed in favor of disaster, the more miraculous will the deed done in freedom appear." Both Arendt and Bolingbroke knew that "it is disaster, not salvation, which always happens automatically and therefore must appear to be irresistible."[78]

Bolingbroke urged his readers to prepare for the unforeseeable and unpredictable advent of a Patriot King. He saw the spread of "universal corruption" as an automatic process that can only spell ruin to the spirit of liberty. But even within and against that process citizens can assert themselves through action. Private men can do little to resist the general contagion. At most, while protesting against the inexorable process of degeneration, they can "keep the spirit of liberty alive in a few breasts". Like Arendt, Bolingbroke was sure that "the faculty of freedom itself" still "remains intact in the epochs of petrification and foreordained doom." He was convinced that the freedom to act will come out of hiding once a Patriot King is raised to the throne. "A Patriot King is the most powerful

---

77 Ibid., 240, 270.

78 Hannah Arendt, *The Human Condition*, (Chicago: University of Chicago Press, 1958), 191, 178; Arendt, *Between Past and Future*, 170.

of all reformers; for he is himself a sort of standing miracle." Precisely because the appearance of a Patriot King is so infinitely improbable, a capacity for performing miracles must be within the range of his faculties.[79]

Of course, no individual, however heroic, can reverse the effects of deeply entrenched social and economic structures. In political theory we repeatedly encounter the problem "of how to express concretely the idea of a collectivity of people by their own conduct rendering themselves helpless to deal effectively with problems resulting from that conduct." Both Arendt and Bolingbroke portray peoples entangled in the web of "universal corruption" or behaving as they must as "paradoxically not free yet free-to-become-free, thus free after all." Both Arendt and Bolingbroke, also frame this issue within a secular frame of reference. Accordingly, Arendt's work on the inexorable "rise of the social" has been likened by Hanna Pitkin to a science-fiction scenario in which the helpless population of planet Earth is attacked by a Blob from outer space. Thinking of "the social as Blob" helps to express but also disguises the logical complexities of a paradox central to "the enterprise of political theory."[80]

A one-sided focus on inexorable economic and political developments always renders us vulnerable to an "attack of the Blob." Political theory always "flirts with twin dangers." On the one hand, the political theorist can be prone to "utopian irrelevance" when he writes "as if absolutely *any*thing were possible here and now." On the other hand, he may succumb to "the immoral and apolitical presentation of people as inanimate objects or instinct-driven animals." In that case, he writes "as if *nothing* were possible for us, the future already determined." Pitkin concludes that "these conundrums ... cannot be resolved or escaped." They are insoluble dilemmas "built right into our ways of talking and thinking about human affairs." If that is true, the diagnosis of corruption in Walpole's England or the rise of the social in our own day must involve both "man's spirit" and "the structural terms of his condition." Moreover, they must be involved *together* in that diagnosis, even though a diagnosis grounded in agency is logically incompatible with one invoking causal necessity.[81]

Both Bolingbroke and Arendt felt the overpowering force of causal necessity in political and social life. They understood that if "one looks at the world in terms of causal processes in time, then the present moment,

79 Arendt, *Between Past and Future*, 168-169; Bolingbroke, "Patriot King", 249, 251.

80 Hanna Fenichel Pitkin, *The Attack of the Blob: Hannah Arendt's Concept of the Social* (Chicago: University of Chicago Press, 1998), 241, 239, 240.

81 Pitkin, *Attack of the Blob*, 242, 245, 246.

and action, disappear." Both writers also feared that "we might be becoming, and forming, the sort of people who cannot act, who lack the desire or the requisite skills and traits for action, particularly for action in concert with others." They concluded that "we urgently need to think also about how to turn this trend around." Accordingly, they tried to discover "what it might take to develop…a character structure more conducive to political engagement and freedom." Bolingbroke dealt with these issues in a manner appropriate to the education of a prince responsible for the welfare of his country. In that context, it becomes obvious that action "has no causes." One cannot program or predict a patriot prince. However careful and controlled an education may be, conduct always *originates* "in the agent 'whose' action it is, so that he deserves the credit or blame, unlike a storm, a chemical process, or the movements of a puppet."[82] That is why action always "looks like a miracle."[83] But the story of a king moved to interrupt our foreordained doom can inspire the rest of us to perform similar wonders.

A New People?

Both Arendt and Bolingbroke associate action with the experience of beginning anew. Bolingbroke, in particular, believed that a Patriot King will return the constitution to its original principles. His miraculous advent will interrupt the process of corruption and the spirit of the constitution will revive. As the Patriot King casts out devils from the body politic, "the orders and forms of the constitution" will be "restored to their primitive integrity." Legal forms will no longer provide a mask or blind behind which tyranny conceals itself. Instead, "[a] new people will seem to arise with a new king." Men will be "conscious that they are the same individuals" but "the difference of their sentiments will almost persuade them that they are changed into different beings." Beware however; the blessing of a Patriot King may be withheld from us. But if fortune does bestow such a gift upon the people, they must be prepared "to receive it, to improve it, and to co-operate with it." In the face of corruption, decay, and despotism, a few faithful remnants of Anglo-Saxon Christian civilization must "keep the cause of truth, of reason, of virtue, and of liberty, alive."

---

82   *Ibid.*, 268, 281.

83   Arendt, *Human Condition*, 246.

Patriots dare not wait upon a miracle; we must "deserve, at least, that it should be granted to us."[84] God helps those who help themselves.

Bolingbroke warned that we "may not expect more from such a king than even he can perform." He can return the spirit and the orders of the constitution to first principles but he cannot prevent their subsequent dissolution. All constitutions carry within them the seeds of their own destruction. "Every hour they live is an hour the less that they have to live." The most that can be done "to prolong the duration of good government" is to seize every favorable opportunity to draw the constitution back "to the first good principles on which it was founded." But no people can count on an endless succession of patriot princes to perform that task. During his reign, the Patriot King can restore the spirit of liberty and promote good government. "The rest his people must do for themselves." If they fail to carry on the enterprise begun by him, they will have only themselves to blame.[85]

Arendt makes the same point when she observes that "the strength of the beginner and leader shows itself only in his initiative and the risk he takes, not in the actual achievement." Action is divided into two parts, "the beginning made by a single person and the achievement in which many join" by seeing the initiative through to its end.[86] Inherent in the action taken by a Patriot King is a principle that will inspire "the deeds that are to follow." That principle will remain "apparent as long as the action lasts." Polybius also saw that the leader depends upon the strength of his followers. "The beginning is not merely half of the whole but reaches out towards the end." The beginning made by the Patriot King is not merely arbitrary. Rather the way he "starts whatever he intends to do lays down the law of action for those who have joined him in order to partake in the enterprise and to bring about its accomplishment."[87]

In principle, Bolingbroke believed the Patriot King will act in opposition to the tyranny of party and faction. He will "espouse no party" but will govern instead "like the common father of his people." His guiding principle will be to overcome the division of his people: "the king we suppose here will deem the union of his subjects his greatest advantage."[88] Applying that principle to our own time, a Patriot King is bound to resist the tyranny of the nation-state which, in every Anglo-Saxon coun-

84 Bolingbroke, "Patriot King", 251, 222.

85 Ibid., 251-252.

86 Arendt, *Human Condition*, 190.

87 Arendt, *On Revolution* (Harmondsworth: Penguin, 1977), 212-213.

88 Bolingbroke, "Patriot King", 259.

try, divides rootless WASPs not just from each other but also from their forbears and descendants. All states presently acting in the name of the Crown have a strong vested interest in the fragmentation of the British peoples, pushing them into widely separated, over-governed, jurisdictions, each possessed of its own statutory citizenship and international legal personality. Only the British monarch, as the embodied voice of history and tradition, retains the spiritual authority to speak for and to all people of Anglo-Saxon descent.

To act in accordance with such a principle will bring a patriot prince into conflict with those who benefit from the tyranny of the nation-state. Bolingbroke warned that "a prince who gives just reasons to expect that his reign will be that of a Patriot King" will not be greeted with universal acclaim. Any move in that direction by an Anglo-Saxon prince will demand great boldness. A patriot prince acting in defence of the common world created by his people is bound to suffer as a consequence. He requires the courage to endure the sometimes hostile and threatening reactions provoked by his own actions.

But the suffering he is forced to accept will bind him more closely to the people at large. Bolingbroke suggested that "many advantages would accrue" to "a good prince" ready "to suffer with the people, and in some measure for them." For one thing, "the cause of the people he is to govern, and his own cause would be made the same by their common enemies." A prince brave enough to speak out in the United States, asserting the right of an Anglo-Saxon king to represent those of his co-ethnics holding American citizenship will be subject to personal and political attack. He will also win sympathy and even admiration from those who see him feeling "grievances himself as a subject, before he had the power of imposing them as a king." Such a prince "would be formed in that school out of which the greatest and the best of monarchs have come, the school of affliction."[89]

To act as a Patriot King is to begin a story. If a patriot prince emerges victorious in the story of his deeds and sufferings "all the vices which had prevailed before his reign would serve as so many foils to glories of it."[90] A Patriot King who musters the courage to act recognizes posterity as a constituent element of the political community. As a practitioner of exemplary history, Bolingbroke was aware that the unchangeable identity of a Patriot King will become tangible only in the story of his life. In other words, the essential character of the Patriot King can be "grasped as a pal-

---

89   Bolingbroke, "Patriot King", 237-240.

90   Arendt, *Human Condition*, 190; Bolingbroke, "Patriot King", 240.

pable entity only after it has come to its end." The heroic actor is ultimately dependent upon the storyteller. The essence of his life comes "into being only when life departs, leaving behind nothing but a story." As a man of action, the Patriot King lives not just for himself but for the sake of an "immortal fame" surviving in the hearts and minds of posterity.[91]

Action in the present establishes a link between the past and the future. The political community cannot be identified solely with the interests of the lives in being at any given moment. Both Bolingbroke and Arendt see in the common world of the *polis* a means of ensuring "that the most futile of human activities, action and speech, and the least tangible and most ephemeral of man-made 'products,' the deeds and stories which are their outcome, would become imperishable." Though separated by centuries, both writers were post-Christian rationalists; both shared the modernist faith in the religion of the Republic. They looked to a trans-generational political community to assure "the mortal actor that his passing existence and fleeting greatness will never lack the reality that comes from being seen, being heard, and, generally appearing before an audience of fellow men."[92] The Anglo-Saxon Christian commonwealths of the twenty-first century, too, will provide a pathway to eternal life. Should WASPs surprise the world by reviving the spirit of the ancient British constitution, the archaic virtues of heroism and chivalry, beauty and grace will once again be woven into the fabric of everyday life.

As with other racial, ethnic, and religious groups, Anglo-Saxon identity will be "forged in the furnace of impending death and dislocation. This is to say that ethnicity is reducible to precisely the reactions against this impending state of wretchedness that build solidarity as a defense against it." Faced with a widening range of external threats, Anglo-Saxon communities will be compelled "to build consensus, solidarity and internal cohesion."[93] In the active recovery of the archaic traditions of a people defended by a popular monarchy, Anglo-Saxon Christians will become a formidable source of spiritual energy. But be warned: like Bolingbroke and his eighteenth century followers, those who pray publicly for a patriot prince will be denounced as dangerous reactionaries and sentimental fools by those plugged into the circuitry of power and privilege.

---

91 Arendt, *Human Condition*, 113.

92 *Ibid.*, 117-118.

93 Matthew Raphael Johnson, "Anarchy, the Ethnos and the State," http://www.rusjournal. com/state.html

Conclusion

Bolingbroke was concerned not with style but with the substantive meaning of political life. In fearing that the new modes of political behavior were draining from the public realm its accumulated reserves of shared meaning, Bolingbroke was not behind but rather ahead of his time. His idea of a Patriot King has become not less but rather more relevant with the passage of time. An Anglo-Saxon king whose authority derives from the ancient British constitution will be free to act in opposition to the all-pervasive behavioral norms of the modern corporate welfare state.[94] The image of a Patriot King breaking with the conventional norms of every-day behavior can inspire all of us to dare the extraordinary, to break with the tyrannical power of the "inevitable" and "inexorable" forces allegedly determining our future. In doing so, we can recover the spirit of liberty and hold it in trust for posterity.

In reading Bolingbroke's *Patriot King*, we can see that it does "not point backward to the historical context or putative intentions" of its now-dead author. Instead, it points "forward, to the hidden opportunities of the present."[95] In fact, taken as a whole, Bolingbroke's political writings carefully rehearse the range of responses that might have been made to what Arendt calls the rise of the social over the past three centuries. Using his own "archaic" vocabulary, Bolingbroke saw in the eighteenth century process of "universal corruption" forms of behavior very much like those described by Arendt in more recent times. Both writers associate the modern political economy with a political system in which an entire people fails to acknowledge its powers and responsibilities.[96]

"Behavior" in Arendt's work and "corruption" in Bolingbroke's political writings are both forms of "action *manqué*, a failure to act where action is called for." The "social" is the macro-level "counterpart to behavior, as politics is to action." The rise of the social was a process of "politics *manqué*, the absence of politics in a context where politics is possible and desirable."[97] Bolingbroke lived through the first phase of the rise of the social. He was so horrified by the experience that his imagination raced forward overtaking events; he foresaw a time when "the social" pushes politics in the classical sense all but completely out of the governmental system.

---

94   Arendt, *Human Condition*, 206.

95   Harlan, *Degradation of American History*, 26.

96   Pitkin, *Attack of the Blob*, 182.

97   Ibid., 182.

In the short run, Bolingbroke and his circle failed to spark a popular spirit of resistance to Walpole's regime. By 1736, Bolingbroke was no longer writing exemplary histories addressed to the public at large. He recognized that the people had been conditioned to behave in accordance with the corrupt norms of the new political economy. In his *Letter on the Spirit of Patriotism*, Bolingbroke looked instead to a natural aristocracy of superior spirits in the hope that they could be persuaded to act for the good of their country. Not long afterwards Bolingbroke realized that "private men" could not reverse the tide of corruption without the intervention of a Patriot King.

In suggesting that the natural leaders of the English polity had been reduced to the status of "private men," Bolingbroke was outracing the political realities of Augustan England. Even in his time, property, including mobile property, still served as the material foundation of public life. Property ownership entitled, perhaps even obliged one to become a "public man." By the twentieth century, this was no longer true. The enormous growth in the number and scale of modern business corporations facilitated the abdication of the public men in both the English and the American ruling class. The separation of ownership and control within the corporate sector led to the appearance of a new class of professional managers. In the public domain, the managerial revolution handed over the business of government to professional politicians and bureaucrats. Government and the corporate sector were then fused together in a single, interdependent system of needs. Within that system of "no-man rule," there is no place for public men of action.[98] The allegedly archaic, anachronistic and obsolescent idea of the Patriot King is now the best available model of the public man capable of moving his fellow citizens to action.

A Patriot King must challenge the automatic processes of the corporate welfare state by helping to establish autonomous Anglo-Saxon Christian commonwealths. Within those zones of ethnoreligious freedom, the king can perform the role assigned to the monarch by Montesquieu in his classic *L'Esprit des Lois*. The fundamental principle of monarchy, according to Montesquieu, is honor. By distributing honors to the best of his subjects, the Patriot King will be able to set a remodelled *republica Anglorum* into motion.[99] Royal authority will not be exercised, as it is now, on the instructions of governments of the day, to reward merely conventional behavior. The prince will exercise his prerogative power to recognize those

---

98 Arendt, *Human Condition*, 40.

99 Cf Montesquieu, *The Spirit of the Laws*, (Cambridge: Cambridge University Press, 1989), 27.

of his people who perform great deeds. By distributing honors in such a manner, a Patriot King can reverse the rise of the social, encouraging the emergence of a novel natural aristocracy of public men (perhaps even women) of action. The object is to reawaken the spirit of freedom essential to the rebirth of Anglo-Saxon Christian commonwealths in the postmodern world.

A patriot prince will join his subjects in demanding the autonomy of Anglo-Saxon institutions and the reconstitution of Anglo-Saxon tribes. Similarly, Anglo-Saxon Christian churches will promote the pooling of resources and the creation of businesses not just to provide co-ethnics with essential goods and services but also to repair the destruction caused by the secular system of political economy. Anglo-Saxon Christian commonwealths will become local, resilient, and networked "structures of survival." They will facilitate the "ethnically-based organization of neighborhoods and town councils," expanding Anglo-Saxon control over local media and economic institutions so as to serve the interests of that ethnoreligious community.[100] In our final chapter we discuss the principles of institutional architecture that should guide the regeneration of such "island communities."

---

100 cf Matthew Raphael Johnson, "Anarchy, the Ethnos and the State."

8.

Palingenesis: The Postmodern Rebirth of Anglo-Saxon Christendom

Over the past three centuries, Anglo-Saxon Protestants around the world have staked their survival, jointly and severally, on states and markets. Cocooned within the cornucopian mythology masking a debt-driven pseudo-prosperity, burning unimaginable quantities of cheap fossil fuels, WASPs are over-invested in organizational frameworks so complex and interdependent as to be unmanageable and unsustainable. A rising tide of disorder and chaos threatens the stability of the transnational market-state, leaving WASPs dangerously dependent upon decaying systems of biopolitical production to sustain their hothouse lifestyle. WASPs face compulsory liberation from the "slavery" of belonging to a nation, an identity, or a people as their historic homelands are overrun by the mobile multitude that claims citizenship in a neo-communist Empire. In short, WASPs are a dying race. Yet they carry the irreplaceable seed-stock for the postmodern rebirth of Anglo-Saxon tribes outside and apart from the interlocking systems of state and corporate power.[1]

Anglo-American corporate welfare states have peaked in wealth, power, and influence. In their rise to ascendancy, modern states "crushed all opposition, from empires to tribal confederations." They "extended their reach to control the economy, personal rights, borders, resources, security, laws, infrastructure, education, and health of their citizens." But, Philip Bobbit writes, "that control is coming to an end." A new environment created by globalization and the internet has swept "aside state power in ways no army could. States are losing control of their borders, economies, finances, people, and communications." Intertwined in a complex tangle of mutual interdependencies, states face serious repercussions

---

1 Philip Bobbit, *Terror and Consent: The Wars for the Twenty-First Century* (New York: Knopf, 2008); *cf* Michael Hardt and Antonio Negri, *Empire* (Cambridge, MA: Harvard University Press, 2000).

for solo action. "To further complicate matters, a new competitive force is emerging in this vacuum of state power." John Robb points to the whole gamut of nonstate actors, "terrorists, crime syndicates, gangs, and networked tribes…stepping into the breach to lay claim to areas once in the sole control of states."[2]

It is not just terrorists, criminal gangs, and other "discrete and insular minorities" who are propelling us toward a "feudal vision of the future."[3] Addicted to economic growth, the system is its own worst enemy. The promise of perpetual prosperity was always an illusion and reality is now biting hard. James Howard Kunstler tirelessly reminds us that we are not far away from the "world-wide power shortage" that will signal the end of the cheap-oil era. The rapid decay of industrial civilization as we know it will generate "political turbulence every bit as extreme as the economic conditions that prompt it." It is not just in the Third World that nonstate actors have acquired the ability to fight states and win. Even in the formerly peaceable kingdoms of the Anglo-Saxon world the onset of what Kunstler calls the Long Emergency will spread chaos and increasingly violent disorder. Even before the onset of the recent global financial crisis, the services that states offer WASPs who happen to be American, Australian, British, Canadian, or New Zealand citizens were in broad decline. Shrinking resources will spark racial, religious, and ethnic struggles; there will be winners and losers. Kunstler predicts that "The Long Emergency is going to be a tremendous trauma for the human race."[4]

Perhaps so, but the Anglo-Saxon race has the most to lose. In such a threat-rich environment, collective survival will depend upon the arts and science of racial self-defence. The stage is set "for the development of nonstate groups that represent the needs of minorities (or at a minimum members of the group) that aren't being served by the states to which they belong." Only socially cohesive peoples will be able "to take control of their own economic and social destiny" by appropriating the power of the state for their own purposes. Already the steady rise of urban ethnic gangs provides visible evidence that such "groups are developing the means of warfare that will allow them to not only survive but also *thrive* at the expense of states."[5] Before long, law-abiding WASP taxpayers will

---

2   John Robb, *Brave New War: The Next Stage of Terrorism and the End of Globalization* (Hoboken, NJ: John Wiley & Sons, 2007), 16-17.

3   *Ibid.*, 20.

4   James Howard Kunstler, *The Long Emergency: Surviving the Converging Catastrophes of the 21ˢᵗ Century* (London: Atlantic Books, 2006), 20.

5   Robb, *Brave New War*, 21.

be presented with ever-more powerful incentives to secede economically and culturally from spiritually corrupt and financially bankrupt corporate welfare states.

Kunstler envisages "the comprehensive downscaling, rescaling, downsizing, and relocalizing of all our activities, a radical reorganization of the way we live in the most fundamental particulars." He warns that "life in the decades ahead…will become increasingly and intensely local and smaller in scale." If their ethnoculture is to survive, WASPs must regenerate binding norms of in-group solidarity. A group survival strategy that relies heavily upon the kinship principle will meet resistance among WASPs accustomed to looking out for number one. Accordingly, the transition will be far from smooth and trouble-free. But the return of archaic life forms "is actually inevitable, whether we go there voluntarily or have to be dragged kicking and screaming into that future." The "cheap oil fiesta" is about to end in tears. "As energy supplies decline, the complexity of human enterprise will also decline in all fields, and the most technologically complex systems will be the ones most subject to dysfunction and collapse." The threat of systemic failure is not confined to national, state, and local governments; complex systems of corporate enterprise (think Walmart) "based on far-flung resource supply chains and long-range transport will be especially vulnerable. Producing food will become a problem of supreme urgency." The chaotic conditions of the Long Emergency will cripple corporate organizations "scaled to operate virtually like sovereign states run by oligarchies." Business corporations "can certainly be reorganized on the small, local community scale," but they "will not be the same as General Motors."[6]

Kunstler, not an especially religious person, nevertheless expects that the church will be the "most visible form of corporate organization" to survive the Long Emergency, if only because a religion of hope does not require endless supplies of cheap and abundant energy. Kunstler's scenario for a hand-made American future harks back to the archaic Anglo-Saxon Christian bioculture of Old England and its early colonial offshoots. But the Old Faith will spring back to life only if and when Anglican churches learn to celebrate rather than bewail their "Anglo-Saxon captivity."[7] At that point, the Church of England will become the nucleus around which a postmodern Anglo-Saxon tribalism crystallizes. When Anglicans return

---

6   Kunstler, *Long Emergency*, 238-239, 259.

7   *Ibid.*, 259; *cf.*, Kevin Ward, *A History of Global Anglicanism* (Cambridge: Cambridge University Press, 2006).

to their ethnoreligious roots, Anglo-Saxon Christians will be well-placed to weather the coming storms.

A New Dark Age

Leading strategic thinkers believe that "in most parts of the world, issues of security and stability" in the coming century will "revolve around the disruptive consequences of globalization, governance, public safety, inequality, urbanization, violent nonstate actors and the like." Some suggest that we are moving into the New Middle Ages. Others caution that a systemic failure "to manage the forces of global disorder...could lead to something even more forbidding—a New Dark Age."[8] To survive such a future intact, powerless and isolated individuals will have to "manufacture a strong community that protects, defends and advances the interests of its members." Even proudly post-ethnic WASPs will need to learn anew how to "build a tribe." An enviably upmarket, fashionably cosmopolitan lifestyle of high-intensity consumption will not only cease to be cool; it will be simply unsustainable. Tribes, on the other hand, are "the most survivable of all organizational types;" indeed, John Robb refers to tribal organization as "the organizational cockroach of human history."[9]

In the Long Emergency everyone will need to find a group of people loyal to him and to whom he is loyal in return. Simple tribes will have to be "built organically from the bottom up," starting by cementing ties to one's "extended family, a connection of blood." By extending "that network to include other families and worthy individuals" sharing a community of language, memory, and tradition, ethnic groups generate a sense of brotherhood between members of an "imagined community." Ethnogenesis is a biocultural process producing an imagined or "fictive" kinship between individuals belonging to different families and clans; the foundation myths of ethnoreligious communities provide individuals with "a sense of connectedness that leads to the creation of loyalty to the group."[10] Story-telling and rites of passage, reciprocal rights and obligations, self-sacrifice and mutual loyalty: all are essential ingredients for the production of tribal organizations, precisely the sort of socially cohesive,

---

8   Phil Williams, "From the New Middle Ages to a New Dark Age: The Decline of the State and US Strategy," : http://www.strategicstudiesinstitute.army.mil/pdffiles/pub867.pdf, 1.

9   John Robb, "Tribes!" March 6, 2009, posted at Global Guerillas: http://globalguerrillas.typepad.com/globalguerrillas/2009/03/manufacturing-fictive-kinship-.html

10   Id.

resilient communities in which Anglo-Saxon Christians will find refuge in the decades to come.

The Church of England gave birth to the Old English nation during the Dark Ages. In the New Dark Age, the ecclesiastical heirs and successors of St Augustine of Canterbury will be called upon to save Anglo-Saxon souls from the satanic forces unleashed by a disintegrating world-system. Whether they like it or not, WASPs cannot remain within the institutional carapace of the corporate welfare state; WASPs must "die to themselves" in the hope that they will be reborn into a global network of Anglo-Saxon Christian tribes. The regeneration of Anglo-Saxon Christendom will unite those who pray with those who work and those who fight in a "palingenetic" form of community. Simply put, Anglo-Saxon Christianity will be revived by "the vision of a radically *new* beginning which follows a period of destruction or perceived dissolution."[11]

Originally coined to denote certain rare biological phenomena, the term "palingenesis" had a rather bad press following its metaphorical translation into the realm of social and political philosophy. The Swiss naturalist Charles Bonnet (1720-1793) characterized the life-cycle of aphids as palingenetic because "every female individual contains within her the 'germs' of all the creatures that originate from her, the one generation within the other." In a more philosophical vein, Bonnet applied the idea of "palingenesis" to every situation in which the birth of an individual is "therefore always a rebirth where the original germ of existence of the living thing reasserts itself." Palingenesis became the central theme in his "intriguing account of the staged or graded development of life on earth."[12]

Because Bonnet's account relied so much on the role of catastrophes and unexpected upheavals in the advance of life, Immanuel Kant roundly denounced the use of palingenesis as a metaphor for political change. A man of the Enlightenment, Kant confidently asserted that the progress of mankind could be guided by the power of secular reason. For him, the concept of "metamorphosis" was the most appropriate biological metaphor to describe successful political change. Kant was "a proponent of political improvement with radical goals but which employs nonradical means." With the spectacle of the French Revolution before his eyes, Kant recoiled from the prospect of palingenetic political transformations: the idea of palingenesis conjured up "the trauma of a political death and the romance of a sudden rebirth, one that, in his view, is far too abrupt to

11 Roger Griffin, *The Nature of Fascism* (London: Routledge, 1993), 33.

12 Howard Williams, "*Metamorphosis* or *Palingenesis*? Political Change in Kant," (2001) 63(4) *Review of Politics* 693, at 707-708.

bring about lasting or desirable political change." Kant refused to accept
that "the birth of a new structure can only take place with the completed
death of the old." Accordingly, he set himself against the ancient philosophers who "believed that the world was born from chaos and 'would also
sink back into the same.'" Metamorphosis, he counselled, "is a kind of natural change which is not simply destructive of past forms." It always leaves
room for an immanent "intelligence" managing the process of change and
development directing both organisms and societies toward higher forms
of life. The Kantian program of political change requires that all human
societies "gradually become republics with full separation of powers leading ultimately to a peaceful worldwide civil society."[13]

Pace Kant, however, no amount of intelligence will save the transnational market-state from catastrophic collapse. If anything, history will
record that the managerial revolution ran onto the rocks through a surfeit
of "intelligence" as a well-credentialed, ostentatiously multiracial, "meritocracy" rushed in to fill the spiritual vacuum left by the simultaneous
disappearance of Christian faith and Anglo-Saxon racial solidarity. Kant,
denying the truth of the Resurrection, and perhaps in fear of death, proposed that mankind somehow transform itself into a perpetual innovation machine. That project is now running on empty. The system of political economy is visibly dying. But, because the *novus ordo seclorum* was,
from the beginning, a monstrous mutation of the archaic Anglo-Saxon
Christian bioculture, its death will not be the end of the world. Anglo-
Saxon Christian tribes will rise phoenix-like from the ruins of political
and economic modernity. Under those conditions, palingenesis will be
personal as well as political; individuals will appear to be altogether different beings as the long-lost impulse toward in-group altruism is revived.
Inspired, perhaps, by the advent of a Patriotic King, whole families will be
reborn into the sacramental community of the Old Faith.[14]

Those who pray for the rebirth of the Anglo-Saxon *Volksgeist* are sure
to attract charges of neo-fascism. One influential academic definition of
fascism provides such accusations with a superficial but spurious air of
plausibility. Roger Griffin has rescued the concept of palingenesis from
obsolescence by classifying fascism as "a genus of political ideology whose
mythic core in its various permutations is a palingenetic form of populist
ultra-nationalism." On his analysis, German National Socialists and Italian
Fascists alike were inspired by a core mythology "welding the 'people' into

---

13   *Ibid.*, 693-694, 699-700.

14   *Cf.*, Viscount Bolingbroke, "The Idea of a Patriot King," in *Bolingbroke: Political Writings*
     David Armitage, ed (Cambridge: Cambridge University Press, 1997), 251.

a dynamic national community under new elites infused with new heroic values." In that generic sense, fascism is "a populist, trans-class movement of purifying, cathartic national rebirth (palingenesis)" aiming to stem the tide of modernist decadence.[15]

A postmodern Anglo-Saxon Christian Commonwealth of necessity will be another palingenetic form of community; it will not emerge through the peaceful metamorphosis of the corporate welfare state. Rather it will offer salvation in the midst of catastrophe and collapse. In that sense, the appearance of a Patriot King will bear some resemblance to the advent of Hitler, Mussolini, or even Roosevelt. The crucial distinction between fascism and Anglo-Saxon Christianity is that fascism is a neo-pagan political religion that renders unto Caesar not just that which belongs to Caesar but all that we owe to God as well.

Fascist doctrine prescribes "an obligatory code of *ethical commandments* for the citizen" and institutes "a collective *political liturgy* in order to celebrate the *deification of the state* and the *cult of the leader*." Anglo-Saxon Christians, no less than Roman Catholics, see in such totalitarian religions "a single aspect of the much larger phenomenon of the re-emergence of the paganism and idolatry…that, in all their cultural and political manifestations" deny the existence of God and deify man.[16] The deification of the corporate welfare state subverts the ethnoreligious integrity of Anglo-Saxon Christianity. Iconic figures such as priests, bishops, or kings are to be revered as holy men not worshipped as gods. Contemporary neo-communism is another political religion, sacralizing the manufactured "diversity" of a borderless Empire. Corporations and the state have shown themselves to be, at best, indifferent to the fate of the Anglo-Saxon race; if Anglo-Saxon Christians know what is good for them, they will reciprocate that sentiment. By extricating themselves from the market-state, Anglo-Saxon Christians can keep the forces of evil at arm's length.

Tribes and Networks in the Transnational Market-State

Christians need not fear the palingenetic process of death and rebirth. Fascists and communists are not alone in their preoccupation with

---

15 Griffin, *Nature of Fascism*, 27, x.

16 Emilio Gentile, "The Sacralisation of Politics: Definitions, Interpretations and Reflections on the Question of Secular Religion and Totalitarianism," (2000) 1(1) *Totalitarian Movements and Political Religions* 18, at 40, 46, 48.

regeneration and the return to a lost past. Griffin points out that, far from being confined to fascist doctrine, "the most obvious well-head of palingenetic myth in the wider sense is religion. The resurrection of Jesus Christ places one such myth at the very center of a whole faith." Metaphysical notions of "death and rebirth pervade the symbolism of baptism, communion, and Easter celebrations." The *political* religions of fascism and communism drew much of their imagery and symbolism from Christian traditions. Even as totalitarian movements plotted the destruction of Christian civilization, they freely and unashamedly mimicked, borrowed, and ransacked the spiritual treasures of the Old Faith. Should the soft totalitarianism of our neo-communist political religion prove to be as ephemeral as the fascist cult of the state, the time will be ripe for the reappearance of an Anglo-Saxon *Volkskirche*.[17]

The regeneration of a world-wide network of Anglo-Saxon tribes will not be a maladaptive throwback to a long-since superseded form of ethnoreligious community. The tribal organizations that Anglo-Saxons build over the next century will be postmodern rather than prehistoric in form and function. Indeed, they will be on the cutting edge of evolutionary development. Such conclusions are supported by macro-evolutionary studies of the way in which people have organized their societies across the ages. David Ronfeldt, for example, suggests "that the historic evolution and increasing complexity of societies has been a function of the ability to use and combine...four forms of governance in what appears to be a natural progression." He describes the four types in the following manner:

1. the kinship-based *tribe*, as denoted by the structure of extended families, clans, and other lineage systems;

2. the hierarchical *institution*, as exemplified by the army, the (Catholic) church, and ultimately the bureaucratic state;

3. the competitive-exchange *market*, as symbolized by merchants and traders responding to forces of supply and demand;

4. and the collaborative *network*, as found today in the web-like ties among some non-governmental organizations devoted to social advocacy.[18]

---

17 Griffin, *Nature of Fascism*, 33; Gentile, "Sacralisation of Politics," 23-24.

18 David F Ronfeldt, "Tribes, Institutions, Markets, Networks: A Framework About Societal Evolution," Rand Corporation: http://www.rand.org/pubs/papers/2005/P7967.pdf, 2.

Ronfeldt sums up the long range evolution of societies in a formula he calls the "TIMN framework." Societies that learn to combine these forms into a system survive and perhaps even prosper. Others will fall by the wayside. "Over the ages, societies organized in tribal (T) terms lose to societies that also develop institutional (I) systems to become T+I societies, normally with strong states. In turn, these are superseded by societies that allow space to develop the market form (M), and become T+I+M societies." We are currently witnessing the rise of the network (N) form. "Power and influence appear to be migrating to actors who are skilled at developing multiorganizational networks, and at operating in environments where networks are an appropriate, spreading form of organization." Rosenfeldt suggests that the network form will inaugurate "a new phase of evolution in which T+I+M+N societies will emerge and take the lead."[19]

Like Kant, Ronfeldt prefers to think of social evolution as a process of metamorphosis, yet such a smooth evolutionary progression is far from a sure thing; catastrophes, chaos, and chance can capsize the most successful system. Indeed, the future may unfold as a very different story of palingenesis. Even now, the dysfunctional, depraved and downright evil character of the global I+M system is an open insult to the constitutional faith of well-meaning WASP conformists. As threats multiply, far-sighted WASPs will build tribal networks to provide themselves with food, shelter, transportation, and security. T+N structures of survival will become increasingly prominent in a dangerous, disorderly, and chaotic world. Success will depend upon the capacity of T+N structures to foster a sense of ethnic kinship across existing class, jurisdictional, and geographical boundaries. Anglo-Saxons who pray, those who work, and those who fight will be integrated into autonomous networks of tribal organizations. A transterritorial confederation of Anglo-Saxon tribes will secede from but retain an arm's length relationship with the market-state represented graphically in the following manner: (T+N)↔(I+M).

Churches, families, and corporations will provide multi-organizational platforms for the reconstruction of the tripartite functionality of archaic Anglo-Saxon Christian societies. As it did during the reign of Alfred the Great, the trinitarian structure of society will resemble the three legs of a stool supporting the majesty of the Crown. Once again, royal authority will become the fountain of justice from which flows a law common to the three estates. Let us finish by considering the constitutional principles upon which the archaic estates of the realm will be reconstituted and governed in years to come.

19 *Ibid.*, 3.

Praying for an Anglo-Saxon Ethnonation

The church will play a constructive role in the constitution of a postmodern Anglo-Saxon Christian commonwealth. Anglicans know in their hearts that the Church of England was born as the national church of the *Angelcynn*. In the dark times to come it will reassert the orthodox Christian doctrine of nations in opposition to the feckless neo-communist theology of the global Anglican Communion. In the nineteenth century, FD Maurice taught that the "form of character…intended for each nation" could only "be developed by the 'spiritual body' within it." For that reason, the Reformation Church of England protested against the pretended transnational authority of the Papacy. Englishmen became Protestants because they recognized their nation as both "a theological fact" and "a providential reality." At the same time, by insisting that Christ remained the sole legitimate head of the universal church, English Protestants were more Catholic than the Pope. Their view was that Roman Catholicism had stripped every *national* church of its iconic role in the tripartite "spiritual constitution" of family, nation, and Church. The Papacy, in setting "aside the reality of the incarnation by asserting its own visible headship," outraged and insulted "the communion of the visible and invisible worlds." Anglicanism provided a church *for* the English people. English Christians were bound "to resist every power, papal, imperial, democratic, which strives to destroy the peculiarities of race, family, individual." Maurice condemned attempts to dissolve the trinitarian unity of family, nation, and church as profane violations of the divine order aiming "to construct a society which shall be an artificial corporation, not a living body."[20]

The coming Anglican Reformation will be grounded in the clear understanding that the preservation and even the separation of tribes, nations, and races are mandated by the Bible. Such a view in no way contradicts the faith of Anglican evangelicals in the primacy and sufficiency of Scripture.[21] Only those blinded by the secular humanist cult of equality can fail to see that "the Bible teaches that mankind is composed not of an amorphous mass of individuals but of nations." Maurice was sure that the "dispersions" and "distinctions" of the nations were "the fulfilment of God's designs for the race which He had made after His own likeness." Others observe that in Genesis 10 we see that "God organized mankind

---

20 Jeremy Morris, *FD Maurice and the Crisis of Christian Authority* (Oxford: Oxford University Press, 2008), 95, 103-105. Maurice, of course, automatically identified the English nation with "its" State, an equation that is now not just utterly untenable but downright risible.

21 *Cf.*, Reginald H Fuller, "Scripture," in Stephen Sykes, ed *The Study of Anglicanism* Revised Edition (London: SPCK, 1998), 90-91.

into discrete nations in the aftermath of the Great Flood." In Genesis
11 the sons of Noah built the Tower of Babel in an attempt to frustrate
God's design thus demonstrating their power and independence. God's
response was to destroy the Tower and scatter its builders "over the face of
all the earth." But, as HA Scott Trask observes, "the scattering was neither
arbitrary nor chaotic. According to the Biblical account, people moved
with their nations in an orderly exodus that fulfilled God's purposes."
Each nation or people received its own lands separated from the others by
territorial boundaries. Clearly, both the Old and the New Testament sanction the love of nations, each grounded in its own distinctive ethnic stock.
Maurice contended that the "New Testament showed the completion or
fulfilment of that which had been partially effected in the Old." While the
one presents the history of "a peculiar nation," the other reveals "a universal Church unfolding itself out of that nation" to take root in other nations
and peoples throughout the ancient world.[22] Thus began the history of
Christendom during the Age of Incarnation. During the second European
millennium, the Age of Disincarnation, the Anglican Church mortgaged
the *Volksgeist* of its parishioners, first to the papacy, then to the state and,
more recently, to its corporate benefactors.

In common with other mainstream Anglo-Saxon Protestant denominations, global Anglicanism urges "Christians to do all they can to restore
mankind's lost unity by tearing down national boundaries, promoting
mass immigration, teaching English as a universal language, and inter-
marrying freely with members of other racial families." This modernist
interpretation of Scripture "repeats the sin of those who built the Tower of
Babel." Indiscriminate and large-scale Third World immigration into formerly Anglo-Saxon countries is antagonistic to the divinely-sanctioned
love of nation. Anglicans, by bestowing their blessing upon the alien
invasion of every Anglo-Saxon homeland, are complicit in "a rebellious
project that defies God's plan for world order based on discrete nations
each residing within its own lands."[23] Such perverted displays of Anglo-
Saxon ethnomasochism rightly inspire disgust and contempt in other
more patriotic peoples. After all, it is through the nation that we enter
into eternal life in the Kingdom of Christ. Maurice claimed that "there
is an immortality for a nation, and that when one of its citizens separates
his interests from its interests he loses the practical sense of his immortality" grounded in "his relation to the righteous and everlasting God."

22   HA Scott Trask, "The Christian Doctrine of Nations," (2001) 12(7) *American Renaissance*
     1, 3-5: http://www.amren.com/ar/2001/07/; Morris, *Crisis of Christian Authority*, 104-105.

23   Trask, "Christian Doctrine of Nations," 4.

In other words, because every "nation exists in the acknowledging of the Righteous God," it must oppose "all attempts to suppress its independence under God."[24] Contemporary WASPs need a church proud to affirm that solidarity with one's kinfolk is no sin.

Russians are fortunate to have such a church. Only recently the bishops of the Russian Orthodox Church declared: "The universal nature of the Church...does not mean that Christians should have no right to national identity and national self-expressions." Therefore, their ancient church calls upon Russians to preserve and develop their Christian culture through the self-awareness of their peoplehood. Every Orthodox Christian belongs to an ethnoreligious community. In a passage of particular significance to members of the Anglo-Saxon diaspora, the bishops affirmed that "the Orthodox Christian is called to love his fatherland, which has a territorial dimension, and his brothers by blood who live everywhere in the world." It should not be a surprise to Anglicans that the New Testament "reaffirms the national and ethnic distinctions of the Old Testament, if anything in stronger and clearer terms." Every Sunday school should remind Anglo-Saxon children (and their parents) that God "made from one [Adam] every nation [*ethnos*] of mankind [*anthropon*] to live on all the face of the earth, having determined their appointed times, and the boundaries of their habitation"[25] The Anglican Church was founded by a monk who followed Christ's mandate to go and "make disciples of all the nations [*ethnē*]."[26] God certainly entered the hearts of medieval Anglo-Saxons; Old England's civilization was saturated from top to bottom with visions of the Redeemer who suffered, died, and was buried, only to rise again on the third day. If godless WASPs want to find him again, they must keep faith with the blood and bone of their ancestors.

Most contemporary Anglicans, however, shrink in horror from the thought that the Holy Spirit was incarnate in the flesh and blood of the Anglo-Saxon peoples. But Jesus Christ was not a generic human being; through his mother Mary's flesh and blood he was born into the tribe of Judah. By the power of the Holy Spirit and the force of law, he was received as the adopted son of Joseph, a lineal descendant of David who, many hundreds of years earlier, had been anointed by God as the King of Israel. Sent to redeem his fellow Jews, Christ suffered death at the hands of their leaders. Because his lordship was rejected by the Jews, the risen Christ found an earthly habitation elsewhere. In the Age of Incarnation,

---

24   Morris, *Crisis of Christian Authority*, 103-105.

25   Trask, "Christian Doctrine of Nations," 5; Acts 17:26.

26   Matthew 28:19

Christian Europe became the New Israel, a spiritual kingdom within which the God-Man was received as the King of Kings. Christ revealed Himself not just in Scriptures and patristic theology but through the faithful works of countless men and women who prayed, fought, and worked to lay the foundations of European civilization. Christendom was constituted within a unique and irreplaceable family of European nations where kings and knights, bishops and humble parish priests, peasants and workers lived in an enchanted world as iconic representations of the Trinity.

In times past, every European ethnonation sought a mystic union with Christ through the medium of its own distinctive bioculture. Until every nation enters into the holy, catholic, and apostolic faith, the "universal brotherhood of man" is little more than a pious hope. There is no such thing as a "human being;" the word is little more than an empty philosophical abstraction. The experience of belonging to particular families, tribes, and nations has always brought Christians closer to God. Those of mixed race, those who "belong" to two or more nations, those, in other words, whose hearts are forever torn are to be pitied. Somewhat like adopted children, they suffer from a sort of spiritual birth defect. By nature, they are only partially and provisionally open to the saving grace that comes through blood and belonging. For that reason, the apostle Paul took pains to assure fellow Jews that there was a place reserved for their ancient ethnonation (Israel) in Christ's spiritual kingdom alongside the Greeks, the Romans and, centuries later, the Anglo-Saxons.[27] Indeed, the Church inspired the birth of the English nation. Today, however, the Church of England blesses those who administer ethno-euthanasia to its comatose namesake nation.

The Next Reformation

The next Protestant Reformation must recall the Anglican Church to its original mission to shepherd the Anglo-Saxon race into the Kingdom of God. Whether the miraculous success of that first mission to the Angles can be repeated in the twenty-first century remains to be seen. Slowly but surely, however, at least three closely related, if still separate strands of Reformed theology are laying the groundwork for a comprehensive challenge to the neo-communist dogmas that now poison the minds of Anglo-Saxon Christians. These counter-movements are known as kinism, preterism, and covenant creationism.

---

27 Trask, "Christian Doctrine of Nations," 7-8.

"Kinism" affirms that the orthodox Christian doctrine of nations is rooted in the reality of racial differences. In opposition to the race-mixing agenda of mainstream Christianity, kinists condemn miscegenation as a sin against the seventh Commandment. In their view, the sin of adultery encompasses much more than illicit sexual intercourse with a married person. They warn "against any and all adulteration, marital or national, as it invariably leads to divided loyalties and a compromising of security in all spheres." They insist that Old Testament laws against hybridisation, unequal-yoking, and bastardisation of families and races were not annulled in the New Testament. "The burden of the law," kinists say, "is thus against inter-religious, inter-racial, and inter-cultural marriages, in that they normally go against the very community which marriage is designed to establish."[28] Most sociobiologists are inclined to agree. Unfortunately, WASP sociobiologists tend to be religious sceptics who are uninterested in either mainstream Christianity or fundamentalist Protestantism. A fusion of kinism and sociobiology can achieve critical mass only when a Reformed Anglicanism brings WASP unbelievers into the Christian fold.

For such conversions to occur, however Christianity must bridge the credibility gap now separating Anglo-Saxon Protestants from their racially-conscious co-ethnics. This is where "preterism" (from the Latin *præter*: past) has an important role to play. Religious sceptics have long had a field day debunking the official creeds promulgated by organized Christianity. In a celebrated lecture, "Why I am Not a Christian," delivered in 1927 to the National Secular Society, Bertrand Russell mocked those still waiting for Christ to return in clouds of glory. Of course, Russell thought it "quite doubtful whether Christ ever existed at all;" but, he continued, "taking the Gospel narrative as it stands," Christ certainly thought that he would come again "before the death of all the people who were living at that time." He went on to cite "a great many texts that prove that." And, indeed, there are many such passages such as Matthew 16:28, to cite but one, in which Christ assures his listeners that "there are some of those standing here who will not taste death before they have seen the Son of Man coming in his kingdom." At long last, however, a growing group of Protestant preachers are seizing that skeptical bull by the horns. Preterists maintain that the prophecies of his return were fulfilled before the last of his apostles died, thereby endowing the historical Jesus with an altogether unexpected and explosive significance. A preterist reading

28 See, for example, Ehud, "A Kinist Elucidation," (Summer 2010) *The Kinist Review* 4-23, available online at: http://www.kinism.net/publications/tkr_summer_2010.pdf; Rousas John Rushdoony, *The Institutes of Biblical Law* Vol. 1 (Phillipsburg, NJ: Presbyterian and Reformed Publishers, 1973), 256-257.

of the Bible suggests that those who look forward to the Second Coming of Christ at "the end of the world" have lost the plot of the Bible story. Having projected Christ's *parousia* into some indeterminate time in the near to distant future, fundamentalist Christians today are no less blind than secular humanists such as Russell to the apocalyptic meaning of the siege of Jerusalem in AD 70. By any standard, the destruction of the Jerusalem temple was an event of world-historical significance; not least of all to Jews since it resulted in the death of over a million of their co-ethnics and forced exile for countless others.[29] Preterism adopts a common sense reading of Scriptures, simply taking Christ at his word. The biblical prophets, together with Christ and his apostles, repeatedly predicted that God would destroy the temple. Even Bertrand Russell would be hard-pressed to deny that biblical prophecy squares with the known history of Old Israel and the destruction of Jerusalem by fire and sword.

In a nutshell, preterists debunk the futurist eschatology which both fundamentalist and mainstream Christians share with secular progressives.[30] Secular futurists retain a naïve faith in the power of science to create heaven on earth through the miraculous powers of technological progress. Their creed is not at all dissimilar to the belief that Christ's triumphal return will inaugurate the Kingdom of God at some as yet future time. The conviction that the "last days" prophesied in the Book of Revelations have yet to come rests upon the canonical authority of the Nicene Creed composed by the Church in the fourth century AD. Many American Protestants believe that when Christ comes again in glory on "clouds of heaven" the dead will be resurrected in the flesh; literal-minded pre-millennialists also expect that after Judgement Day Christ will establish a physical kingdom over which he will rule for a literal thousand years from a physical throne in a restored temple geographically located in the city of Jerusalem. Preterists dismiss such predictions of an apocalyptic "Rapture" event. They contend that the clear text of Scripture shows that all of the Biblical prophesies of a new heaven and new earth, not just those in Revelations, were fulfilled in AD 70. In August of that year, Christ came (the *parousia* or Second Coming) to oversee the destruction of the temple in Jerusalem, the physical center of the old heaven and old earth occupied by God's first people. In Revelation, we see the Old Covenant world of

---

29 Bertrand Russell, *Why I am Not a Christian* (New York: Simon & Schuster, 1957), 16; Flavius Josephus, *The Jewish War* rev ed (Harmondsworth: Penguin Classics, 1984).

30 A comprehensive discussion of the differences between fulfilled (preterist) and unfulfilled (futurist) eschatology can be found in David Green, ed *House Divided: Bridging the Gap in Reformed Eschatology. A Preterist Response to When Shall These Things Be?* (Ramona, CA: Vision Publishing, 2009).

Israel sinking into lakes of fire while the New Covenant world enters into history. The physical temple in Jerusalem makes its exit in a spectacular cataclysm; a new creation becomes incarnate in the church, the ecclesiastical Body of Christ. There the Bible story ends.

Preterism confronts the embarrassing contradiction exposed by Russell between the historical creeds and the plain language of the Scriptures. In fact, it is ridiculously easy to identify Bible passages in which Christ and his apostles promise that He will return "soon" or "quickly," and certainly before the present generation passed away. If the preterist reading of Scriptures is hermeneutically sound, Christ's *parousia* did not entail the physical end of planet Earth. Nor does Genesis have to do with the creation of the material universe. Instead, from beginning to end, the Bible tells the story of God's first, habitually unfaithful, people, the nation of Israel. The Book of Genesis describes the creation of a covenant world, the "old heaven" and the "old earth," not the origins of the planet Earth and all living things upon it. But that Old Covenant world ended in AD 70; afterwards every province of Christendom inherited the New Covenant world promised by the Son of God. No longer does God rest within a physical temple in a particular city; rather, every faithful Christian nation serves as a shrine of the indwelling Holy Spirit. In circumstances where Christians are held captive by the forces of the anti-nation, however, such theologies have subversive implications.

Indeed, preterism is closely related to a third deviant strand of theological thinking bubbling away in the Christian underground. "Covenant creationism" contends that the end of the Bible story is foretold in its beginning, in the Book of Genesis.[31] This approach to Biblical hermeneutics flatly denies that Genesis was written as an account of the physical creation of the universe. Nor was it intended to explain the origins of mankind. From this perspective, Darwin's evolutionary theories are entirely consistent with the view that Genesis deals, not with the origins of mankind at large, but with the first men made after the image of God; the people whose cosmic role was to represent God to the rest of creation.[32] Adam, therefore, was not the first human being but merely the (bad) seed from which the intermittently holy nation of Israel was destined to spring. Covenant creationism lends implicit support to the allegedly heretical hypothesis "that Adam might not be the progenitor of the entire human

---

31 The clearest exposition of "covenant creationism" and of its connection to preterism is: Timothy P Martin and Jeffrey L Vaughan, *Beyond Creation Science: New Covenant Creation From Genesis to Revelation* (Whitehall, MT: Apocalyptic Vision Press, 2007).

32 John H Walton, *The Lost World of Genesis One: Ancient Cosmology and the Origins Debate* (Downers Grove, IL: IVP Academic, 2009), 69.

race and there might be non-adamic peoples in existence."[33] Preterism and covenant creationism reveal that there is no necessary conflict between the science, whether in astronomy, geology, or paleoanthropology, and a biblically-grounded Christian faith. A materialist or scientific cosmology is interested in the physical structure of the world not in the divine purposes that it may serve.

By contrast, the first chapter of the Bible's first book "was never intended to be an account of material origins." According to John Walton, Genesis 1 reflects an ancient cosmology; it "was intended as an account of functional origins" of the cosmos inhabited by a holy nation made in the image of God. Its priestly authors viewed "the cosmos as a temple." Later in the history of Old Israel, the Jerusalem temple came to be conceived as a mini-cosmos within which God was at rest in the holiest inner sanctum. Within the cosmic order each of the elements of creation, light and darkness, the waters and the dry land, the birds of the air, the beasts of the field, the fish of the sea, together with man and woman, had its own distinctive function to perform. Taken as a whole, the Bible is a story about God's purposes in the covenantal world of Israel, from the first Adam, who was expelled from the Garden of Eden, until the apocalyptic return of the last Adam in AD 70. "In the biblical way of thinking, the objects and phenomena of the world function the way they do because of God's creative purposes." The creation story in Genesis 1 is consummated when the heavens and earth are completed (in Genesis 2:1-2) by the inauguration of the cosmic temple where God takes "up his residence and from where he runs the cosmos."[34] In Jerusalem, the temple was made by hand as the physical representation of the cosmos created by God. Following the stone-by-stone destruction of the Jerusalem temple in AD 70, the New Covenant creation came into being as a spiritual kingdom within which the Body of Christ was the numinous temple of a "new heaven" and "new earth."

Just as preterism gives rise to covenant creationism, the latter leads reformed theology back full circle to kinism. The Old Covenant bound the holy nation of Israel to God; the New Covenant extended the grace of God to every nation (*ethnos*) of the known world. The leaves of the tree of life in the New Jerusalem were to serve "for the healing of the nations."[35] Old Israel was no more. Only a remnant was saved to carry the holy seed of Israel unto the nations. As the faith spread from Jewish Christians

---

33 David N Livingstone, *Adam's Ancestors: Race, Religion, and the Politics of Human Origins* (Baltimore, MD: Johns Hopkins University Press, 2008), 24.

34 Walton, *Lost World*, 132, 144, 146.

35 Revelations 22:2-3.

to the Gentile peoples of the Roman Empire, the catholic and apostolic church created a New Israel. Jews who reject Christ stand outside the New Jerusalem; many became its sworn enemies.

Covenant creationism packs a powerful kinist punch. Implicitly at least, it counsels Christians to embrace ethnoreligious realism, insisting that there can be no seamlessly Judeo-Christian tradition of ecumenical harmony. Christians and Jews who reject Christ cannot both be God's people. On Judgement Day, Christ sentenced the stiff-necked synagogue of Satan to spiritual death.[36] Accordingly, for more than eighteen centuries, every Christian nation adjured Jews within their midst to recognize their Redeemer, thus ending their age-old rebellion against God. In sharp contrast to Jews, Anglo-Saxons eagerly entered into the new covenant world.

Attuned to racial differences, kinists understand the powerful biocultural affinity between the early Christian church and the pagan tribes of Anglo-Saxon England as well as the prominent place occupied by covenants in tribal social structures. Conversely, once their churches downplay the importance of *blood* covenants to the spiritual life of both family and nation, the ancestral attachment of Anglo-Saxon Protestants to the Body of Christ is bound to fade away. Because our recently-established civil religion denies that faith is passed on through the blood of a large, partly-inbred extended family, the proposition nation can never become a holy nation. By contrast, the Christian nation is a macro-organism closely related to the kinist "trustee family;" both rest upon a covenant between the dead, the living, and the unborn. The living members of the trustee family "see themselves as trustees of the family blood, rights, property, name, and position for their lifetime. They have an inheritance from the past to be preserved and developed for the future."[37] The trustee family is an archaic Christian idea that will revive in the New Dark Age. The next Reformation will almost certainly depend upon the reservoirs of trust generated when such families come together to create resilient local communities capable of surviving the coming collapse.

Rescuing Proletarian Families

Whether one takes a biblical or biocultural view of the matter, the family rather than the individual must be the molecular building block of

---

36   See, Chapter one, "The Synagogue of Satan," in E Michael Jones, *The Jewish Revolutionary Spirit and Its Impact on World History* (South Bend, IN: Fidelity Press, 2008).

37   RJ Rushdoony, "The Trustee Family," (Winter 1977-78) 4(2) *Journal of Christian Reconstruction: Symposium on the Family*, 12.

postmodern Anglo-Saxon tribalism; what Robert Nisbet called "the key link of the social chain of being." Nisbet warned that neither intellectual growth nor social order nor "the roots of liberty can possibly be maintained among a people unless the kinship tie is both strong and has functional significance and symbolic authority." The first great contribution of kinship to society, according to Nisbet, is "the sense of membership in and continuity of the social order, generation after generation." No less important is "the spur to individual achievement, in all areas, that the intimacy of the family alone seems to effect."[38] It is no accident that the modern corporate welfare state has worked tirelessly to crush the family beneath its destructive weight and, to date, it has very largely succeeded.

Not every form of the family possesses functional importance while generating symbolic authority. Certainly, the proletarian family does not. Frédéric Le Play, a nineteenth century French critic of the Enlightenment, observed that "the populations of workers that live under the new industrial regimes in the West" were dominated by an especially unstable family form. Typically, the proletarian family is formed by "the union of two spouses…grows through the birth of children. Later, it shrinks when these children, lacking obligation towards parents and kin, establish themselves elsewhere." When the parents die, "the families are dissolved." Having left the paternal house and gained his inheritance, each child "enjoys the fruits of his labors himself." No longer having "any care for the needs of his kin, if he is skilled he will soon gain a higher social position." If unskilled or prone to vice, the grown child will find himself riding the down escalator. Particularly in France, the proletarian form of the family spread "among the wealthy classes because of a forced equality of inheritance."[39]

As an alternative to the proletarian family, Le Play advocated a variant on the "trustee family" that he called the "stem family." Such families fuse kinship and private property in such a way as to promote the dignity of labor and the restoration of authority within households. The distinguishing features of the stem family are "liberty of testament balanced by a strong custom of handing on the inheritance whole and entire." Even children "who go abroad seeking fortune with their inheritance" remain rooted in the family. "If the designated heir dies prematurely, the younger children are always ready to renounce a brilliant future and to return to the family home to fill the void that has opened." Writing in 1864, Le Play

---

38 Robert Nisbet, *Twilight of Authority* (New York: Oxford University Press, 1975), 260, 253.

39 Frédéric Le Play, "On the Family," in Christopher Olaf Blum, *Critics of the Enlightenment: Readings in the French Counter-Revolutionary Tradition* (Wilmington, DE: ISI Books, 2004), 228.

was still able to hold up the English and North American family as the best working model of the stem family.[40]

Today, we can only shake our heads in disbelief. During the twentieth century, middle class WASP families were proletarianized to the point where they lost any resemblance to Le Play's ideal. Family homes are routinely flipped for short-term financial gain while feminism flattens the natural differences between husbands and wives, fathers and mothers, even men and women. Law decrees that marriage and the family are little more than evanescent products of instantly revocable personal choices. In these dark circumstances, postmodern Anglo-Saxon tribes need to recover the depth of being that once welled up from the interior life of households and families in Old England and their colonial offshoots in America and Oceania.

Strange as it seems now, Le Play looked to the Anglo-Saxon household of the mid-nineteenth century as a working model of the stem family. Le Play reported that the laws and customs governing marriage and inheritance in nineteenth century England were highly favorable to "unity of action within the family as well as a judicious division of responsibility." Whenever marriages are fruitful, it seemed a law of nature that mothers will be "kept at home by the duties of maternity." The "true function of the woman," therefore, "is to govern the family home." Fathers delegate their authority to mothers acting within that clearly circumscribed domain. The responsibility of husbands and fathers was to "look after the exterior property and defend it against encroachment, exercise the duties of a profession and fight for the interests related to it, and, finally, uphold the rights of the family before commune, province, and state."[41] Le Play identifies the family home as the proprietary foundation for unity within the extended family in both town and country. The family home is no less important to those who pray and those who fight than it is to those who work. But those who work are in immediate need of property that lends itself to productive uses if they are to escape the chains of dependency that bind the proletarian to his job or, still worse, his social welfare entitlements. The Anglican Church has a special responsibility to reverse the flattening of family life among Anglo-Saxon Protestants. It can and should do that by helping its communicants to establish family farms, workshops, and businesses. Such a model of Christian charity would provide the material basis for the renaissance of the kinship principle among Anglo-Saxons living through the Long Emergency.

---

40   *Ibid.*, 229.

41   *Ibid.*, 240-241.

"The salient fact about life in the decades ahead," according to Kunstler, "is that it will become increasingly and intensely local and smaller in scale." As energy supplies contract, the production of food will require more human and animal labor. The economy for "decades to come will center on farming."[42] Anglo-Saxon tribalism will find fertile soil in the countryside. Rural areas almost everywhere remain regions where Anglo-Saxons are still comparatively thick on the ground. But even in towns and cities, it is possible to provide material support for the growth of Anglo-Saxon stem families by encouraging the development of regulatory guilds among craftsmen, technicians, and professionals. Self-governing guilds will not be directly involved in production but will instead "provide a measure of organization and support to small owners" whether tradesmen, retailers, manufacturers, or professionals. Such self-governing bodies will concern themselves with assuring supplies of raw materials, disseminating technological advances, conducting training and apprenticeship programs, ensuring equitable prices and preventing undue concentration of property and market shares.[43] Given such a widespread reversion to archaic forms in the world of work, the pathological progress of the proletarian family can be halted, even reversed.

Bodies Politic in a Christian Commonwealth

Within contemporary proletarian families, individuals are conceived as the basic building blocks of society. Within the Anglo-Saxon Christian tribal networks of the future, the family will become the dominant metaphor for society at large. The three estates of the realm will be bound together in an organic unity. The resulting body politic will resemble "a large, partly-inbred extended family."[44] Conversely, each family will take on some of the attributes of a body politic. Under such circumstances, it may be time to re-open the nineteenth century debate on "the subjection

---

42 Kunstler, Long Emergency, 239.

43 Thomas Storck, "Capitalism and Distributism: Two Systems at War," in Tobias J Lanz, Beyond Capitalism & Socialism: A New Statement for an Old Ideal (Norfolk, VA: IHS Press, 2008), 80; Arthur J Penty, "Distributism: A Manifesto," in Distributist Perspectives: Essays on the Economics of Justice and Charity, Vol II (Norfolk, VA: IHS Press, 2004), 94-95.

44 Steve Sailer, "It's All Relative: Putting Putting Race in its Proper Perspective," 2 August, 2008: http://www.vdare.com/sailer/presentation.htm

of women."[45] In a world made by hand, the archaic division of labor rooted in the relative strength of men and women will re-assert itself with all the force of natural law.[46] In 1873, James Fitzjames Stephen stood against the tide in contesting John Stuart Mill's confident assertion that "the equality of married persons before the law...is the only means of rendering the daily life of mankind, in any high sense, a school of moral cultivation." Mill, anticipating the progressive wave of the future, quickly occupied the moral high ground. Today's proletarian family faithfully mirrors Mill's dictum that marriage is a contract between equals; indeed, Mill's equally high-minded epigones stipulate that such contracts may now join any two or more persons of either sex in the matrimonial state. Radically unstable modern families long ago delegated the task of "moral cultivation" to the state and the corporate media. Such cavalier disregard for the formative influence of family life will not survive the Long Emergency. Credibility will be restored to Stephen's archaic notion that marriage is best understood, in law and morals, "as a contract between a stronger and a weaker person involving subordination for certain purposes on the part of the weaker to the stronger."[47] That the stronger person will be a man, and the weaker, a woman, once went without saying.

To conceive the family as "the real molecule of society" is to imply that all of the atomic particles within that structure are bound together in an autonomous order.[48] Individual family members submit themselves to the overriding interests of the household. If the household is indeed a body politic writ small, it must speak with one voice. Under such circumstances, there will be good reason to reconsider the principle of universal suffrage which fragmented the family, destroying its moral strength and political unity. Not coincidentally, it was the putatively democratic institution of universal suffrage that facilitated the replacement of the Anglo-Saxon *people* by a *population* of atomized, deracinated individuals. Importantly, universal suffrage also trivialized politics into a perennial quarrel over who gets what, when, where, and how, calling into question the very existence of a shared public interest, whether within the microcosm of the family or in the commonwealth as a whole.

---

45 See especially, John Stuart Mill, "The Subjection of Women," in *id.*, *On Liberty and Other Essays*, John Gray, ed (Oxford: Oxford University Press, 2008); and, James Fitzjames Stephen, *Liberty, Equality, Fraternity* (Indianapolis, IN: Liberty Fund, 1993).

46 *Cf.*, James Howard Kunstler, *A World Made by Hand* (New York: Grove Press, 2008).

47 Stephen, *Liberty, Equality, Fraternity*, 135-142.

48 Nisbet, *Twilight of Authority*, 260.

Anglo-Saxon tribal organizations will return to archaic forms of household suffrage. By treating each family as an autonomous, self-governing, body politic, household suffrage will allow Anglo-Saxon tribes to engender in-group solidarity from the bottom up. Individuals will assess their social, political, and biocultural interests as members of a group acting in concert. The head will rise out of the private realm of the household into the public realm where he will represent not just his individual interests but the interests of the family as a whole.

The right to vote or to win office in tribal organizations will reside not in individuals but in the heads of every independent household. This arrangement will not sacrifice the republican principle of political equality; each individual still carries equal political weight so long as household heads exercise the number of votes corresponding to the number of souls subject to their jurisdiction. In other words, single persons forming a household on their own will receive one vote. Childless couples on the other hand will have two votes on condition that the couple nominates a head of household to vote on its behalf. Couples with children will receive three or more votes depending on the number of children in the household. Every additional child living at home, of any age, entitles the head to an additional vote.

Any household unwilling to nominate a head empowered to act as a surrogate for all its members will forfeit its right to vote. How to select the head will be a matter for each household. The person selected to serve as household head for purposes of voting or holding office in the tribal council need not be the same person acting as household head in the governance of other bodies corporate and politic. Whoever serves as head of household must represent the interests of their families but they must also be *seen* to be representing those interests, faithfully and well. Members of the head's family as well as his neighbours have an interest in knowing how the household votes are cast. In other words, the theory and practice of household suffrage may well be opposed to the secret ballot. Those who vote on behalf of others must display both their good faith and the courage of their convictions.

Biblical authority and archaic political traditions alike suggest that heads of household should be men, if only to rekindle a sense of manly responsibility among feminized WASPs. Prudential considerations will justify exceptions to this rule. To grant each household the freedom to determine whether it is to be represented by a male or a female head is not simple deference to the lingering influence of feminism. Anglo-Saxon societies always have been distinguished by the relatively high status accorded to women. Both prudence and tradition suggest that households should be free to govern their own internal affairs, each according to its own lights. Restoring civic responsibility to the family and the household is a significant step toward the reconstitution of autonomous, self-governing Anglo-Saxon Christian commonwealths.

The appearance of such tribes will not meet with universal approval; powerful and dangerous enemies will be ranged against them. The Anglo-Saxon tribal network must develop the capacity to defend itself against domestic disorder and external attack. It will not be for much longer that such core functions can be consigned to the care of crumbling corporate welfare states.

Corporate Warriors

Already the centralization of security in the hands of the state has brought "us to the brink of a police state for very little benefit." Intrusive methods of intelligence gathering, for example, are counter-productive not just because they are immoral and unconstitutional but also because they are ineffective and destructive of social cohesion, already stretched to the limit. John Robb suggests that for security to work, it needs to be affordable, efficiently allocated, socially broad-based and participatory. On all counts, the centralized state fails the test.[49] States assert a monopoly over both the legitimate use of violence and the power to tax. The security they provide, therefore, comes at a price dictated by the supplier. All other things being equal, states prefer to raise taxes and limit protection. "Under monopolistic auspices the price of justice and protection must rise and its quality must fall." A centralized state has few incentives to limit its own power or to safeguard individual life and property. In determining "*how much* security to provide…a government's answer will invariably be the same: *to maximize expenditures* on protection…and at the same time to *minimize* the *production* of protection." In addition, the judicial monopoly enjoyed by the state degrades the quality of justice as "the definition of property and protection will continually be altered and the range of jurisdiction expanded to the government's advantage."[50] Secession from inefficient, unaffordable, and authoritarian state systems of collective security will become a real option for Anglo-Saxons in the coming century.

---

49 Robb, *Brave New War*, 157, 163.

50 Hans-Hermann Hoppe, "Government and the Private Production of Defense," in *id.*, *The Myth of National Defense: Essays on the Theory and History of Security Production* (Auburn, AL: Ludwig von Mises Institute, 2003), 344-345.

Fortunately, Anglo-Saxon societies built up a stock of biocultural capital that will ease the adaptation of WASPs to the brave new world of privatised security.

By comparison with European absolutism, both early modern England and the first American republic were stateless societies. Only from the mid-nineteenth century onwards did urbanization and industrialization foster dependence upon taxpayer-funded protection. Nor did the households of Old England look to kinship networks as the chief line of defence against external aggression. Covenant played a crucial role; warriors were bound to the chief of their *comitatus* by reciprocal vows of fealty and protection—a non-kinship based form of reciprocity. Similar traditions of mutual exchange between unrelated individuals were the essential precondition for the eventual emergence of a free market society in England. Countless routine contractual relationships between strangers over centuries built up an immensely valuable stock of biocultural capital. Englishmen learned that they could trust each other to honor promises of mutual support. Those lessons have not been entirely forgotten. In the decades ahead, heads of Anglo-Saxon households will "partake of the advantages of the division of labor and seek better protection of his property than that afforded by self-defense by cooperation with other owners and their property."[51] Covenant will once again become an important dimension of group solidarity in the Anglo-Saxon Christian commonwealth.

Police protection will be provided by people or firms who do not rely upon coercion to gain revenue or arrogate to themselves a compulsory monopoly of security services. In principle, any member of the tribal network will be able to "buy from, sell to, or otherwise contract" with other members "concerning protective and judicial services." Moreover, anyone can "at any time unilaterally discontinue any such cooperation with others and fall back on self-reliant defense or change one's protective affiliations." Hans-Hermann Hoppe nominates insurance companies as the most likely candidates "to offer protection and defense services." After all, it is in every insurer's financial interest to provide efficient protection. Clearly, "the better the protection of insured property, the lower are the damage claims and hence an insurer's costs." Competitive insurers can be depended upon to levy high premiums in high-crime neighborhoods and to lower prices in low-crime areas. Governments, of course, do the exact opposite; in fact, they typically subsidize crime-ridden inner-city slums at the expense of suburbanites. The predictable but paradoxical

---

51 *Ibid.*, 345.

consequence of government protection policies is to erode "social conditions unfavorable to crime while promoting those favorable to it." [52]

A global, multi-organizational network of Anglo-Saxon tribes will provide a profitable platform for insurance companies able to deliver on their promises of protection. To find and retain clients, Anglo-Saxon insurance companies "must possess the economic means—the manpower as well as the physical resources—necessary to accomplish the task of dealing with the dangers, actual or imagined, of the real world." With the entire Anglo-Saxon diaspora as their base of operations, insurance companies will be able to disperse their property holdings across wide territories and beyond the boundaries of a single state. With their finger in many pies, insurance agencies have a manifest interest in effective protection and will be big enough to provide it.[53] Insurance companies possessing great wealth and police powers backed by military muscle, however, can become "too big to fail."

Kunstler expects that "corporate enterprise in the Long Emergency may revert to being more public in nature and far less sovereign in power."[54] Anglo-Saxon insurance companies in the security business will recover their archaic status as public service corporations. It is essential that they do not develop delusions of sovereign grandeur. Fortunately, insurance companies, unlike governments, have few incentives to disarm those they promise to protect. As we are learning to our discomfiture, unarmed populations can be taxed and exploited by the state with relative ease. Nobody would pay voluntarily to be protected "by someone who required as a first step" that the client "give up his ultimate means of self-defense." Insurers are far more likely to "encourage the ownership of weapons among their insured by means of selective price cuts."[55]

A broad-based and participatory security system can also be encouraged through the constitutional reformation of corporate governance.[56] Anglo-Saxon tribal networks can breathe new life into the archaic, early American republican model of the corporation as a civil body politic. In other words, insurance agencies can be constituted as little republics designed to balance the private interests of their shareholders against the public responsibilities attached to membership in a joint enterprise pos-

52 Ibid., 345, 361.

53 Ibid., 345-348.

54 Kunstler, Long Emergency, 259.

55 Hoppe, "Government Production of Defense," 367.

56 See generally, Andrew Fraser, Reinventing Aristocracy: The Constitutional Reformation of Corporate Governance (Aldershot: Ashgate/Dartmouth, 1998).

sessed of both economic wealth and physical power. In Old England those who disposed of military power constituted a warrior nobility. Within a postmodern network of Anglo-Saxon tribes, those who acquire a substantial share in the ownership of security firms will become eligible for membership in a revamped civic aristocracy.

All shareholders who possess a significant, legally prescribed threshold stake in defence corporations will be admitted, on the basis of equality, to the corporate senate. Such corporations produce protection for customers, wealth for shareholders, and power for managers; they also generate risks for other members of the tribal public. A shareholder senate competent to accept political responsibility when corporate strategies turn sour must be built into the operating constitution of the enterprise. Thus, the proprietary interests of owners will be embedded in a civic process of decision-making open to all substantial shareholders willing to take up that challenge. The self-interested pursuit of long-term shareholder wealth will be harmonized with the responsible management of socially shared risks within a corporate body politic designed to overcome the separation of ownership from control.

Members of such a shareholder senate will not be "nominated from above or supported from below." Rather this novel civic aristocracy "would select itself." Shareholders who select themselves to participate in corporate governance will be those who care and those who take the initiative. The right to be heard in the conduct of senate business will be confined to those who "have demonstrated that they care for more than their private happiness and are concerned about the state of the world." Whatever authority they acquire will rest "on nothing but the confidence of their equals." This equality would not be "natural," but rather "political." It will not be something with which members of the senatorial elite will have been born; it will be "the equality of those who [have] committed themselves to, and now [are] engaged in a joint enterprise."[57] Shareholder senates will counter-balance the power of professional managers. Novel forms of in-group altruism will re-embed the economy in a complex web of social relationships. By such means, a sense of honor can be regenerated within the governing circles of Anglo-Saxon societies. Those who fight can be depended upon to defend to the death such archaic codes of honor.

Kings are expected to honor those who distinguish themselves from the ordinary run of mankind, whether as workers, priests, or soldiers. But they must also be seen to do justice by all manner of men, whatever their personal qualities. The emergence of Anglo-Saxon Christian

---

57 Hannah Arendt, *On Revolution* (Harmondsworth: Penguin, 1977), 277-280.

commonwealths will be the occasion for the renaissance of the Old English traditions of the common law.

Royal Justice and the Common Law

Christian faith, kinship, and covenant, taken together, represent the archaic core of Anglo-Saxon bioculture. The three elements were bound together by a common law that flowed from the royal fountain of justice. English kings were law-givers but the law was not created by imperial decrees or codes handed down from above. Rather, the common law emerged from the bottom-up, or at least from the middle ranks of English society, through case-by-case adjudication of claims and counter-claims advanced by private litigants. The common law tradition placed both Old England and the early American republic within the matrix of a *legal* civilization. Lawyers and judges were not always or even often popular figures but they made an important contribution to the sense of ethnic kinship between rulers and ruled in both England and America. The common law transcended class differences. Royal justice will foster a similar sense of in-group solidarity among Anglo-Saxons in the twenty-first century and beyond.

In the early American republic, lawyers were not just a learned profession but the closest thing to an aristocracy that could be found in the First (Federal) Republic. Indeed, Tocqueville thought the aristocratic character of the legal profession was much more distinctly marked in both England and the United States than in other countries. In those days, both the English and the Americans had retained the law of precedents; that is to say they continued "to found their legal opinions and the decisions of their courts upon the opinions and decisions of their predecessors." The legal profession was the very model of a transgenerational community that bound the interests of those of us in the here and now together with the interests of the dead and the unborn. Laws, according to Tocqueville, were "esteemed not so much because they [were] good" but "because they [were] old."[58]

Particularly in England, lawyers and judges worked to preserve the traditional fabric of their society, ensuring that changes would "square with the intentions and complete the labors of former generations." Even in America, the legal profession helped to bind together the disparate elements of a dynamic social order. Because lawyers belonged "to the people

58   Alexis de Tocqueville, *Democracy in America* Vol I (New York: Vintage, 1945), 286, 288.

by birth and interest" but "to the aristocracy by habit and taste," they served "as the connecting link between the two great classes of society."[59] Among the members of that natural aristocracy, the governing professional ideal was the image of the public-spirited lawyer-statesman. It went without saying, therefore, that the lawyer was distinguished from ordinary men by the spirit of citizenship. Through an extended apprenticeship in judgement, the best lawyers acquired their defining character trait: prudential wisdom. Their "special talent for discovering where the public good lies and for fashioning those arrangements needed to secure it" gave lawyers a powerful awareness of the shared destiny that linked the profession to their people as a whole.[60]

Despite their lengthy and expensive academic training, lawyers who serve the transnational market-state no longer belong to a "learned profession." Law is a business. Like any other business, law firms are driven by the economic imperatives of billable hours and the bottom line. Following the rise of the corporate law firm, legal practice became commercialized, de-professionalized and bureaucratized. In place of the practical wisdom of the lawyer-statesman, we have today the "expertise" of the "transactional specialist."[61] If we are to revive the original principles of the ancient British constitution, the legal profession must be reconstituted as a natural aristocracy of lawyer-statesmen. This can be done by restoring to lawyers the opportunity to act as independent, public-spirited citizens.

A world-wide, multi-organizational network of Anglo-Saxon tribes will create much work for lawyers and courts. Just as urban craftsmen and technicians will be encouraged to form guilds to regulate their common affairs, the legal profession must recover its archaic corporate identity. Judges, of course, will be selected from the ranks of the practicing profession. All lawyers admitted to practice in a court will be eligible for membership of an electoral college convened to nominate candidates for judicial office in that court. Formal appointment of judges will, however, remain in the gift of the king or his vice-regal representative. Once appointed, judges will be paid not by the king—who will lack the taxation powers of a state—but by the Church, protective service corporations, and private litigants. Judges will be independent professionals bound to adhere to standards promulgated by their own judicial guild.

---

59 Ibid., 286-288.

60 Anthony T Kronman, *The Lost Lawyer: Failing Ideals of the Legal Profession* (Cambridge, MA: Harvard University Press, 1993), 14.

61 Ibid., 283-291.

Prudence will restrict membership in the electoral college to independent members of the practicing profession, that is to say, to the partners of established firms or solo practitioners. Taken together such reforms provide a constitutional alternative to the pernicious influence of state and corporate power within contemporary legal professions. To ensure that the legal profession and the judiciary share a community of interest with their fellow citizens, provision will be made as well for popular recall of judges. After a period of, say, seven years following nomination by the profession and appointment by the king, heads of household constituting the relevant electorate will either confirm that appointment or remove the judge from office.[62]

Once confirmed in office, judges will continue to dispense justice in the name of the king; but they will do so under the watchful gaze of those who pray. Legal education will be provided by colleges and universities founded and maintained by the church. The common law crafted by the legal professions will regulate commercial life and safeguard property rights within the complex network of tribal organizations; it will also reinvent the canon law, the province of the ecclesiastical courts of Old England. Law will be the capstone of constitutional unity within an autonomous Anglo-Saxon Christian civilization; equity will articulate "the norms of right living" binding upon the common conscience of Anglo-Saxons everywhere.

* * *

Whether Anglo-Saxons are to be reborn as a people of destiny in the twenty first century is, of course, impossible to know. We can, however, pray for the coming of the day when Anglo-Saxons of all ranks and conditions, in America and around the world, rise to hail their Patriot King. By imagining the whole of life—at work and at play, at home, school, and church, in law and even politics—as a form of prayer, the Old Faith will help to hasten that happy moment.

God save the King!

---

62 *Cf.*, Andrew Fraser, "Beyond the Charter Debate: Republicanism, Rights, and Civic Virtue in the Civil Constitution of Canadian Society," (1993) 1(1) *Review of Constitutional Studies* 27.

Subject Index

absolutism, royal – 100, 103

adaptive utilitarianism – 177, 204, 323-4

administrative state, lineaments of (see also fraternity; managerialism; New Deal) – 97, 136,160, 234, 240, 247, 272, 284, 306, 336, 341, 380

altruism, role of – 17, 21, 181, 183-4

American Adam – 174, 195, 207, 216, 220-1, 270

American Jewish Congress – 315

American republic, and Christianity – 8, 233, 271, 276, 282, 315

American republican tradition (see American civil religion)

ancient constitution – 30, 90, 95-97, 100-1, 104-7, 109, 144, 146-9, 156, 159, 332-7, 357-8, 362-3,

Angelcynn – 46, 50, 64, 204, 224, 382

Anglican Church – 64, 96, 194, 202, 207, 212, 225, 292, 339, 358, 375, 383-5 *passim*, 392

Anglo-Protestant culture (see also bioculture, Anglo-Saxon) – 22, 27-31, 268

Anglo-Saxons – see *Angelcynn;* bioculture, Anglo-Saxon; church, of Anglo-Saxons; Church of England; inner-directed; kinship networks; liberty; magicorelicious-directed; other-directed; tradition-directed; sacral kingship; self-government

Anglosphere – 29, 188

anti-discrimination (see also antiracism) – 29, 30

Antifederalists – 272-3, 275, 283,

anti-racism – 200-3

anti-semitism – 185, 238, 268-9

Australia – 9, 12, 15, 18, 20, 222, 239-40, 359, 363

Australia, republican movement – 342, 357-361 *passim*

authority

and American civil religion– 302-3, 305, 333, 340,

and corporations –195, 235-6, 243-50 *passim*, 257-60, 267, 268, 371, 379, 381, 398, 399,

and natural rights – 136-7, 139

and parliamentary monarchy – 139, 142-4, 155, 358

and Puritanism – 124 -34 *passim*

and Southern churches – 289-292 *passim*

charismatic (see also *heilerfüll* – 42-44, 72- 73, 86-7, 96, 112, 137, 359,

China – 61, 84, 116

debate between spiritual (papal) and temporal (royal)– 65, 74- 76, 78-9, 81, 83-7, 93-104 *passim*, 118, 188-95 *passim*, 210, 276

ecclesiastical – 46-48, 50, 74, 77, 79-80

legal-rational – 73, 75, 79, 81, 83, 93, 96, 101, 101, 105, 159 managerial (see humanism, corporate; managerialism)

religious, in Anglo-Saxon societies – 46-50, 65, 72

source in tradition (origins) – 95-8, 100, 335, 341-2

bioculture

Anglo-Saxon (see also covenant) – 14, 17, 19, 21, 22, 27-65 *passim*, 145, 169,187-8, 206, 221-2, 224, 253, 261, 312, 323, 331, 339, 341, 375, 378, 385, 397, 400

Jewish – 8

Black liberation theology – 224, 312, 321, 326, 323, 326

blackness, phenomenon of – 216

blood feud – 31, 35- 38, 40-41, 52, 70

Book of Genesis – 149, 184-85, 197,382-3, 388-9

Book of Revelations – 387

bourgeoisie, Anglo-American – 254, 257-8, 267, 272, 303,

Canada – 9, 10, 12, 15, 18, 20, 174, 222, 238, 339

canon law – 68, 75, 76, 80, 86, 192, 235, 402

capital

biocultural – see bioculture, Anglo-Saxon

cultural – *223*, 258

 social – 15, 162, 222, 236, 250, 275, 306

Capitalism

and Christianity – 231-3, 235, 241, 252-3

Anglo-Saxon provenance of – 252

finance – 349

Puritan spirit of – 112, 113, 130, 229, 276

capitalist modernization (see also corporation, role of; proletari-

anization) – 29, 122, 144-5, 154, 161-2, 215, 218, 221, 228, 230-6 *passim*, 233-5, 247-53, 255, 260, 262, 275, 284, 291, 300, 304, 309,319, 330, 336-7, 341, 363

Carolene Products case – 313

Catholic theology – see Henry VIII; Milbank; papal monarchy; Papal Revolution; Roman Catholic Church; scholastic rationalism

Catholic, ethnic enclaves – 14-15, 219, 276, 311-2, 317

character of Anglo-Saxons – see inner-directed; magicoreligious-directed; other-directed; tradition-directed

China, ancient civilization and traditions of – 30, 57-8, 60-3, 73, 82-4, 116

chivalry, ideals of – 56, 119, 121-2, 137, 301, 303-4, 369

Christendom

Anglo-Saxon – 14, 16, 19, 20, 22, 46 -50, 65-8, 72, 112-3, 118, 121, 124, 190-2, 194, 298, 301, 311, 323, 332, 373-402 *passim*

Western – 81-5 *passim*, 170, 188, 204, 271, 276, 278, 385

Christian doctrine of nations – 19, 382, 386

Christian socialism – 231-2, 235,

Christianity (see also Anglican Church; Church of England; covenant theology; ethnotheology; papal monarchy; Papal Revolution; Puritan Revolution; religion; Roman Catholic Church)

Anglo-Saxon – 19, 42, 47, 48-49, 60, 65, 67-9, 72-3, 75, 77, 81, 87, 96, 112, 114, 117,

orthodox, evangelical mission of –

204, 212

Church of England – 94, 95, 107, 120, 123, 124, 139, 175, 194, 209, 212, 237, 254, 339, 357, 375, 377, 382, 385

Church, of the Anglo-Saxons – 16, 19, 30, 33, 45, 46-50, 64, 67, 74, 80, 81, 86, 95, 174, 179, 187, 200, 204, 205, 207, 225-6, 228, 358, 372, 382, 384, 390

citizenship –18, 27, 64, 151, 152, 217-9, 245, 271, 275, 293-4, 312, 330, 336, 368, 373, 401

civic humanism – 8-11 passim, 108-11 passim, 119, 150-2 passim, 158, 155, 156, 158, 160, 239, 249, 280-2 passim, 337, 348, 352

civic nationalism (see also ethnonationalism; nationalism; white nationalism) – 10, 11, 8, 57, 64, 162, 177, 217, 221, 226, 267, 320, 323-5, 359

civil body politic – 236-9 passim, 244-8 passim, 250, 398,

civil religion (see also civic humanism; equality; fraternity; humanism, secular; state, and nation; theology, political)

American – 8, 14, 15, 17, 94, 96,195, 219, 219, 225, 241, 255, 260, 269, 270-326 passim, 332-3, 326, 390

Jewish – 315-7, 324

civil rights revolution – 11, 220, 260, 269, 299, 319

civil war, American –122, 129, 172-3,214, 217-9, 230,269, 272-3, 275, 285, 287-96, 299, 307,

civil war, English – 107, 109, 130-1, 138, 156

comitatus, defined (see also sacral kingship, Anglo-Saxon) – 35

Commission on Law and Social Ac-

tion (CLSA) –315

common law, role of – 50, 68, 75, 86, 87, 98-102 passim, 105-7 passim, 110, 157, 215, 245, 247, 248, 250, 270, 311, 333, 335, 400-2 passim

communism (see also Marxism; neo-communism; socialism) – 220, 220, 228, 232, 318, 380

Communists,

Jewish – 318, 320

Negroes – 319, 320

Conservatism – 18, 157, 222, 241-2, 244-5, 247, 275, 284, 288, 293, 298, 307-9, 313, 321

constitution, mixed and balanced – 105, 108-10, 113, 151, 274

constitutional patriotism – see American civil religion

contract, role of (see also marriage; social contract) – 29, 114, 125, 128, 170, 208, 215, 217, 236-7, 252, 254, 397

corporatism – 276, 336-8

corruption – 123, 128, 138-41, 145-8, 150-15, 168, 170, 323, 345, 350, 354, 356, 362, 364-6, 370-1

cosmopolitanism – 8, 20, 21, 162, 238, 252, 260-69, 277-80, 282, 305, 376

covenant

and American civil bodies politic – 135-7, 236-40, 242, 247

and Anglo-Saxon bioculture (see also covenant theology) – 29, 49, 72, 136, 155, 170, 209, 211, 236, 238-9, 325, 397, 400

and Constitution (see also American civil religion) – 273, 286, 288, 324

and corporations – 236, 248-9

creationism – 385-390 passim

theology, of Puritans (see also Puritan Revolution) – 211-12, 236, 239, 247, 288

creationism – see covenant creationism

critical race theory – 322

culture of critical discourse (see also New Class; managerialism) – 257-61

Darcy v Allein - 105

Darwinism (see also selection) – 177, 181, 189, 195-200, 206

deism – 156, 278, 285

democracy
    and Anglo-Saxons – 33, 44
    cosmopolitan – 162, 266, 359
    in America – 254, 283
    Jeffersonian – 243, 284, 291

demography, and WASP decline – 18-20, 64, 171-2, 178, 180, 265, 300, 359

despotism – 103, 142, 159-60, 168, 336, 366

discrimination, ethnic and racial – 299, 300,310, 312, 314, 319, 322

diversity, problem of – 7, 11, 17, 148, 162, 171, 202, 226, 229, 276, 300, 310-312, 324, 329-30, 332-38 passim, 342, 357, 379

divine right of kings – 98-100, 109, 360

double majesty – 88-93 passim, 97, 106, 110, 119, 156

Dr Bonham's case - 106

Eastern Orthodox tradition – 175, 188

Ecclesia
    corporate – 254-61 passim
    role and transformation of – 189, 190-2, 194, 200-2, 206, 209-10, 217, 221, 223, 229, 237, 242, 246-7, 249, 253-4, 276, 290, 292, 306, 311-2, 323, 326

egalitarianism – see equality

Eigenkirchensystem – 49

Eigenklostersystem – 40

Enlightenment values (see also reason/rationalism; tradition) – 168, 177, 186, 188, 271, 276-8, 282, 290, 341-2, 377, 391

equality
    and Anglicanism – 225,
    ideological role of – 253, 270, 271, 275, 281, 282, 293-299, 303, 309, 310, 312, 313, 329, 332, 382, 391
    in English constitutionalism – 103-5 passim, 118
    of rights – 250, 334, 391, 394
    political – 395, 399
    racial – 218, 222, 275, 322
    social – 148, 235, 275, 310

Ethical Culture movement – 263-4

ethnoculture
    Anglo-Saxons (see also homo Americanus) – 28, 56, 149, 168, 169, 170, 176, 178, 182, 214, 222, 223, 226, 279, 281, 300, 301, 305, 337, 339, 340, 357, 369, 375
    Jewish – 14, 28

ethnonation
    Anglo-Saxon (see also Alfred the Great; Angelcynn) – 7, 12- 16 passim, 23, 30, 42, 49-57, 50-57, 65, 167, 177, 187, 203, 207, 225, 276, 280, 306, 331, 339, 357, 363, 382-385
    Jewish –13, 14, 56, 315, 226, 315, 385

ethnonationalism, Negro – 13, 319-323, 325

ethnotheology
    Jewish (see also civil religion, Jewish) – 173, 226, 315-17, 325

of Negroes – 325
orthodox Christian – 16, 19, 22,
   149, 170-71, 223-7 *passim*, 235,
   317, 325
evangelical revivalism – 241-3, 245,
   247-50, 253, 256, 285-7, 292, 382
evil – 70, 117, 131, 159, 190, 197-8,
   203, 207, 211, 222, 232, 235, 248,
   288-9, 357, 379, 381
evolution – see bioculture
family
   Chinese – 61-2
   proletarian – 390-34
   role of – 32, 40-1, 43, 45, 47, 56,
      58, 61, 112, 125, 127, 148,
      155, 160, 183, 204, 211, 237,
      261, 302-4, 358, 376, 382, 390,
      393-6
fascism – 200, 204, 378-80
Federalists – 216, 242-7 *passim*, 279,
   283-5
feminism – 220, 275, 302-4, 312,
   392, 395
feudalsim, English – 39, 53-54, 56,
   74, 76, 85-86, 88-9, 103-5, 119,
   155, 193, 209, 298, 335
Fourteenth Amendment – 219, 275,
   293-296 *passim*, 299, 303, 308,
   313
Frankfurt School – 233
fraternity, ideal of – 270, 271, 275,
   281, 306-9, 311-4 *passim*, 317,
   322, 326, 329, 331
free labor (see also slavery) – 214,
   230, 231, 287, 295, 296
genetic interests
   and religion – 197, 204, 323
   ethnic (see also bioculture, Anglo-
      Saxon) – 145, 177, 204, 323
Gens anglorum – 46-47, 49, 174
Glorious Revolution – 139, 141,
   156-7, 348

Great Schism – 188, 226
Harvard College/University – 28,
   223
Heilerfüllt (see also kingship, Anglo-
   Saxon) – 43, 64, 87, 137
historians – 33, 56, 110, 119, 148,
   150, 179, 208, 212, 307, 344-7,
   352, 354
Holy Trinity – 186, 191, 194-5, 359,
   385
homo Americanus – 10, 15, 20, 163,
   167-227 *passim*, 238, 271
homo oeconomicus – 138
household, role of – 34-6, 98, 105,
   109, 111, 143, 160, 211, 237, 240,
   258-9, 332, 391-2, 394-7, 402
human rights, universal – 64, 221-2,
   228, 248
Humanism
   corporate – 256, 259-61
   secular/political – 9, 10, 17, 64-65,
      66, 131, 188-9, 196, 198, 228,
      262, 331, 345
hybridity – 21
identity politics – 14, 18, 20, 23, 171,
   222, 224, 301, 304, 334, 357
identity
   and citizenship – 10, 312
   Anglo-Saxon (see also bioculture,
      Anglo-Saxon) – 8, 11, 12, 16,
      18, 21, 27, 30, 47, 52, 53, 55-
      57 *passim*, 66, 67, 87,148, 149 ;
      Part Two, *passim*
   race and – 148, 214, 216, 221
immigration, impact of (see also
   demography) – 9, 19, 20, 28,
   63-4, 162, 203, 205, 218-20, 300,
   305, 383
incarnation – 68, 77-81, 123, 186,
   192, 194, 198, 200-1, 205, 228,
   302, 382-4
Individualism, Anglo-Saxon Protes-

tant tradition of (see also equality; liberty; Puritan) –12,15, 20, 29-30, 33-35, 40, 55, 61-2, 65,69, 70- 72, 81-86, 94, 106, 112, 124-6, 128-30, 134-9, 152-4, 156, 159, 161-2, 174, 182, 184, 196, 210-1, 217, 221, 246, 249-50, 252, 256, 266, 277, 286, 291-2, 296-7, 332-5, 394, 397

inner-directed Anglo-Saxon character – 19, 68, 111-2, 129 -30, 140, 156, 162, 221, 238, 256, 258-9, 261-2, 297

intellectuals
  Anglo-Saxon and Protestant – 13, 15, 17, 18, 20, 27, 28, 30, 55, 117, 167, 178, 304,
  Catholic – 14
  Jewish – 10, 13-14, 17, 202, 263-4, 266-7, 275, 314, 320
  Negro – 13, 17, 28, 319-20
  progressive – 20, 126, 256, 258-9, 264, 303-6, 324-5, 349-51

Israel (state) (see also Old Covenant Israel; state, Jewish) – 317-18, 325

Jewish homeland – 11

Jews – see also civil Judaism; ethnotheology, of Judaism; cosmopolitanism; ethnonation, Jewish)
  and identity – 8, 17, 56-7, 173, 225-6, 263, 265, 314, 316-7, 326
  and American identity politics – 11-15, 17, 173, 223, 260, 264, 269, 306, 311, 314-20, 323
  and Christianity – 54, 56-57, 201, 206, 266-7, 315-8, 321, 325-6, 384-5, 387, 389-90
  and corporate welfare state – 10-11, 266, 314
  and Negroes – 13, 17, 173, 319-20

and New Deal – 313-4
and tradition – 317
Anglophobia of – 7, 15, 30, 318
as minority – 268-9, 312
beliefs of – 82-3, 263-4, 316, 318, 320
economic behavior of – 54-6, 173
ethnic interests of – 8, 9, 11, 13-15, 172-3, 184-5,201, 225-6, 254, 265, 317-18
ethnocentrism of – 30, 173, 254, 264-5, 268, 311, 317-8, 331
evolutionary group strategy of (see also Jews, ethnic interests of) – 173, 185, 225, 268
in England – 54-6, 172
pariah status of – 8, 10, 172

Judaism
  Orthodox – 55, 77, 185, 203, 224-25
  Reform - 263

Judeo-Christian tradition – 54, 238, 311, 390

jus gentium – 333

kingship, Chinese – 61, 116,

kinism – 385-390 *passim*

kinship networks (see also tribes; kinism) – 7, 10, 15, 30, 32, 34-43 *passim*, 52, 56, 58-59, 61, 71, 81, 114, 127, 136, 162, 170, 175, 183-4, 205, 217, 236, 282, 340, 375-6, 380-1, 384, 391-2, 397, 400

Kirchenstaat – 65, 76, 79, 190, 204

knights – 53, 91, 119, 193, 385

law, ecclesiastical (see also canon law; common law) – 74, 80, 246, 402

lawyers (see also canon law; common law)
  Jewish – 314-6
  Negro – 321
  role of – 93, 98, 102, 110, 215, 257,

281, 284-85, 293, 314-6, 322, 363, 400-2

Leviathan – 13, 136, 168, 279, 306

liberty

and equality – 275, 283, 293, 297, 300, 334

and fraternity – 313

and property rights – 297-98

and religion – 211, 240, 242, 263, 277, 280, 281, 366

Anglo-Saxon tradition of – 29, 33, 35, 39, 53, 81, 98, 101, 104-6, 110, 140, 143-4, 145-53 *passim,* 156-7, 161, 270, 273, 275, 280, 297, 332, 354, 360-7 *passim,* 370, 391

in French revolution – 270-1

modern – 155-159 *passim,* 161, 334

republican – 273, 275, 280-83 *passim,* 287-293, 312, 329, 331

Long Emergency – 168, 374-6, 392-4, 398

magicoreligious-directed character of Anglo-Saxons – 42, 48, 49, 65, 67, 69, 72, 73, 75, 81, 87

Magna Carta – 53-55, 91, 105

managerial multiculturalism (see managerialism; multiculturalism)

managerial revolution (see managerialism)

managerialism (see also multiculturalism) – 226, 229, 253, 256, 260, 267, 269, 272, 275, 306-12, 371, 378

managers, scientific – 256-8

Manifest Destiny – 217, 286

Männerbund – see *comitatus*

market-state, transnational – 163, 220, 222-3, 255, 269, 275, 306-7, 336, 357, 363, 373, 378-81, 401

marriage (see also households) – 32, 35, 41, 93, 127, 180, 237, 332, 386, 392, 394

Marxism (see also materialism; proletarianization) – *12,* 220, 229-33, 235, 250-3, 298, 309, 319, 350

materialism – 83, 103, 105, 107, 121-2, 130, 132, 174, 178, 221, 228, 253, 275, 301, 320, 324, 389,

men

Anglo-Saxon – 32, 34, 37-38, 40-41, 52, 53-54, 58, 63, 81, 302, 332, 372, 392, 394-96

role of (see also comitatus, warriors, proletarianization) – 11, 32, 127, 211, 220, *223,* 258-9, 302-6 *passim,* 392, 394

monarchy

constitutional – 339, 357, 360, 363

Parliamentary – 139

principle of – 371

role of (see also Papal Revolution; kingship, Anglo-Saxon) – 18, 54, 67, 90-2, 103, 107, 110, 129, 138, 271, 339-40, 342-4, 357-63 *passim,* 369

monogamy – 34-5

morality

and slavery – 289, 291

Christian – 121, 125, 138, 148, 152, 181, 226, 230, 246, 281, 290

Germanic – 35

multiculturalism (see also anti-discrimination) – 18, 20-21, 174, 226, 310-11, 330

multiracial society, impact of (see also managerialism) – 13, 15, 27, 64, 162, 205, 226, 310-11, 330, 334, 359, 378

Nation of Islam – 320

nation of nations – 12
National Association for the Advancement of Colored People – 321
National identity, English – 95, 149, 150, 168, 178
nationhood, English – see ethnonationalism
Negroes – see also anti-racism; black liberation theology; Communists; equality; ethnonationalism
and capitalism (see also slavery) – 172, 179, 214-6, 217-9, 229-31
and Christianity – 320-1
and identity politics – 12, 14, 17, 28, 173, 223, 229-30, 254, 260, 269, 279-80, 299, 306, 312-3, 319-24
criminality of – 15
integration – 219-20,269, 303, 305, 319-20
neo-Communism – 220-222 passim 227, 229, 276, 329-30, 379
neo-feudalism – 336
New Class – 258, 309, 371
New Covenant – 16, 388-9, 390
New Deal – 269, 275, 306-9, 311-15
New Israel – 385, 390
New Testament – 72, 290, 310, 316, 383-4, 386
Nicene Creed – 192, 387
Norman Conquest – 30, 31, 52, 53, 65, 67, 68, 73, 86-88, 146
novus ordo seclorum – 22, 113, 163, 174, 216-17, 248, 271, 378
oaths – 30, 36, 56, 57-64 passim, 71, 81, 91, 93, 114, 156
Obama, administration – 20, 272,
Old Covenant Israel – 16, 49-50, 72, 225, 238-40, 387-9
Old English Church – 188, 204, 205
Old Faith – 16, 66, 176, 186, 192,
206, 229, 276, 302, 311, 375, 378, 380, 402
Old Testament – 49, 72, 150, 183, 200, 238-9, 283, 290, 383-4, 386
ordeal, trial by – 59-60, 81
other-directed Anglo-Saxon character – 7, 19, 174, 187, 258, 260-2, 265, 267, 269, 305, 323-4
Papal monarchy – 75, 76, 77, 78, 80, 94, 118, 175, 186, 191-2, 196, 204, 226
Papal Revolution – 30, 65, 67-68, 74-77, 85, 96, 113, 118, 122, 168, 174, 193, 202, 226
Patriot King (see also Bolingbroke) – 329-372 passim; 379, 402
political economy – 17, 20, 148, 151, 154, 160, 196, 213, 226-7, 229, 233, 240-1, 252, 254, 319, 335, 338, 348, 354, 362, 370-2, 378
political theology (see theology, political; race, political theology of)
polity, ecclesiastical – 94-98 passim, 111, 123, 189, 190, 209-10, 221, 223, 332
prerogative
royal – 76, 93, 95, 97-9, 101, 104-6, 119, 141, 146, 160-1, 191, 345, 362, 371
seigneurial – 41, 98
preterism – 385-389 passim
private property, role of – 38, 59, 86, 97-9, 101, 103-106, 109-10, 112, 136-9, 143-4, 155, 159, 200, 207, 217, 240, 242-4, 247, 250-1, 258, 275, 280, 294, 297-8, 304, 313, 335, 348-50, 371, 390-3, 396-8, 402
progressive movement – 66, 83, 208, 256, 259, 262-4, 275, 293, 299, 302-6, 308, 324, 340, 349, 387, 394

proletarianization (see also family, proletarian) – 215, 221, 229-32, 234-5, 266, 302, 392

prophecies, Biblical – 16, 149, 225, 386,

proposition nation – 9, 12, 162, 254, 315, 390

Protestant ethic (see also Puritans; Weber) – 17, 229, 255-6, 321

Protestant Reformation – 123, 210, 385

Pseudomonas fluorescens – see wrinkly spreader

purgatory - 79

Puritan Revolution (see also covenant theology) – 65, 67, 68, 95, 105, 107, 108, 110-3 *passim*, 120-31 *passim*, 133, 136, 138, 157, 158, 170, 174, 207, 208, 211, 212, 239, 240, 288

race
  and Christianity (see also kinism) – 200, 382, 385, 386, 388-9
  Anglo Saxon (see also *Angelcynn*) – 7, 8, 15, 17, 18, 27, 31, 32, 46, 167, 169, 171-45, 178, 180, 207, 228, 266, 268, 276, 301, 302, 305, 343, 373, 374, 379, 385
  as biocultural phenomenon – 11, 17, 31, 179, 181, 197, 201, 225
  issue of – 9, 15, 21, 171-4, 176, 200, 214, 263, 299-300, 338
  Jewish – 318
  political theology of (see also civil rights revolution; citizenship; corporatism; equality; fraternity; managerialism; Negroes; white nationalism) – 293, 299, 312, 322, 329, 330
  "social construction" of – 17, 180, 202, 310,

racial discrimination – see discrimination

racism – 66, 170, 185, 228, 265, 267, 268, 325
  Scientific – 300-1

Radical Orthodoxy (see also Baker, Milbank) – 167, 186-8, 190,193, 197-8, 200-7, 217, 224-5, 231, 233

rainbow republicanism – 311-3, 331, 338, 357

rationalism (see also rationality; scholasticism)
  legal – 102, 105 (see also authority, legal-rational)
  post-Christian (see also deism; Enlightenment; managerialism; Marxism) – 101, 107, 143, 149, 159, 174-5, 177-8, 186-8, 190, 193, 195, 212, 220-1, 228, 231, 241, 251-4, 256, 271, 277-8, 285, 301-2, 310, 321, 323-4, 331, 369

rationality, for ancients – 159, 187

reason, role of (see also rationalism; truth) – 34, 60, 67-8, 74, 78, 97, 102, 105, 132, 143, 159, 174-5, 177, 186, 188, 190, 193, 195, 212, 221, 241, 254, 277-8, 285, 333, 335, 360, 366, 368, 377

religion, evolutionary utility of – 18-19, 181, 184-6 , 222-3, 223

Republic, First (Federal) – 280-283 passim, 288,

Republic, Second (Bourgeois) – 272, 275, 293-7 passim, 299-300, 302-3, 305, 313

Republic, Third (Managerial/Therapeutic) – 293, 306-9

republica Anglorum – 65, 66-107 *passim*, 108, 109, 111, 113, 118-21, 123, 126, 129, 131, 371 *res publica* - 110-11, 119, 131

Roman Britain – 30, 31

Roman Catholic Church – 74, 78, 82, 83, 85, 93, 123, 235, 379, 382

Russian Orthodox Church – 384 (see also Eastern Orthodox tradition)

sacral kingship, Anglo-Saxon – 30, 42-46, 51, 64, 67, 69, 71, 72, 74-77 *passim*, 85, 87, 90, 96, 97,

salvation

  personal – 249

  religious – 14, 16, 47, 79, 87, 94, 103, 107, 124-5, 128, 132, 147, 191, 194, 211, 247, 362, 364, 379

  secular – 217, 221, 276, 312, 320, 324

scholasticism – 67, 76-80, 81, 85, 91, 131,174-5, 187-8, 191, 193, 195-6, 205, 241, 277

Scientific Revolution – 186

secular humanism – see humanism, secular/political

secular utility , religion of – 19, 181, 185, 197, 212, *222*, 223

selection

  group – 175-6, 179, 181-3, 186, 200, 202, 204, 205-6, 214, 224-5,

  natural (see also Darwinism) – 34, 84, 130, 173, 183, 196-9, 206

self-government, Anglo-Saxon commitment to – 33-46 *passim*, 98

selfish gene – 18

selfishness – 152, 178, 181-4, 199, 271, 273, 359

Ship Money case – 104, 104

slavery, Negro (see also proletarianization) – 122, 214-221 *passim*, 229-31, 275, 287-291, 295, 299

social contract theory – 336, 357

social gospel – 49, 67, 256

social order, trifunctional – 50, 113-22 *passim*, 124, 129, 133, 135-6, 138-9, 156, 158, 163, 193-4, 209, 235, 287, 332, 369, 377-8, 381-2, 385, 392, 402

social sciences, role of – 160, 188, 257, 259, 297, 302

socialism – 232, 235

sociobiology – 18, 21, 167, 175, 176, 178, 181, 185-86, 189, 200, 207, 225-26, 323, 386

sovereignty – 97, 103, 108, 115, 117, 120, 138, 158, 201, 207

  consumer – 171

  of Parliament – 107

  parcellized (see also ancient constitution) – 88-92, 336

  political theology of (see also theology, political) – 11, 85-93 *passim*, 219, 278 (see also religion of the Republic)

  popular – 108, 218, 274, 278, 282, 309, 336

Standing Orders – 237, 240, 241-3

state of nature – 130-1, 134-5, 198, 239

state

  and church (see also *Kirchenstaat*) – 75-76, 79, 126, 170, 188, 190, 191-2, 195, 204, 207, 210-11, 17, 227, 273, 278, 290, 315, 340, 383

  and Crown – 100, 104, 340

  and nation – 94, 148, 168, 217-8, 221, 226, 279, 293-4, 314, 334, 368

  and nonstate actors – 373-4, 376

  and people – 108, 161, 279, 284, 297-8, 309, 361

  corporate welfare (see also market-state) – 11, 14, 15, 17, 19,

64, 67, 88, 162, 168, 222, 226, 229, 258, 261, 276, 313, 319, 323, 329, 334, 354, 363, 369, 371, 373, 377, 390, 391, 396

Jewish – 11, 263, 317, 325

of courts and parties – 284-8

role of (see also administrative state; authority, legal-rational; market-state; New Deal; political economy) – 9, 11, 19, 30, 34, 37-38, 50, 52-53, 61, 64-65, 67, 71, 75-76, 79, 88, 96, 115, 139-40, 144, 154-5, 161, 188, 190, 204, 210, 211, 217, 227, 244, 269, 272-3, 290-1, 300, 303-5, 315, 358, 368, 394, 396

states' rights – 274, 291

statesmen-legislators – 98, 100-01, 145, 154, 240-1, 243, 279, 283-4, 401

Stuart regime – 97, 99, 103, 107, 110, 141, 348

suffrage – 220, 295, 303, 308, 394-5

Supreme Court – 218, 244, 285, 295-6, 299, 307-8, 312-3, 316, 322

synagogue of Satan – 325-6, 390

Tailors of Ipswich case – 106

Talmud – 317-8, 325

Temple of Jerusalem – 16, 387-89

theology

black liberation – see black liberation theology

political (see also ethnotheology; race, political theology of; sovereignty; Chapter 6) – 85-93 *passim*, 134-8, 170, 216-220, 223, 269, 275-6, 288-92, 293, 301, 310-11, 313, 322

rationalist (see also Puritans) – 67-8, 77, 79-81, 82, 124, 205

Three Estates – 53, 92, 109, 274, 349, 381, 393

tradition (see also Western legal tradition)

and ancient constitution – 107, 109

and constitutional interpretation – 313, 353

and monarchy – 340-3, 345, 358 , 360, 368-9

Anglo-Saxon (see also kingship; warriors) – 32, 33, 42, 44-45, 47, 52, 60, 73, 89, 117, 120, 129, 395-6

Christian (see also Puritans) – 14, 28, 111-3, 121, 123-9 *passim*, 175-6, 193, 202, 282, 287-8, 302, 304, 324-5, 332, 359, 380

English common law – 86, 93, 98-99, 101-3, 107, 311, 400

of Anglo-Saxon constitutional patriotism – 8, 9, 54, 161-2, 176, 288

civic republicanism (see also civic humanism)– 8, 9, 11, 29, 108-11, 119, 133, 137-8, 145, 150, 155-6, 161, 239, 280, 282

of natural theology (see also Darwinism) – 177, 196

role of – 341-3, 351, 376

tradition-directed Anglo-Saxon character – 19, 57, 65, 68, 73-75, 82, 89, 94-98, 107, 111-13, 129, 138, 209, 261

tribes

and tribalism, role of – 7, 15, 16, 18, 23, 28, 66, 115, 117, 162, 171, 181, 214, 226, 239, 277, 329-74 *passim*, 376, 379-81, 395, 397, 402

Anglo-Saxon – 16, 15 18, 19, 21, 23, 30-48 *passim*, 50, 54, 66, 69, 72, 87, 88, 120, 176, 332, 344, 373, 375-8 *passim*, 380,

385, 390-3 *passim*, 395, 396-9
passim, 401-2
truth, and Christianity – 78, 123,
131, 190, 199-201, 205,210,232,
277, 321,326, 378
truth
role of in Anglo-Saxon culture –
59-60, 190, 260, 366
significance of – 59, 60, 78, 123,
131, 190, 199-201, 205, 210,
232, 260, 277, 321, 326, 366,
378
Tudor Revolution – 92-5, 97, 110,
119, 157, 348, 358
universal church – 76, 88, 382-4
universalism (see also cosmopolitanism; equality; humanism,
secular) – 34, 67, 103, 105, 162,
221, 231, 257, 263
utilitarianism (see also adaptive
utilitarianism; secular utility) –
122, 129, 155
virtue, civic – 10, 17, 137, 143, 144,
148-55, 159, 226, 243, 245, 249,
250, 286, 348
Volksgeist, Anglo-Saxon – 18, 19,
22, 45, 49, 66, 178, 206, 225, 276,
378, 383
Volksgemeinschaft – 204
warriors
and Puritans – 128
and tradition – 121-2, 304
Anglo-Saxon – 31, 35-7, 40-3, 47,
66, 89, 115, 119, 170, 236-7
corporate – 396-400 *passim*
Western legal tradition – 60, 68, 76,
81
white indentured servants – 215-6
white man's country – 167-227 *passim*, 292, 311
white nationalism – 67, 170, 216-
222, *223*, 279

white pride – 222
White Republic/Commonwealth –
170, 173, 179, 220, 223, 280, 339,
358-9
white skin privilege – 218-9, 299-
300, 319, 322
white supremacy – 185, 219, 222,
322, 326
white theology (see also black liberation theology) – 322
whiteness – 216, 218, 221-3, 321,
326
whites
and citizenship – 211, 217-8, 221,
290
as ethnic group – 14-15, 17, 20-21,
28, 168-9, 172-3, 211, 216,
218-9, 221-3, 229, 263, 301,
306,
women, role of – 7, 11, 32, 34, 127,
220, 259, 302-06, 314, 377, 392-
96
women's movement– 220, 302-06,
308, *311*, 314, 332, 334, 372, 392
wrinkly spreader (WS) – 181-2, 184,
198
Zionism – 11

Name Index

Ackerman, Bruce – 309

Adam – 184, 197-98, 384, 388-9

Adams, John – 273

Addams, Jane – 262

Adler, Felix – 263-4

Adler, Rabbi Samuel – 263

Alfred the Great – 16, 32, 42, 48-51, 58, 65-68, 73, 116, 117, 355-7, 381

Arendt, Hannah – 8-11, 109, 111, 113, 160-1, 173, 238-9, 271, 332, 343, 344, 364-7, 369, 370

Aristotle – 70, 109, 150, 159, 205, 245, 347

Armitage, David – 351, 355

Augustine (of Canterbury) – 46, 48, 67, 198, 224, 234, 377

Bacon, Francis – 100-3, 107

Baker, Anthony – 200-1, 205-6

Baltzell, E Digby – 266-69

Becket, Thomas – 75

Bede, Venerable – 46, 47, 49, 50, 357

Bellah, Robert – 286, 324,

Berle, Adolf A. – 234-5

Blair, Tony – 203

Bloch, Marc – 36

Boethius – 116

Bolingbroke, Viscount (Henry St John) – 140-53, 155-58, 160-1, 332, 344-56, 358-371

Bonnet, Charles – 377

Bourne, Randolph – 256, 264-5, 267, 269, 305-6

Brooke, John – 346

Brown, Norman O – 231

Burke, Edmund – 157-8

Burnham, James – 309-10

Burtt, Shelley – 148-9, 153

Calhoun, John C - 219

Calvin, John – 122, 123, 125, 126

Capone, Al – 267

Cavanaugh, William – 217

Charlemagne – 191, 192

Charles I – 109, 110,

Clark, JCD – 347

Cnut – 53

Coke, Edward – 101-2, 105-06

Colley, Linda – 347

Commons, John R – 256

Cone, James – 321-2, 326

Constant, Benjamin – 158-59, 161

Cromwell, Oliver – 53, 108, 129, 157, 172

Cruse, Harold – 12, 13, 14, 17, 18, 280, 319-21

Dabney, Robert Lewis – 303, 308

Dale, Thomas – 170

Darwin, Charles –174-5, 181, 186, 195-8, 388

David – 50, 384

Dawkins, Richard – 185

Depew, David J – 205

Dewey, John – 256, 262, 264, 304-5

Du Bois, WEB – 321

Duns Scotus – 193, 196

Edward I – 56-57

Edward the Confessor – 53, 90, 91, 95

Elizabeth I – 93, 355
Elizabeth II – 340, 359
Eve – 184
Fausette, Richard – 184-5, 197
Feldman, Stephen – 316
Ferguson, Adam – 241
Field, Stephen – 295-6, 298
Fitzhugh, George – 122
Fortescue, John – 92
Francis, Samuel – 309, 310
Franklin, Benjamin – 138
Freud, Sigmund – 56, 57
Freyr – 115
Garrison, William Lloyd – 288
Garvey, Marcus – 13
Genovese, Eugene – 230
George III – 345
Gilman, Charlotte Perkins – 303
Ginsberg, Benjamin – 314
Gordon, Thomas – 153
Gottfried, Paul Edward – 310
Grant, George – 18, 23
Grant, Madison – 213, 301
Greenberg, Cheryl Lynn - 13
Gregory the Great – 46, 48, 75, 224
Griffin, Roger – 380
Gross, David – 341-42
Guthrum – 356
Habermas, Jürgen – 342
Hamilton, Alexander – 243, 283
Hampden, John – 104
Hanson, Donald – 110
Hardt, Michael – 329-30,
Harlan, David – 353-5
Harlan, John (Justice) – 299-300, 322
Harold II – 53
Harrington, James – 150, 156-7, 348
Haskell, Thomas - 256
Hengist – 170
Henry I – 53, 91
Henry II – 75, 86, 87, 89, 91
Henry IV (France) - 360

Henry VII – 97
Henry VIII – 92-94, 97, 188
Hertzberg, Arthur – 315, 317
Higham, John – 20
Hirschman, Albert O – 154
Hobbes, Thomas – 130-9, 170, 198,
    348
Hooker, Richard – 94-97, 102, 111,
    120-1, 124, 127
Hoppe, Hans-Hermann – 397
Horsa – 170
Hughes, Thomas – 341
Hume, David – 152
Huntington, Samuel P – 22, 27, 28,
    29, 176, 223
Indra – 114
James I – 98, 99, 100, 101
James II – 139, 348
James, William – 256, 260, 264, 321
Jay, John – 279-80
Jefferson, Thomas – 243, 273
Jesus Christ – 16, 23, 45-46, 48, 58,
    74, 78-80, 86, 94-95, 120, 123-4,
    126, 128, 132, 133, 170, 175, 189,
    192, 194, 200-1, 204-5, 206, 209-
    10, 225, 232, 235, 242, 249, 254,
    276-7, 281, 288, 317, 324-5, 358,
    380, 382-90
John I – 53, 91
Johnson, Andrew – 295
Johnson, Lyndon – 220, 315
Jones, E Michael – 14, 318, 319
Joseph – 384
Josey, Charles Conant – 301
Jupiter – 114
Kant, Immanuel – 335, 377-8, 381
Kaufmann, Eric – 20, 21, 22, 261, 263
Kennedy, John F – 220, 315
Kerby, Robert L – 291-2
King Ine of Wessex – 31
Kotkin, Joel – 16, 23
Kramnick, Isaac – 349-52, 354-5

Kramnick, Isaac – 349-52, 355
Kunstler, James Howard – 374-75, 393, 398
Lawson, Gary – 306-07
Le Play, Frédéric – 391-92
Lee, Robert E – 292
Lincoln, Abraham – 217, 288-9, 293, 314,
Locke, John – 170, 333
MacDonald, Kevin – 35, 185
Macfarlane, Alan – 82
Machiavelli, Nicolo – 151, 361-2
Malthus, Thomas – 196
Marcuse, Herbert – 232, 233
Mars – 114, 115
Marx, Karl – 8, 220, 229, 231-3, 235, 250, 252-3, 298
Mary – 384
Maurice, FD – 382-83
McCarraher, Eugene – 231-32
McNeill, William H - 338
Mead, Sidney – 278
Medved, Michael – 318
Meyer, Donald - 256
Milbank, John – 188-90, 194-5, 199, 200, 202-5, 231-3, 235, 241, 251
Mill, John Stuart – 394
Miller, Perry – 208
Milton, John – 127
Montesquieu, Charles-Louis de Secondat – 335, 371
More, Thomas – 110
Namier, Lewis Bernstein– 347, 355
Negri, Antonio – 329-30
Newton, Isaac – 195-6
Niebuhr, Reinhold – 267, 326
Nisbet, Robert - 391
Noah – 383
Odin – 114
Paine, Tom – 332, 335
Parsons, Theophilus (Chief Justice) – 246

Phillips, Andrew – 204
Pitkin, Hanna – 365
Plato – 115, 120, 133, 205
Pocock, JGA – 9, 242, 351-5
Pollard, Justin – 356
Polybius – 150, 367
Pope Alexander II – 68, 74
Pope Gregory VII – 74
Quirinus – 115
Robb, John – 376
Robertson, Wilmot – 234, 255
Romulus – 115
Ronfeldt, David – 380-81
Roosevelt, Franklin D – 275, 306-9, 314, 379,
Ross, Edward A – 300, 301, 304
Royce, Josiah – 304
Russell, Bertrand – 386-8
Russell, James C – 36
Salter, Frank – 177, 204, 323
Saul – 50
Schäfer, Peter - 317
Skinner, Quentin – 352-3, 355
Skowronek, Stephen – 285
Smith, Adam – 196, 233, 240
Smith, Anthony – 147
Smith, Thomas – 108, 109, 110
Solomon – 50
St Germain, Christopher – 93
St John, Henry – see Bolingbroke
St Matthew – 16, 386
St Paul – 385
St Peter – 190, 193
Stephen I - 91
Stephen, James Fitzjames - 394
Stewart, James – 240, 241
Stoddard, Lothrop – 301
Story, Joseph – 244
Stubbs, William (Bishop) – 53
Sumner, William Graham – 297-9, 301
Sunic, Tomislav – 238-9

Sutherland, Lucy – 346
Tacitus – 31, 33-36, 40, 42, 137
Tawney, RH – 229, 233,
Thor – 114
Toombs, Robert – 292
Toqueville, Alexis de – 284, 286-7,
    400
Toynbee, Arnold – 234
Trask, HA Scott – 383
Trenchard, John – 153
Tully, James – 332-9
Tyr – 114
Ullman, Walter – 19
Walpole, Robert – 140-2, 150, 155,
    345-6, 350, 354, 365, 371
Walton, John – 389
Ward, Cynthia – 337
Washington, Booker T – 13, 321
Washington, George – 271, 273, 279
Weber, Bruce H – 205
Weber, Max – 72, 229, 233
Weil, Simone – 232
William and Mary – 139
William I/William the Conqueror –
    53, 74, 75, 87, 88, 90, 91, 332
William of Orange – 348
Williams, Rowan (Archbishop of
    Canterbury) – 178, 203
Wilson, David Sloan – 185
Woocher, Jonathan – 314
Wood, Gordon – 271, 282

ABOUT ARKTOS

ARKTOS is the result of a novel idea that was arrived at simultaneously by several individuals scattered across many parts of the globe, causing us to combine forces to bring this idea to fruition. The basis of this idea is our common observation that there are a growing number of individuals who believe that something has gone terribly wrong with the modern world. As with the people who make up Arktos itself, some see this primarily as a political or sociological issue, while others believe that the root of the problem lies in a spiritual or metaphysical decline. Still others may see these two factors as being interrelated.

Arktos is founded on the proposition that there is a common thread that links all of these individuals and ideas together, regardless of the particulars, and that the primary obstacle to realizing any genuine change or renewal over the past half-century has been the internal squabbles over these differences which neutralised many such groups and movements from within. As such, Arktos does not seek to propagate any specific ideology, system of beliefs or viewpoint. We do not seek consistency. Rather, we want to provide the resources for individuals of many different inclinations to find alternatives to the onslaught of modernity. We leave it to the Fates to decide which of these seeds will bear fruit in the future.

The resources we offer will vary widely. Our books, both those of other publishers which we offer through our retail section and those we publish under our own imprints, *Traditio* (for our more spiritually-inclined texts) and *Eos* (for our sociopolitical works), lay the foundation in their presentation of both alternative visions of the world, as well as practical guidebooks on how to live outside the prevailing culture. We also seek to continue to develop our music and lifestyle sections to reflect the interests of those we serve. Every item in the Arktos catalogue has been carefully reviewed and selected by our committee to fulfil a need which we believe exists in the subculture of anti-modernity.

We hope you will find inspiration in these words of T. E. Lawrence: *'All men dream: but not equally. Those who dream by night in the dusty recesses of their minds wake in the day to find that it was vanity: but the dreamers of the day are dangerous men, for they may act their dream with open eyes, to make it possible.'*

If you enjoyed this book, then we can certainly offer you other books, music or other varieties of items that will suit your taste. Please visit us at **www.arktos.com**.